IET PROFESSIONAL APPLICATIONS

Modelling Enterprise Architectures

Other volumes in this series:

Modelling Enterprise Architectures

Jon Holt and Simon Perry

The Institution of Engineering and Technology

Published by The Institution of Engineering and Technology, London, United Kingdom

© 2010 The Institution of Engineering and Technology

First published 2010

The Institution of Engineering and Technology
Michael Faraday House
Six Hills Way, Stevenage
Herts, SG1 2AY, United Kingdom

www.theiet.org

British Library Cataloguing in Publication Data
A catalogue record for this product is available from the British Library

ISBN 978-1-84919-077-0 (paperback)
ISBN 978-1-84919-078-7 (PDF)

Typeset in India by MPS Ltd, A Macmillan Company
Printed in the UK by CPI Antony Rowe, Chippenham

This book is dedicated to my sister, Donna - the original bogey-biter!

JDH

To Sally, with all my love.

SAP

Contents

Acknowledgements

The origin of this book was an initiative that was funded and run by the IET and the NCC known as EA-SE, Enterprise Architecture and Systems Engineering, back in 2007. Through this project, I had the pleasure of meeting Nigel Bragg of the NCC who really pioneered the initiative and kept its head above water for the year that the project lasted. So it's a big thank you for Nigel and the several hundred people who were involved in the workshops and had to put up with me forcibly extracting their requirements for EA.

Thanks should also go to some of our enduring clients who have let us loose on their organisations, such as Duncan and Alec and many others.

The last year or so has been one of monumental change for me, and one of the biggest acknowledgements for this work, and all the work that I have done over the last 12 years must be Brass Bullet Ltd and all who sailed in her. Sadly, Brass Bullet Ltd is no more, but her spirit lives on as a small part of Atego and I look forward to the next few years and all the challenges and opportunities that this will throw up for me, Simon and Mike.

Many thanks, as ever, got to Mike and Sue Rodd who still manage to exert an uncanny control over my destiny, even after all these years. It's over 20 years since I first worked with Mike and Sue taught me how to string a sentence together. Who'd have thought where we would all end up?

Finally, my undying love and thanks go to my beautiful wife Rebecca, my wonderful (mostly) children: Jude, Eliza and Roo, and my two cats: Olive and Betty.

Jon Holt, April 2010

As is often the case Jon has said (almost) everything that needs to be said, but I would like to echo his thanks to Nigel Bragg. The EA-SE project forced Jon and me to think about what an enterprise architecture really is. Applying our ideas to our own organisation helped to crystallise our thoughts and the result is this book.

The last 18 months have been interesting times, and not the most conducive to writing a book, so I would like to give special thanks to Mike Brownsword for being a sounding-board for our thoughts and ideas and helping to bring this project to a successful conclusion. I would also like to thank all those that were part of Brass Bullet Ltd and whose support enabled Jon and me to spend time writing.

Finally, as always, extra special thanks and all my love go to my wife Sally. Her love and encouragement continue to keep me sane (and I have the certificate to prove it).

Simon A. Perry, April 2010

Chapter 1

Introduction

Architecture is not all about the design of the building and nothing else,
it is also about the cultural setting and the ambience, the whole affair.

Michael Graves

1.1 Enterprise architecture

The world of business and commerce is changing. As technology advances at a rate of knots and the geography of global working becomes less and less relevant, so the need to run an effective business becomes more and more important. Businesses grow at an alarming rate, often overnight. Interest in particular field can explode resulting in massive, instantaneous business expansion or, rather sadly, the reverse can often happen. New technologies, the increase in power and performance of existing technologies and even legislation can result in businesses going broke at an equally alarming rate. Even when business expansion is more measured, this is often through acquisition of other businesses which brings a whole new swathe of problems with it.

It is essential, therefore, that a business can be managed and controlled in way that makes its behaviour as predictable as practically possible and which allows for the flexibility of an uncertain future. To manage and control the change associated with any business, there is a need for enterprise architecture (EA).

EA is one of those areas where everyone seems to have an opinion, yet few people seem to be able to agree as to exactly what is EA and what does it mean to them.

This book is aimed at helping people to develop their own EAs through modelling. This book provides a description of modelling techniques, in terms of the notation and the approach to applying it, along with a solid approach to modelling EAs. This is an approach that is focussed on modelling and, hence, can be used in conjunction with any number of established techniques or processes for EA development and maintenance. This book is not intended to replace these techniques, but to serve as an enabler to actually realise the EA.

1.2 The need for EA

1.2.1 Introduction

The fundamental need for EA comes from the need to manage business change. As has already been discussed, we live in a world of constant business flux and one of increasing competition. If we cannot run our businesses effectively, then somebody else will overtake us.

1.2.2   Manage business change

An effective EA must be able to represent all aspects of the business for three different eras – the present, the future and the visionary eras.

- Present. The present EA represents the current situation of the business. Where is the business, who is involved and so on. The present EA needs to be a blunt and realistic view of the business, warts and all. It is all too tempting to present an overly rosy view of the business when creating and defining an EA. It is arguably fine to present a slightly better view of a business when facing the outside world – after all, who wants to admit to potential clients that there are problems or shortfalls with the business or, indeed, that the business is failing. When looking inwardly, however, it is essential that the true picture of the business is captured. There is no point lying to yourself as this self-delusion will only lead to disappointment and possibly failure in the future. Be harsh, be blunt and above all be realistic.
- Future. The future EA reflects where the business will be in the short to mid-term future. It is difficult to put an exact time frame on what is meant by 'future' as it will be different for different types of business. As a guide, think about aspects of the business that you know are likely to change and also that you would like to change. The future EA should be an initial target for where the business should be in a few years.
- Visionary. The visionary EA is the ultimate goal of where the company wants to be. This should form the main target and, hence, drive for the company and will impact on all aspects of the businesses.

Everything in this book that describes modelling EAs can be applied at each of these three eras.

1.2.3   Professionalism

Professionalism must underlie everything that we do. It does not matter what your background is, or what level you sit in the business, professionalism is the key.

Think of professionalism as the key enabler for confidence. Confidence exists at several levels:

- Customer confidence. This is the obvious one. If our customers have confidence in our business then they will use and re-use our products and services. Not only this, but the customer will also be happy to recommend our business to others. This will happen because we have a relationship with the customer that extends beyond the simple contract. We will treat them with respect and offer services and products that meet all their requirements and exceed their expectations. In short, we will be professional.

- Internal business confidence. Working with professionals brings up the level of confidence within any team. Teams should work together to achieve the business goals of the company. Teams should be aware of one another and aware of the contribution that each brings to the business.
- Self confidence. At the end of the day, businesses are made up of people. It is dangerous to think of the business as 'people' however, as you should really think of 'people' as a group of individuals. Individuals need to feel valued, motivated and respected. The ability of each individual should be known and measured. Where this measure falls short of the expected norm, then solutions should be offered.

It is fine to discuss professionalism in terms of the worthy goals of confidence, but confidence is one of those things that is easy to talk about, but difficult to measure in any realistic way. How, therefore, can professionalism be measured? The answer lies in two areas, in terms of capability and competency.

- Capability. The term 'capability' is defined here as being the ability of a business or business unit. This may be the entire organisation or may be a team within the organisation, or anywhere in between. Capability will tell your customers exactly what you can do, whether this relates to services or products. Capability can be measured by looking at the process behind a capability. In the case of a service, processes should be defined that state exactly what approach will be taken to deliver the service. In the terms of a product, then the process will define the approach taken to develop, deliver and support that product. In the world of capability, process is the king, and there are many ways to assess and measure capability, such as: Capability Maturity Model Integration (CMMI), etc.
- Competency. If capability describes the ability of an organisation, then competency defines the ability of an individual. Individuals have job titles which will have a number of roles associated with them. With each role it is possible to identify a number of skills that are required, which go together to form a competency scope. Individuals may be assessed against these scopes and produce a competency profile that reflects their current competency levels. Competency assessment will identify the knowledge, skills and attitude of the individual according to their roles. Competency is also the cornerstone of continued professional development and hence is a very powerful mechanism when it comes to professional registration, such as chartered status.

Bearing in mind that both competency and capability reflect the ability of something, then it is clear that there is some sort of link between the two. Competency is the key enabler for capability. It is possible to have a number of processes in place that do everything that you want your company to do, but if there are no competent people to support this, then this capability can never be realised.

To conclude, therefore, professionalism is key to everything that we do as a business. Professionalism leads to confidence at every level and professionalism can be demonstrated in two ways. The first is through capability that reflects the ability of the organisation (or unit) and measured in terms of process. The second is through competency that reflects the ability of an individual and that can be measured by using a single, or a set of, appropriate competency frameworks. Competency is the key enabler for capability.

Professionalism will constrain everything that we do in business.

1.2.4   Understand change

It is essential to understand change. This is quite difficult however as, by the very nature of the beast, change is highly changeable! However, to understand the change and how it will potentially affect the business, there are three steps that must be carried out: identify the change drivers, assess the impact of the change and define strategy for solutions.

The first step is to identify change drivers. It is impossible to identify all the possible drivers for business change, but there are a few key areas that may be considered.

- Mergers and acquisitions. Companies merge and buy one another all the time. Every company, at some point in time, may be traceable to someone having a good idea and wanting to exploit it. Most companies, however, do not just evolve and grow over time in a linear fashion, but achieve changes through merging with other businesses or buying them. Clearly, this can be a massive change. Several questions must be asked, such as are the business goals congruent between the companies, what are their capabilities and competencies, what products or services do each offer and so on. There are several reasons why a company may consider a merger or acquisition; to obtain the following market share, products or services, a client base or individuals. Each has their own pro's and con's but it is essential to understand why the merger or acquisition is happening. Of course, there are many sensitivities to be borne in mind as the human aspect of business change cannot be ignored. With any merger or acquisition, there is the imminent threat of redundant roles or capabilities, which can lead to large impact on the moral of the staff.
- In sourcing and outsourcing. In sourcing and outsourcing are big issues at the moment – particularly outsourcing. When people hear the words 'outsourcing' they immediately think of foreign countries and job losses. Although this is far from always being the case, this is a very human way to react. When we talk about outsourcing, it is not the job itself that is being outsourced but the process behind the job.
- New technologies. Technology changes at a very rapid pace and not always in a linear fashion. One example that is used elsewhere in this book is that of data storage. The amount of data that can be saved easily and conveniently has increased exponentially over the last 20 years, whilst the cost has decreased. Apart from this, the technology has also undergone some step changes. Any business that works in this area must be able to predict (as much as possible)

where and when the technology will change and, hence, adapt to the new technologies.
- Political and legal changes. Every business must operate within the constraints of the country and government that it sells its products and services into. In many cases, the laws and politics between different countries will not be the same, so a service that may be delivered in one way in one country, may have to be tailored before it can be delivered in another country. In terms of legislation, the obvious areas to think about are technological ones, such as Electromagnetic Compatibility (EMC) compliance, etc. but what about other changes that may affect the organisation? Consider, for example, the recent smoking ban in public places in many countries, how will this affect productivity if some people will now be spending part of their day walking outside, or in some cases off-site to get their infusion?

Of course, this is not an exhaustive list, but it tries to demonstrate that it is often not the immediately obvious changes that have the biggest influence on the business.

1.2.5   Assess the impact of the change

Once change drivers have been identified, what is to be done about them? There are two main aspects of the change that need to be considered:

- The immediate impact of change. When talking about the immediate impact of the change, we are referring to what aspects of the business are immediately affected. In the case of the smoking ban example discussed previously, some of the immediate impacts will be the removal of smoking areas and ash trays (an infrastructure requirement), the erecting of signs and notices (a legal requirement) and the dissemination of the new rules and policy (an internal management requirement).
- The wider-reaching impact. When talking about the wider-reaching impact, we are referring to the less obvious, but equally valid impact on the business. As was mentioned earlier, what will the impact be on the efficiency of the business if people are losing part of their working day to walk to smoking areas? In some cases, this may not be much of an issue, but in the situation where the entire site is made non-smoking, will people be walking off-site to smoke? Apart from the efficiency and timing issues here, what about security? If the business operates on a secure site, then is there an impact because people are now walking on and off-site four or five times per day? What about the public perception of the business? It is quite off-putting when turning up at a building to be greeted by a hoard of smokers standing directly outside the building and does nothing for the professional image of the company. Also, how are the new rules to be enforced? And so on.

One of the problems with change is being able to assess just which other areas of the business are impacted by the change. One of the benefits that an effective EA will bring is the ability to be able to assess the impact of any change across the entire organisation. One of the great benefits of systems modelling is that different parts of the model can be related together and that the traceability and dependences between the various parts can be explored. When this modelling is applied to the business, the resulting EA can be fully navigated and the impact of any change fully realised, or as much as the EA covers.

1.2.6   Define a strategy for solution

Once a change driver has been identified and the impact of the change has been assessed, then a solution needs to be found. There are two ways to look at defining the strategy for the solution:

- Solving the immediate problem. This involves looking at the change and its impact and seeing what can be done to solve it. For example, with the smoking example, the possible solutions to be considered in the strategy may be: putting up signs, removing smoking areas, putting out email to all employees and maybe pointing people towards resources to help them stop smoking.
- Looking for potential advantages. Any change to a business may have an impact on a positive or negative way. We tend to just think of the negative aspects of change, because these are the ones that come back to bite us. However, what about the potential advantages? In the case of the smoking example, maybe the company previously had dedicated smoking rooms that can now be used for other purposes as an additional resource. The cost of cleaning may very well decrease as the cost of simple cleaning compared to de-fumigation may be considerable. Also, the cost of maintenance of the room – if there was air conditioning in the smoking room, does this need of be on all the time now or can money be saved by reducing the numbers of hours per day that it is powered?

Remember here that we are talking about the strategy for the solution, rather than the specific solutions themselves. In the case of solving the immediate problem, people will often think of immediate solutions, whereas when looking for potential advantages, it is possible, and indeed desirable, to think far more strategically.

1.2.7   Understand business need

It is essential that we question 'why' we do everything that we do in business. If we do not understand the need for doing something, then it is highly unlikely that we will do a good job of creating a business doing it. This all boils down to understanding requirements at every level of the business. Why do we produce a product of service? Who wants it? What benefit will they get? And so on.

One of the underlying themes in this book is about understanding the requirements for everything that we do. Many people may think that they understand why they do things, but when this is explored, the world is usually far more complex than they had originally anticipated.

In fact, requirements are so important to realising an effective EA, that there is an entire chapter dedicated to the subject.

1.2.8   Manage infrastructure

Every business will have an infrastructure, whether the business is a multi-national with offices all over the world, or whether the business is run out of somebody's bedroom. The scale and complexity of the infrastructure will vary enormously, but it is important that it is understood and managed.

Perhaps of all the areas of EA, this is the one that most people will immediately think of, as many aspects of the infrastructure can be easily visualised. These are the areas that are well-managed, or easy to manage, but the problem comes in when we consider aspects of the infrastructure that are less easy to manage. Consider the following list: buildings, computers, people, competency and roles. Now try to visualise each of them.

The first three items in the list, buildings, computers and people are easy to visualise, as they are 'things' that we can see, touch and interact with. As a result of this immediate visualisation, these items tend to be easier to manage, but what about the other items on the list? What does 'competency' look like and what does a 'role' look like? This is far more difficult to achieve and it is not immediately apparent how to visualise each one. Even worse, if something can be visualised, will it be visualised in the same way by all people who view it? The answer to this question is a resounding 'no'!

An effective EA will allow all aspects of the business infrastructure to be visualised in a uniform and controlled manner. An effective EA will present a number of views on the same information (depending on who needs the information) but each will be presented in a consistent and coherent manner.

1.2.9   Ensure whole life cycle is covered

The issue of life cycles is surprisingly complex. Most people will have an idea of what a life cycle is at a high level. Many will be able to define a life cycle using hilarious quips, such as 'cradle to grave', 'lust to dust' and even 'sperm to worm', but are these accurate reflections of what a life cycle is or just throw-away phrases?

A life cycle starts when the first idea has been generated and ends when the 'thing' is fully retired and taken out of service in a safe manner. There are two discussion points here:

- 'When the first idea has been generated'. This does not mean when the first draft of requirements has been generated, or when the first contract has been agreed, but when the idea first comes up. In some cases, depending on what the 'thing' is, these may coincide with the requirements, but this is not a hard-and-fast rule. Consider a human being – when does the life cycle begin? Some may argue it is when the child is born, but what about the nine months in the womb? Some may argue that it is the point of conception, but do some people not plan to have children years in advance, and some others may require medical help to conceive? The starting point of the life cycle is not at all clear-cut and, once more, will be dependent on the type of 'thing' that it is applied to.

- 'When the system is fully retired'. This does not mean when people stop using the system, nor does it mean when the system has been put away into storage. Again, more though is required. Consider once more the case of a human being and, in particular, the case of the now-deceased Jeremy Bentham. Jeremy Bentham was a world-renowned philosopher and juror in the 18th and 19th centuries and is credited as being one of the spiritual fathers of UCL (University College of London, in the UK) and whose personal doctrine was one of Utilitarianism, the promotion of the principle of 'the greatest happiness of the greatest number'. The point of considering Bentham here though has less to do with the impact of his works during his life, but more to do with his impact on UCL after his death. In his will, Bentham requested that his skeleton be preserved, dressed in his own clothes and be surmounted by his preserved head. Although the head is now wax (due to the imperfect 19th century preservation process and the behaviour of drunk students) the so called 'auto-icon' of Bentham is, to this day, displayed in the foyer of the South Cloisters building of UCL. Another condition of his will was that he (his preserved body, anyway) should be in attendance at all meetings of the College Council, and that the auto-icon is wheeled into the Council Room so that he can sit amongst the present-day members. This is recorded in the official minutes as 'Jeremy Bentham – present but not voting'. At what point, therefore, should we consider Bentham's life cycle to be over?

The previous two points have been mainly concerned with the concepts of defining a life cycle, but these can be thrown into disarray by thinking about what the life cycle applies to. The truth is that many life cycles will exist depending on what the 'thing' under consideration is.

- Project life cycles. Project life cycles are perhaps, along with product life cycles, one of the more obvious example of 'things'. We tend to have rigid definitions of the terminal conditions of a project, such as start and end dates, timescales, budgets, resources, etc. and so a project life cycle is one that most people will be able to identify with.
- Product life cycles. Again, another quite obvious one is to consider the life cycle of a product. It is relatively simple to visualise the conception, development, production, use and support and disposal of a product.
- Programme life cycles. Most projects will exist in some sort of higher-level programme. Each of the programmes will also have its own life cycle and, clearly, this will have some constraint on the life cycles of all projects that are contained within it.
- System procurement life cycles. Some systems may have a procurement life cycle that applies to them. From a business point of view, this may be a better way to view a product, or set of products, than looking at the product life cycle alone.
- Technology life cycles. Any technology will have a life cycle. For example, in the world of home computers, the accepted norm for removable storage was magnetic tapes. This was then succeeded by magnetic discs, then optical discs,

then solid-sate devices and then virtual storage. Each of these technologies has its own life cycle.

- Equipment life cycles. Each and every piece of equipment will have its own life cycle. This may start before the equipment is actually acquired and may end when the equipment has been safely retired. Stages of the equipment life cycle may describe it's current condition, such as whether the equipment is in use, working well, degrading and so on.
- Business life cycle. The business itself will have a life cycle. In some cases, the main driver of the business may be to remain in business for several years and then to sell it on. Stages of the life cycle may include expansion or growth, steady states, controlled degradation and so on.

This list can go on and on, but it is not the length of the list here that should cause the most concern, it is the interaction of these life cycles where things really start to get complex. Imagine a rail transport system and then look at the list above. How many of these different life cycles could be applied in some way to a rail system? If you try hard enough, then it is possible to imagine each of them being relevant. Now try to imagine how each of these life cycles impacts each of the others. Now the situation starts to get really complicated.

Any EA will have its own life cycle but it is not enough to just consider the life cycle of the EA, but to appreciate that there will exist many other life cycles, all of which will have some impact and indeed form complex interactions with the life cycle of the EA itself.

1.3   Modelling enterprise architectures

A key enabler for many problems associated with business is modelling. The field of business process modelling is one that is well documented and that is now reaching a certain level of maturity. An example of this is the 'seven views' approach that defines a set of views that must be considered to model any process effectively [1].

The idea of looking at something from a number of different points of view is not a new one and any collection of views may be thought of as an architecture. Architectures may be used to describe the technical aspects, the physical aspects and the logical aspects of a system – in fact any viewpoint that meets the requirements of an interested stakeholder. By applying the key concepts of modelling and viewpoints to an entire business it is possible to create an EA.

1.4   Understanding the 'why' of enterprise architecture

1.4.1   Introduction

One common theme that has emerged from the discussion presented so far in this book is that of needing to know 'why'. To put this a bit more formally, this comes down to understanding the requirements at every level business. To engineer any solution, it is essential to understand the initial requirements. To know whether one has achieved what one has set out to achieve, it is essential to understand the requirements.

Unfortunately, too many attempts at EA either fail or deliver no benefits (fail) as the original requirements for the exercise were not known in the first place. This is somewhat akin to the 'old lady who swallowed a fly.'

1.4.2   I know an old lady who swallowed a fly

EA is often seen as a good solution to a number of business problems. The thing is, however, that it is essential to understand the problem that the solution is being applied to and to understand why and how it solves the problem. Many EAs have been put into place without understanding why they are needed in the first. This is rather like the old lady from the old nursery rhyme who swallowed a fly.

1.4.3   I don't know why she swallowed a fly

Why did the old lady swallow a fly? What was she trying to achieve? Unfortunately, we never find out. The old lady goes further and further through an ever-increasing array of solutions to a problem that is never defined.

Begin by asking a few fundamental questions.

- Why do you want an EA?
- What will it be used for?
- Who will be using it?

It is essential that the 'why' of an EA is considered and by this we really mean carrying out a proper requirements capture and analysis exercise, rather than just generating a wish-list. When engineering any type of system, the first step is always to get a good idea of exactly what the requirements are for that system. An EA must be treated just like any other system and it must be engineered accordingly. Bear in mind that the EA is a business-critical system – can you afford to get it wrong?

One output of a good requirements exercise is the production of one or more context. A context provides a set of inter-related requirements for a system (in this case an EA) *from a particular point of view*. Bear in mind that there will be many stakeholders interested in the EA and each of them, potentially, has a different point of view on what the EA is all about, how it can be used and what benefits will be realised by the EA. These different viewpoints will result in conflicts, common interest and overlapping requirements for the EA and all of these must be resolved. For example, consider the IT staff and the business development staff in an organisation. Do they both need an EA in place? The answer is, in all probability, 'yes'. Do they each want the same things from the EA? The answer is, in all probability, 'no'.

Clearly, it is essential that all stakeholders are identified at this point and that an understanding of the 'why' for each stakeholder, or stakeholder group, is arrived at.

1.4.4 *I know an old lady who swallowed a spider (that wriggled and jiggled about inside her)*

When confronted with a fly in the stomach, the temptation is to look for tried and tested approaches to fly removal, such as spiders, but is this suitable?

When confronted with a topic like EA, the temptation is to look for best-practice approaches that people have followed before and that have a number of success stories associated with them. Indeed, there are many excellent frameworks and standards for EA (e.g. References 2–4, etc. see for more discussion) that represent best practice but each of these must be tailored for any business and their suitability assessed. There is no point in simply applying a perceived solution to a problem when the problem is not understood in the first place. Just because a particular EA works for one business does not necessarily mean that it will work for another – only when the requirements are the same will this be the case. Also, the reality is that any two given businesses, even if they are perceived to be very similar, will inevitably have different business requirements.

These best-practice models each have their own strengths and weaknesses and all have been applied very successfully on many projects. Each of these best-practice models has its own set of requirements which will give an insight as to where their use may be effective and appropriate. Each of these best-practice models do work (hence, they are referred to as 'best practice') but they should each be treated as tools in a toolbox and it is essential to choose the right tool for the right job.

1.4.5 *I know an old lady who swallowed a bird/cat/dog*

Spiders in the stomach bring their own problems. There may be a clearly under-stood and logical progression of eating slightly larger animals to solve the problem, but does the old lady actually understand the nature of her problem or, for that matter, her own physiology.

Once the 'why' of an EA is understood, it is essential to be able to relate this to the business. Key to understanding the business is having a common understanding of the key terms and concepts in that business.

For example, in many industries it is important to have a very clear picture of what the core capabilities are – whether this takes the form of services (such as local government, healthcare, etc.) or products (such as manufacturing, systems development, etc.). This may seem obvious, but is it usually the 'obvious' where many assumptions and ambiguities creep in. This may be as obvious as ensuring that there is a consensus on the core terminology and language that is being spoken in the organisation. As an example of this, ask three different people exactly what is a 'service' and it is highly probable that you will receive at least two different definitions. Following on from this, any capability should be able to be demon-strated through a sequence of processes, whether these are carried out by people, teams or products. Processes are essential for any business but these processes cannot be truly realised without competent people to realise them. This brings up the whole issue of people, job titles, roles and their relevant competencies.

The point here is that there are many key concepts and that their definition and understanding is very complex. This results in the need for an ontology for the EA where such concepts and terms are captured and defined. Also, notice that although key business concepts have been discussed, no mention (as yet) has been made of IT systems.

Efficient and effective communication is key to realising an appropriate EA, whether this is between team, individuals, organisations or, indeed, technical systems. When talking about communication, it is important that we consider 'stakeholder communication' as any stakeholder, whether on the customer side, supplier side or even an independent, external stakeholder will have a need to both communicate and be communicated to.

1.4.6   I know an old lady who swallowed a goat/cow

Goats are renowned for eating anything – but would a goat eat a dog? Cows are herbivores, so the eating of goats is simply not consistent with a cow's normal behaviour. By focussing too much on identifying larger and larger mammals, is the old lady losing sight of her goals and losing touch with reality?

Given that architectures are all about views, it is surprising that EA is often considered from a very narrow point of view where only the IT aspects of an EA are produced. Before we go any further, let it be made clear that the IT aspects of an EA are absolutely essential to the successful running of any business but the scope of EA is certainly a lot wider. For example, many examples of EA that exist in real life are focussed on ensuring that the IT systems (including machines, applications, data, etc.) are aligned with the business requirements of that organisation, which is correct. However, as has been discussed in the previous section there is far more to EA than the IT aspects.

Most organisations have a good understanding of what the IT capabilities of the business are. They understand the hardware that exists or is required, the applications, operating systems and the data requirements. However, it is essential that this can be looked at in relations to the capabilities and, hence, the processes that are required by the business, whether these processes relate directly to services or to the development of products. It is by establishing the relationships between these diverse concepts that we begin to create a true EA.

The visual manifestation of an EA is through describing a number of views. Views are actually very easy to generate, but there must be a reason why the views are needed. It is all too easy to generate a set of random views that are not contributing to meeting the requirements of the EA. Also, all these views must be consistent with one another or the result is a set of pictures rather than a true model to represent the EA.

1.4.7   I know an old lady who swallowed a horse

1.4.7.1   She's dead of course!

There are a few key points that emerge from the points presented in this section:

- Understanding why – understand your requirements for your EA from different points of view. Each stakeholder may have a different set of requirements and these must be resolved.
- Speak a common language – understanding the terms and concepts is essential – generate an ontology.

- Views must have a purpose – do you understand which of the EA requirements that they are satisfying.
- Views must be consistent – they must form part of a model and not be just a set of pictures.

Solutions are a great and necessary part of EA, but bear in mind that all solutions lend themselves to particular problems. And simply applying bigger solutions (fly, spider, bird, cat, dog, goat, cow and horse) is not necessarily the best approach.

Also, it should be remembered that whatever solution you throw at a problem, it will come with its own set of required resources. It is all too easy to end up with a house full of dead bodies, hay and horse dung.

1.5   Understanding requirements

Unfortunately, understanding requirements is by no means a trivial matter. It is not good enough to just have a brainstorming session and then write down a list. Requirements must be fully engineered and it must be appreciated that if the requirements are not understood, then the EA will not be effective. This may sound harsh, but this is a lesson learned the hard way from the world of engineering. We do not want to just fabricate an EA, we want to engineer it, and that means the requirements must be understood.

There is a whole chapter dedicated to understanding requirements in this book.

1.6   Conclusions

This chapter has introduced the subject of EA and has discussed the main need for an EA. Alongside all these great-and-good generic reasons why an EA is required, there is the very pragmatic issue of why you, as an organisation or individual, want the EA and what is needed from it. The requirements for the EA is one of the central themes in this book and the use of modelling is proposed as a pragmatic and effective means of meeting these requirements.

References

1. Holt, J. *A Pragmatic Guide to Business Process Modelling.* 2nd edn. Chippenham: BCS Publishing; 2009.
2. Zachman, J. *John Zachman's Concise Definition of the Zachman Framework.* California: Zachman International; 2008. Available from http://www.zachmaninternational.com/concise%20definition.pdf [Accessed 01 Feb 2010].
3. The Ministry of Defence Architectural Framework, 2007. Available from http://www.mod.uk/modaf.
4. The Open Group Architectural Framework (TOGAF), version 9. Available from http://www.opengroup.org/architecture/togaf9-doc/arch/ [Accessed 01 Feb 2010].

Chapter 2
Modelling

People can have the Model T in any colour – so long as it's black.

Henry Ford (1863–1947)

2.1 Introduction

This section introduces the concept of modelling and includes a discussion on why modelling is so important and why we need to model. It also introduces a number of basic concepts that will be referred to constantly throughout the rest of the book.

2.2 Why we model

It is vital to understand the reasons why we must model things. To justify the need for models, a number of simple examples will be considered. These examples aim to justify modelling in general terms and not simply with regard to enterprise architectures (EAs), which demonstrate the need for flexibility when modelling – indeed, the three examples used here are not related to EAs. The examples are taken from Reference 1 and were created by the master of modelling, Grady Booch; they are based on Booch's doghouse, house and office block examples.

2.2.1 The kennel (doghouse)

For the first example of modelling, consider the example of building a kennel. A kennel is a small house where pets, usually dogs, can spend some time outside without being exposed to the elements. The basic requirement for a kennel is to keep the dog happy. This will include building a structure that is waterproof and large enough to fit the dog inside. To fit inside, there must be an entrance in the kennel that is larger than the dog itself. The inside should also be large enough for the dog to be able to turn around to leave. Dogs are particularly bad at walking backwards, which makes this last point crucial. Finally, the dog should be comfortable enough to sleep in the kennel and thus some bedding or cushions may be in order.

Figure 2.1   The kennel (doghouse)

If you were about to build this kennel, then consider for a moment the basic skills and resources that you would require. You would be wise to have the following:

- Basic materials such as timber, nails, etc. The quality is not really that important as it is only for a dog. This might involve looking for any old pieces of wood around the house or even making a trip to a hardware store.
- The money needed to pay for the kennel would be your own, but is unlikely to be a large outlay. In terms of your personal income, it would be a fraction of a week's salary – perhaps the cost of a social evening out.
- Some basic tools, such as a hammer, a saw, a tape measure, etc. Again, the quality of the tools need not be wonderful, providing they get the job done.
- Some basic building skills. You need not be a skilled craftsman, but basic hand-to-eye coordination would be an advantage.

At the end of the day (or weekend), you will probably end up with a kennel that is functional and in which the dog would be happy to shelter from the rain.

If the kennel was somewhat less than functional and the dog was not very happy with its new accommodation, you could always start again (after destroying the first attempt) and try a bit harder, learning from past mistakes. It would also be possible to destroy the doghouse and then to deny all knowledge of ever having built one in the first place, thus avoiding embarrassment later. Alternatively, you could get rid of the dog and buy a less demanding pet such as a tortoise, as there is no need to build a kennel for an animal that carries its own accommodation on its back. After all, the dog is in no position to argue or complain.

This is Booch's first example of modelling: the kennel or, for our trans-Atlantic readers, the doghouse.

2.2.2 The house

Consider now, maybe based on the resounding success of your kennel, that you were planning to build a house for your family. This time the requirements would be somewhat different. There would need to be adequate space for the whole family in which to sit and relax. In addition, there would have to be adequate sleeping arrangements in the number of bedrooms that are chosen. There would need to be a kitchen, maybe a dining room and one or more bathrooms and toilets. As there will be more than one room, some thought should be given to the layout of the rooms in terms of where they are in the house and where they are in relation to one another.

Figure 2.2   The house

If you were to build a house for your family, you would (hopefully) approach the whole exercise differently from that of the kennel:

- You would have to start with some basic materials and tools, but the quality of these resources would no doubt be of a higher concern than those used for the kennel. It would not be good enough to simply drive down to a local hardware store and pick up some materials as the quantity would need to be far greater and it would not be possible to guess, with any degree of accuracy, the amount of materials required.
- Your family would also be far more demanding and vocal than the dog. Rather than simply guessing your family's requirements, it would be more

appropriate to ask them their opinions and perhaps get a professional architect in to listen to and discuss their needs.

- Unless you have built many houses before, it would be a good idea to draw up some plans. If you were hiring skilled craftsmen to do the job, you would certainly have to draw up plans to communicate your requirements to the builders. These plans may require some input from an architect in order that they achieve a standard that may be used effectively by the people who will be building the house.
- The house would also have to meet building regulations and require planning permission. This may involve contacting the local council or government representative and possibly applying for permission to build. This in turn would almost certainly involve submitting plans for approval before any work could be started.
- The money for the house would probably be yours, and thus you would have to monitor the work and ensure that people stick to the plans to get the job done in time, within budget and to meet your family's original requirements. The scale of the financial outlay is likely to be in the order of several years' salary and would probably be borrowed from a bank or building society and would thus have to be paid back, regardless of the outcome of the project.

If the house turns out not to suit the requirements, the consequences would be more serious than in the case of the kennel. The house cannot be knocked down and started again as the kennel could, because considerably more time and money would have gone into the house building. Similarly, you cannot simply get a less demanding family (in most cases) and living with the consequences of failure is not worth thinking about!

This is Booch's second example: the house.

2.2.3   The office block

Taking the two building projects that have been discussed so far even further, imagine that your ambition knows no bounds and that you decide to build an entire office block.

Consider once more the resources that would be required for this, the third and final building project.

- It would be infinitely stupid to attempt to build an office block by yourself.
- The materials required for building an office block would be in significantly larger quantities than the house. The materials would be bought direct from source and may even need to be brought in from specialist suppliers, perhaps even in different counties or countries.
- You will probably be using other people's money and thus the requirements for the building will probably be their requirements. In addition, their requirements will no doubt change once you have started building the tower block.

Figure 2.3   The office block

- More permissions are required to build an office block than a house and many more regulations must be considered. Consider, for example, environmental conditions that the office building may have to meet – the building must not block anyone's light, it will be required to blend in with its surroundings, or it may be deemed too ugly for a particular area.
- You will have to carry out extensive planning and be part of a larger group who are responsible for the building. Many teams will be involved from different areas of work (builders, plumbers, electricians, architects, etc.), all of whom must intercommunicate.

If you get the right teams involved and enjoy a degree of luck, you will produce the desired building.

If the project does not meet the investor's requirements, you would face severe repercussions, including the potential of no further work and the loss of reputation.

This is Booch's third example: the office block.

2.2.4   The point

These three examples from Booch may seem a little strange and somewhat trivial at first glance; however, there is a very serious and fundamental point behind all of this.

Nobody in their right mind would attempt to build an office block with basic DIY skills. In addition, there is the question of resources, and not only in terms of the materials needed. To build an office block, you would need the knowledge to access the necessary human resources (including people such as architects, builders, crane operators, etc.), plenty of time and plenty of money.

The strange thing is that many people will approach building a complex system with the skills and resources of a kennel-builder, without actually knowing if it is a kennel, house or office block. When contemplating any complex system, you should assume that it will be, or has the potential to turn into, an office block building. Do not approach any project with a 'kennel' mentality. If you approach a project as if it were an office block and it turns out to be a kennel, you will end up with a very well-made kennel that is the envy of all canines. If, however, you approach a project as if it were a kennel and it turns out to be an office block, the result will be pure disaster!

One of the reasons why it is so easy to misjudge the size and complexity of a project is that, in many cases, many elements of the system will not be tangible or comprehensible. Consider integrated circuits: who can say, simply by looking at an IC, how many transistors are inside it? Is it a processor or a simple logic gate? Consider software: simply by looking at a DVD it is impossible to judge the size or complexity of the information contained on it. In terms of size, this could range anywhere from a single kilobyte to several gigabytes. Even if you have an idea of the type of application that is on the DVD, it is still difficult to judge the size of the software. Take, for example, software that may help people write letters: this may be a simple line editor program that may be a few kilobytes of information or it could be a full-blown office application that may not fit on to a single DVD. The fact is that all projects that involve complex systems will have an intangible element about them, whether it is a control system, a process or whatever.

The important term that is used here is 'complexity' rather than size, as size is not necessarily a reflection of the complexity of a system. The next section discusses complexity in more detail.

2.3   The three evils

Projects fail and disasters occur for many reasons. However, there are three underlying reasons why things go wrong, the 'three evils' of *complexity*, a *lack of understanding* and *communication* issues.

2.3.1   Complexity

The concept of complexity will be illustrated in two ways – one that emphasises the importance of relationships, and one that uses a brontosaurus to visualise the nature of the evolution of complexity.

For the first example, consider five boxes that may represent five elements within a system, for example an organisation, as shown in Figure 2.4(a). Each

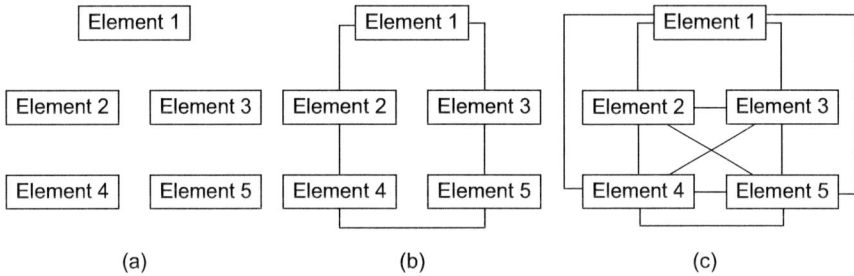

Figure 2.4 Complexity manifesting through relationships

element may represent almost anything, ranging from a text sentence that represents business goals, to a department that makes up an organisation, to processes that are used by the organisation, etc. Each of these elements may very well be understood by whoever is reading the diagram, but this does not necessarily mean that the organisation and what it does or is capable of doing is understood.

Consider now Figure 2.4(b) and it is quite clear that this diagram is more complex than the previous one, although nothing has changed in the elements themselves, only the relationships between them.

Consider now, Figure 2.4(c) where it is, again, obvious that this diagram is more complex than its predecessor and far more complex than the first.

In fact, the more relationships that are added between the elements, then the higher the complexity. More and more lines could be drawn onto this diagram and the complexity will increase dramatically, despite the fact that the complexity of each of the five elements has not actually increased as such.

The point here is that just because someone understands each element within a system, this does not, by any means, mean that the system itself is understood. The complexity of a system manifests itself by relationships between things – in this case the system elements. It should be borne in mind, however, that these elements may exist at any level of abstraction of the system, depending on what they represent. Therefore, the complexity may manifest itself at any point in the system. The complexity of the whole of the system is certainly higher than the complexity of the sum of its parts.

This may be thought of as being able to see both the woods *and* the trees.

The second way that complexity is illustrated is through the concept of the 'brontosaurus of complexity'. In this slightly bizarre analogy, complexity is visualised as a brontosaurus, in that the complexity of a system at the outset is represented by the dinosaur's head and, as the project life cycle progresses, this complexity increases (travelling down the neck), increases even further (through the belly) before reducing and finally ending up at the tail of the brontosaurus (Figure 2.5).

This fits with the shape of the brontosaurus that is '*thin at one end, much much thicker in the middle, and then thin again at the far end*' [2]. The perceived

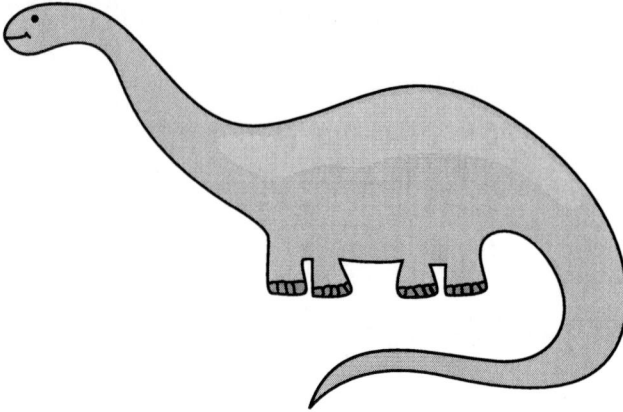

Figure 2.5   A brontosaurus

complexity of a project is almost always low to begin with, but balloons during the analysis of a project, as the understanding of the full impact of the requirements and the constraints is fully understood. By the time the problem is fully understood, then a project is well-and-truly in the 'belly of the brontosaurus', whereas when the design begins and becomes optimised, then the project should be heading towards the 'tail of the brontosaurus'. By applying the brontosaurus of complexity analogy, it is shown that one must go from the head (initial ideas and requirements) to the tail (system) but that it is impossible to do this without going through the belly of the brontosaurus.

Consider the situation when a project is at the head of the brontosaurus, then this may be visualised as the illustration in Figure 2.4(a). As the complexity of the project increases and we move down the neck of the brontosaurus so the complexity increases, as shown in Figure 2.4(b). In fact, the more relationships that are added between the system elements (and, hence, the more interactions between them) then the closer to the belly of the brontosaurus we actually get.

Many projects will fail because the project never leaves the belly or, in some cases, is left even higher up in the neck. If a project stays in the head or neck, then there is a large danger of the system being over-simplified and the complexity inherent in the system is never uncovered until it is too late. If the project remains in the belly, however, then the complexity has been realised, but it has not been managed effectively. Unfortunately, when a project is in the belly of the brontosaurus, then it may seem to the project personnel that the world is at an end and that there is no understanding of the project as a whole. Successfully developing a system is about being able to see the brontosaurus as a whole and that there is life after the belly.

In a final twist to this analogy, there is major difference between complexity and the brontosaurus. Complexity is difficult to visualise, but definitely exists in any system. A brontosaurus, on the other hand, is easy to visualise but never actually existed (it was demonstrated in 1974 that the brontosaurus was actually the apatosaurus).

2.3.2   Lack of understanding

EAs are being created by many organisations. However, many organisations set about creating EAs without any clear understanding of the needs, problems and solution surrounding an EA. This was discussed in Chapter 1 and is briefly commented on here.

A lack of understanding regarding the needs for an enterprise often mean that large amounts of time and money are wasted in producing EAs that, if they get completed at all, often do not address the needs of the organisation and are then seen as a waste of resources.

Knowing why an EA is needed is therefore essential, but allied to this is knowing the problems associated with the generation of the EA. A lack of understanding of the problems involved, even if the needs are understood, again can lead to an EA that is not fit for purpose. Problems that are often encountered include: having access to all the information necessary to generate the EA, having the tools and techniques in place to enable the EA to be created, knowing how to maintain the EA and ensure that it is used (and used correctly).

Finally, there is often a lack of understanding regarding the solution. Even with the needs clearly articulated and the associated problems understood and addressed, many organisations jump into EAs by generating large numbers of views without due consideration of what the views are for, that is what part of the solution are they addressing. If views are created that are not needed or that are incomplete or inconsistent or that do not present information in a readily usable form then the EA is likely to be seen as a waste of time and will not be used.

Of course, these examples are merely a representation of some ways that a lack of understanding can manifest itself in the creation of an EA – there are many other places where problems may occur.

2.3.3   Communication

The third of the three evils is the problem of communication or, more correctly, *ineffective* communication. The richness and complexity of human communication is what separates humans from other species. One of the earliest recorded examples of project failure is that of the Tower of Babel, as described wonderfully by Fred Brookes [3]. The Tower of Babel started life as a very successful project and the first few stages of the project went off without a hitch and the project was running on schedule, within budget and was meeting all the project requirements. However, one of the key stakeholder's requirements was not considered properly which was to cause the downfall of the project. When the stakeholder intervened in a divine fashion, the communication between project personnel was effectively destroyed.

Communication problems may occur at any level of the organisation or project, for example:

- Person-to-person level. If individuals cannot communicate on a personal level, then there is little hope for project success. This may be because people have different spoken languages, technical backgrounds or even a clash of personalities.
- Group-to-group level. Groups, or organisational units within an organisation, must be able to communicate effectively with one another. These groups may be from different technical areas, such as hardware and software groups, or the groups may span boundaries, such as management and technical groups, or marketing and engineering, for example. Such groups often use language specific to themselves, making inter-group communication difficult.
- Organisation-to-organisation level. Different organisations speak different languages – each will have their own specific terms for different concepts, as well as having an industry-specific terminology as well. When two organisations are working in a customer–supplier relationship, the onus is often on the supplier to speak the customer's language so that communication can be effective, rather than the customer having to speak the supplier's language. After all, if the supplier won't make an effort to speak the customer's language, it is quite likely that they will not remain customers for very long.
- System-to-system level. Even non-human systems must be able to communicate with one another. Technical systems must be able to communicate with technical systems, and also with financial systems, accountancy systems, environmental systems, etc.
- Any combination of the above. Just to make matters even more confusing, just about any combination of the above communication types is also possible.

These problems, therefore, lead to ambiguities in interpreting any sort of communication, whether it is a spoken language or an application-specific or technical language.

2.3.4   The vicious triangle

Having established that these three evils exist, matters become even worse. Each of these three evils does not exist in isolation, but will feed into one another. Therefore, unmanaged complexity will lead to a lack of understanding and communication problems. Communication problems will lead to unidentified complexity and a lack of understanding. Finally, a lack of understanding will lead to communication problems and complexity.

The three evils, therefore, form a triangle of evil that it is impossible to eliminate. In fact, the best that one may hope for is to address each of these evils in their entirety and try to minimise each one. In fact, it is important to always consider these three evils at all stages of a project and when looking at any view of a system, include EAs.

2.4 Modelling

Having considered why modelling is so important and having discussed the three evils, it is time to introduce a definition of modelling and some of the principles associated with it that form the foundations for the rest of the book. Modelling allows us to identify complexity, aid understanding and improve communication – all important if a successful EA is to be developed.

2.4.1 Defining modelling

To understand modelling, it is important to define it. We define a model as a *simplification of reality* [1]. It is important to simply reality in order to understand the system. This is because, as human beings, we cannot comprehend complexity.

If a model is a simplification of reality, there are many things then that may be thought of as a model:

- Mathematical models, such as equations that represent different aspects of a system that may be used as part of a formal analysis or proof.
- Physical models, such as mock-ups, that may be used to provide a picture of what the final system will look like or may be used as part of a physical simulation or analysis.
- Visual models, such as drawings and plans that may be used as a template for creation or the basis of analysis.
- Text models, such as written specifications that are perhaps the most widely used of the tools at our disposal. Regarding text as a model can be initially quite surprising but the second that we start to describe something in words; we are simplifying it to understand it.

This is by no means an exhaustive list, but it conveys the general message.

It is important to model so that we can identify complexity, increase our understanding and to communicate in an unambiguous (or as unambiguous-as-possible) manner.

To model effectively, it is essential to have a common language that may be used to carry out the modelling. There are many modelling approaches that exist, including graphical, mathematical, textual, etc. but, regardless of the approach taken, there are a number of requirements for any modelling language:

- the choice of model
- the level of abstraction
- connection to reality
- independent views of the same system

Each of these are considered below.

2.4.2   The choice of model

The choice of model refers to the fact that there are many ways to solve the same problem. Some of these will be totally incorrect but there is always more than one correct way to solve the problem at hand. Although all these approaches may be correct, some will be more *appropriate* and, hence, more correct for the application. For example, if one wanted to know the answer to a mathematical equation, there are several approaches open: you may simply ask someone else what the answer is, you may guess the answer, you may apply formal mathematical analysis and formulae or you may enter the equation into a mathematical software application. All may yield a correct answer, but the most appropriate approach will be application-dependent. If you were merely curious to the answer to the equation, then guessing or asking someone else may be entirely appropriate. If, on the other hand, the equation was an integral part of the control algorithm for an aeroplane, then something more formal would be more appropriate.

It is important that we have a number of different tools available to choose the most appropriate solution to a problem, rather than just relying on the same approach every time.

Therefore, one requirement for any modelling language is that it must be flexible enough to allow different representation of the same information to allow the optimum solution to be chosen.

2.4.3   The level of abstraction

Any system may be considered at many different levels of abstraction. For example, an office block may be viewed as a single entity from an outside point of view. This is known as a high level of abstraction. It is also possible to view a tiny part of the office block, for example the circuit diagram associated with a dimmer light switch in one of the offices. This is what is known as a low level of abstraction. As well as the high and low levels of abstraction, it is also necessary to look at many intermediate levels of abstraction, such as each floor layout on each level, each room layout, the lifts (or elevators), the staircases and so on. Only by looking at something at high, low and in-between levels of abstraction is it possible to gain a full understanding of a system.

Therefore, the second requirement for any modelling language is that any system must be able to be represented at different levels of abstraction.

2.4.4   Connection to reality

It was already stated that, by the very nature of modelling, we are simplifying reality and there is a very real danger that we may over-simplify to such a degree that the model loses all connection to reality and, hence, all relevant meaning.

One type of modelling that is very easy to lose the connection to reality is that of mathematical modelling. Mathematical modelling is an essential part of any engineering endeavour, but it can often be seen as some sort of dark art as very few people possess a sufficient knowledge as to make it usable and, indeed, many people are petrified of maths! Consider the example of the mathematical operation of differentiation that is used to solve differential equations. As every school child knows, differentiation can be applied in a quite straightforward manner to achieve a result. What this actually means in real life, however, is entirely another matter for discussion. Differentiation allows us to find the slope of a line which, when taken at face value, and particularly when at school, can be viewed as being utterly meaningless. To take this example a little further, we are then told that integration is the *opposite* of differentiation (what is the opposite of finding the slope of a line?) which turns out to be measuring the area underneath a line. Again, when first encountered, this can be viewed as being meaningless. In fact, it is not until later in the educational process when studying subjects such as physics or electronics that one realises that finding the slope of a line can be useful for calculating rate of change, velocity, acceleration, etc. It is this application, in this example, that provides the connection to reality and hence helps communicate 'why'.

The third requirement for any modelling language, therefore, is that it must be able to have a strong connection to reality and, hence, to meaningful observers who, in many cases, should require no specialist knowledge, other than an explanation, to understand the meaning of any model.

2.4.5   Independent views of the same system

Different people require different pieces of information, depending on who they are and what their role is in the system. It is essential that the right people get the right information at the right time. Also, for the purpose of analysing a system, it is important to be able to observe a system from many different points of view. For example, consider the office block again where there would be all different types of people who require different information. The electricians require wiring diagrams – not colour charts or plumbing data; the decorators require colour charts and not wiring diagrams and so on.

There is a potentially very large problem when considering things from different points of view and this is consistency. Consistency is the key to creating a correct and consistent model and, without any consistency, it is not possible to have or demonstrate any confidence in the system.

The fourth requirement, therefore, for any modelling language, is that it must allow any system to be looked at from different points of view and that these views *must* be consistent.

2.5   The UML

The previous sections have identified many requirements for modelling and have justified why modelling is so important. To model successfully, a common language is required and that common language which is used throughout this book is the Unified Modelling Language (UML).

The UML is a general-purpose modelling language that is intended for software-intensive systems. This definition is far too restricting however. The UML is a language and can thus be used to communicate any form of information and should not be limited to software. The main aim of this book is to take the UML and apply it to the modelling of EAs.

2.5.1   Background to the UML

The UML was defined in 1997 and was developed to simplify and consolidate the many existing methods which were developed throughout the 1970s, 1980s and 1990s. With so many modelling languages and methodologies being developed and used, one of the main reasons for modelling – that of communicating effectively – was being destroyed as, in a bizarre Babel-like scenario, everyone ended up speaking different languages when they were actually trying to solve this problem. There was thus a huge industrial need to consolidate all these techniques into a single, usable, flexible language. In addition, by making the UML a language rather than a methodology (a language with an inherent process), it became more generally acceptable and far more powerful than its predecessors.

The creation of the UML was driven by industry to address different life cycles, notations, industries and business domains and, given that the UML is now probably the most widely used modelling notation in the world, it has proved a great success at meeting these industrial drivers.

Another contributing factor to its success is that it is non-proprietary so that it is not owned by a single organisation. The Object Management Group retains ownership and responsibility for the UML standard itself and, as such, it is in the public domain. Indeed, an earlier version of UML is now an ISO standard [4]. For more details on the history of UML see Reference 5.

2.5.2   The UML model

Any UML model has two aspects. These two aspects of the model are the 'structural' and 'behavioural' aspects of the model. It is vital that both of these aspects exist for any system, otherwise the system is not fully defined.

The structural aspect of the model shows the 'things' or entities in a system and the relationships between them. It is crucial to remember that the structural aspect of the model shows 'what' the system looks like and 'what' it does, but not 'how'. The structural aspect of the model may be thought of as a snapshot in time of any system.

The behavioural aspect of the model shows the 'how'. The behavioural aspect of the model demonstrates how a system behaves over time by showing the order in which things happen, the conditions under which they happen and the interactions between things.

Each of these two aspects of the model must exist. Understanding the need for these two aspects is absolutely fundamental to understanding the UML. The structural aspect of the model may be realised by six UML diagrams: class diagrams, object diagrams, package diagrams, composite structure diagrams, deployment diagrams and component diagrams. The behavioural aspect of the model may be realised using seven UML diagrams: state machine diagrams, use cases, interaction diagrams (sequence, communication, interaction overview and timing diagrams) and activity diagrams. Structural and behavioural modelling is the subject of the next chapter, while each of the 13 diagrams is discussed in more detail in Chapter 4.

References

1. Booch, G., Rumbaugh, J. & Jacobson, I. *The Unified Modeling Language User Guide*. 2nd edn. Boston, MA: Addison-Wesley; 2005.
2. Elk, A. The brontosaurus sketch, *Monty Python's Flying Circus*. BBC TV; 1974.
3. Brookes, F.P. *The Mythical Man-month*. Boston, MA: Addison-Wesley; 1995.
4. International Standards Organisation. ISO 19501, Information technology – Open Distributed Processing – Unified Modeling Language (UML) Version 1.4.2. ISO Publishing; 2005.
5. Holt J. *UML for Systems Engineering – Watching the Wheels*. 2nd edn. London: IEE Publishing; 2004 (reprinted IET Publishing; 2007).

Chapter 3

Introduction to the notation

There is nothing more difficult to take in hand, more perilous to con-
duct or more uncertain in its success than to take the lead in the
introduction of a new order of things.

Niccolo Machiavelli (1469–1527), The Prince (1532)

3.1 Introduction

Modelling is fundamental to everything that is presented in this book. A brief
introduction to modelling has been discussed in Chapter 2, along with a set of
requirements for any modelling language.

To produce any sort of real model of an enterprise architecture (EA), it is essential
that the model is looked at in terms of two aspects: both the structural and the behavioural aspects of the enterprise must be considered to generate a complete EA.

This chapter looks at both structural and behavioural modelling in turn and introduces the Unified Modelling Language (UML) syntax along with the main concepts
that must be understood to model effectively. Only the briefest of syntax will be looked
at in this chapter. For a more detailed description of the UML syntax, see Chapter 4.

3.2 Structural modelling

The structural aspect of the model shows the 'things' or entities in a system and the
relationships between them. It shows 'what' the system looks like and 'what' it
does, but not 'how'. The structural aspect of the model may be thought of as a
snapshot in time of the system.

It is worth noting that the word 'system' used here and throughout the book is
used simply to refer to the subject of the model. As a reader of this book your 'system'
will be the EA that you are developing – a system that is made up of both
'hard' systems, such as IT infrastructure and software, production lines, etc., and 'soft'
systems, such as business processes, capabilities, competencies, etc. The UML is not
restricted to modelling 'hard' systems and by the end of the book you will see that the
UML is powerful enough to model both types of system.

The UML has six diagrams that can be used to realise structural aspects of the
system. They are shown in the Figure 3.1.

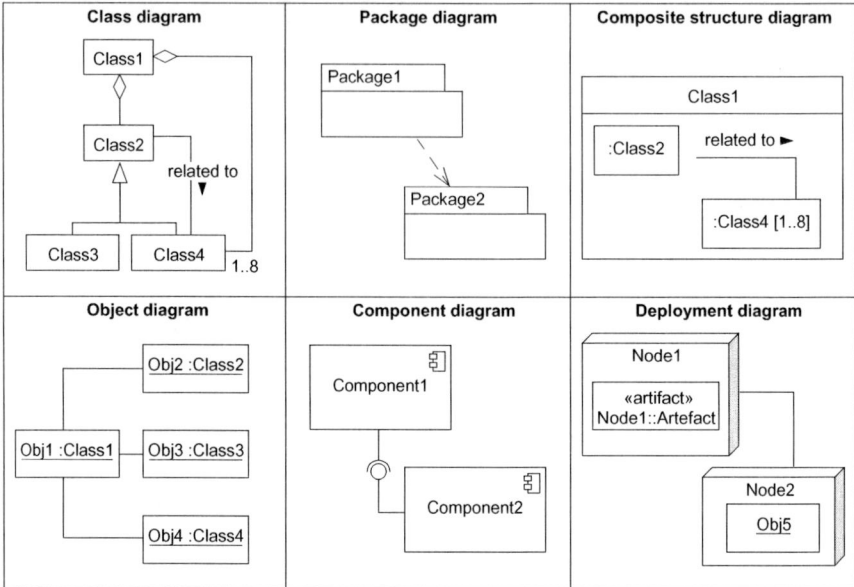

Figure 3.1   Types of UML structural diagrams

Figure 3.1 shows the six types of diagram that can be used to realise the structural aspect of the model: class diagram, package diagram, composite structure diagram, object diagram, component diagram and deployment diagram.

To illustrate the concepts behind structural modelling, one of the six structural diagrams will be used to show some simple examples. The diagram chosen is the class diagram as this forms the backbone of the UML. In addition, the structural modelling principles that will be shown in this section with reference to class diagrams can be applied when using any type of structural diagram.

3.3   Structural modelling using class diagrams

3.3.1   Introduction

The class diagram is, arguably, the most widely used diagram in the UML. Class diagrams have a long history and are present in some shape or form in all of the other methodologies that contributed to the definition of the UML. The class diagram is also the richest diagram in terms of the amount of syntax available to the modeller. As with all UML diagrams, it is not necessary to use every piece of syntax, as experience has shown that 80 per cent of any modelling task can be achieved by using approximately 20 per cent of class diagram syntax. The simplest (and wisest) approach is to learn the bare minimum syntax and then to learn more as and when circumstances dictate.

3.3.2 Basic modelling

There are two basic elements that make up a class diagram – the 'class' and the 'relationship'. Clearly, there are many ways to expand on these basic elements, but provided that they are understood clearly and simply, the rest of the syntax follows on naturally and is very intuitive.

A 'class' represents a type of 'thing' that exists in the real world and, therefore, should have a very close connection to reality. Classes are almost always given names that are nouns (or noun phrases), as nouns are 'things' and so are classes. This may seem a trivial point, but it can form a very powerful heuristic when assessing and analysing systems as it can be an indicator of whether something may appear as a class on a model.

The second element in a class diagram is a relationship that relates together one or more class. Relationships should have names that form sentences when read together with their associated classes. Remember that the UML is a language and should thus be able to be 'read' as one would read any language. If a diagram is difficult to read, it is likely that it is not a very clear diagram and should perhaps be 'rewritten' so that it can be read more clearly. Reading a good UML diagram should not involve effort in the same way that any sentence should not be difficult to read.

Now that the basics have been covered, it is time to look at example class diagrams. It should be pointed out that from this point, all diagrams that are shown will be UML diagrams. In addition, although some of the diagrams may seem trivial, they are all legitimate and correct diagrams and convey some meaning – which is the whole point of the UML.

Figure 3.2 shows two very simple classes. Classes are represented graphically by rectangles in the UML and each must have a name, which is written inside the rectangle. To understand the diagram, it is important to read the symbols. The diagram here shows that two classes exist: 'Class 1' and 'Class 2'. This is one of the first UML diagrams in the book and, if you can read this, then you are well on the way to understanding the UML.

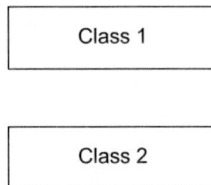

```
┌─────────────────────┐
│                     │
│       Class 1       │
│                     │
└─────────────────────┘


┌─────────────────────┐
│                     │
│       Class 2       │
│                     │
└─────────────────────┘
```

Figure 3.2   Representing classes

Figure 3.3 shows how to represent a relationship between two classes. The type of relationship shown in this diagram is known as an 'association' and is a general type of relationship that relates together one or more class. The association is represented by a line that joins two classes, with the association name written somewhere on the line. This diagram reads: two classes exist: 'Class 1' and 'Class 2' and 'Class 1' associates 'Class 2'.

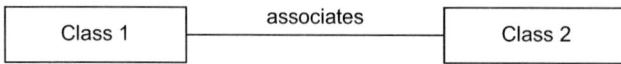

Figure 3.3   Representing a relationship

Figure 3.4 shows an example that is based on real life. The diagram reads: there are two classes: 'Dog' and 'Cat' where 'Dog' chases 'Cat'.

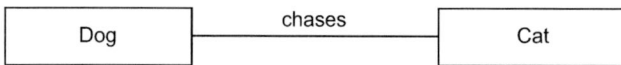

Figure 3.4   Examples of classes and associations

This illustrates a very important point concerning classes, as classes are conceptual and do not actually exist in the real world. There is no such thing as 'Cat', but there do exist many examples of 'Cat'. A class represents a grouping of things that look and behave in the same way, as, at one level, all examples of 'Cat' will have a common set of features and behaviours that may be represented by the class 'Cat'. What this class is really representing is the blueprint of 'Cat', or the essence of 'Cat'.

Another important point illustrated here is that every diagram, no matter how simple, has the potential to contain a degree of ambiguity. Figure 3.4 is ambiguous as it could be read in one of two ways, depending on the direction in which the association is read. Who is to say that the diagram is to be read 'Dog' chases 'Cat' rather than 'Cat' chases 'Dog', as it is possible for both cases to be true. It should be pointed out that for this particular example the world that is being modelled is a stereotypical world where dogs always chase cats, and not the other way around. Therefore, there is some ambiguity as the diagram must only be read in one direction for it to be true. To remove this ambiguity, a mechanism is required to indicate direction.

The simplest way to show direction is to place a direction marker on the association that will indicate which way the line should be read, as shown in Figure 3.5. The diagram now reads 'Dog' chases 'Cat' and definitely not 'Cat' chases 'Dog' and is thus less ambiguous than Figure 3.4.

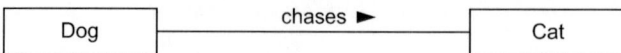

Figure 3.5   Showing direction with a direction marker

The second way to show direction is to define a 'role' on each end of the association, as shown in Figure 3.6. In this case, the two roles that have been defined are 'chaser' and 'chasee', which again eliminates the ambiguity that existed in Figure 3.4.

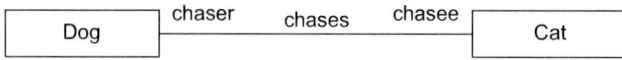

| Dog | chaser | chases | chasee | Cat |

Figure 3.6   Showing direction with role names

Figure 3.7 introduces a new association called 'dislikes'. This time, however, the lack of direction is intentional as both statements of 'Dog' dislikes 'Cat' and 'Cat' dislikes 'Dog' are equally true. Therefore, when no direction is indicated, it is assumed that the association can be read in both directions. That is the association is said to be 'bi-directional'. However, such bi-directional associations do nothing to remove ambiguity. When looking at Figure 3.7, the reader is forced to consider whether the association is intended to be bi-directional or whether the directionality has been accidentally omitted from the diagram. For this reason, it may be better to annotate the diagram with a 'note' as shown in Figure 3.8.

| Dog | dislikes | Cat |

Figure 3.7   Bi-directional associations

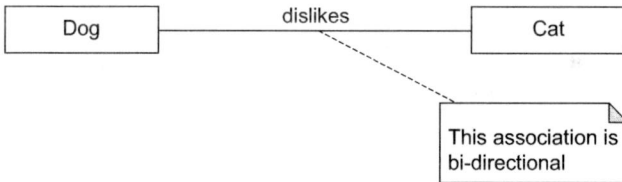

| Dog | dislikes | Cat |

This association is bi-directional

Figure 3.8   Removing ambiguity in bi-directional associations

The note in Figure 3.8 is used to show that the association is bi-directional, helping to remove ambiguity from the diagram. It would be desirable to show bi-directional associations with two direction markers at each end of the association name, pointing in opposite directions. Unfortunately the UML syntax does not allow this.

Another reason why the diagram may be misunderstood is because there is no concept of the number of cats and dogs involved in the chasing in the previous diagrams. Expressing this numbering is known as 'multiplicity', which is illustrated in Figure 3.9.

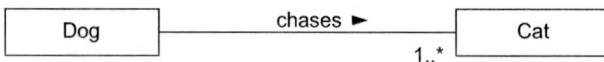

| Dog | chases ► | Cat |
1..*

Figure 3.9   Showing numbers using multiplicity

Figure 3.9 shows that each 'Dog' chases one or more 'Cat'. If no number is indicated, as in the case of the 'Dog' end of the association, it is assumed that the number is 'one'. Although the number is one, it does not necessarily indicate that there is only one dog, but rather that the association applies for each dog. The multiplicity at the other end of the 'chases' association states '1..*', which means 'one or more' or somewhere between one and many. Therefore, the association shows that each 'Dog' chases one or more 'Cat', and that each 'Cat' is chased by only one 'Dog'.

Figure 3.10 shows a case where the multiplicity has been changed, changing the entire meaning of the model. In this case, the diagram is read as: one or more 'Dog' chases one or more 'Cat'. This could mean that a single dog chases a single cat, a single dog chases any number or a herd of cats, or that an entire pack of dogs is chasing a herd of cats.

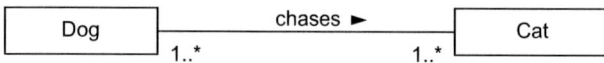

Figure 3.10   Showing numbers using multiplicity (continued)

Which of the two examples of multiplicity is correct? The answer will depend on the application that is being modelled and it is up to the modeller to decide which is the more accurate of the two.

It is important to note that if no multiplicity has been indicated, then the association end carries a default value of '1'. However, this can lead to some problems as in the case when the number is omitted by accident, rather than design, which leaves the multiplicity unspecified. It is suggested therefore, in the UML specification that the number '1' should be included in all diagrams to show that the lack of number is not an omission. The only real argument against this is that it can render some diagram far less readable. The final decision of whether or not to include the number 1s lies with the modeller.

The modeller must decide on the appropriate multiplicity, which may require changing as the model evolves. The common multiplicities are as follows:

0..1 which indicates an optional value

1 which indicates exactly one

0..* which indicates any number, including zero

* same as 0..*

1..* which indicates 1 or more

In fact, any subset of the non-negative integers can be used to specify a multiplicity. If, for example, a dog can chase between 1 and 3 cats, then the multiplicity at the 'Cat' end of the association in Figure 3.10 would be changed to '1..3'.

3.3.3   Adding more detail to classes

So far, classes and relationships have been introduced, but the amount of detailed information for each class is very low. After all, it was said that the class 'Cat' represented all cats that looked and behaved in the same way, but it is not defined anywhere how a cat looks or behaves. This section examines how to add this information to a class by using 'attributes' and 'operations'.

Consider again the class of 'Cat', but now think about what general attributes the cat possesses. It is very important to limit the number of general attributes that are identified to only those that are relevant, as it is very easy to get carried away and over-define the amount of detail for a class.

For this example, suppose that we wish to represent the features 'age', 'weight', 'colour' and 'favourite food' on the class 'Cat'. These features are represented on the class as 'attributes' – one for each feature – as shown in Figure 3.11.

Cat
age
weight
colour
favourite food

Figure 3.11   Attributes of the class 'Cat'

Attributes are written in a box below the class name box. When modelling, it is possible to add more detail at this point, such as the visibility of the attribute, type, default values and so forth. As attributes represent features of a class, they are usually represented by nouns and they must also be able to take on different values. For example, 'colour' is a valid attribute, whereas 'black' would not be in most cases, as 'black' would represent an actual value of an attribute rather than an attribute itself. It is possible for 'black' to be an attribute, but this would mean that the attribute would have a Boolean type (true or false) to describe a situation where we would only be interested in black cats and not any other type.

Attributes describe how to represent features of a class, or to show what it looks like, but they do not describe what the class does, which is represented using 'operations'.

Operations show what a class does, rather than what it looks like, and are usually represented by verbs. In the case of the class 'Cat' we have identified three things that the cat does, which are 'eat', 'sleep' and 'run'. These are shown in Figure 3.12.

Operations are represented in the UML by adding another rectangle below the attribute rectangle and writing the operation names within it. Operations may be defined further by adding extra detail – for example, arguments, return values and visibility.

The class 'Cat' is now fully defined for our purposes and the same exercise may be carried out on any other classes in our system to fully populate the model. It should also be pointed out that the classes may be left at a high level with no

Cat
age
weight
colour
favourite food
eat()
sleep()
run()

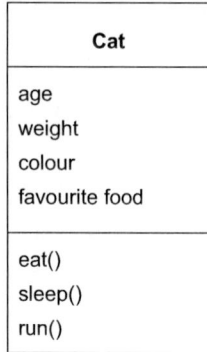

Figure 3.12   Operations of the class 'Cat'

attributes or operations. As with everything in the UML, only use as much detail as is necessary, rather than as much as is possible.

3.3.4   Adding more detail to relationships

The previous section showed how to add more detail to classes, while this section shows how to add more detail to relationships, by defining some special types that are commonly encountered in modelling. There are four types of relationship that will be discussed here: 'association', 'aggregation', 'specialisation' and 'dependency', which represent the majority of the most common uses of relationships.

Associations have already been introduced and shown to be a very general type of relationship that relate together one or more class. Therefore, they will not be discussed in any further detail, so the next three sections cover each of the other special types of relationship.

3.3.4.1   Aggregation and composition

The second type of relationship is a special type of association that allows assemblies and structures to be modelled and is known as 'aggregation'.

Figure 3.13 provides an example of aggregation. Aggregation is shown graphically in the UML by a diamond shape and when reading the diagram is read by saying 'is made up of'. Starting from the top of the diagram, the model is read as: 'Cat' wears 'Collar'. The direction is indicated with the small arrow and there is a one-on-one relationship between the two classes. The multiplicity here is implied to be one to one as there is no indication.

The 'Collar' is made up of (the aggregation symbol) a 'Bell', a 'Belt' and a 'Buckle'. The 'Bell' is on the 'Belt' and the 'Buckle' is on the 'Belt'. The 'Bell' is made up of (the aggregation symbol) a 'Clasp', a 'Donger' and a 'Sphere'.

This is the basic structure of the bell and allows levels of abstraction of detail to be shown on a model.

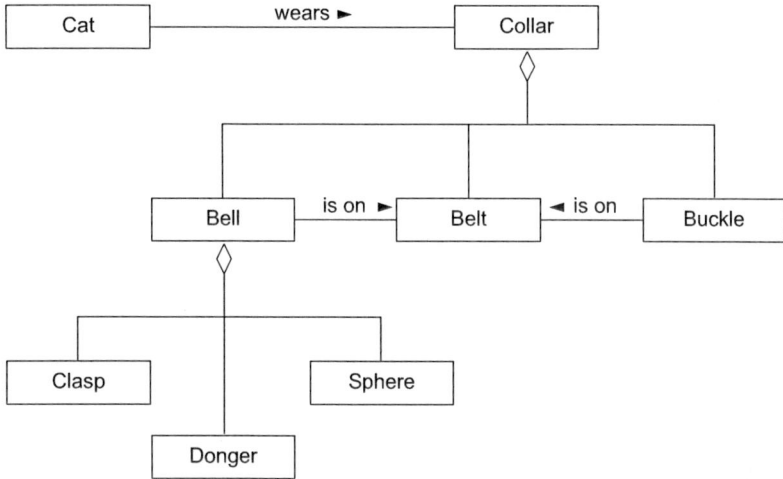

Figure 3.13 Example of aggregation

It is worth noting here that the 'tree' layout of the aggregations beneath 'Collar' and 'Bell' is a notational convenience. There are actually six aggregations in the diagram, three under each of 'Collar' and 'Bell'. When the multiplicity at the diamond end are the same, then the aggregations can be overlain in this manner. If the multiplicities are *not* the same, then the aggregations must be shown as separate relations. In most cases, the multiplicity at the diamond end of an aggregation is usually '1' but need not be. The following two diagrams illustrate this further.

The diagram in Figure 3.14 shows a typical railway 'Carriage' that is made up of four 'Door', six 'Window' and two 'Bogie'. (A bogie is the structure underneath a carriage at both ends to which axles and wheels are attached through bearings.) Since the multiplicity at the diamond end of the aggregation is '1' (remember, this is the default multiplicity if none is shown) the three aggregations can be overlaid into the 'tree' style as shown.

In the United Kingdom there are some train sets that are made up of carriages that share bogies as shown in Figure 3.15.

As can be seen in the diagram, each bogie is shared between two carriages. The class diagram has been updated to show this by changing the multiplicity at the diamond end of the aggregation between 'Carriage' and 'Bogie' to '2'.

Now, since this has a different multiplicity to the other two aggregations, it cannot be overlain on top of the other two (which can still be overlain) and must be shown separately. If it *were* overlain then it would be impossible to tell which of the three aggregations the '2' applied to.

There is also a second special type of association that shows an aggregation-style of relationship, known as 'composition'. The difference between composition and aggregation is subtle but very important and can convey much meaning. The simplest way to show this difference is to consider an example, as shown in Figure 3.16.

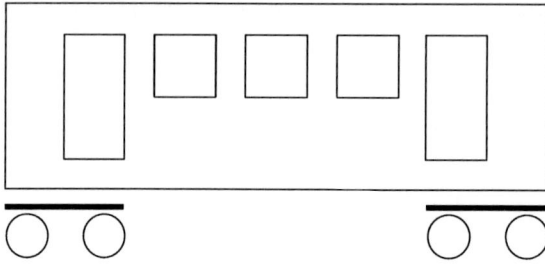

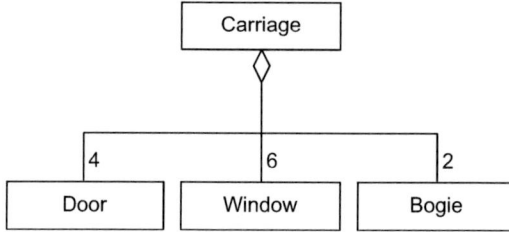

Figure 3.14   Overlaying aggregations – identical multiplicities

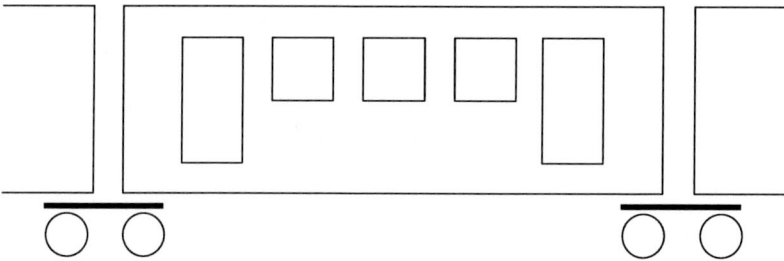

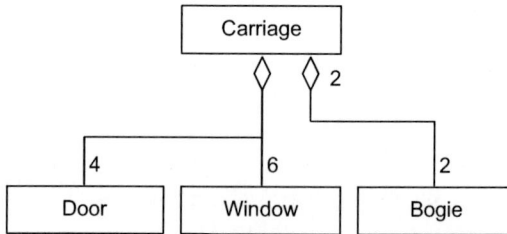

Figure 3.15   Overlaying aggregations – different multiplicities

Figure 3.16 shows the structure of the humble garden fork. It can be seen that a 'Garden Fork' is made up of a 'Head', a 'Shaft' and a 'Handle', with the 'Head' and 'Handle' attached to the shaft.

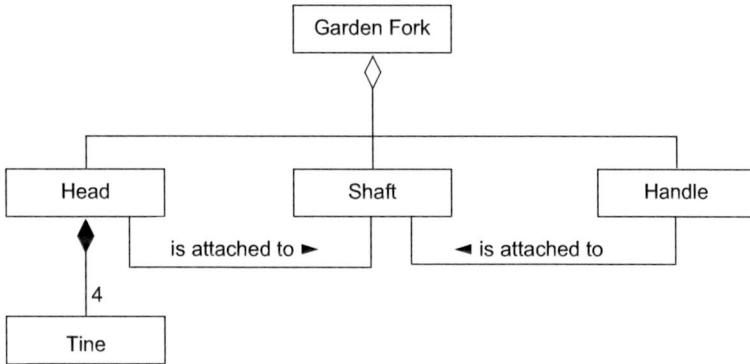

Figure 3.16   Example of the difference between composition and aggregation

The 'Head' is made up of four 'Tine', but this time the diamond under 'Head' is solid in contrast to the empty diamond in the aggregations under 'Garden Fork'. The solid diamond indicates that the relationship is a 'composition' rather than an aggregation. This means that the component parts (in this case 'Tine') represent meaningful concepts but may *not* exist in their own right.

In terms of the 'Garden Fork' this means that if any of the 'Handle', 'Shaft' or 'Head' are damaged or worn out, they can be replaced. However, if a 'Tine' is damaged it cannot be replaced (at least not without some rather tiresome welding!), but requires the replacement of the entire 'Head'. The 'Tine' is an integral part of the 'Head' rather than being an independent part in its own right, although it represents a meaningful concept which, in the case of a garden fork, can be touched and, if one is not careful, felt! Such a class may have its own attributes and/or operations, even when used as part of the composition relationship.

Aggregations and compositions are often used to show *structural hierarchies*, with aggregations used to show 'replaceable units' and compositions to show the structure of the *least* replaceable units in the hierarchy.

3.3.4.2   Specialisation and generalisation

The third special type of relationship is known as 'specialisation' or 'general-isation', depending on which way the relationship is read. 'Specialisation' refers to the case when a class is being made more special or is being refined in some way. Specialisation may be read as 'has types' whenever its symbol, a small triangle, is encountered on a model. If the relationship is read the other way around, then the triangle symbol is read as 'is a type of', which is a generalisation. Therefore, read one way the class becomes more special (specialisation) and read the other way, the class becomes more general (generalisation).

Specialisation is used to show 'child' classes, sometimes referred to as 'sub-classes', of a 'parent' class. Child classes inherit their appearance and behaviour from their parent classes, but will be different in some way to make them special. In UML terms, this means that a child class will inherit any attributes and operations that its parent class has, but may have additional attributes or operations that make the child class special.

As an example of this, consider Figure 3.17, which shows a rather science-fiction inspired definition of the different types of life known to man.

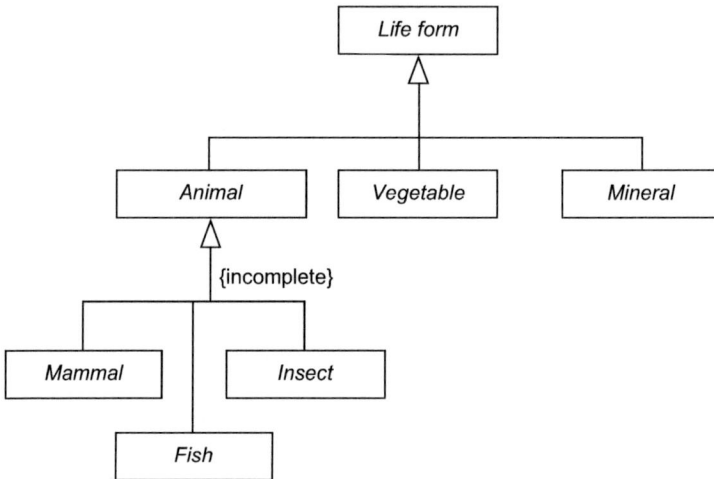

Figure 3.17   Life-form hierarchy

The top class is called 'Life form' and has three child classes: 'Animal', 'Vegetable' and 'Mineral', which makes 'Life form' the parent class. Going down one level, it can be seen that 'Animal' has three child classes: 'Mammal', 'Fish' and 'Insect'. Notice now how 'Animal' is the parent class to its three child classes, while still being a child class of 'Life form'.

Also notice the use of '{incomplete}' on the specialisations beneath 'Animal'. This is an example of a UML *constraint* that constrains the diagram in some way or adds extra information to the diagram. Constraints are one of the standard extension mechanisms for the UML. The constraint '{incomplete}' indicates that there are additional child classes of 'Animal' that are not shown on the diagram.

The diagram may be read in two ways:

1. From the bottom up: 'Mammal', 'Fish' and 'Insect' are types of 'Animal'. 'Animal', 'Vegetable' and 'Mineral' are all types of 'Life form'.
2. From the top down: 'Life form' has three types: 'Animal', 'Vegetable' and 'Mineral'. The class 'Animal' has three types: 'Mammal', 'Fish' and 'Insect'.

At this point it is worth noting another piece of UML syntax that can be used on class diagrams and which can be seen in the diagram in Figure 3.17. Notice how each of the classes in the diagram have class names that are in *italic* font. This indicates that the classes are what are known as *abstract* classes. An abstract class is one which cannot have an instance – a 'real-life' example (see the section on object diagrams in Chapter 4 for a discussion of instances) but which still exists as a valid concept. For the diagram in Figure 3.17, this means that there are no examples of things that are just mammals, or animals or life forms, etc. You could not go into a pet shop and buy a 'mammal' because 'mammal' is an *abstract* concept; rather you would have to buy a cat or dog or rabbit, etc. If this seems an unduly pedantic piece of notation, do not worry about using it. Many people who model success-fully using the UML never use abstract classes.

This example has explained how to read class diagrams containing speciali-sations, but has not covered one of the most important concepts associated with generalisation and specialisation, that of inheritance. This is best illustrated by considering the diagram in Figure 3.18.

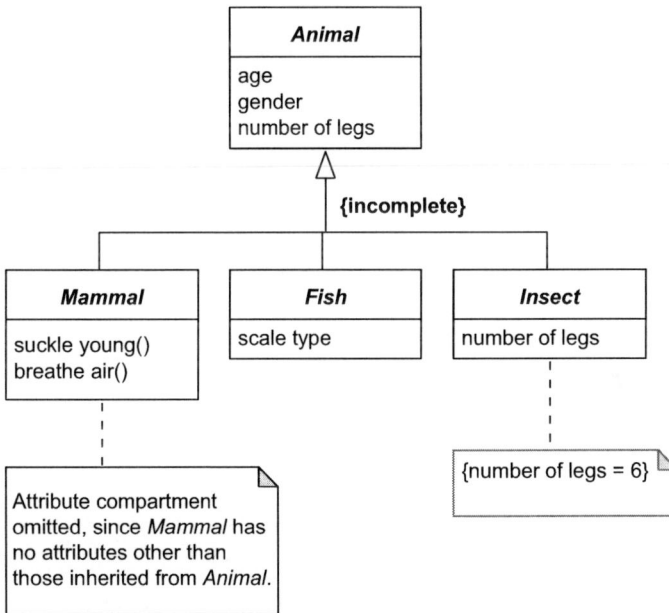

Figure 3.18   Example of inheritance

Figure 3.18 shows an expanded version of Figure 3.17 by adding some attri-butes and operations to the classes. It shows that the class 'Animal' has three attributes: 'age', 'gender' and 'number of legs'. These attributes will apply to all types of animal and will therefore be inherited by their child classes. That is to say that any child classes will automatically have the same three attributes. This inheritance also applies to the behaviour of the parent class. If some operations had been defined for the class 'Animal', these would also be inherited by each of the child classes. What makes the child class different and therefore an independent class in its own right is the addition of extra attributes and operations or constraints on existing attributes. Let us consider an example of each one of these cases.

The class 'Mammal' has inherited the three attributes from its parent class. Inherited attributes (and operations) are not usually shown on child classes. In addition, it has had an extra two operations identified, which the parent class does not possess: 'breathe air' and 'suckle young'. This is behaviour that all mammals possess, whereas not all animals 'breathe air' and 'suckle young'. These operations are why mammals are special compared to animals generally.

The class 'Fish' has inherited the three attributes from its parent class (which are not shown), but has had an extra attribute added that its parent class will not possess: 'scale type'. This makes the child class more specialised than the parent class.

The class 'Insect' has no extra attributes or operations but has a constraint on one of its attribute values. The attribute 'number of legs' is always equal to six, as this is in the nature of insects. The same could be applied to 'mammal' to some extent as 'number of legs' would always be between zero (in the case of whales and dolphins) and four, while 'number of legs' for 'fish' would always be zero.

From a modelling point of view, it may be argued that the attribute 'number of legs' should not be present in the class 'animal' as it is not applicable to fish. This is fine and there is nothing inherently wrong with either model except to say that it is important to pick the most suitable model for the application at hand. Remember that there are many correct solutions to any problem, and thus people's interpretation of information may differ. In the same way, it would also be possible to define two child classes of 'Animal' called 'Male Animal' and 'Female Animal', which would do away with the need for the attribute 'gender', as shown in Figure 3.19.

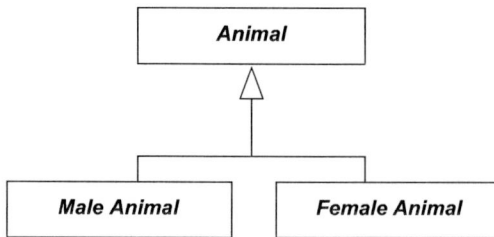

Figure 3.19   Another way to model gender

Figure 3.19 shows another approach to modelling the gender of an animal, which uses specialisation to define male and female sub-classes of 'Animal' rather than using an attribute to define gender. Which approach is the better of the two, the one shown in Figure 3.18 or the one shown in Figure 3.19? Again, it is necessary to pick the most appropriate visual representation of the information and one that you, as the modeller, are comfortable with.

As a final example, let us revisit our old friend the cat who is undeniably a life form, an animal and also a mammal. This gives three layers of inheritance, so that the class 'Cat' may now be represented as in Figure 3.20.

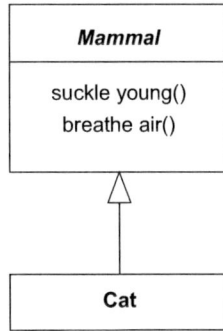

Figure 3.20   A cat's inheritance

Figure 3.20 shows part of the life-form hierarchy extended to include the 'Cat'. Here, it can be seen that 'Cat' is a type of 'Mammal' and therefore inherits all the features and behaviour from its parent class. These are not shown on the diagram, nor are the attributes of 'Animal' inherited by 'Mammal'.

The full attributes and operations of 'Cat' inherited from its parent classes are shown in Figure 3.21.

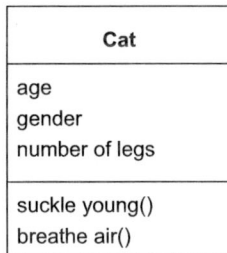

Figure 3.21   A cat's inheritance – expanded

The class 'Cat' is shown in Figure 3.21 with all the inherited attributes and operations from its parent classes. Note the inclusion of the three attributes that are inherited from 'Animal', which, although the class is not included on this particular diagram, still influences the child classes, no matter how far removed.

3.3.4.3   Dependencies

The final type of relationship that will be discussed is that of the 'dependency'. A dependency is used to show that one class is dependent somehow on another. This means that a change in one class may result in a change in its dependent class. A dependency is represented graphically by a dashed line with an arrow on the line end. For example, consider the simple diagram in Figure 3.22.

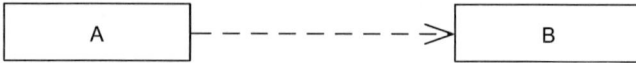

Figure 3.22   A simple dependency

In this example, class 'A' is dependent on class 'B'. This means that any change to class 'B' may result in a change to class 'A'.

By their very nature, dependencies are quite weak relationships and really need to be further adorned using stereotypes to add any real meaning. Many diagrams use the dependency in conjunction with stereotypes, such as the use case diagram and the package diagram where stereotyped dependencies are used to show the relationships between use cases and packages – how one use case *depends* on another or how one package *depends* on another. The use of dependencies on use case diagrams is discussed further in Section 3.5 and dependencies are also discussed in more detail in Chapter 4.

3.3.5   Other structural diagrams

This chapter is intended to introduce structural modelling as a concept, but has so far only considered one of the six structural diagrams: the class diagram. However, the concepts introduced here, that of things and the relationships between them, applies to each of the structural diagrams. Therefore, if you can understand the concepts used here, then it is simply a matter of learning some syntax and some example applications for the other types of diagram. Indeed, this is achieved in Chapter 4 where each of the 13 UML diagrams is described in terms of its syntax and its typical uses. The important thing to realise about all six types of structural diagram is that they all represent the 'what' of a system. The other five diagrams are the package diagram, composite structure diagram, object diagram, component diagram and deployment diagram.

3.3.6   Using class diagrams to understand the UML

As stated earlier, class diagrams are probably the most widely used of the structural diagrams available in UML. To explore the power of structural modelling, we conclude this section by looking at how class diagrams can be used to understand the UML itself. We begin with a summary of this section presented as a class diagram.

The diagram in Figure 3.23 shows a summary of UML models and how they may be realised using the various types of diagram.

A 'Model' is constructed using the 'UML' which is made up of 13 'Diagram'. Each 'Model' has two 'Aspect'. There are two types of 'Aspect' – a 'Structural Aspect' and a 'Behavioural Aspect'. Six 'Diagram' realise the 'Structural Aspect' and seven realise the 'Behavioural Aspect'.

The actual types of diagram are not shown here, but are shown in Figure 3.23, which introduces a package that groups together the various types of structural diagrams.

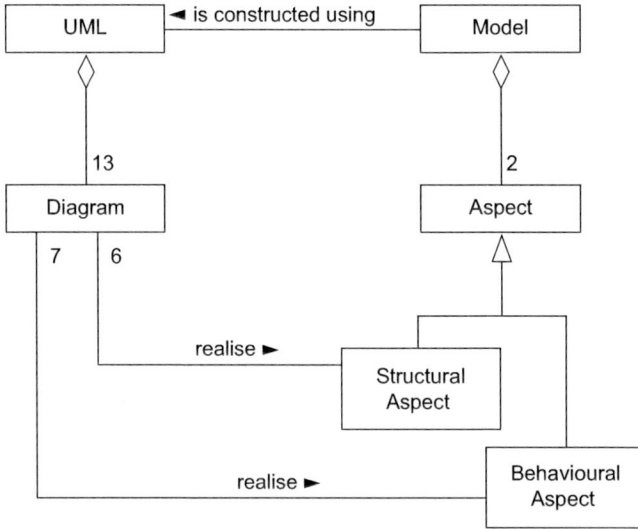

Figure 3.23   Summary of UML models and their associated diagrams

The diagram in Figure 3.24 shows that the package 'Structural Diagrams' (a simple grouping representing the UML structural diagrams) contains 'Class Diagram', 'Package Diagram', 'Composite Structure Diagram', 'Object Diagram', 'Component Diagram' and 'Deployment Diagram'. Thus a simple UML class diagram, itself a UML structural diagram, is being used to model the types of structural diagrams that are available in UML – the UML is being used to model itself!

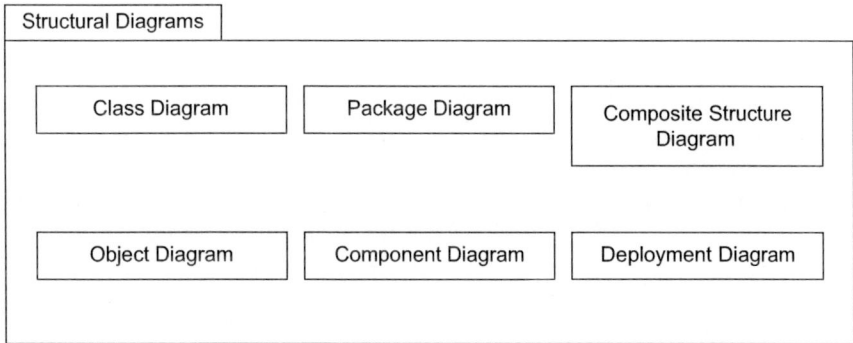

Figure 3.24   Types of structural diagrams

The actual elements that make up the class diagram can also be modelled using a class diagram. This is a concept known as the 'meta-model', which will be used extensively throughout this book.

Remember that the UML is a language and should be able to be read and understood just like any other language. Therefore, the model in Figure 3.25 may be read by reading class name, then any association that is joined to it and then another class name.

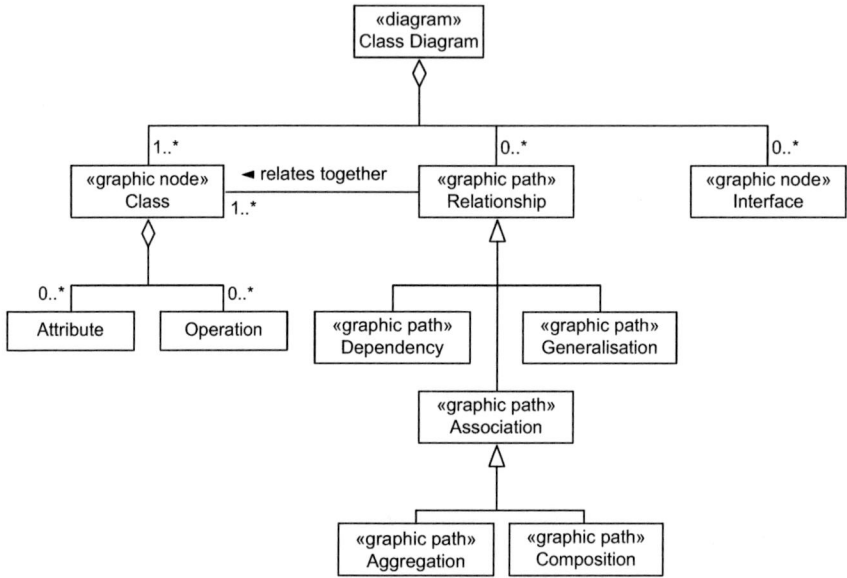

Figure 3.25   Partial meta-model for class diagrams

Reading the diagram, we see that: a 'Class Diagram' is made up of one or more 'Class', zero or more 'Interface' and zero or more 'Relationship'. It is possible for a class diagram to be made up of just a single class with no relationships at all; however, it is not possible to have a class diagram that is made up of just a relationship with no classes. Therefore, the multiplicity on 'Class' is one or more, whereas the multiplicity on 'Relationship' is zero or more.

Each 'Relationship' relates together one or more 'Class'. Notice that the word 'each' is used here, which means that for every single 'Relationship' there are one or more 'Class'. It should also be noted that the multiplicity on the 'Class' side of the association is one or more, as it is possible for a 'Relationship' to relate together one 'Class' – that is to say that a 'Class' may be related to itself.

Each 'Class' is made up of zero or more 'Attribute' and zero or more 'Operation'. This shows how classes may be further described using attributes and operations, or that they may be left with neither.

There are three main types of 'Relationship'.

1.   'Association', which defines a simple association between one or more 'Class'. There are also two specialisations of 'Association': namely the

'Aggregation' and 'Composition' used to model structural hierarchies as discussed earlier in the text.

2. 'Generalisation', which shows a 'has types' relationship that is used to show
    parent and child classes.

3. 'Dependency', which shows that one class is dependent on another. Any class
    that is dependent on another may have to change if the other class changes.

This meta-model concept may be extended to include all the other types of
structural diagram and this is the approach adopted in Chapter 4 to introduce all the
other UML diagram types, where meta-models are discussed in more detail.

3.4   Behavioural modelling

The previous section introduced structural modelling, one of the two basic types of
modelling using the UML. This section introduces the second basic type of modelling that is behavioural modelling.

Behavioural models may be realised using seven types of UML diagram, as
shown in Figure 3.26. The seven types of behavioural UML diagram are: use case
diagrams, sequence diagrams, communication diagrams, state machine diagrams,
activity diagrams, timing diagrams and interaction overview diagrams.

As was discussed in the Section 3.3, structural modelling defines the 'what' of
a system: what it looks like, what it does (but not *how*) and what the relationships
are. If structural modelling tells us 'what', then behavioural modelling tells us
'how'. This 'how' is described by modelling interactions within a system. These
interactions may be modelled at many levels of abstraction with different types of
behavioural diagram suited to modelling the different levels of abstraction. These
levels of abstraction may be categorised as follows:

*   Interactions may be modelled between objects or between subsystems. In
    UML, such models are realised using the four types of interaction diagram:
    communication, timing, interaction overview or sequence diagram.
*   Interactions may also be modelled at a slightly lower level of abstraction by
    considering the interactions within a class or its associated objects. Modelling
    the behaviour over the lifetime of a class, or an object, is achieved by using
    state machine diagrams. State machine diagrams are concerned with one, and
    only one, class and its objects, although it is possible to create more than one
    state machine diagram per class.
*   The lowest level of abstraction for modelling interactions is concerned with the
    interactions within an operation. Interactions within an operation are modelled
    using activity diagrams. Activity diagrams may also be used to model inter-
    actions at a higher level of abstraction, which will be discussed in greater detail
    later in this book.
*   The remaining level of abstraction is at the highest possible level, which is the
    context level of the project, where high-level functionality of the system,
    as defined by its requirements, and its interaction with the outside world, as

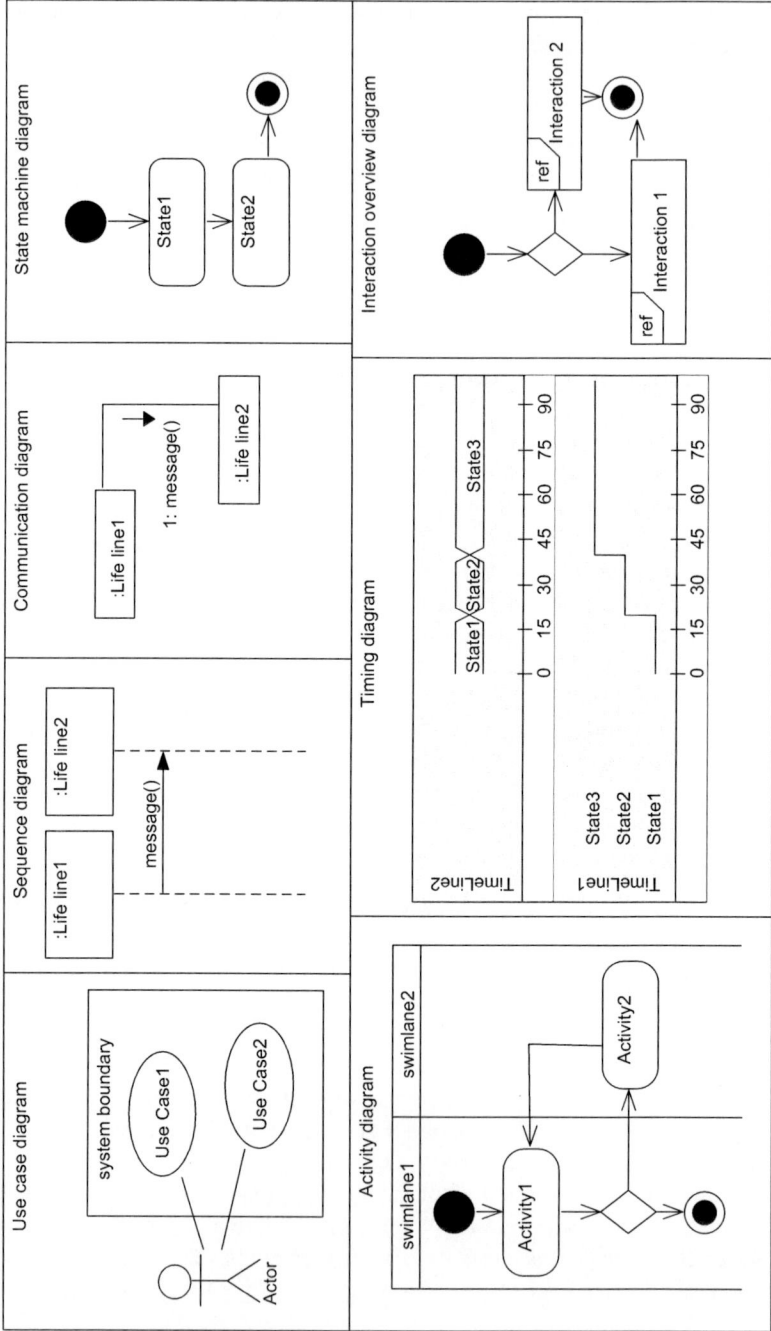

Figure 3.26   Types of UML behavioural diagrams

represented by the project stakeholders, is modelled. These high-level inter-actions are realised using use case diagrams.

As discussed previously in Chapter 1, understanding *why* we are developing an EA is a key issue that has to be addressed. That is the *requirements* for the EA have to be captured and understood. Requirements, as will be seen throughout the book, are key to developing an effective EA. Requirements are modelled in UML using use case diagrams and, given the importance of requirements to the development of EAs, the use case diagram will be used to illustrate behavioural modelling.

For additional and in-depth discussion of behavioural modelling using state machine diagrams rather than use case diagrams, see References 1 and 2.

3.5 Behavioural modelling using use case diagrams

3.5.1 Introduction

The use case diagram, as stated earlier in text, is used to model the *requirements* for the EA being developed, allowing the enterprise architect to address such questions as *why* an EA is needed and *what* an EA must give to an organisation. Use case diagrams are key for understanding the EA and so relate to all the other diagrams used to model an EA. For more information on using use case to model require-ments, see Chapter 6.

3.5.2 Basic modelling

A use case diagram consists of four basic elements: use cases, actors, relationships and system boundaries. Use cases are used to capture the requirements of a system, actors are used to model the stakeholders that have an interest in the system, rela-tionships are used to relate together use case and actors and a system boundary is used to define the context of the system. Each of these elements will be looked at in more detail, starting with the use case.

The use case is the basic unit of the use case diagram and is represented gra-phically by an ellipse which contains the name of the use case written as a verbal phrase. This verbal phrase is a short description of the requirement that the use case is representing. Figure 3.27 shows two use cases: 'Deliver course' and 'Teach new skills' that represent two requirements relating to an organisation that delivers training courses.

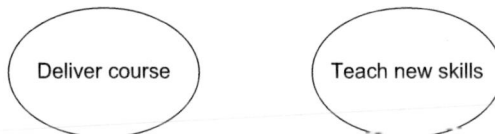

Figure 3.27   Representing use cases

As well as capturing the requirements for a project or system, it is also necessary to model the stakeholders involved in the project. Stakeholders represent the *roles* of the people, organisations, things or other systems that have an interest in the project and are modelled in UML on a use case diagram using actors, as shown in Figure 3.28.

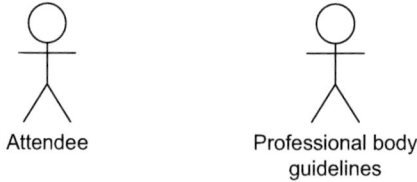

Figure 3.28   Representing actors

An actor is represented on a use case diagram by a 'stick man' labelled with the name of the stakeholder written below. The name 'actor' and the 'stick man' symbol are, unfortunately, perhaps the most confusing and misleading name and symbol used in UML since such a name and visual representation suggests to anyone looking at a use case diagram that an actor represents a person. It does not. Keep in mind that an actor is used to model a stakeholder and that a stakeholder represents the *role* of a person, organisation, thing or other system that have an interest in the project. Figure 3.28 uses two actors to represent two very different stakeholders. 'Attendee' is used to represent the role of a person who is an attendee on a training course, whereas 'Professional body guidelines' is used to represent the role of a set of guidelines that may govern how a course is delivered. The word 'role' must be stressed here, as one of the most common mistakes made on use case diagrams is to label actors with names representing actual people or organisations or position or systems. This is wrong. It is the *role* that the person, organisation, system, etc. takes that is important.

Having the requirements and stakeholders of a system captured on a use case diagram is all well and good, but what makes the use case diagram powerful is the ability to relate use cases to each other and to the actors. This is done using relationships as shown in Figure 3.29.

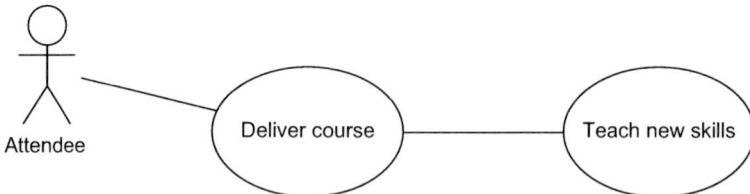

Figure 3.29   Representing relationships

The most basic relationship used on a use case diagram is an association which is shown graphically, as on class diagrams, by a line. However, unlike on a class diagram, an association on a use case diagram has neither multiplicities nor a name and direction, but is a simple unadorned association.

Such an association is drawn between two use cases to show that the requirements, modelled by the use cases, are related. Where a stakeholder has an interest in a requirement, the association is drawn between the actor representing the stakeholder and the use case representing the requirement.

Figure 3.29 shows the same two use cases as seen previously, but this time the association between them shows that the requirements represented by the use cases are somehow related. It also shows that the 'Attendee' stakeholder role has an interest in the 'Deliver course' requirement. The diagram can be read thus: 'Attendee' has an interest in the 'Deliver course' use case which is related to the 'Teach new skills' use case.

Just as with class diagrams, other types of relationship are available for use on a use case diagram. These are discussed in Section 3.5.3.3.

The final element used on use case diagrams is the system boundary, an example of which is shown in Figure 3.30.

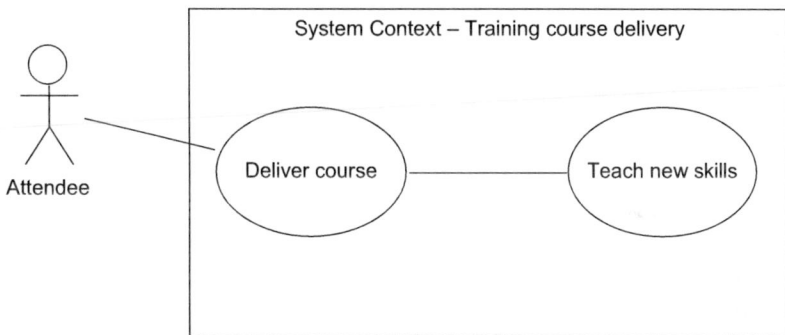

Figure 3.30   Representing contexts

The system boundary is represented graphically on a use case diagram as a rectangle surrounding the use cases but *not* the actors. It defines the boundary of the system. That is everything inside the boundary is part of the system; everything outside the boundary (the actors) is outside the system.

A system boundary defines a *context* for the system taken from a single viewpoint. This is a crucial point. Since a context is drawn from a single point of view it is possible, and indeed desirable, to model multiple contexts for the system. Such contexts include:

• Business context
• System contexts (project, product, etc.)
• In fact, contexts drawn from the point of view of *any* stakeholder.

It is important to differentiate between the different contexts and, for this reason, a system boundary should be labelled to indicate the context it represents, as can be seen in Figure 3.30. It is also important to trace between the various contexts. This is discussed further in Chapter 6.

Having looked at the various elements that make up a use case diagram, it is time to put them all together in an example.

3.5.3   *Behavioural modelling – a simple example*
3.5.3.1   **Introduction**
The diagram in Figure 3.31 shows the results of a requirements gathering exercise carried out by an organisation that delivers training courses.

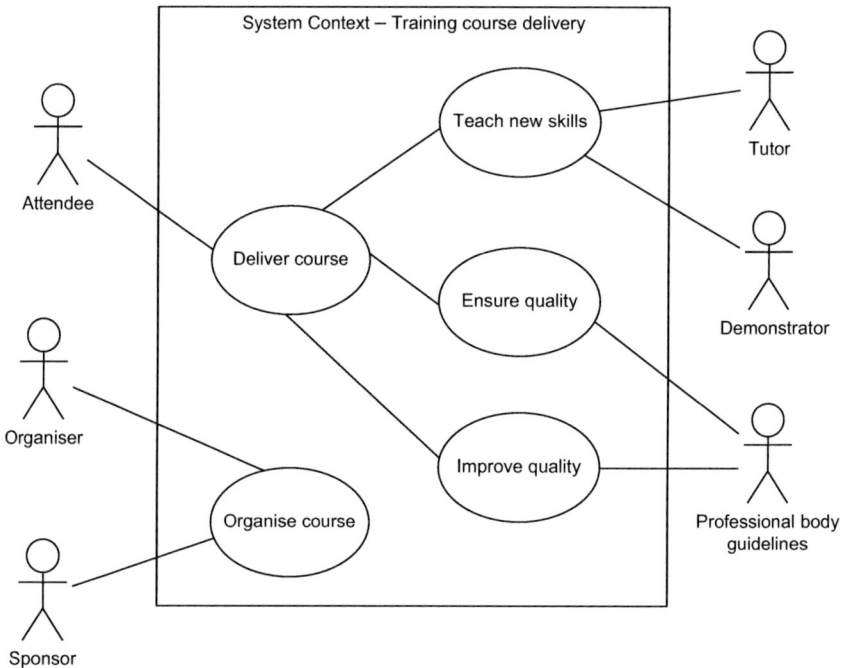

Figure 3.31   Example of use case diagram – training organisation context

The high-level requirements have been identified, along with the relevant stakeholders, for the *system* context – that being training course delivery. Simple association relationships have been added between related use cases and between actors and the use cases they have an interest in. Each of these requirements will need to be further decomposed to fully understand the system and this is considered below.

3.5.3.2   **Focusing on a single requirement**
The use case that will be taken and used for this example is that of 'Organise course'. When thinking about how to decompose this requirement, it is very

tempting to over-decompose. This can lead to all sorts of problems as it is quite easy to go too far and to end up with the system decomposed to such a level as to solve the problem, rather than state the requirements.

It is important, therefore, to know when to stop decomposing use cases. To understand when to stop, it is worth looking at the formal definition of a use case, which states that a use case must have an observable effect on an actor. Therefore, consider each use case and then ask whether it actually has an effect on an associated actor. If it does not, it is probably not appropriate as a use case. 'Prevent unauthorised entry' would be a valid use case for a system that must only allow authorised users to access the system; 'Enter user name and password' would *not* be a valid use case for the system since this describes a particular solution to preventing unauthorised access.

By thinking about the further requirements that must be met to organise a course, the use case 'Organise course' can be decomposed as shown in Figure 3.32.

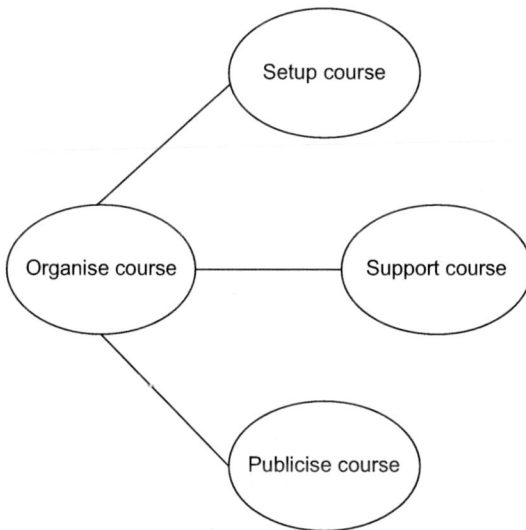

Figure 3.32   Focusing on a single requirement

As can be seen, 'Organise course' has been decomposed into three use cases: 'Setup course', 'Support course' and 'Publicise course'.

Further consideration of the diagram may lead to additional new use cases that are also applicable to the decomposed model, but that have slightly different relationships compared to the 'decomposed into'-style relationship that is shown in this diagram. The three new use cases are 'Cancel course', 'Organise in-house course' and 'Organise on-site course'. These are shown in Figure 3.33, with their relationships to the other use cases indicated by simple associations.

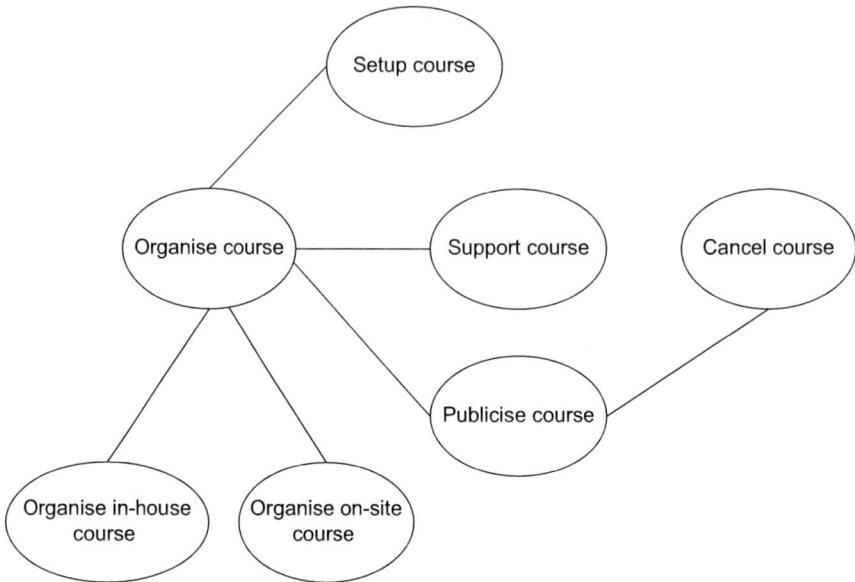

Figure 3.33   More populated requirements

Figure 3.33 shows the updated use case diagram that has been populated with the new requirements. The new use cases are as follows:

- 'Organise in-house course' and 'Organise on-site course'. These represent two different ways in which the course may be organised: sometimes the clients will come to the organisation, on other occasions the organisation will go to the client. Although the courses will still need to be set up in similar ways, there are differences in the way they are organised. For example, when delivering an on-site course then hotels will need to be booked for the course tutor. For this reason, it is important to distinguish between the two types of course. These two requirements are directly associated with the original 'Organise course' requirement.
- 'Cancel course'. If the publicity for the course is not successful and too few people have registered, the course would be economically unviable for the organisation. In such an event, the course must be cancelled. This new requirement is related directly to the 'Publicise course' use case.

As is shown in Figure 3.33, these three new use cases have been related to the other use cases using the association. However, the descriptions of these three new use cases show that the relationships that they have to the other use cases in the diagram is different to the basic decomposition-style relationship already seen. Unfortunately it is impossible to differentiate between them from the information given in Figure 3.33. What is needed is a way of adding information to the diagram by making clear the different types of relationships involved. Fortunately the UML has a way of showing this, as considered in the next section.

3.5.3.3   Other types of relationship

To differentiate between the different types of relationship in Figure 3.33, UML has three additional types of relationships that can be used on use case diagrams. These relationships are shown in Figure 3.34.

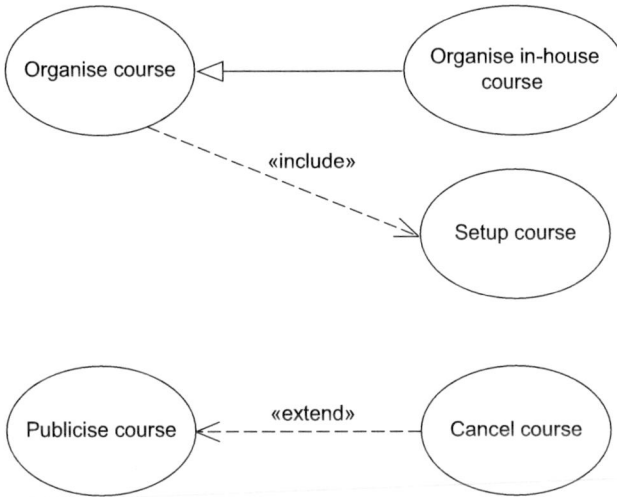

Figure 3.34   Other types of relationship

The '«include»' dependency is used to model requirements that maybe split of from another requirement and is perhaps the most common relationship employed on a use case diagram to model the decomposition of requirements. It is used to model common functionality within a use case and allows for the decomposed use cases to be used by another part of the system. The included use case is *always* part of the parent use case. That is to meet the requirements of the parent use case, the requirements of the included use cases also have to be met. However, it is possible for the included use cases to be requirements in their own right that happen to provide functionality that also forms part of the parent use case. The direction of the arrow on the '«include»' dependency should make sense when the model is read aloud. This part of Figure 3.34 is read as 'Organise course' includes 'Setup course'.

The '«extend»' dependency is used when the functionality of the base use case is being extended in some way. It is used when the functionality of a use case *may* change, depending on what happens when the system is running, and is typically used to model special cases, exceptions and error handling. Unlike an included use case which is *always* part of the parent use case, an extending use case is *sometimes* part of the parent use case. An example of this is when the 'Cancel course' use case is implemented. Most of the time this use case is not required. However, there may be circumstances in which it is required. This is represented by the '«extend»' stereotype, but it is important to get the direction of the relationship correct, as it is the opposite of the '«include»' direction. Always remember to read the diagram and the direction of the relationship makes perfect sense. In Figure 3.34, 'Cancel course' extends 'Publicise course'.

The final type of relationship is the specialisation–generalisation relationship. This is exactly the same as when used for class diagrams and is used to model use cases that are specialisations of a parent use case, inheriting the base functionality described by the parent use case and specialising it with additional or different functionality of their own. Figure 3.34 shows that 'Organise in-house course' is a type of 'Organise course'.

These other types of relationship may now be applied to the requirements diagram in Figure 3.33 to add more value to the model, as shown in Figure 3.35.

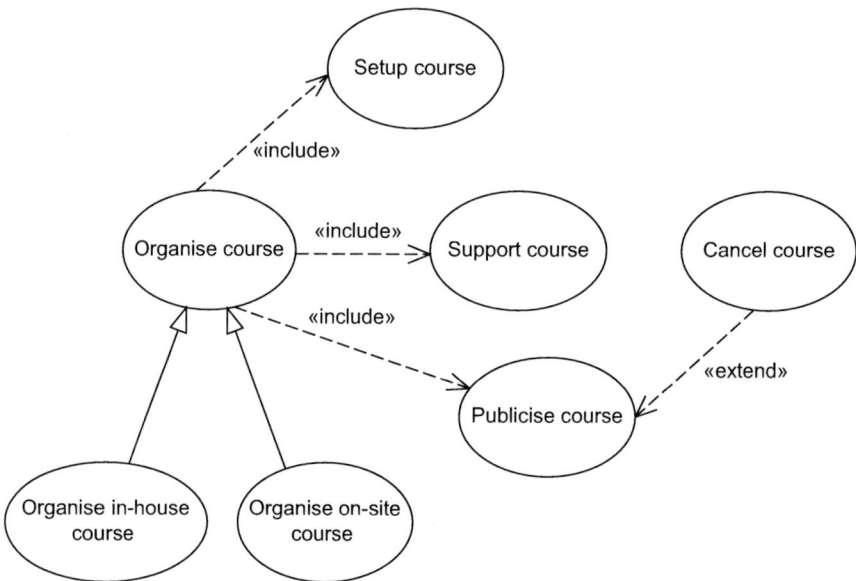

Figure 3.35   The complete diagram

Figure 3.35 shows that the main use case 'Organise course' has two types: 'Organise in-house course' and 'Organise external course'. The 'Organise course' use case has been decomposed, using '«include»' relationships, into three lower-level use cases: 'Setup course', 'Publicise course' and 'Support course'. The 'Publicise course' use case may be extended by the 'Cancel course' use case.

Because 'Organise in-house course' and 'Organise external course' are types of 'Organise course', they too include the three use cases: 'Setup course', 'Publicise course' and 'Support course' that are included by 'Organise course'.

Sometimes, when modelling, a model could be made clearer by using new types of relationship that are not part of standard UML. Fortunately there are mechanisms within the UML that allow us to define such new relationships. This is discussed in the following section.

3.5.3.4   Showing constraints

When modelling requirements, it is important that *non-functional* requirements are captured. Non-functional requirements *constrain* functional requirements; that is they may limit functional requirements in some way. For this reason non-functional requirements are sometimes known as *constraints*.

Since constraints are just a type of requirement, they too are modelled as use cases. However, to make clear which other requirements they constrain it would be good if we could relate constraints to other requirements with relationships specifically designed to represent constraints. Unfortunately the UML does not have such a relationship. However, it *does* have an extension mechanism that allows such a relationship to be defined, using a modelling mechanism called *stereotyping*. A full discussion of the definition and usage of stereotypes is beyond the scope of this book (see Reference 3 for details).

In brief, stereotypes allow the definition of a new type of UML element which must be based on an existing UML element. Whenever the new element is encountered an assumption is made about its semantic meaning. This assumed meaning is captured in an 'assumption model' which is defined as part of a *profile*, as shown in Figure 3.36. Such a diagram would be accompanied by a description of the intended meaning for the stereotype.

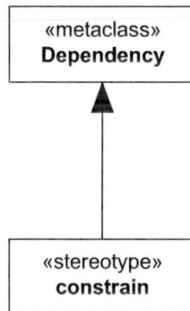

Figure 3.36   Defining a new dependency

Figure 3.36 defines a new stereotype, 'constrain' that can be applied to a dependency. Whenever the term '«constrain»' is encountered on a dependency in a model it is assumed that we are using a new UML element whose definition must be explicitly recorded somewhere, typically on a diagram such as Figure 3.36 which forms part of a profile.

Armed with this new relationship, we can now make explicit which requirements are constrained by others, as shown in Figure 3.37.

Figure 3.37 shows how the newly defined UML element has been used to show that the requirements 'Ensure quality' and 'Improve quality' constrain the requirement 'Deliver course'. 'Ensure quality' and 'Improve quality' are non-functional requirements and any use case connected to another with a '«constrain»' dependency is a non-functional requirement.

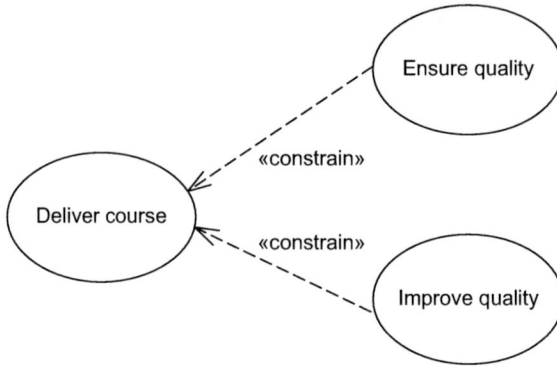

Figure 3.37   Showing constraints

3.6   Identifying complexity through levels of abstraction

3.6.1   Introduction

Having introduced structural and behavioural modelling, this section discusses one of the important themes that run through the book, namely *complexity*.

Complexity is one of the three evils of engineering and is one of the funda-mental reasons why we need to model, as discussed in Chapter 2. In this section, two systems will be compared in terms of their complexity which will be identified by looking at the system from different levels of abstraction using different UML diagrams. Although you have not yet been introduced to many of these diagrams, the intention here is not to discuss the syntax and semantics of the diagrams (that will be discussed in Chapter 4). Rather the diagrams are introduced to discuss levels of abstraction and the modelling issues that arise from this example.

3.6.2   The systems

Imagine a situation where you are put in charge of developing two systems, neither of which you have any domain knowledge of and so you have to rely on descrip-tions of each systems to gain an understanding of them. This is a prime application for modelling – there is a lack of understanding about the two systems, there is no indication of how complex each is and this information will need to be commu-nicated to the project teams.

The two systems that have been chosen to illustrate how modelling can be used to help understand the complexity of systems and to show where the complexity manifests itself have been taken from the domain of board games: chess and Monopoly. If you are *not* familiar with these games, then so much the better. If you are, then try to think about them as completely unfamiliar systems.

Before beginning to model these two systems, ask yourself a simple question – which is the more complex, chess or Monopoly? Take a moment to consider this before reading on.

3.6.3   Structural view

Often when confronted with new systems the first, and normally the easiest, aspect of the system to model is the *structural* aspect. This is often done using class diagrams and the diagram in Figure 3.38 shows a simple class diagram representation of each of the two systems.

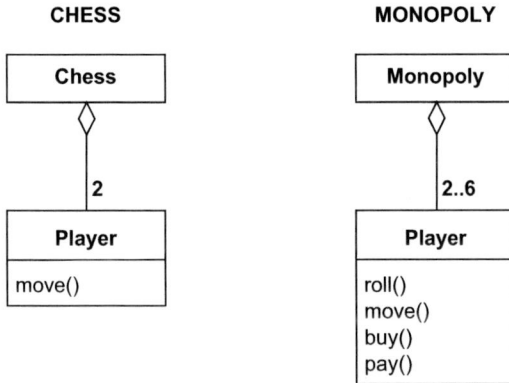

Figure 3.38   Comparing complexity – class diagrams

Having modelled the structural aspect of each system, the class diagram can be used to help answer the question of which of the two is more complex.

The two systems have a lot in common, as can be shown by the identical pattern in each system's class diagram – each game is made up of a number of 'Player'. In terms of complexity, at least as far as can be identified from this structural model, there is really not much to choose between the two. If forced to choose one, then 'Monopoly' could be considered more complex than 'Chess', as it has a higher multiplicity on the class 'Player' (more players in the game) and it has four operations compared to one in 'Chess' (more things that can be done in the game).

Is this sufficient to conclude that 'Monopoly' is more complex than 'Chess'? Since we have only considered the structural aspect of each system the answer has to be *no*. Further modelling of each system is needed, but this time the behavioural aspects of the systems need to be captured. As each of the 'Player' classes has at least one operation, a state machine diagram could be used to start the behavioural modelling.

3.6.4   Behavioural views

Simple state machine diagrams for 'Chess' and 'Monopoly' have been created and are shown in Figure 3.39. The complexity of the two systems will now be considered by comparing these two state machine diagrams.

A direct comparison of the two state machine diagrams in Figure 3.39 again seems to suggest that 'Monopoly' is more complex than 'Chess' as there are more

CHESS   **MONOPOLY**

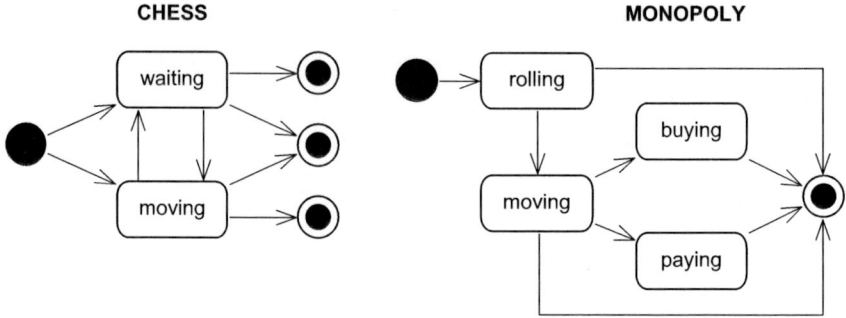

Figure 3.39   Comparing complexity – state machine diagrams

states in the state machine diagram for 'Monopoly', reflecting the number of different things that a player can do in a game of 'Monopoly' (rolling, moving, buying and paying).

However, 'Monopoly' only has two more states than 'Chess' and both diagrams have the same number of transitions between states. So, once more, deciding which game is the more complex is not an easy decision to make.

Further behavioural modelling is needed. This time the behaviour will be modelled at a higher level of abstraction than the state machine diagram using the communication diagram.

The communication diagram in Figure 3.40 shows a higher level of behaviour for both the 'Chess' and 'Monopoly' examples and shows a typical playing scenario for each of the two games.

CHESS   **MONOPOLY**

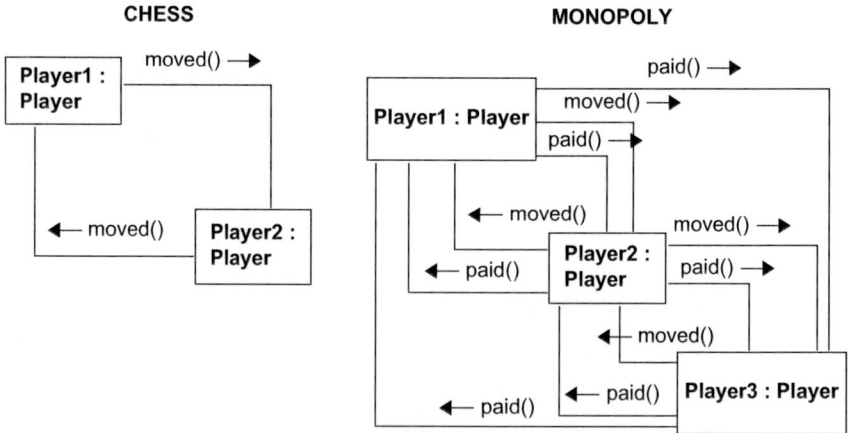

Figure 3.40   Comparing complexity – communication diagrams

In the scenario shown, 'Chess' still appears to be the more simple of the two – there is only one interaction going each way between the two 'Player' lifelines, resulting in a total of two interactions.

In the case of 'Monopoly', there are more interactions on the diagram. Each 'Player' passes the control of the game onto the next player, which results in a single interaction between each subsequent lifeline. Also, any 'Player' can pay money to any other 'Player', which results in an extra six interactions for this scenario with three players, and an extra 30 interactions in the scenario with six players!

When comparing these two views, it is clear that the 'Monopoly' diagram is the more complex of the two and it would be reasonable to assume that 'Monopoly' is a more complex game than 'Chess'. However, there is one final diagram that we can use to model the games at their lowest level of abstraction, the activity diagram.

The diagram in Figure 3.41 shows the lowest level of abstraction for both examples using activity diagrams.

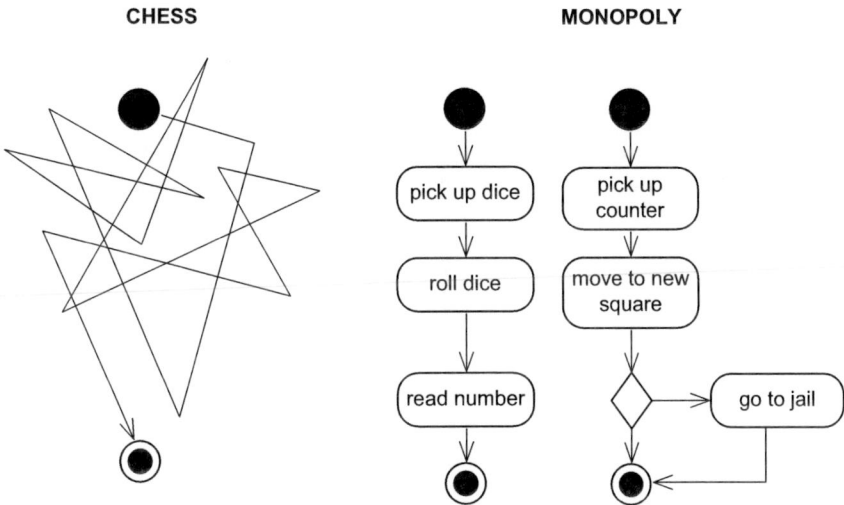

Figure 3.41   Comparing complexity – activity diagrams

In the case of 'Chess', a single activity diagram is used to describe the behaviour of the single operation from the class diagram, that of 'move'. Bearing in mind that the 'move' activity describes all the planning, strategies and movement of the chess pieces, this would result in a very complex diagram indeed – represented in the diagram by a tangled mess.

In the case of 'Monopoly', there are more activity diagrams needed (four in total, one for each operation – only two are shown here) but each activity diagram is so simple as to be almost trivial.

The diagram in Figure 3.42 shows each of the three behavioural views for each example alongside one another so that they can be compared directly.

The diagram shows all the behavioural diagrams that have been produced for the two games. In summary, the following conclusions were drawn:

● When comparing the original class diagrams, there was not much to choose between the two, but 'Monopoly' was slightly more complex than 'Chess'.

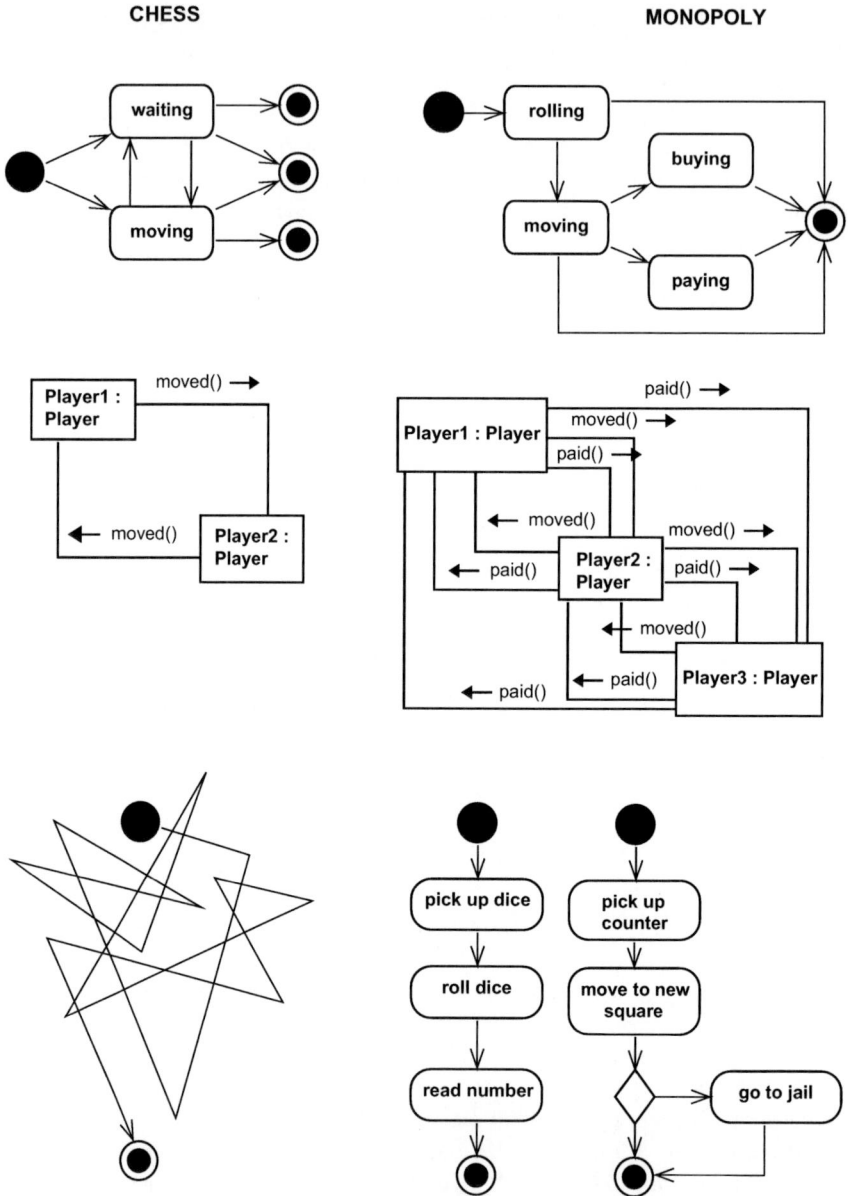

CHESS   MONOPOLY

Figure 3.42   Summary of views to assess complexity

- When comparing the state machine diagrams, again there was not much to choose between the two, but once again the state machine diagram for 'Monopoly' was deemed to be more complex than the one for 'Chess'.

At this stage, there is nothing to really distinguish between the two games. In each diagram 'Monopoly' was deemed slightly more complex than 'Chess', but only marginally so. It is interesting to see how things change quite dramatically when the systems are looked at from higher and lower levels of abstraction.

- When looking at the higher level of abstraction, using the communication diagram, it was very clear that 'Monopoly' was far more complex than 'Chess'.
- When looking at the lowest level of abstraction using the activity diagram, it was very clear that 'Chess' was far more complex than 'Monopoly'. Indeed, the activity diagram for the 'Chess' *move()* operation was so complex that it could not be drawn easily.

There are a number of conclusions that may be drawn at this point concerning, not just complexity, but also general modelling:

- The complexity of the systems manifested itself at different levels of abstraction. In the case of 'Chess', the complexity manifested itself at the lower levels of abstraction, whereas in the 'Monopoly' system, complexity abounded at the higher levels. This actually makes a nonsense of the question of which is the more complex system. None is 'more' complex as such, but in each system the complexity manifested itself at different levels of abstraction.
- If any of these views was taken individually and compared, there is no way whatsoever that any realistic comparison could be made between the two systems. For example, just comparing class diagrams gives no real insight into each system. This may seem obvious, but many people will construct a class diagram and then state that this is the model of their system. To understand any system and to create a useful model, both the structural and behavioural aspects of the model must be looked at.
- Even when both the structural and behavioural aspects of the model are realised, it is essential to look at the model at different level of abstraction for the system to be understood, since the complexity may manifest itself at any level and by not looking at a system at all levels of abstraction the complexity may be missed.
- It is also possible that the complexity of the system changes depending on the point of view of the stakeholder. For example, imagine a passenger train system (again), and imagine it now from two different stakeholders points of view – the engineers involved in train development and the signalling engineers. The train development engineers may view the system in a similar way to the chess system, in that the complexity occurs at a low level of abstraction, as individual trains are very complex machines but, at a higher level, they simply drive along a set of rails. The signalling engineers may view the same system in a similar way to the Monopoly system, in that each train is viewed as a simple system as a train is a machine that goes backwards or forwards along the rails. However, stopping these simple machines from colliding and making them run on time is a very complex undertaking.

It is essential when modelling, therefore, to look at both the structural and behavioural aspects of the system and to look at the system at different levels of abstraction. In this way, areas of complexity may be identified and hence managed. It is also important to look at the system in different ways and from different stakeholders' points of view, which helps to keep the connection to reality for all stakeholders.

3.7   Conclusions

This chapter has looked at the two aspects of modelling that are necessary in UML – structural and behavioural modelling. Class diagrams were used to discuss structural diagrams and use case diagrams were used to introduce behavioural modelling.

It was seen that to have a complete model it is necessary to look at the system at different levels of abstraction. Only when a number of these views exist can one start to have a concise, correct and coherent model.

Key to all of this, of course, is consistency, that leads to a good, correct, concise and consistent model, which leads directly to confidence in the system. Confidence means that the system is understood and can be communicated to other people.

Remember:

UML + consistency = model

UML – consistency = pictures

When modelling, try to remember and understand these concepts, and then try to remember the syntax, not the other way around.

References

1. Holt, J. *UML for Systems Engineering – Watching the Wheels*. 2nd edn. London: IEE Publishing; 2004 (reprinted IET Publishing; 2007).
2. Holt, J. & Perry, S. *SysML for Systems Engineering*. London: IET Publishing; 2008.
3. Rumbaugh, J., Jacobson, I. & Booch, G. *The Unified Modeling Language Reference Manual*. 2nd edn. Boston, MA: Addison-Wesley; 2004.

Chapter 4

UML diagrams

Concern for man himself and his fate must always form the chief interest of all technical endeavor. Never forget this in the midst of your diagrams and equations.

Albert Einstein (1879–1955)

4.1 Introduction

This chapter introduces the 13 types of diagram that may be used in the Unified Modelling Language (UML). The information in this chapter is kept, very deliberately, at a high level. There are several reasons for this:

- The main focus of this book is to provide practical guidelines and examples of how to use the UML efficiently and successfully for an enterprise architecture (EA). It is, therefore, a deliberate move to show only a small subset of the UML language in this chapter. In reality, it is possible to model a large percentage of any problem with a small percentage of the UML language.
- Experience has shown that the most efficient way to learn, and hence master, the UML is to learn just enough to get going and then to start modelling with it. This chapter aims to give just enough information to allow readers to start using the UML. As readers progress and find that they want to express something beyond their present understanding, they are referred to the many books that are devoted entirely to the UML and its very rich syntax. References 1–3 are probably the most popular examples of such texts.

Each of the UML diagrams has a section devoted to it in this chapter. For each diagram type there is an overview, discussion of the diagram elements, together with examples and a summary of how to use the diagram when modelling an EA.

A note on spelling: While British English is used throughout, the reader may notice that the US English spelling of 'artifact' is used in this chapter. This is because the definition of the UML uses this US English spelling in its definition and it is this spelling that is used in all the major UML modelling tools.

4.2   The structure of UML diagrams

Each diagram in the UML has the same structure, which is intended to provide a similar appearance for each, as well as making cross-referencing between diagrams simpler. The structure of each diagram is shown in the diagram in Figure 4.1.

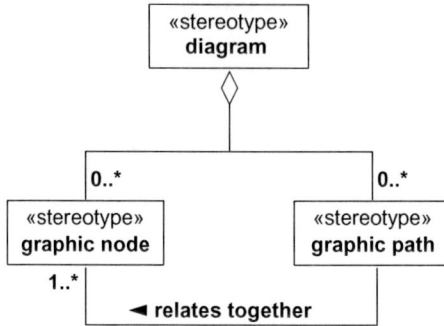

Figure 4.1   Structure of each UML diagram

The diagram in Figure 4.1 shows that each 'diagram' is made up of zero or more 'graphic node' and zero or more 'graphic path'. Each 'graphic path' relates together one or more 'graphic node'. Of course, a diagram with zero graphic nodes or paths would be of little use, being an empty diagram, but would still be a valid UML diagram.

Examples of graphic nodes already met include classes on class diagrams and use cases on use case diagrams. Examples of graphic paths include aggregations on class diagrams and «include» dependencies on use case diagrams.

The text '«stereotype»' on the classes in Figure 4.1 is itself an example of a stereotype. As discussed briefly in Chapter 3, stereotypes are a mechanism by which the UML can be extended. Stereotypes are discussed further in Section 4.3.

4.2.1   Frames

Any UML diagram may have an optional graphic node known as a 'Frame' that encapsulates the diagram and that has a unique identifier to make identification of, and navigation between, diagrams simpler. An example of a frame is shown in the diagram in Figure 4.2.

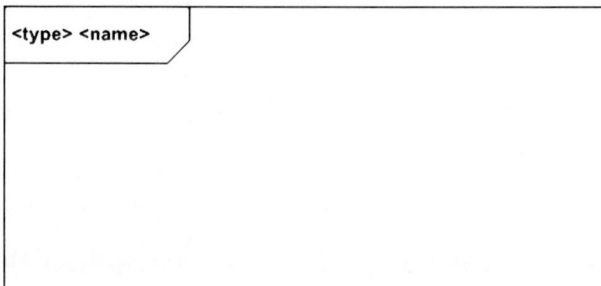

Figure 4.2   Example of a frame in UML

The diagram in Figure 4.2 shows the symbol for a frame – a large rectangle that will contain all the view elements in a particular diagram. The irregular pentagon in the upper left-hand corner contains two references – one to the type of diagram and one to the name for the diagram.

Although there are no standard abbreviations for the diagram types, typical abbreviations that are used are shown in the following list:

- Activity diagram – ad
- Class diagram – cd
- Communication diagram – commd
- Component diagram – cmpd
- Composite structure diagram – csd
- Deployment diagram – dd
- Interaction overview diagram – iod
- Object diagram – od
- Package diagram – pd
- State machine diagram – smd
- Sequence diagram – sd
- Timing diagram – td
- Use case diagram – ucd

It should also be noted here that when naming diagrams that represent EA views, the diagram name should describe the view and should include the word 'view' in the name. This convention is followed throughout the chapter.

4.3   Stereotypes

Stereotypes are, by far, the most widely used of all the UML extension mechanisms and represent a powerful way to define new UML elements by tailoring the UML meta-model, which is described further in Section 4.4.

To use stereotypes effectively, it is first necessary to be able to spot one within a model. Visually, this is very simple, as stereotypes are indicated by enclosing the name of the stereotype within a set of double chevrons. The name of the stereotype is displayed either inside the symbol (in the case of the stereotype applying to a graphical node) or above symbol (in the case of the stereotype applying to a graphical path).

Figure 4.3 shows a UML use case. However, in this case the use case shown here is *not* a regular UML one, but it is a stereotyped use case as can be seen from the word 'capability' inside the chevrons above the use case name. The English phrase that should be used when reading stereotypes is 'that happens to be a'. Therefore, to read the diagram in Figure 4.3, one would say 'there is a use case called "Provide training"' that happens to be a capability. Of course, we are assuming here that the person reading the diagram actually understands what the term 'capability' means in the context of this model.

A stereotype can be defined as a tailored version of any type of UML element that exists within the UML meta-model. A stereotype *must* be based on an existing

Figure 4.3   Stereotyped use case

UML element; it is *not possible* to define a brand new element from scratch, it must be based on an existing element. Some stereotypes are already defined within the UML, such as «include», «extend» that are defined as special types of dependency as seen in Chapter 3.

Stereotypes are defined by tailoring the UML meta-model. Elements from the UML meta-model are taken and then special types of them are declared that represent the stereotype, as seen in the diagram in Figure 4.4.

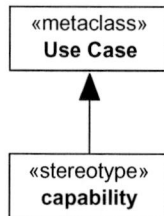

Figure 4.4   Defining the 'capability' stereotype

The diagram in Figure 4.4 shows the definition of a stereotype. The diagram shows two classes, 'Use Case' and 'capability' that are related together by a special type of specialisation known as an extension. An extension is used specifically when defining stereotypes. An extension is represented graphically by a filled-in triangle – very similar to the generalisation symbol.

The element that is being stereotyped is 'Use Case'. The most important point to realise at this point is that 'Use Case' is taken *from the UML meta-model.* The element 'Use Case' modelled here as a class represents the abstract notion of a use case that is found in the UML meta-model. This is indicated by the stereotype «metaclass». In other words, the class 'Use Case' is the representation of use case from the UML language itself.

The new UML element to be defined, in this case 'capability', is shown in a similar way to a child block on a specialisation but using the extension relationship. However, this time it happens to be a stereotype, as indicated by «stereotype». In addition to the graphical definition, it is usual to provide a textual description of the stereotype that describes its intended use.

Now, whenever we see a UML use case that happens to be a capability, as shown in Figure 4.3, we know that it is not a regular UML use case, but a special type as indicated by the «capability» stereotype. Practically, we now have a short-hand way to show that a particular use case is actually a capability, rather than a regular use case.

The definition of stereotypes is, in fact, an almost mechanical process:

1. Draw two classes.
2. Write the stereotype «metaclass» in one class and the stereotype «stereotype» in the other.
3. Connect the two classes with an extension relationship, with the arrowhead on the class with the «metaclass» stereotype.
4. Label the class containing the «stereotype» stereotype with the name of the desired stereotype.
5. Label the class containing the «metaclass» stereotype with the name of the UML element that the new stereotype is to be applied to.

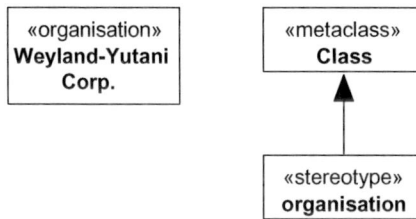

Figure 4.5   Another example of stereotype usage and definition

As another example, say we want to be able to stereotype a class with the stereotype «organisation», perhaps to show that any classes so marked represent business organisations. In step 4 above the class will be named 'organisation'. The class in step 5 will be named 'class'. See Figure 4.5 for an example of the use of the «organisation» stereotype and its definition.

4.4   The UML meta-model

This chapter also introduces the concept of the UML meta-model. The UML meta-model is a model of the UML constructed using the UML – the UML is completely modelled using the UML. The UML meta-model itself is concerned with the modelling elements within the UML, how they are constructed and how they relate to one another. The full UML meta-model is highly complex and, to someone without much UML experience, can be quite impenetrable. The meta-models presented in this book show highly simplified versions of the actual meta-model to aid communication and group different aspects of the model according to each diagram – something that is not done in the actual meta-model.

4.4.1   Diagram ordering

So far, we have looked at two of the diagrams in some detail (see Chapter 3) when class diagrams and use case diagrams were used to illustrate structural and behavioural modelling; these diagrams are shown again in this chapter for the sake of completeness and also to introduce the meta-model using diagrams that are already well known.

The chapter first covers the structural diagrams then the behavioural diagrams. Within these groupings there is no significance in the ordering of the diagrams. Therefore, the various sections of this chapter which describe the 13 UML diagrams may be read in any order.

4.5   Overview of the UML diagrams

As discussed previously in Chapter 3, every model of a system should capture the two aspects of the system being modelled: a *structural* aspect that models the 'what' of the system and a *behavioural* aspect that models the 'how' of the system. The diagrams in the UML mirror this structural and behavioural split, consisting of both structural and behavioural diagrams as shown in the diagram in Figure 4.6.

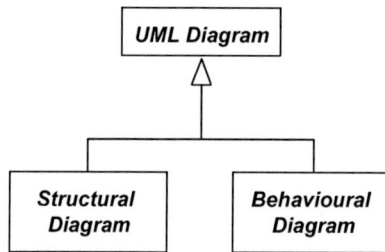

Figure 4.6   UML diagram aspects

Figure 4.6 shows that there are two main types of 'UML Diagram' – the 'Structural Diagram' and the 'Behavioural Diagram'. Each of these two types will be discussed briefly in the following sections before being looked at in more detail in the remainder of this chapter. Note the use of italics in the class names to indicate that the three classes are *abstract* classes, as discussed in Chapter 3.

4.5.1   Structural diagrams

The UML has six types of structural diagram as shown in Figure 4.7.
The six types of UML 'Structural Diagram' are as follows:

- Class Diagram
- Object Diagram
- Package Diagram
- Composite Structure Diagram
- Component Diagram
- Deployment Diagram

These diagrams are described completely in Sections 4.6–4.11.

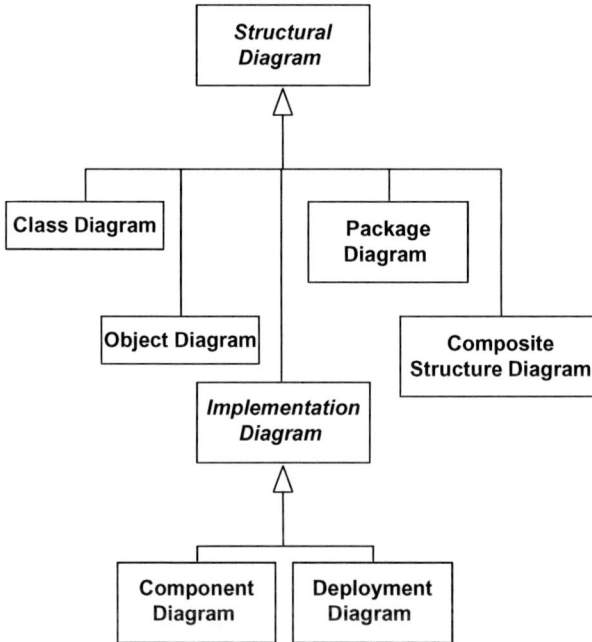

Figure 4.7   Types of UML structural diagram

Figure 4.7 shows that the 'Component Diagram' and 'Deployment Diagram' are types of the abstract 'Implementation Diagram' (as indicated by the use of italics in the class name). This is a term that is used in some UML texts to indicate that the 'Component Diagram' and 'Deployment Diagram' are often used to model elements of the implementation of a system. This grouping and name betray the software origins of the UML and the heavily software-based nature of most UML texts. While it is true that the 'Component Diagram' and 'Deployment Diagram' are often used at the implementation stage of a project, that is not the only time that they can be used. Component diagrams are often used, for example, when modelling high-level system architectures and are thus often one of the *first* UML diagrams to be used.

As an *aide-memoire* to the structural diagrams, Figure 4.8 shows the six diagrams with each represented using a selection of the notation used on that diagram.

Having briefly introduced the structural diagrams, the next section does the same for the seven UML behavioural diagrams.

4.5.2   *Behavioural diagrams*

The UML has seven types of behavioural diagram as shown in Figure 4.9.

The seven types of UML 'Behavioural Diagram' are as follows:

- State Machine Diagram
- Activity Diagram
- Use Case Diagram
- Sequence Diagram

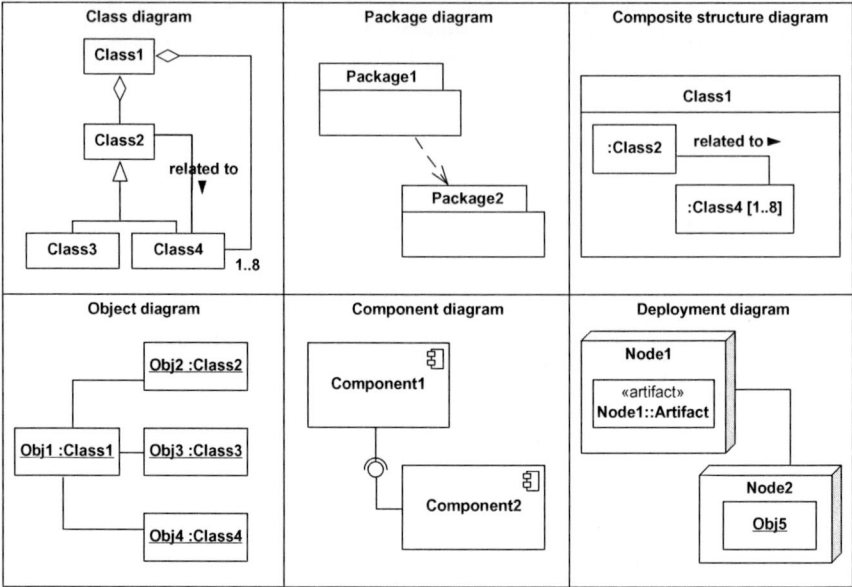

Figure 4.8   Aide-memoire to the UML structural diagrams

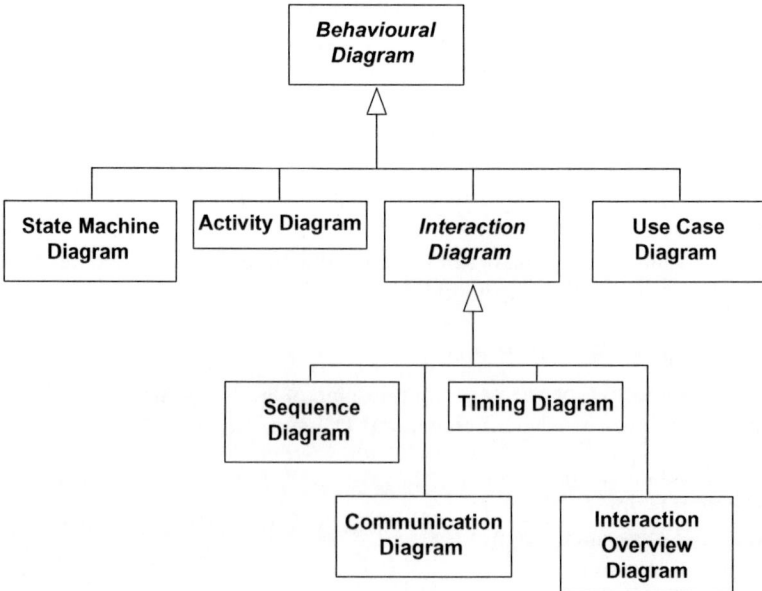

Figure 4.9   Types of UML behavioural diagram

- Communication Diagram
- Timing Diagram
- Interaction Overview Diagram

These diagrams are described completely in Sections 4.12–4.15.

Figure 4.9 shows that the 'Sequence Diagram', 'Communication Diagram', 'Timing Diagram' and 'Interaction Overview Diagram' are types of the abstract 'Interaction Diagram' (again, note the use of italics in the class name). This is a generic term applied to these diagrams to emphasise that they are used to model interactions *between* system elements. Each of these four diagrams is generally used to model different *scenarios* that a system must support.

As with the structural diagrams, an *aide-memoire* to the behavioural diagrams is shown in Figure 4.10 with each of the seven diagrams represented using a selection of the notation used on that diagram.

With all 13 UML diagrams briefly introduced, the remainder of the chapter discusses each of the diagrams in more detail, starting with the class diagram.

4.6 Class diagram

4.6.1 Overview

This section introduces the first of the 13 UML diagrams: the class diagram. The class diagram was introduced in Chapter 3 to illustrate structural modelling, so this section should really only serve as a recap. Class diagrams realise a structural aspect of the model of a system and show what conceptual 'things' exist in a system and what relationships exist between them. The 'things' in a system are represented by classes and their relationships are represented by the various types of relationship seen in Chapter 3.

Class diagrams are used to visualise conceptual, rather than actual, aspects of a system. Classes themselves represent abstractions of real-life entities. The actual real-life entities are represented by objects (also known as instances) and any object must have an associated class that defines what it looks like and what it does. Objects are discussed in more detail in the 'Object Diagram' section which follows this section on 'Class Diagrams'.

4.6.2 Diagram elements

Class diagrams are made up of two basic elements: classes and relationships. Both classes and relationships may have various types and have more detailed syntax that may be used to add more information about them. However, at the highest level of abstraction, there are just the two very simple elements that must exist in the diagram. Classes describe the types of 'things' that exist in a system, whereas relationships describe what the relationships are between various classes.

Figure 4.11 shows a high-level meta-model of class diagrams. The meta-model for class diagrams is created using a class diagram, which makes it a class diagram of a class diagram. All future meta-models in this book will also be realised using class diagrams.

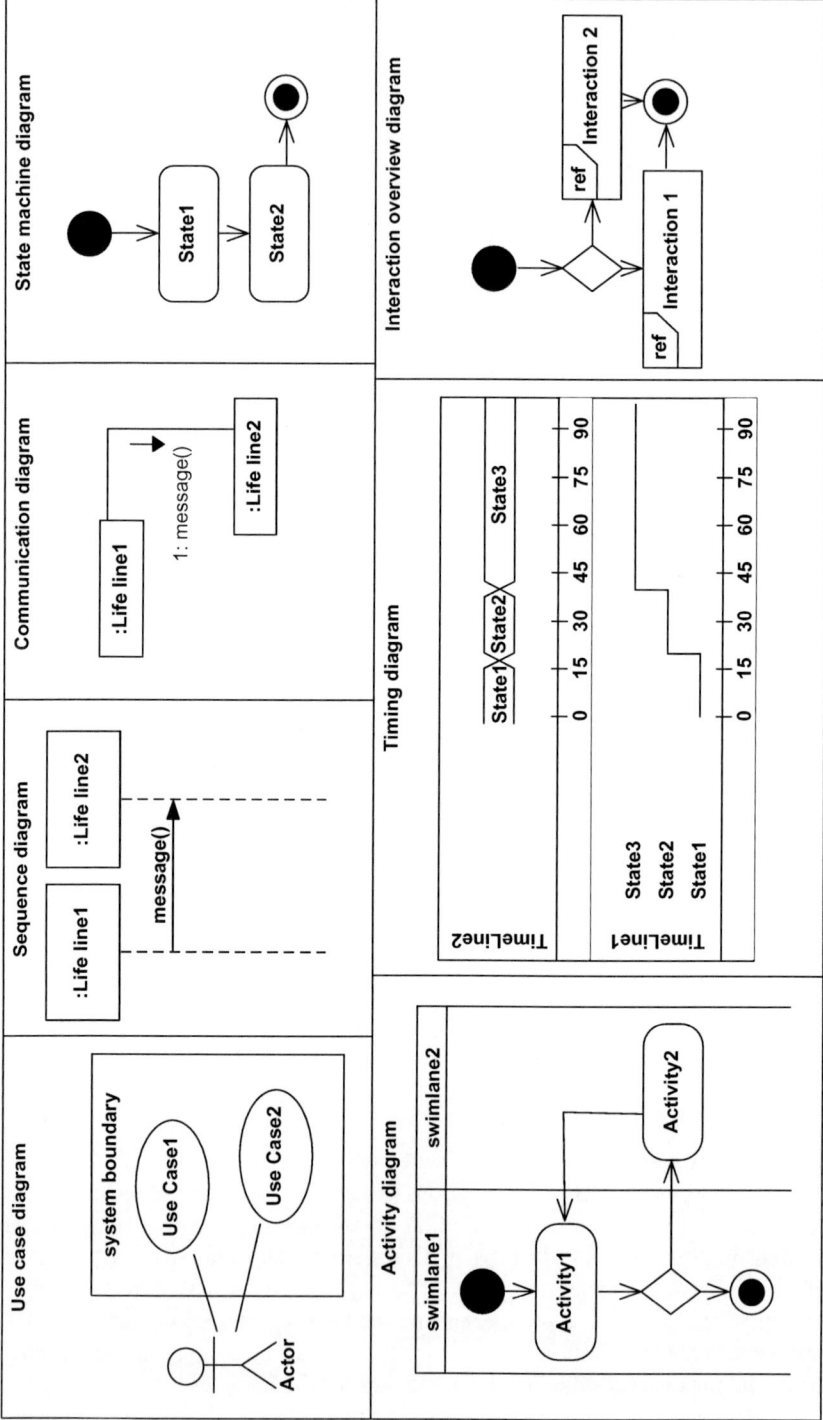

Figure 4.10   Aide-memoire to the UML behavioural diagrams

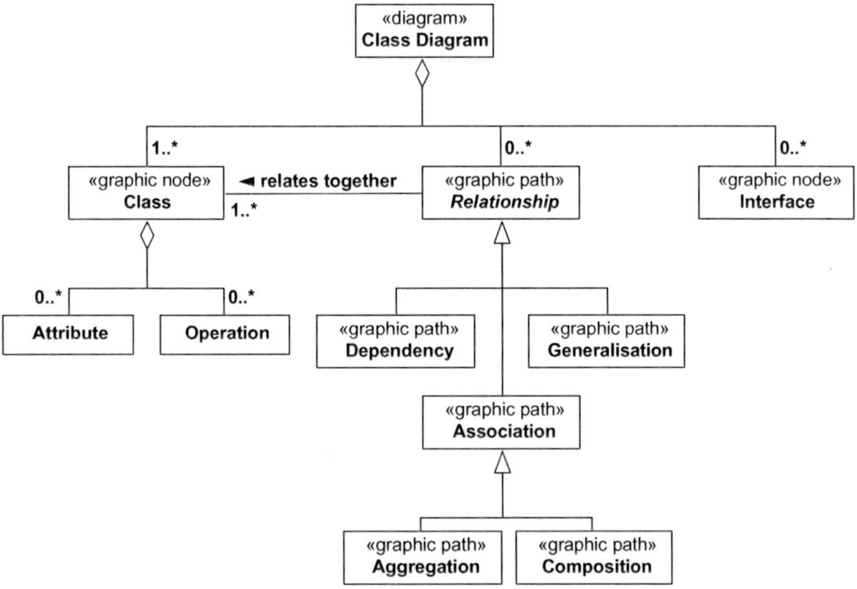

Figure 4.11   Partial meta-model for class diagrams

Figure 4.11 shows that a 'Class diagram' is made up of one or more 'Class', zero or more 'Interface' and zero or more 'Relationship'. It is possible for a class diagram to be made up of just a single class with no relationships at all; however, it is not possible to have a class diagram that is made up of just a relationship with no classes. Therefore, the multiplicity on 'Class' is one or more, whereas the multiplicity on 'Relationship' is zero or more.

Each 'Relationship' relates together one or more 'Class'. Notice that the word 'each' is used here, which means that for every single 'Relationship' there are one or more 'Class'. It is also interesting to note that the multiplicity on the 'Class' side of the association is one or more, as it is possible for a 'Relationship' to relate together one 'Class' – that is to say that a 'Class' may be related to itself.

An 'Interface' is a special type of class and is used to define the interfaces seen on a component diagram. Interfaces and components will be discussed in more detail in Section 4.10.

Each 'Class' is made up of zero or more 'Attribute' and zero or more 'Operation'. This shows how classes may be further described using attributes and operations, or that they may be left with neither.

There are three main types of 'Relationship':

1. 'Association', which defines a simple relationship between one or more 'Class'. There are also two specialisations of 'Association', the 'Aggregation' and the 'Composition'.
2. 'Generalisation', which shows a 'has types' relationship that is used to show parent and child classes.
3. 'Dependency', which is the weakest type of relationship and is used to show that one class depends in some way on another.

All of these relationship types were discussed in Chapter 3.

Notice how the meta-model, even at this very high level, describes all the concepts that were introduced in Chapter 3. Imagine how this model may be expanded upon to show that, for example, each attribute has a type, default value, etc.

Each of these diagram elements may be realised by either graphical nodes or graphical paths, as indicated by their stereotypes. The notation used is shown in Figure 4.12.

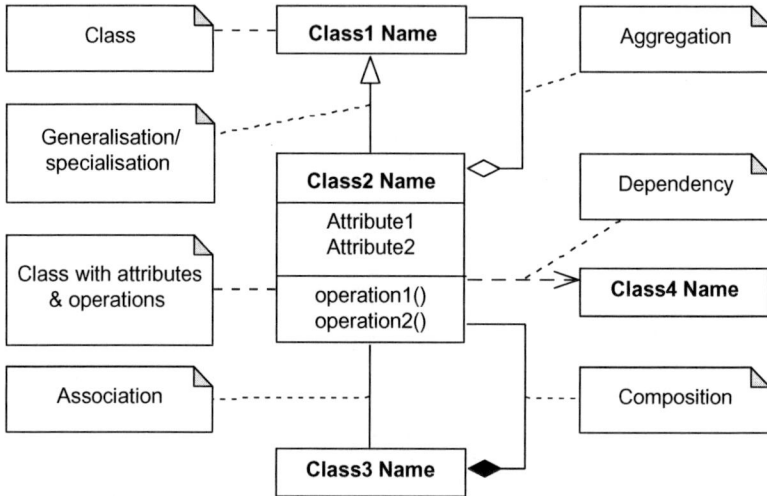

Figure 4.12   Graphical symbols for elements in a class diagram

The diagram in Figure 4.12 shows the graphical symbols used to represent elements in a class diagram. The basic symbol is the class that is represented by a rectangle. Rectangles are also used to show other types of element in the UML, so it is important to be able to differentiate between a class rectangle and any other sort of rectangle. A class rectangle will simply contain a single name, with no colons and underlining. When attributes and operations are present, classes are easy to identify as they have two additional rectangles, drawn underneath the class name, with the names of the attributes and operations contained within. Relationships are shown by a simple line, with slight variations depending on the type of relationship. For example, a specialisation has a distinctive triangle symbol shown next to the parent class whereas a simple association has no such additional symbol. The annotation on the diagram is an example of the use of the UML 'note', which is meant to represent a piece of paper with a turned-down corner. It should also be noted that this diagram is itself a class diagram.

4.6.3   Example EA views realised using a class diagram

Having looked at the meta-model and notation used on class diagrams, a number of example of their use in modelling EAs will now be given.

Figure 4.13 shows the EA ontology, as seen previously in Chapter 1. In this diagram classes are used to model the terms and concepts relevant to the

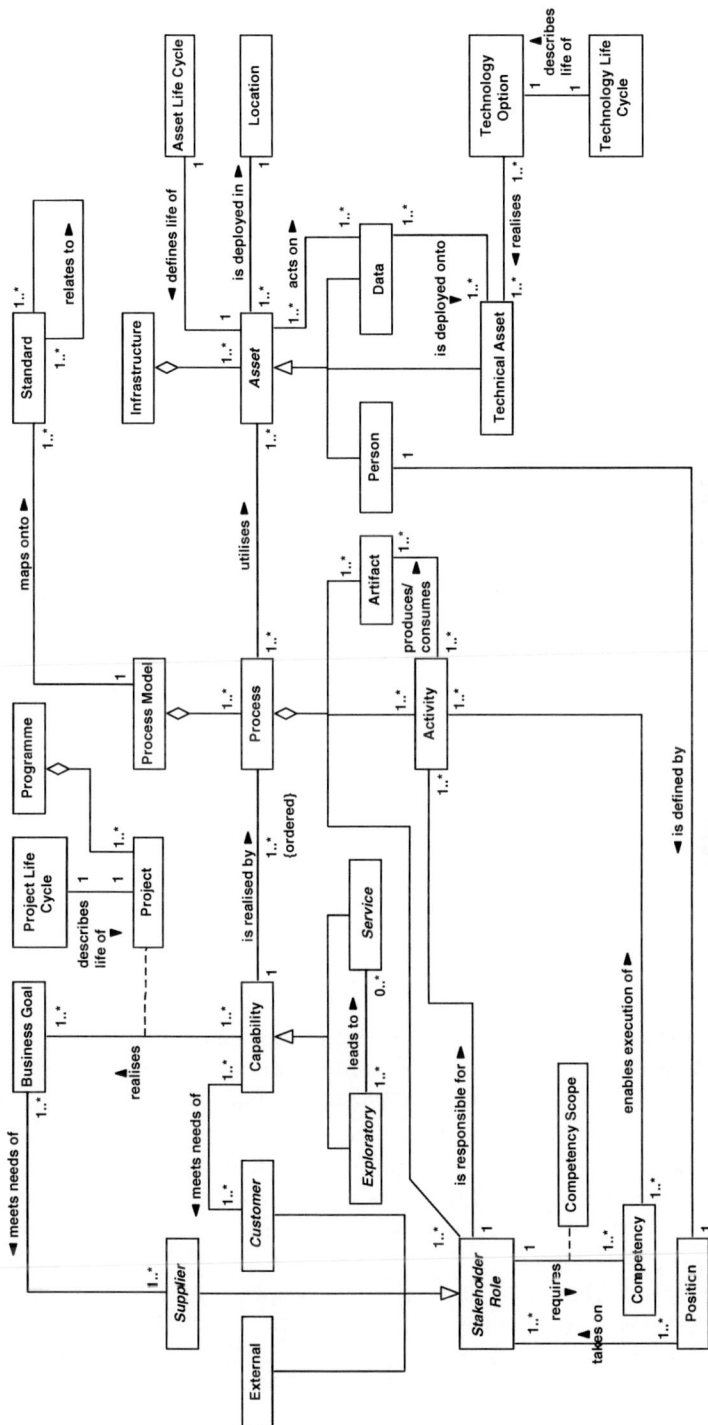

Figure 4.13 The EA ontology

organisation, with relationships showing how the concepts are related to each other. Capturing concepts relevant to a system (in this case the system is an organisation) is a common use for class diagrams.

It is worth commenting here on the use of two new pieces of notation not seen when class diagrams were discussed in Chapter 3, namely ordering and association classes.

The association between 'Capability' and 'Process' has the constraint '{ordered}' at the 'Process' end of the association. This part of the diagram is read as 'Capability', and is realised by one or more *ordered* 'Process'. What this means is that each capability has a number of processes associated with it that realise the capability but to do so the processes are in a particular order when associated with the capability. The class diagram does not specify what the ordering is. Such information would need to be shown on other UML diagrams, such as object or sequence diagrams.

The second piece of notation, association classes, can be seen on the associations between 'Capability' and 'Business Goal' and between 'Stakeholder Role' and 'Competency'. Each of these associations has a third class attached to the association by a dashed line. For the 'Capability' to 'Business Goal' association this class is 'Project' and for the 'Stakeholder Role' to 'Competency' association this class is 'Competency Scope'. Each of these classes is an example of an *association class*. An association class is a class in its own right, but they also add some extra information, such as attributes and operations, to the associations to which they are attached. They are read in the following way: One or more 'Capability' realises one or more 'Business Goal' *via* 'Project'.

Association classes are frequently used when creating meta-models (see Section 4.4) and further examples will be seen in some of the UML diagram meta-models as seen in this chapter.

A common use for class diagrams when developing EAs is for views showing how a business is organised. An example from a typical small training organisation is shown in Figure 4.14.

Figure 4.14, the Business Organisation View, shows the use of class diagrams to model the organisation of a business in terms of its positions and reporting lines. Each class represents a position within the organisation, as indicated by the names of the classes. Specialisation–generalisation relationships are used to show types of position and associations which are used to show reporting lines and responsibilities that one position has in relation to another.

Note that some of the classes have a number of attributes shown. In this diagram the attributes are used to model the stakeholder roles that a position takes on, with each attribute representing a role. This is consistent with the relationship between 'Position' and 'Stakeholder Role' that is shown in Figure 4.13. Each attribute is named and is followed by the *type* of that attribute. This type will either be a standard type that is built in to the UML, such as Integer or Boolean, or will be the name of a class defined elsewhere in the model that defines the type. For example, 'Managing Director' has an attribute 'Assessor' of type 'Primary Assessor'.

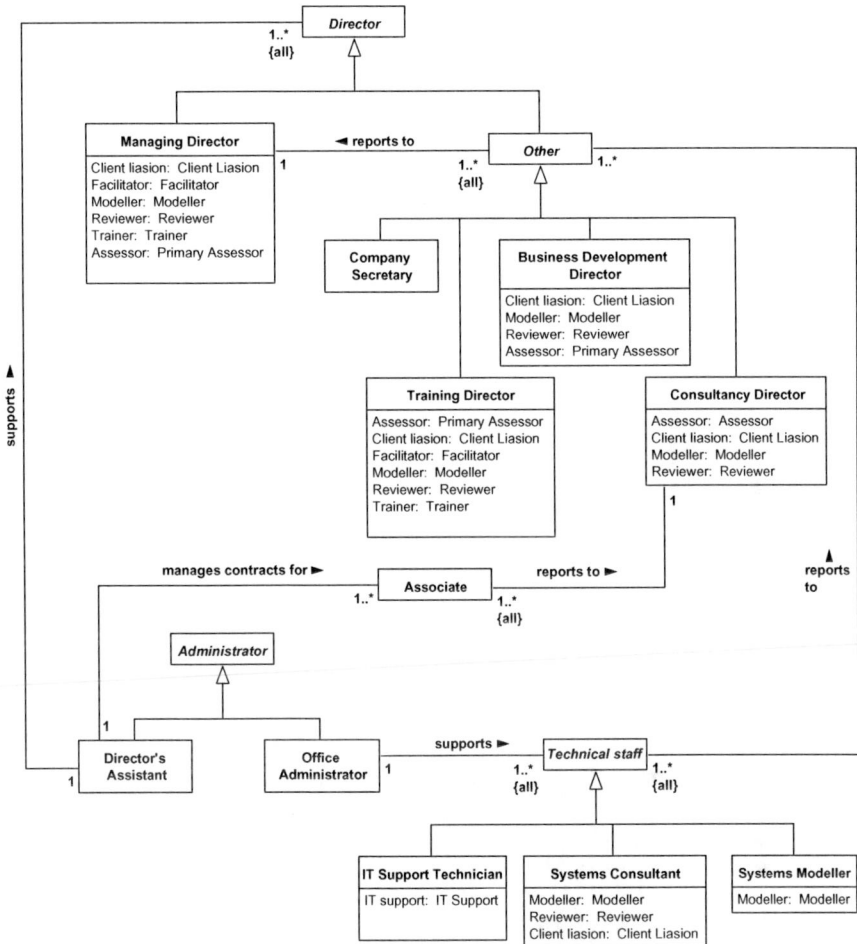

Figure 4.14   Business organisation view

Figure 4.14 shows the positions in the organisation. To model the people associated with each position, an object diagram is needed (see Section 4.7). Before turning to object diagrams, it is worth looking at some more examples of the use of class diagrams for modelling an EA. Figure 4.15 shows how class diagrams can be used to help model aspects of an organisation's infrastructure.

Figure 4.15 describes the various types of asset that make up the infrastructure in the authors' organisation, presented in the form of a taxonomy. The diagram shows that 'Infrastructure' is made up of one or more 'Asset' of which there are two types: 'Person' and 'Technical Asset', the latter broken down into a large number of sub-types covering 'Network', 'Hardware' and 'Software' assets.

Each 'Technical Asset' has its requirements defined by an 'Asset Specification' which defines the key attributes of an asset. It also has one or more 'Technology

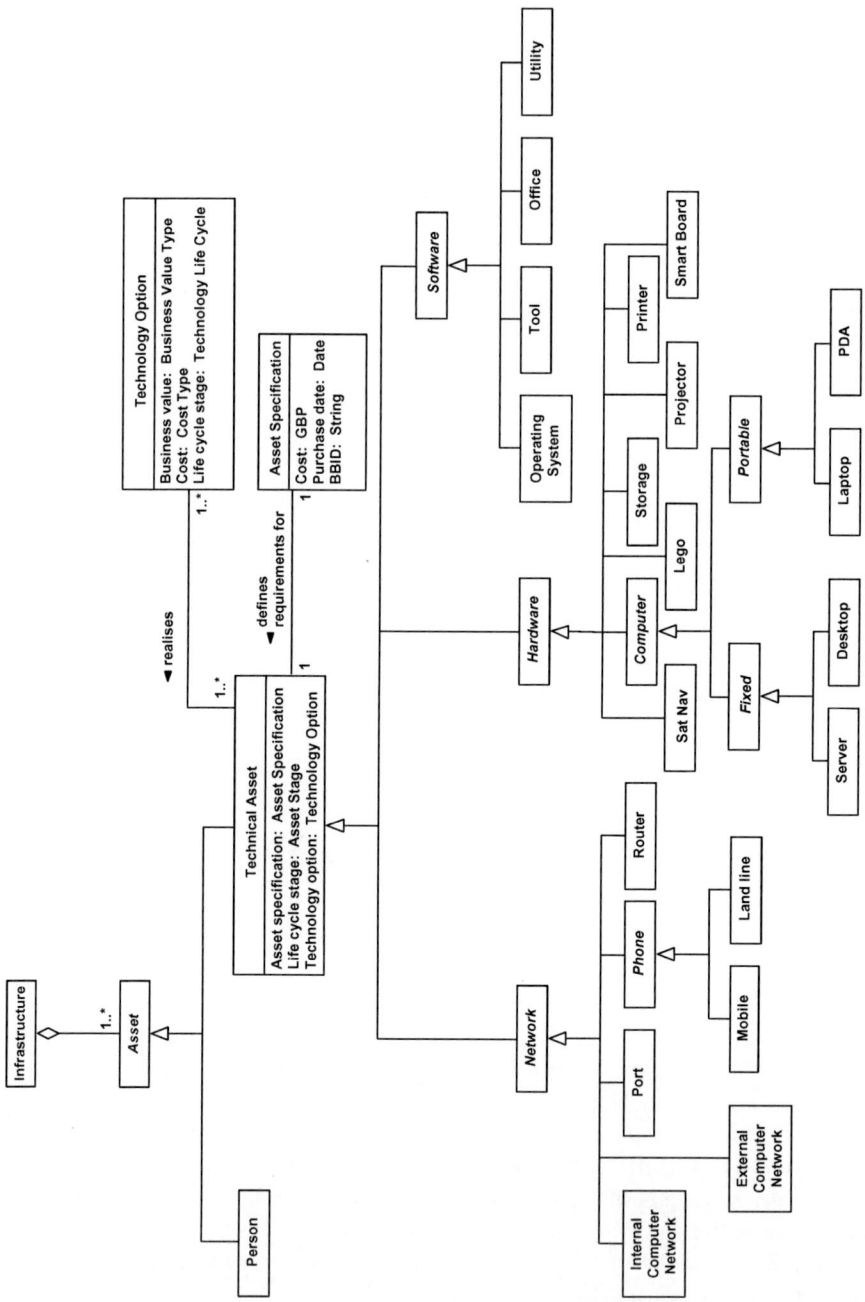

Figure 4.15 Infrastructure view (infrastructure taxonomy)

Option' that describes a type of technology that may be used to realise a particular 'Technical Asset'. The 'Technical Asset' class has attributes to hold references to the 'Technology Option' and 'Asset Specification' (which have attributes of their own). It also has an attribute to represent the life cycle stage that the asset is currently in.

Before looking at the possible life cycle stages for a 'Technical Asset', as well as those for a 'Technology Option', it is worth introducing another piece of notation for class diagrams that is useful for defining types for attributes that can take on one of a number of restricted values, so-called *enumerated* types.

The 'Technology Option' in Figure 4.15 has an attribute 'Business value' of type 'Business Value Type'. This attribute can only take on the value 'low', 'medium' or 'high'. So how is 'Business Value Type' modelled to ensure this? The way to do this is shown in Figure 4.16.

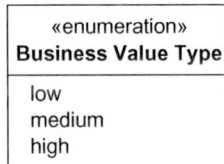

«enumeration» **Business Value Type**
low medium high

Figure 4.16   Modelling enumerated types

An enumerated type is modelled as a class that has the stereotype '«enumeration»'. This indicates that the type being modelled is an enumeration which can only take on one of a list of so-called enumeration literal values. Attributes are used to model these enumeration literal values, with one attribute per value. Each attribute is named with the name of the enumeration literal value and has no data type associated with it. The order of the attributes also defines the order of the enumeration literal values which can be compared for equality or relative position in the list of literals. If desired, an enumerated type can also have operations defined on it, but these operations can only take literals as arguments and return literals as results.

The diagram shows that 'Business Value Type' is an enumerated type. Elements typed by 'Business Value Type' can take on one of the values of 'low', 'medium' or 'high' and that the value 'low' is the lowest in relative ordering, with 'high' being the highest.

Having looked at this additional piece of notation, it is time to look at how the life cycle stages for assets and technology options seen in Figure 4.15 can be modelled.

Figure 4.17 is another example of the use of a class diagram for showing taxonomies. In this case, the taxonomies define the stages for an 'Asset Life Cycle' and a 'Technology Life Cycle'.

Note here that the *pattern* in the diagram is the same for each of the two types of life cycle shown. They both are made up of one or more stage and each stage has

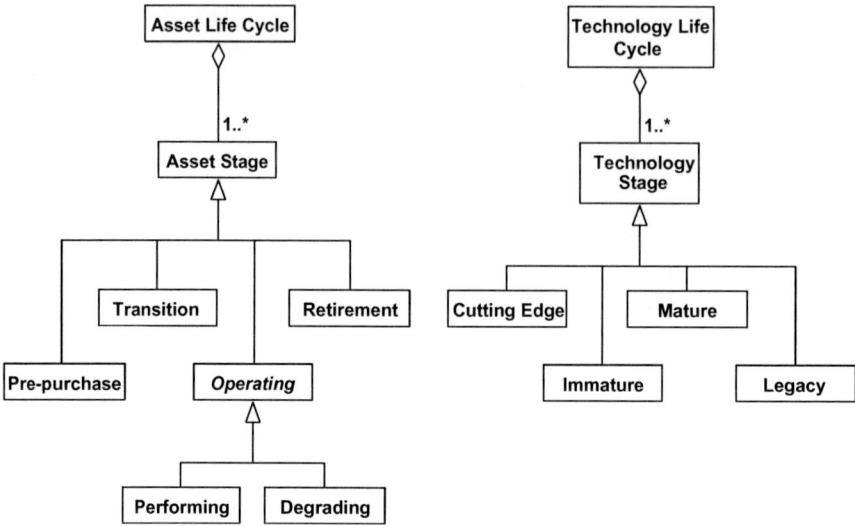

Figure 4.17   Infrastructure life cycle view

a number of types associated with it. This is a common pattern encountered frequently when defining life cycles.

It must also be noted that this diagram does *not* define the life cycle for a particular asset or technology option. This diagram is a structural diagram that simply defines the possible stages that make up such a life cycle. To see the actual stages in the life cycle for a particular asset, a behavioural diagram would be needed. See Section 4.15.4 on 'Timing Diagrams' for an example.

Another common use of class diagrams in EA modelling is for defining the capabilities that an organisation has. This is an important view in an EA as it is the capabilities that define what an organisation can do and hence, at least for commercial organisations, how it can make money. An example is shown in Figure 4.18.

Figure 4.18 shows that 'Capability' has two types, 'Exploratory' and 'Service'. Each of these are abstract capabilities, as indicated by the italic class names, and are broken down into a number of concrete capabilities. One or more 'Exploratory' capabilities lead to zero or more 'Service' capabilities.

As seen previously, each 'Capability' is realised by one or more ordered 'Process'. 'Capability' has an attribute, 'Process owner', that contains the initials of the member of staff who owns the processes associated with a capability. Each concrete capability has two lines of text of the form:

   ::Capability
   Process owner = XYZ

where XYZ are the initials of the member of staff who owns the processes that realise the capability.

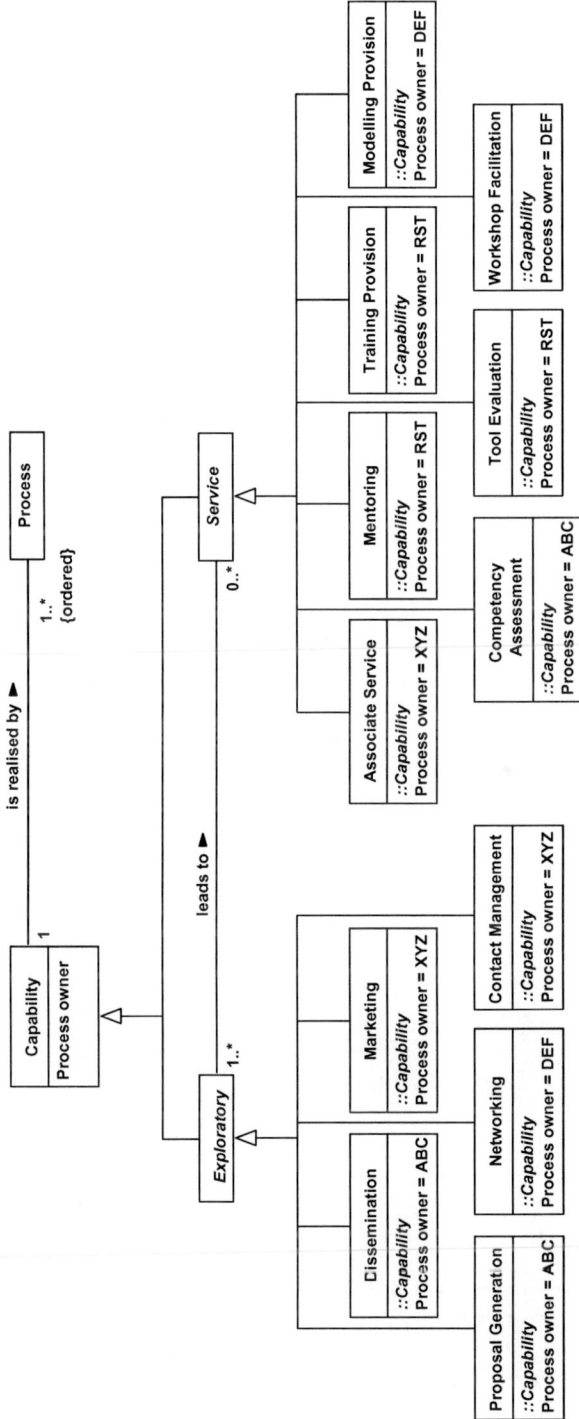

Figure 4.18 Capability definition view

The second of these lines shows how an *initial value* may be set for an attribute. The first line, the text '::Capability' above the attribute name 'Process owner', shows that 'Process owner' is not an attribute defined in the concrete capability but that it is inherited from the 'Capability' class. This is useful when a class inherits attributes from a number of parent classes at different levels in a type hierarchy and the attributes are given initial values. It shows, by grouping inherited attributes by their source class, just where in the type hierarchy they are inherited from. This is particularly useful if the parent classes are not shown on the diagram.

The final example of a class diagram in this chapter shows how class diagrams can be used to help an organisation model its business processes (see Figure 4.19).

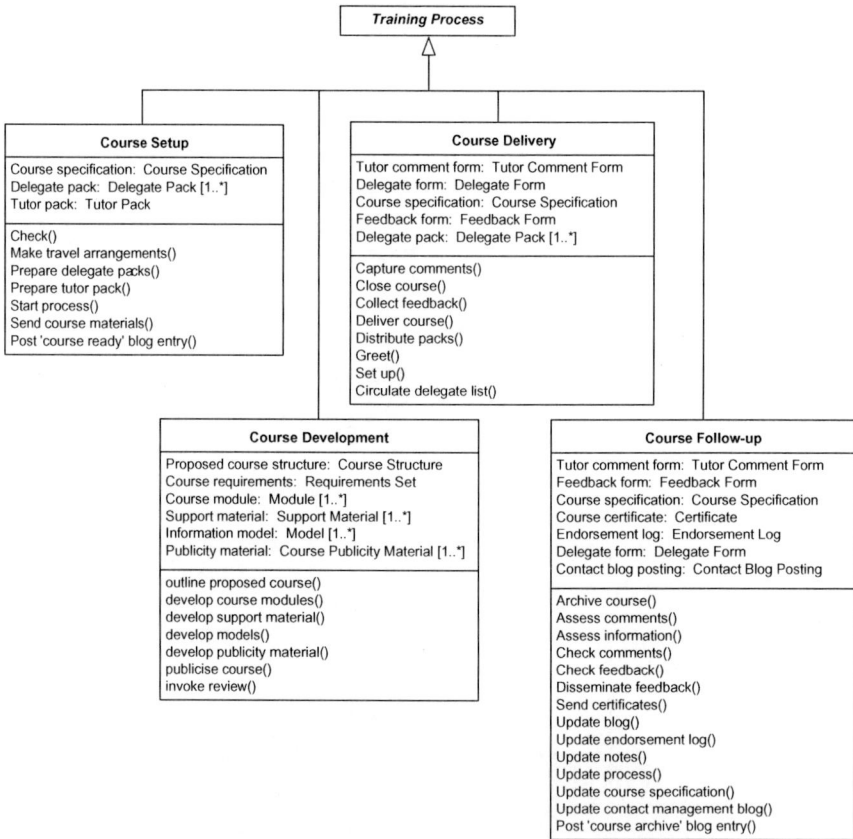

Figure 4.19   Process content view (training)

Figure 4.19 shows a so-called 'process content view', one of seven views that can be produced to allow business processes to be modelled in a complete and consistent manner. For information on the approach behind this see Reference 4.

The diagram shows a small selection of the processes in a small training organisation; specifically it shows the training processes. As can be seen from the diagram there are four types of 'Training Process': 'Course Setup', 'Course Development', 'Course Delivery' and 'Course Follow-up'.

The convention used here is that each process is modelled as a class. The artifacts that are produced and consumed by a process are modelled as attributes of that process. The activities that are undertaken in a process are modelled as operations of the process. The intent of this diagram is to serve as a declaration of the available processes and the artifacts and activities associated with each process and is key to ensuring the consistency of the complete process model, as described in Reference 4. Since this is a structural diagram it does not show *how* each process is carried out. For that a behavioural diagram is needed, such as an activity diagram, and an example is given in Section 4.13.3.

4.6.4 Summary

Class diagrams are used to show abstractions of 'things' and their relationships. Choose names so that:

● Class names are nouns
● Attribute names are nouns
● Operation names are verbs
● Associations read like sentences.

When modelling EAs, typical views that can be modelled using class diagrams include:

● EA meta-model that identifies the high-level concepts that are needed to understand and develop an EA
● EA ontology that identifies the EA concepts and their relationships
● Process content views that identify business processes
● Business organisation views that show the structure of an organisation
● Life cycle views that define life cycle stages for infrastructure assets
● Infrastructure taxonomy views that identify types of infrastructure assets and their relationships
● Stakeholder views that identify organisational stakeholders.

Class diagrams show 'things' at the conceptual level. The next diagram shows 'things' at the actual level.

4.7 Object diagram

4.7.1 Overview

This section introduces the object diagram. Object diagrams realise a structural aspect of the model and are heavily related to class diagrams. The definition of an object is that it is an instance of a class and object diagrams will represent instances of class diagrams. Objects represent real-life examples of the conceptual classes found in class diagrams and relate very closely to real life. Object diagrams also have strong relationships with component and deployment diagrams (both structural) as well as all types of interaction diagram (communication, sequence, interaction overview and timing diagrams).

4.7.2   Diagram elements

Object diagrams are made up of two main elements: objects and links. An object is defined as an instance of a class. In the same way, links are instances of associations. A high-level meta-model for the object diagram is shown in Figure 4.20.

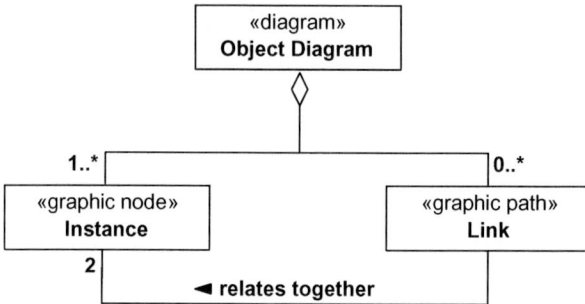

Figure 4.20   Partial meta-model for object diagrams

Figure 4.20 shows that an 'Object diagram' is made up of one or more 'Instance' and zero or more 'Link'. Also, each 'Link' relates together two 'Instance'. When instances are identified, it is usual to assign a value to each attribute as each instance represents a real-life example of a class and must have values completed for the attributes. Each of these diagram elements may be realised by either graphical nodes or graphical paths, as indicated by their stereotypes and are illustrated in Figure 4.21.

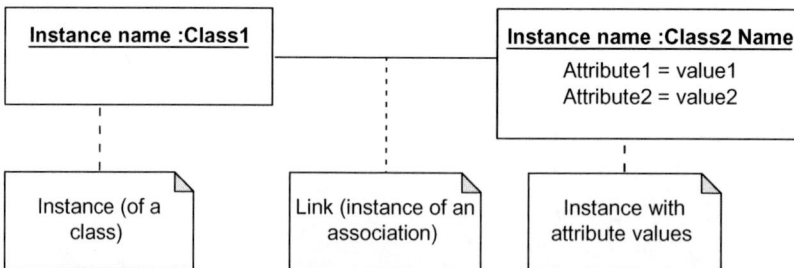

Figure 4.21   Graphical symbols for elements in an object diagram

Figure 4.21, itself an object diagram, shows the notation used on object diagrams. The basic symbol for an instance is a rectangle containing the instance name and the class that it is an instance of, separated by a colon. Most importantly, this text is underlined. This is crucial as, by omitting the underling, it means that the symbol represents a *part* or even a *class*. Parts are discussed in Section 4.8 on 'Composite Structure Diagrams'.

Object diagrams are very heavily dependent on class diagrams, as each object requires an associated class from which its appearance and behaviour can be taken. This is illustrated in Figure 4.22, which shows a meta-model of how classes and objects are related.

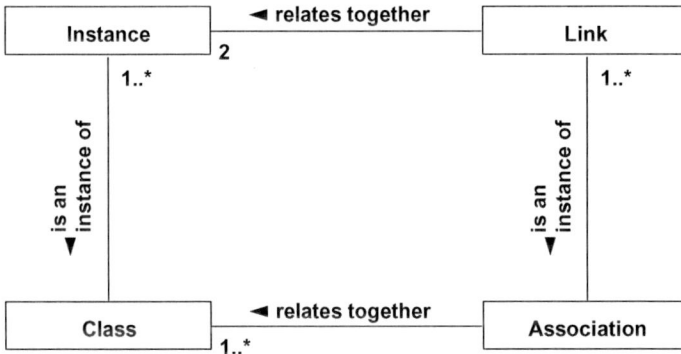

Figure 4.22   Relationships between object diagram elements and class diagram elements

Figure 4.22 shows that a 'Link' relates together two 'Instance'. One or more 'Instance' is an instance of a 'Class' and one or more 'Link' is an instance of an 'Association'. Notice how the top and bottom half of Figure 4.22 have both been seen before in Figures 4.20 and 4.11. This is an example of seeing patterns emerge from different models that can give a whole new view of a particular piece of information when shown together and with the addition of a few extra relationships.

4.7.3   Example EA views realised using an object diagram

As discussed previously, object diagrams are perhaps the least used of all the 13 UML diagrams. The main aim of an object diagram is to enforce the connection to reality between the conceptual class diagram and the real-life system that it is representing. They show examples or *instances* of classes and are useful for establishing the connection to reality that can sometimes be hard to see when faced with a complex class diagram.

When modelling EAs, object diagrams are particularly useful for representing such things as the actual people who hold positions within an organisation or actual pieces of equipment used within an organisation. Examples of both of these uses are given, starting with a business organisation view that shows details of the people who hold positions within the organisation.

Figure 4.23 shows instances of a selection of the classes seen on the Business Organisation View in Figure 4.14. Each of the objects corresponds to one of the positions in Figure 4.14. These positions, such as 'Training Director', are all sub-types of the class 'Position' which was omitted from Figure 4.14, but which is now shown in Figure 4.24.

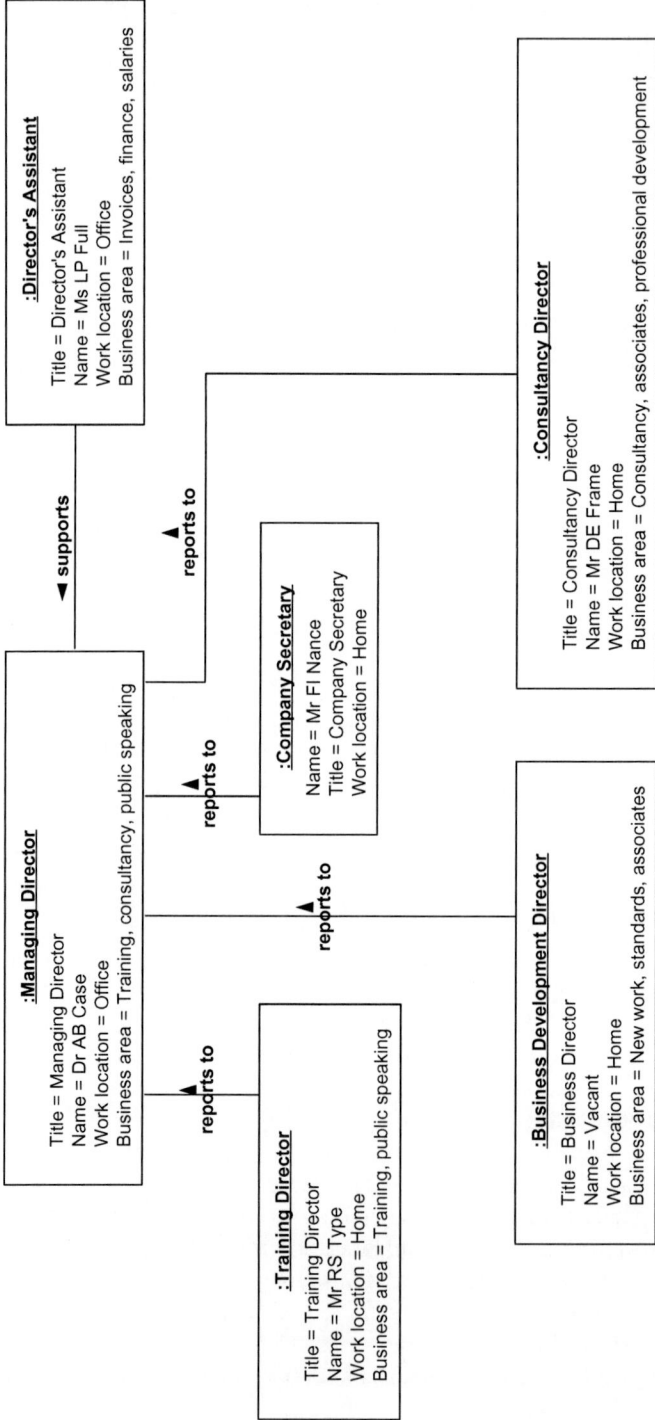

Figure 4.23 Business organisation view (business person view)

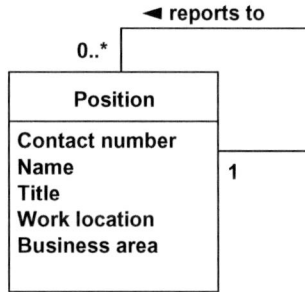

Figure 4.24   The 'Position' class

Figure 4.24 shows that a 'Position' reports to zero or more 'Position' and has a number of attributes that capture information about that 'Position', such as a contact telephone number, name of the person in the position, business areas that they are responsible for, etc.

As can be seen in the object diagram in Figure 4.23, each object has values set for these attributes. Note also that some of the attributes (e.g. 'Contact number') have been omitted from the diagram for reasons of confidentiality. This ability to suppress attributes means that slightly different versions of such a diagram could be produced: one containing 'Contact number' for internal use, and one with 'Contact number' suppressed for external publication. The links between the objects correspond to the associations between the classes in Figure 4.14.

Having looked at an object diagram that details instances of positions, the next example details instances of equipment – technical assets – and shows how they may be grouped by type of equipment on an object diagram.

Figure 4.25 shows instances of technical assets from the Infrastructure Taxonomy View seen in Figure 4.15. Each object represents an actual, physical technical asset. Attributes have been assigned values to indicate the life cycle stage and, in some cases, technology option for each asset.

A requirement for this diagram was to be able to group technical assets into broad categories representing the types of asset represented. This has been done by using packages to visually group the technical assets into categories representing 'Computers', 'Printers', 'Comms' and 'Misc. Equipment'. This use of packages to group model elements on diagrams is perhaps the most common way that packages can be used. Packages do have a diagram of their own in UML and this is discussed in Section 4.9.

4.7.4   Summary

Object diagrams show instances of things and their relationships. When creating object diagrams, check consistency with related class diagrams.

When modelling EAs, typical views that can be modelled using object diagrams include:

- Business person views that show actual people and the positions and responsibilities that they hold in an organisation

Computers		
Sidious :Desktop Life cycle stage = Performing		
Windu :Desktop Life cycle stage = Performing		
:Desktop Life cycle stage = Degrading		
Sony1 :Laptop Life cycle stage = Degrading		
Coruscant :Server Life cycle stage = Degrading		
C3PO :Laptop Life cycle stage = Performing		
R2D2 :Laptop Life cycle stage = Performing		

Printers		
Epsom Photo 1290 :Printer Life cycle stage = Performing Technology option = Inkjet		
OKI :Printer Life cycle stage = Performing		
OKI old :Printer Life cycle stage = Retirement		
Fax :Printer Life cycle stage = Performing		

Comms		
Death Star :Router Life cycle stage = Performing		
Wine :Port Life cycle stage = Performing		

Misc. Equipment		
Obi Wan :Projector Life cycle stage = Performing		
Training :Smart Board Life cycle stage = Performing		
Demo kit :Lego Life cycle stage = Degrading Technology option = RCX		
User kit 1 :Lego Life cycle stage = Performing Technology option = NXT		
User kit 2 :Lego Life cycle stage = Performing Technology option = NXT		

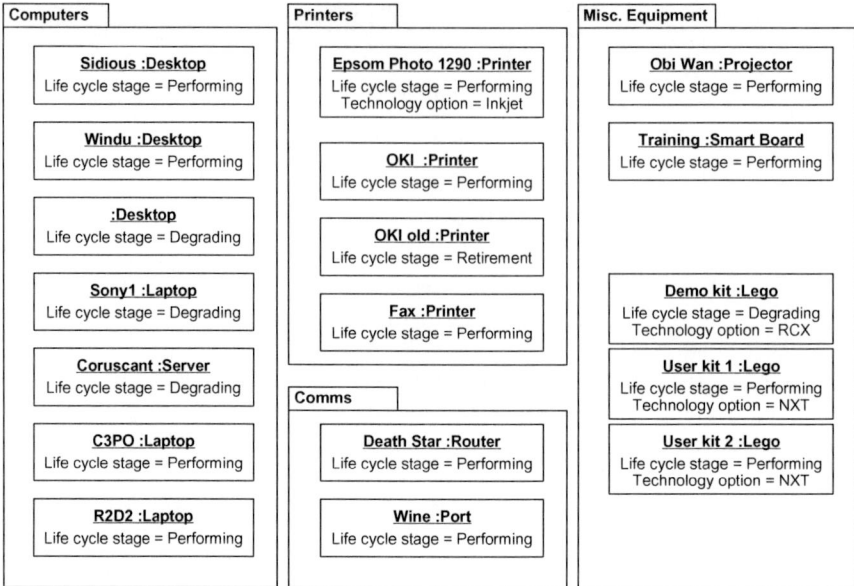

Figure 4.25   Infrastructure deployment view (Swansea assets)

- Asset views that identify infrastructure assets and their associated life cycle stages and technology options.

Although object diagrams show instances of things, we often want to look at so-called *prototypical* instances. This is one of the uses of the diagram considered in the next section.

4.8   Composite structure diagram

4.8.1   Overview

The composite structure diagram realises a structural aspect of the model and allows compositions and aggregations to be represented within the boundaries of a *part* without the need to show the aggregation or composition relationships explicitly. This means that an emphasis may be put on the logical relationships between elements of the composition, rather than the structural breakdown itself. This adds a great deal of value, as it forces the modeller to think about the logical relationship between elements, rather than simply which classes are part of which other classes.

There is another use for the composite structure diagram which is to show *collaborations*, that is relationships amongst instances that interact to implement a desired functionality. While collaborations are useful in general systems modelling, they are less useful in modelling EAs. Indeed, the EA of the training organisation used as a basis for discussion in this chapter does not use any collaborations to represent the views of the EA. For this reason they have been omitted from this book. For information on collaboration see References 1, 3 and 5.

4.8.2   Diagram elements

The basic elements within a composite structure diagram are the *part*, *port* and *connector*. A *part* is an element that describes a collection of UML elements, such as classes or instances of classes. A partial meta-model for composite structure diagrams is given in Figure 4.26.

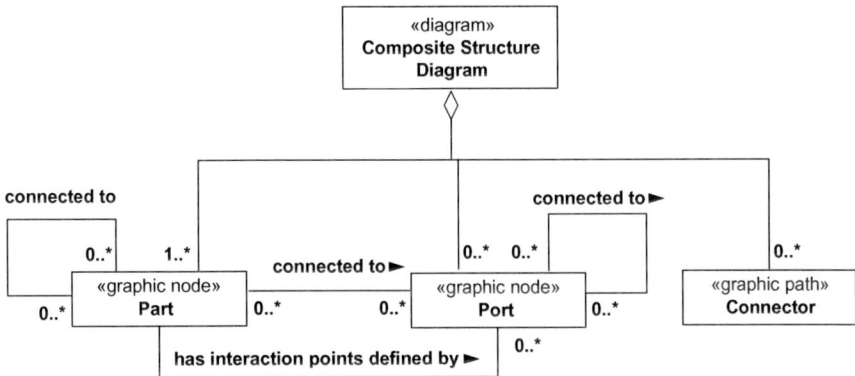

Figure 4.26   Partial meta-model for composite structure diagram

The diagram in Figure 4.26 shows the partial meta-model for the composite structure diagram. It can be seen that a 'Composite structure diagram' is made up of one or 'Part', zero or more 'Port' and zero or more 'Connector'. A 'Part' has interaction points defined by zero or more 'Port'. Each 'Part' is connected to zero or more 'Part' or zero or more 'Port' which themselves can be connected to zero or more 'Port'. This connection is made via the 'Connector'.

Ports do not have to be used on a composite structure diagram as parts can be directly connected. However, if it is important to capture the interaction points between parts then ports should be used. They are similar in concept to the ports found on a computer, such as USB ports, which are, in the case of computers, physical points through which the computer interacts with external systems.

Each of these diagram elements may be realised by either graphical nodes or graphical paths, as indicated by their stereotypes and are illustrated in Figure 4.27.

Figure 4.27 shows the symbols for each of the elements in a composite structure diagram. The symbol for a part looks similar to that of an instance, the difference being that the part has no underlining present. This is the graphical clue that identifies an instance. The part has a part name and a type (which will normally be the name of the class that identifies the type of the part). Ports are added onto a part by using a small rectangle and they too have a name and a type.

When parts are shown nested inside a class (a so-called composite class), the nesting represents the fact that the composite class is made up of the parts. This is best explained with a diagram.

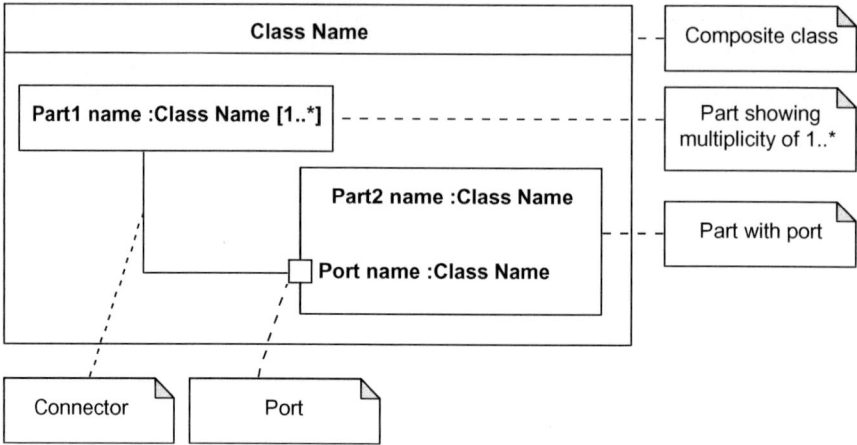

Figure 4.27   Graphical symbols for elements in a composite structure diagram

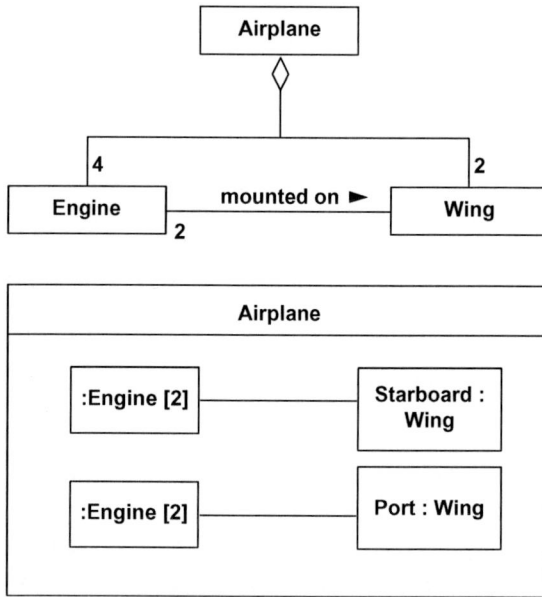

Figure 4.28   Showing aggregation through parts

The top of Figure 4.28 shows a simple class diagram that models the structure of a very simple airplane. The 'Airplane' is made up of four 'Engine' and two 'Wing'. Two 'Engine' are mounted on each 'Wing'.

The bottom of the diagram shows the same structure, but this time modelled as a composite structure diagram. 'Airplane' is represented by the composite class which contains four parts, two each for the 'Engine' and 'Wing'. In the case of the 'Wing' parts, these have been named to identify them as representing the starboard and port wings. The connector between the 'Engine' and 'Wing' parts corresponds to the association between the corresponding classes on the class diagram.

The nesting of the parts corresponding to the 'Engine' and 'Wing' classes inside the composite class 'Airplane' has the same meaning on the composite structure diagram as does the aggregation on the corresponding class diagram. However, because the relationship is now shown by nesting, there is now no longer anywhere to show the multiplicities that appear on the aggregations or the association. To show the multiplicity of a part on a composite structure diagram, it is written in square brackets after the part name and type, as can be seen in the case of the 'Engine' parts in the bottom part of Figure 4.28. If no multiplicity is shown it defaults to a multiplicity of '1'.

4.8.3 Example EA views realised using a composite structure diagram

Where class diagrams are very useful for modelling the structure of hierarchical elements through use of aggregation or composition, there is often the need to model so-called *prototypical instances* of objects that conform to the class diagram. While such representations *can* be achieved using object diagrams, as described in Section 4.7, they are not very good at capturing the whole-part nature of such elements. Fortunately, this is a perfect use for composite structure diagrams and a number of examples are considered in Figure 4.29.

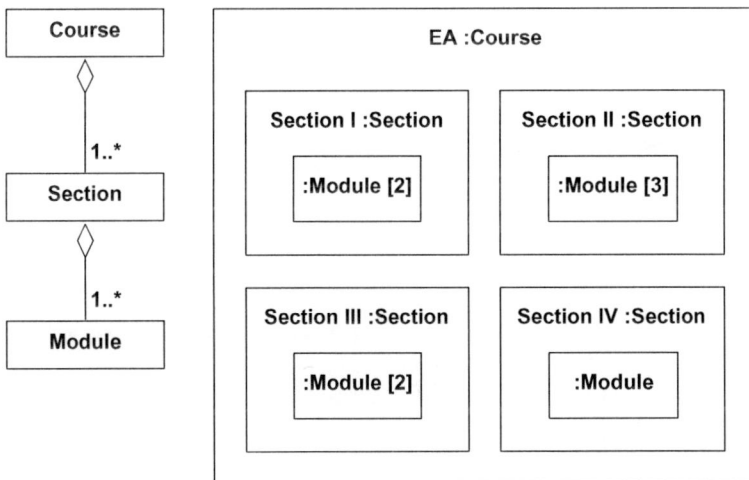

Figure 4.29 Information view (EA course structure)

When developing an EA, the composite structure diagram is particularly suited to representing information about artifacts that are produced and consumed by an organisation's processes. These are typically represented on a number of 'information views'. (See Reference 4 for a full description of a pragmatic approach to process modelling.)

Figure 4.29 shows one such information view which combines a class and composite structure diagram. The left-hand side of the diagram shows three classes that represent the structure of training courses developed and delivered by the organisation: 'Course' is made up of one or more 'Section' and each 'Section' is made up of one or more 'Module'. This is sufficient to represent the generic structure of courses, but what if the structure of a particular course is needed?

The right-hand side of the diagram shows this through a composite structure diagram. UML parts are used to show the structure of a particular course, in this case an EA course. It shows that the EA course is made up of four 'Section', which are named 'Section I' to 'Section IV', and the number of 'Module' in each 'Section'. Thus it can be seen that 'Section I' has two 'Module' whereas 'Section IV' has only a single module.

The composite structure diagram can also be used to show how artifacts are assembled together, both generically and for specific uses. Consider, for example, a number of different artifacts that are distributed as part of material distributed on a training course. Figure 4.30 shows the structure of a 'Delegate Pack' for courses given by the organisation.

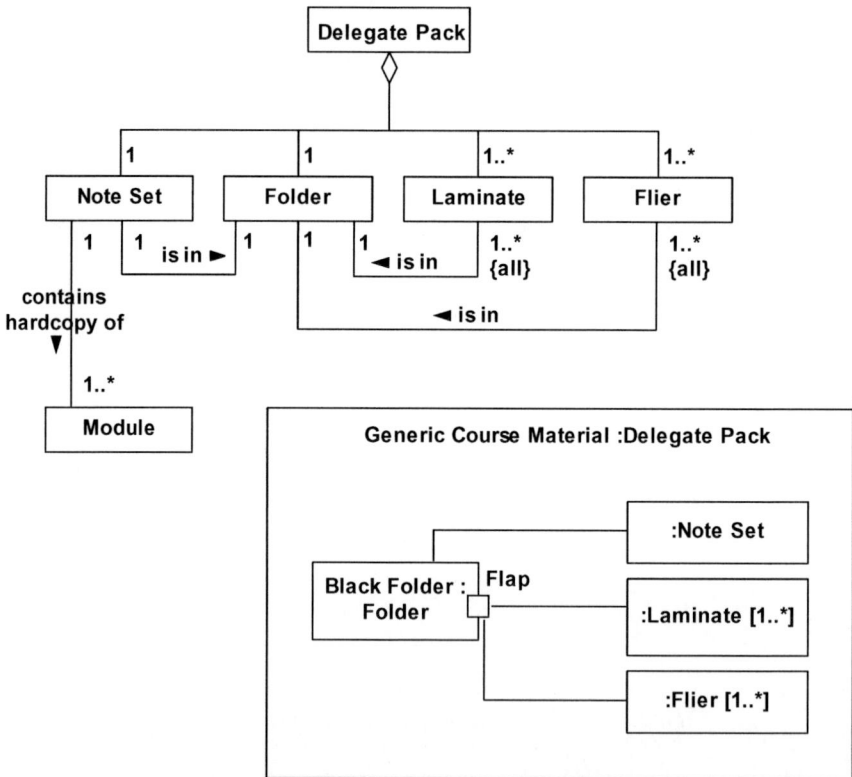

Figure 4.30   Information view (course material)

The top part of Figure 4.30 uses classes to show that a 'Delegate Pack' is made up of a 'Note Set', a 'Folder', one or more 'Laminate' and one or more 'Flier'. It also shows that the 'Note Set' is in the 'Folder' along with each 'Laminate' and

'Flier' and that the 'Note Set' contains hardcopy of one or more 'Module'. The constraint '{all}' is used to indicate that all of the laminates and fliers in the pack are actually in the folder. If this constraint is omitted it would be possible for a pack to contain three laminates, say, but with only one or two of them being in the folder.

The bottom part of the diagram uses a composite structure diagram to show how all these elements of a 'Delegate Pack' are assembled for a generic course. The 'Note Set' is directly linked to the 'Folder', here shown to be a 'Black Folder', using a connector. Each 'Laminate' and 'Flier' is also linked to the 'Folder' but this time a port (the small square labelled 'Flap') is used to show that they are placed in a flap in the folder. This diagram may seem trivial but, in fact, forms a useful part of the 'Course Setup' process introduced in Section 4.6.3 and considered further in Section 4.13.3. It provides useful guidance to the person responsible for assembling course material, ensuring that each 'Delegate Pack' is correctly assembled.

While the composite structure diagram in Figure 4.30 shows the organisation for a generic course, a similar diagram can be produced for a specific course. An example of such a specific use is given in Figure 4.31.

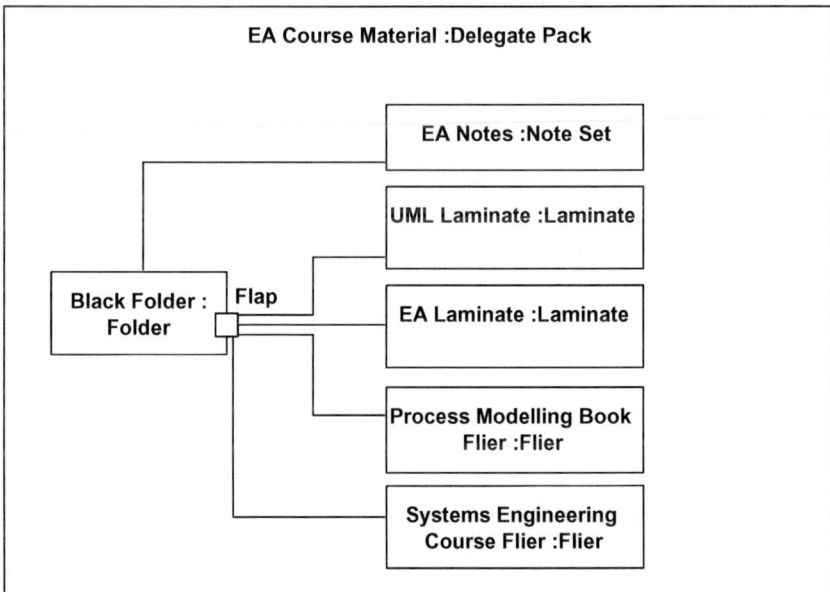

Figure 4.31   Information view (EA course material)

For an EA course, the material is assembled as shown in the composite structure diagram in Figure 4.31. Here, rather than generic parts representing multiple items, for example, ':Laminate [1..*]' as seen in Figure 4.30, specific items have been identified by naming each UML part. Thus it can be seen that for an EA course the 'Delegate Pack' contains the 'EA Notes', a 'UML Laminate', an 'EA Laminate', a 'Process Modelling Book Flier' and a 'Systems Engineering Course Flier', again with the laminates and fliers placed in the flap of the folder as indicated by the connection to the 'Flap' port.

4.8.4   Summary

Composite structure diagrams are used to break down complex compositions and aggregations. They are related to class diagrams and interaction diagrams.

When modelling EAs, typical views that can be modelled using composite structure diagrams include:

- Information views that show the structure of organisational information such as training material.

Any model needs to be structured so that related model elements are grouped together. The diagram discussed in the next section allows the structure of a model to be so represented.

4.9   Package diagram

4.9.1   Overview

Package diagrams simply identify and relate together packages. The concept of the package is exactly the same as when used on other diagrams – each package shows a collection of diagram elements and implies some sort of ownership.

4.9.2   Diagram elements

The syntax for the package diagram is very simple and can be seen in Figure 4.32.

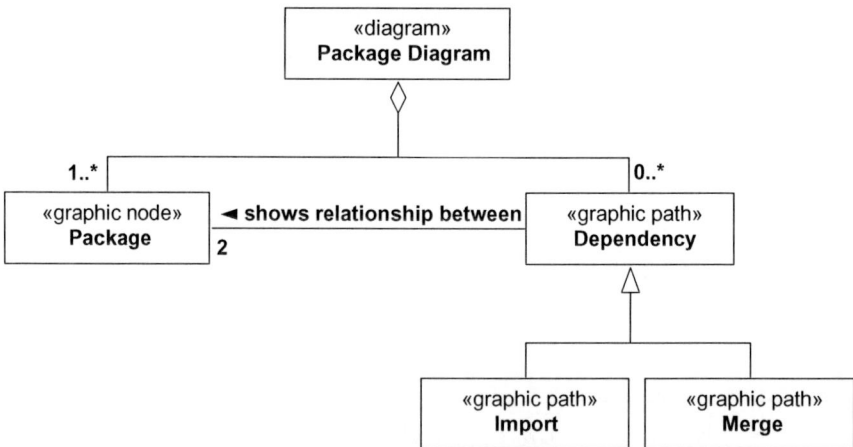

Figure 4.32   Partial meta-model for package diagrams

The diagram in Figure 4.32 shows the partial meta-model for the package diagram. It can be seen that there are two main elements in the diagram: the 'Package' and the 'Dependency'. There are two main types of 'Dependency' defined: 'Import' and 'Merge'.

Each of these diagram elements may be realised by either graphical nodes or graphical paths, as indicated by their stereotypes and are illustrated in Figure 4.33.

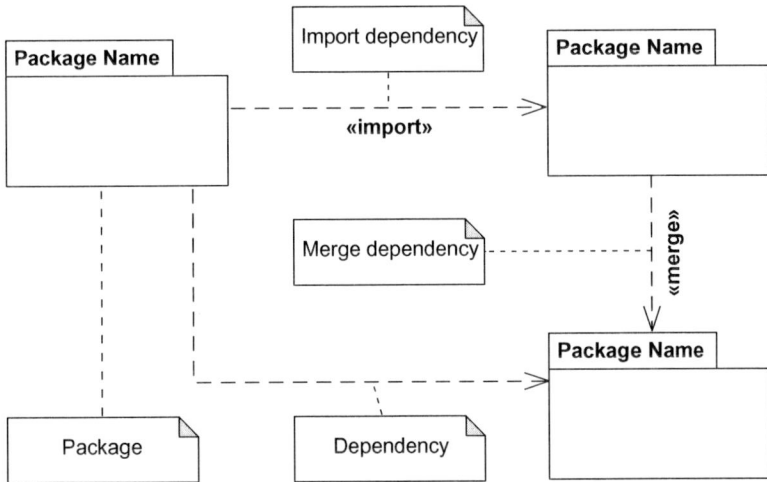

Figure 4.33 Graphical symbols for elements in a package diagram

The package diagram in Figure 4.33 shows that there are really only two symbols on the diagram. The graphical node representing package symbol is a rectangle with a smaller tag rectangle on the top left-hand edge. This is similar to the folder icon that can be seen in Windows systems and has a very similar conceptual meaning. The name of the package can either be shown in the tag (as seen here) or, in the case of long names, will often be shown inside the main rectangle.

The main graphical path in the package diagram is a dependency that has two basic stereotypes defined – «import» and «merge». The «merge» stereotype means that the package being pointed to (target) becomes part of the other package (source), with any elements with the same name being taken as specialisations of the source package elements. An «import», on the other hand, implies that the target package still remains its own package as part of the source package. Any element name clashes are resolved with the source package taking precedence over the target package. Other stereotypes will often be defined for the dependencies on a package diagram.

4.9.3 Example EA views realised using a package diagram

Package diagrams are typically used to show relationships within a model at a very high level and while *packages* are used frequently in UML, for example, to package elements on diagrams such as the class diagram, package *diagrams* tend to be used less often than the other 12 UML diagrams.

Since packages are used to organise a UML model, package diagrams are often used to show the dependencies between the different organisational parts of the model. An example is given in Figure 4.34.

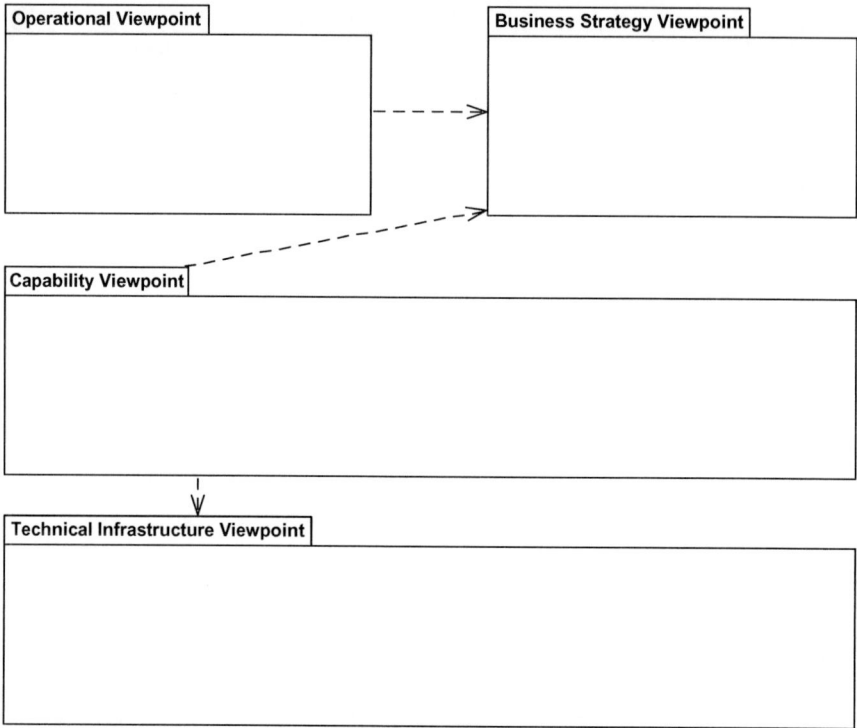

Figure 4.34   EA view quagmire – dependencies

Figure 4.34 is a version of the so-called 'EA View Quagmire' which is discussed in detail later in the book in Chapter 5. For now it is sufficient to know that the quagmire shows all the views in an EA, grouped into viewpoints (views and viewpoints were introduced in Chapter 1).

Figure 4.34 shows the four viewpoints in the EA of the training organisation, with each viewpoint represented by a package. In this diagram the views within each viewpoint have been omitted for clarity. For the full quagmire diagram showing all the views, see Chapter 7 or Appendix A. Dependencies have been used to show how the four viewpoints depend on each other: the views in the 'Operational Viewpoint' depend on those in the 'Business Strategy Viewpoint'; the views in the 'Capability Viewpoint' depend on those in the 'Business Strategy Viewpoint' and the 'Technical Infrastructure Viewpoint'.

Where part of a UML model imports information from other models or makes use of UML profiles (collections of stereotypes and model elements tailored for a particular application domain or for a particular modelling approach), this can be shown using package diagrams as shown in Figure 4.35.

Figure 4.35 shows that a 'Process Model' is importing the elements and definitions from 'MODAF' and 'TOGAF' profiles to make use of such elements within the process model. MODAF and TOGAF are examples of other 'architectural

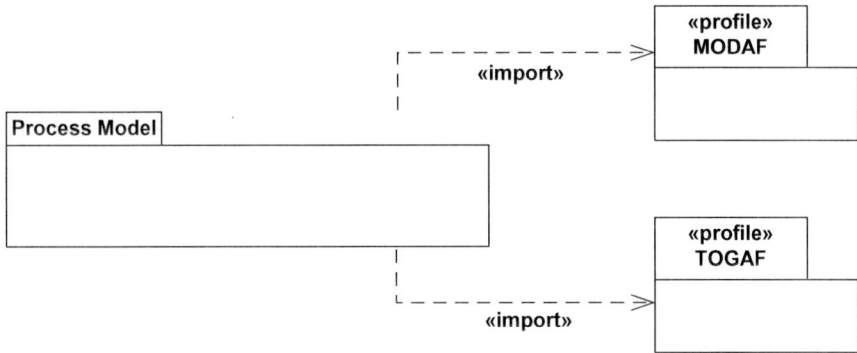

Figure 4.35   Process view – Process Model links to MODAF and TOGAF

frameworks' often used in EA and related modelling. They are described further in Chapter 8.

4.9.4   Summary

Package diagrams show the ownership of modelling elements and are related to most UML elements.

When modelling EAs, typical views that can be modelled using package diagrams include:

- EA meta-model, to show how related EA meta-model concepts are grouped and related
- EA view quagmire, to show how EA views are organised into viewpoints
- Process views, to show how business processes use concepts and elements from modelling profiles such as TOGAF and MODAF.

Whereas package diagrams can be used to organise a model and show ownership of model elements, the next diagram shows how those elements can be put together into larger elements that are characterised by their interfaces.

4.10   Component diagram

4.10.1   Overview

This section introduces component diagrams that realise a structural view of a system. Component diagrams are often perceived as being used at later stages of system development when it comes to packaging up the final product and delivering to the customer and for this reason they are often grouped with deployment diagrams as *implementation* diagrams. However, they are also very useful for modelling legacy systems or for modelling high-level architectures which will usually happen towards the beginning of a project. Component diagrams show real-life aspects of a system and have strong relationships to both class and object diagrams. The simplest way to summarise why a component diagram is used is to imagine buying any product that is packaged in a box. The component diagram, basically, shows 'what's in the box' using both components and artifacts.

4.10.2   Diagram elements

The elements that make up a component diagram are shown in the diagram in Figure 4.36.

Figure 4.36 shows a partial meta-model for component diagrams. There are three main elements that make up a component diagram which are: one or more 'Component', zero or more 'Interface' and zero or more 'Connector'.

A 'Component' is the *specification* of a replaceable module in a system that is defined in terms of its interfaces. A component, therefore, is not the actual physical entity that exists in real life, but the specification of that entity. Components are realised by one or more 'Artifact'. An artifact is the actual physical entity that exists in real life and that meets the specification defined by the component.

An 'Interface' describes the set of services provided by and required by a particular component.

From the diagram, it can be seen that a 'Component' is made up of zero or more 'Port', zero or more 'Part' and zero or more 'Connector'. There are two types of 'Connector' in a component diagram: an 'Assembly Connector' connects together two internal parts and/or ports, whereas a 'Delegation' connects together an internal part or port with an external port of the component.

All these elements may be realised by graphic paths or nodes using the symbols shown in Figure 4.37.

The diagram in Figure 4.37 shows the graphical notation for the elements in a component diagram. The component can be drawn in two ways, either as a rectangle with the stereotype «component» or a rectangle with a small icon in the top right corner. Both examples are shown in Figure 4.37.

Parts and ports are shown using the same notation as used on the composite structure diagram. An assembly connector between internal ports and/or parts is represented by a solid line. A delegate connector between an internal port or part and an external port is shown by a directed solid line.

A provided interface is represented using a 'ball and stick' or 'lollipop' notation. If a component has a provided interface it means that it provides the operations of the interface as services which other components can use.

A required interface is represented using a 'socket' or 'cup' notation. If a component has a required interface it means that the component *requires* the use of another component which provides the same interface to function.

Required and provided interfaces can be connected in two ways, either by showing the ball or the provided interface plugged into the socket of the required interface, or by showing a dependency from the required to the provided interface. Required and provided interfaces can only be connected if they are of the same type, as indicated by the name of the interface.

While the required and provided interface notation show which interfaces are required and provided by which components, it does not define the interface. This

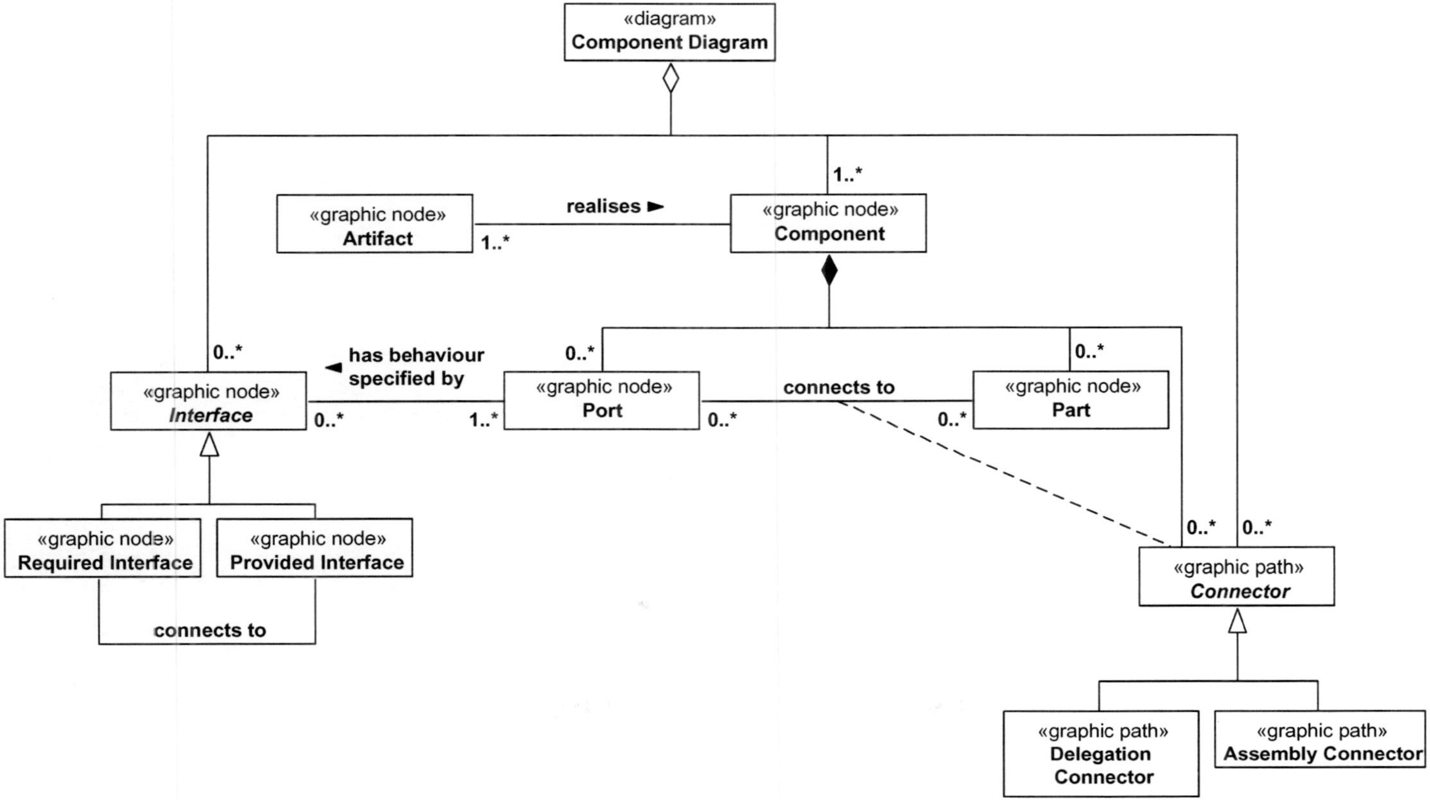

Figure 4.36 Partial meta-model for component diagrams

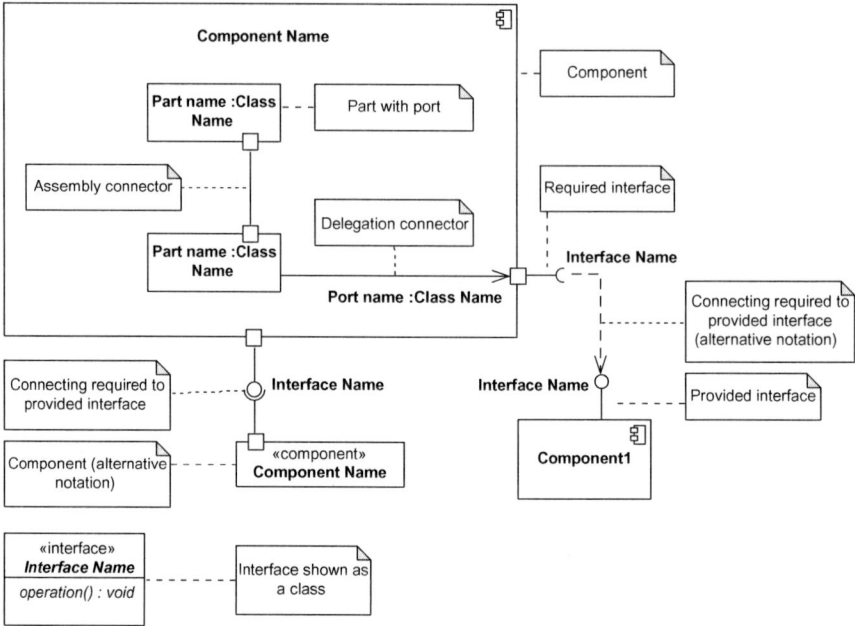

Figure 4.37   Graphical symbols for elements in a component diagram

is done using a special class, stereotyped «interface», that defines the operations of the interface (representing the services that the interface can provide). Note that an interface can only have operations. It *cannot* have attributes.

4.10.3   Example EA views realised using a component diagram

Since component diagrams focus on a structural representation of a system which places the emphasis on the interfaces between system elements and the ports through which they are connected, they are particularly suited to representing infrastructure views of an EA. Two such examples are given in Figure 4.38.

Figure 4.38 shows a generic representation of the hardware that makes up a computer network. Components have been used to represent both the network, here modelled as a simple 'Office network', as well as the equipment connected to the network. The multiplicity of each component is shown on the right-hand side of the component. Thus on the network modelled there are one or more 'Office Desktop PC' and 'Printer', zero or more 'Laptop', a single 'Server' and 'WiFi Port' and an optional 'Storage' device. Ports are used to show the connection points between the equipment and the network, again here modelled generically as 'Network:Network Port'. Note the omission of type from the ports on the 'Office network'. The interface between each item of equipment and the network is modelled as a generic 'Network Interface'. Since the interface is bi-directional, it has to be modelled as a provided and required interface at both ends of the connection. Note the use of the alternative notation which uses a dependency to connect required to provided interfaces.

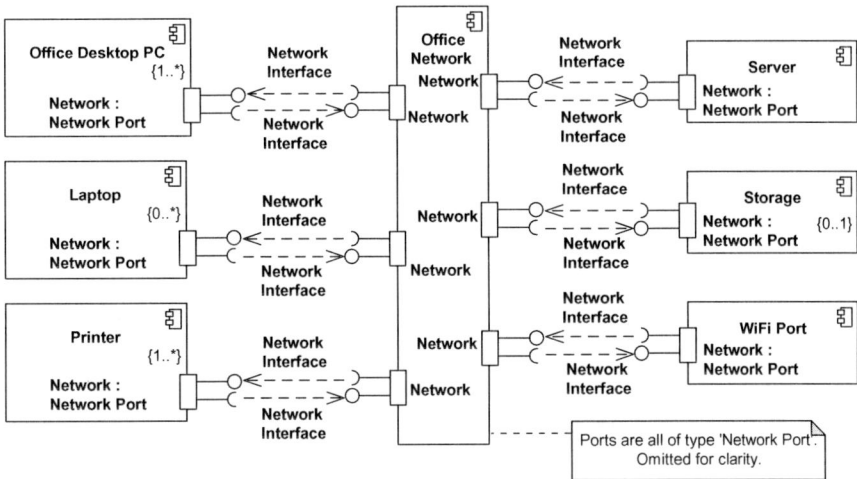

Figure 4.38 Infrastructure configuration view (network configuration)

Although Figure 4.38 models a computer network at a very high level, the generic 'Network Port' and 'Network Interface' could be refined as required to show more specific types of port and interface such as 'RJ-45: Ethernet Port' and 'Ethernet Interface'. Also the diagram treats each of the equipment items as a black box but it is possible to show elements inside a component through nested components or nested parts. Figure 4.39 makes use of this notational facility to show the software contained in computers used on training courses.

Figure 4.39 shows a 'Presentation Laptop' connected to a 'Projector' via a 'Video' interface linking the 'Video Out' port on the 'Presentation Laptop' to the 'Video In' port on the 'Projector'. It can also be connected to an optional 'Smart Board' via a bi-directional 'Smart Interface'. Similarly, the 'Workshop Laptop' is connected, via a 'USB Port' and the 'Lego Interface', to the 'USB Port' on one or more 'NXT Brick'. (This is the programmable Lego 'brick' used in Lego Mindstorms robotic kits.) Note the use of the two notations for connection required and provided interfaces and the alternative component notation used for 'Projector'.

Unlike the diagram in Figure 4.38 which showed each piece of equipment as a black box, this diagram shows some of the software on the 'Presentation Laptop' and 'Workshop Laptop'. The 'Presentation Laptop' as one copy of 'MS Office' and optionally has the 'Smart Board' software installed. The 'Workshop Laptop' has the 'Lego NXT Software' installed. Each of these pieces of software is modelled as a part and they are all typed to show the type of software that they are, either 'Office' software or 'Tools'. These types have been seen previously; they are all defined on the 'Infrastructure Taxonomy' diagram seen in Section 4.6 on 'Class Diagrams'.

Each of the software items is connected to an external port of the laptop on which it is installed. This is shown by the bi-directional delegation connectors connecting the UML parts and ports. This shows that the software communicates

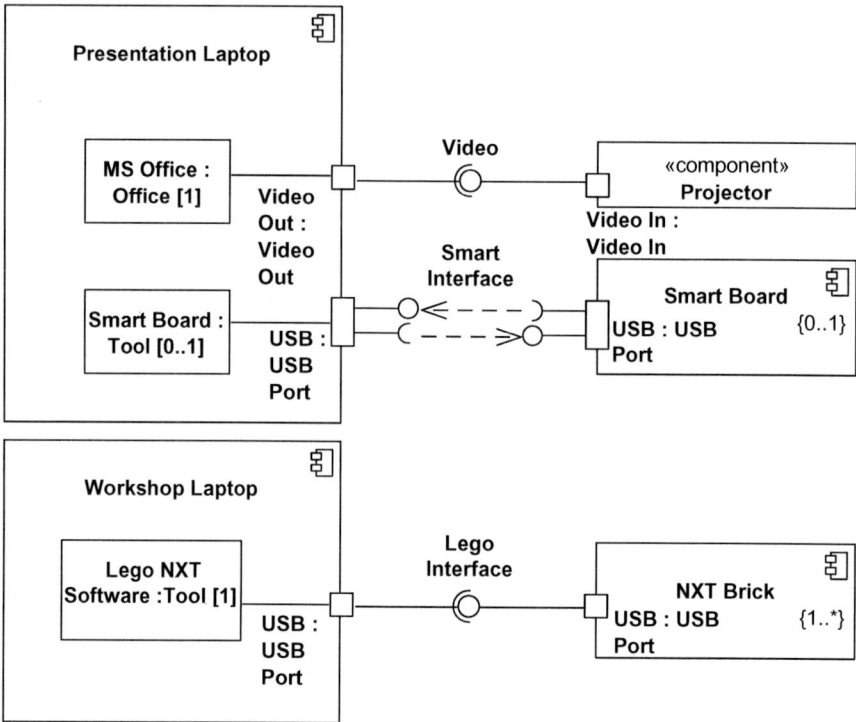

Figure 4.39   Infrastructure configuration view (PC configuration)

through the port and across the interface with the equipment connected at the other end of the interface. Thus the 'Lego NXT Software' communicates via the 'USB Port' on the 'Workshop Laptop' through the 'Lego Interface' with the 'NXT Brick' via its 'USB Port'. For the 'Smart Board' software the communication is bi-directional; that is it can be initiated by either end of the connection – either the 'Smart Board Tool' or the 'Smart Board' itself.

4.10.4   Summary

Component diagrams show 'what's in the box'. They are useful for modelling the connectivity of black-box components, where the focus is on the components and their interfaces rather than on the internals of the components. They are related to structural and interaction diagrams.

When modelling EAs, typical views that can be modelled using component diagrams include:

• Infrastructure configuration views that show how infrastructure assets are configured and connected together.

If component diagrams show 'what's in the box', then the next diagram shows 'where to put the pieces'.

4.11   Deployment diagram

4.11.1   Overview

This section introduces deployment diagrams, which realise a structural aspect of the model of the system. Like component diagrams, deployment diagrams are often hailed as being used towards the end of a project life cycle when the system has been packaged up, although this is often not the case. If a component diagram shows 'what's in the box', it is the deployment diagram that shows 'where to put the pieces'.

4.11.2   Diagram elements

Deployment diagrams are made up of two main elements: nodes and relationships. Nodes represent real-world aspects of a system and show where artifacts that realise components are housed. A partial meta-model for the deployment diagram is shown in Figure 4.40.

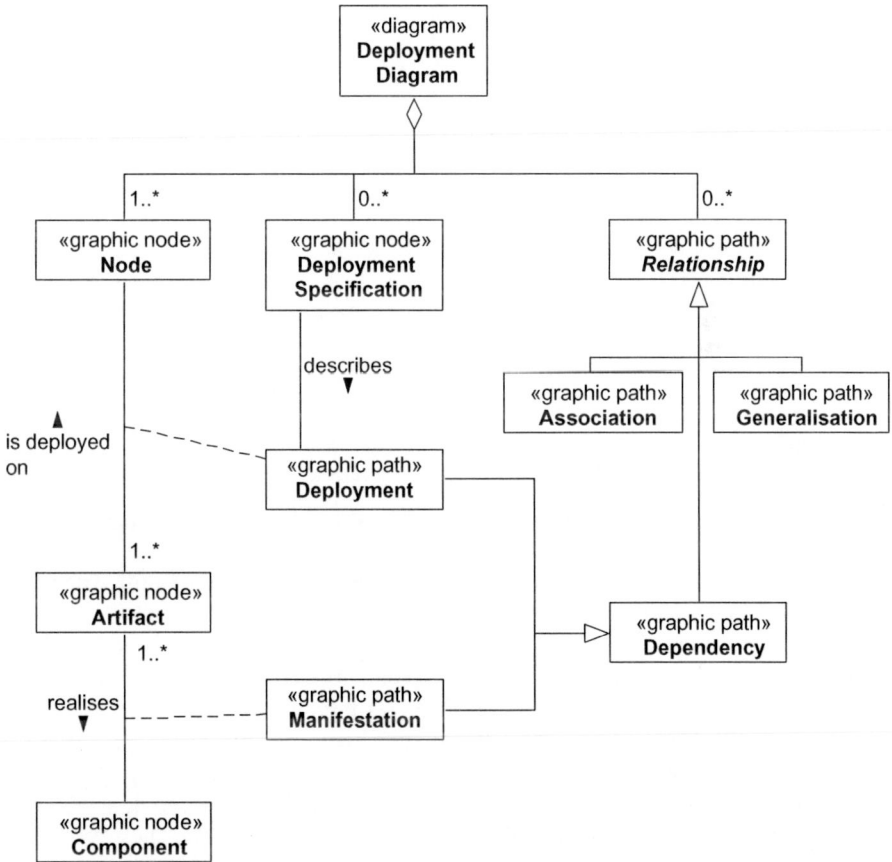

Figure 4.40   Partial meta-model for deployment diagrams

Figure 4.40 shows that a 'Deployment Diagram' is made up of one or more 'Node', one or more 'Relationship' and zero or more 'Deployment Specification'. There are three types of 'Relationship': 'Association', 'Generalisation' and 'Dependency'. The 'Association' and 'Generalisation' relationships are the same as for all structural modelling but the 'Dependency' relationship has two specialisations defined – 'Manifestation' and 'Deployment'. The 'Manifestation' relationship describes the relationship between a component and its associated artifacts so may be thought of as a type of realisation. The 'Deployment' relationship describes an artifact being deployed onto a particular node. Such a deployment may have a 'Deployment Specification' associated with it that describes features of the deployment.

Each of these diagram elements may be realised by either graphical nodes or graphical paths, as indicated by their stereotypes and are illustrated in Figure 4.41.

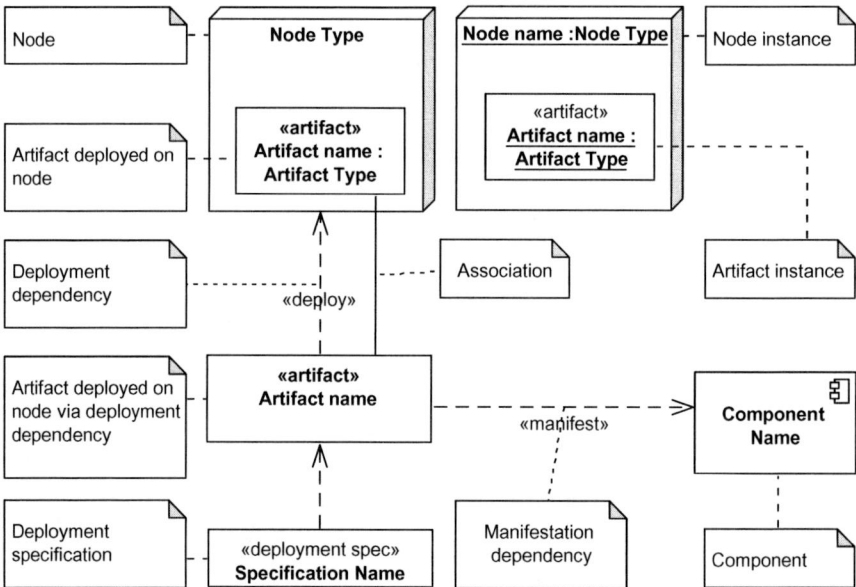

Figure 4.41   Graphical symbols for elements in a deployment diagram

The graphical notation for a deployment diagram is straightforward. The main elements are the *node* and the *artifact*.

A node is represented as a cuboid and simply represents the concept of the *location* where the artifacts that realise a system are deployed. This can be a geographical location, a physical location such as a building or other system or hardware, an organisation or a piece of software such as an operating system. In the strict definition of the UML as applied to software systems, the definition of a node is more restricted than this (see References 1 and 3), but pragmatically people have been using nodes with this much wider definition since the advent of the UML.

As seen earlier in the text in Section 4.10 on 'Component Diagrams', an artifact realises a component. Artifacts are deployed onto nodes in two ways: either the artifact is drawn inside the node onto which it is deployed or it is drawn outside with a deploy dependency from the artifact to the node. Examples of both are shown earlier in the text. A deployment specification can be related to an artifact with a dependency. The deployment specification details any parameters relevant to the deployment of the artifact onto a node. To show the component that an artifact realises, a manifest dependency is drawn from the artifact to the component.

Artifacts can have names and types and it is possible to show both artifacts and *instances* of artifacts on the diagram. If this is confusing, consider the example of a video game console. The console and its handsets can be modelled as a component diagram. Many companies make third-party handsets that can be used with a console. These would be artifacts that manifest the handset component. The actual handset that is used with an actual console is an instance of that artifact.

Associations can also be shown on deployment diagrams between artifacts and/or nodes. An example is shown in Figure 4.41.

4.11.3   *Example EA views realised using a deployment diagram*

Like component diagrams, the deployment diagram is of great use in modelling organisational infrastructure. However, whereas the component diagram is best suited the way infrastructure is connected through ports and interfaces, the deployment diagram comes into its own when representing where infrastructure items are located – that is where they are *deployed*. Two examples illustrate their use.

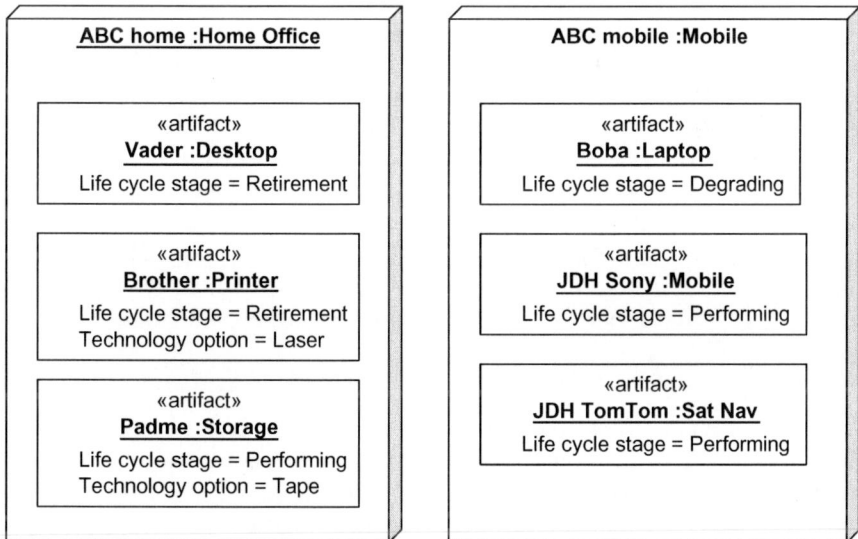

Figure 4.42   Infrastructure deployment view (ABC equipment)

Figure 4.42 shows two nodes, 'ABC home:Home Office' and 'ABC mobile: Mobile'. Each of these nodes is used to represent the set up of the equipment used by one of the authors, one representing his home office, the other the equipment he uses when 'on the road'. While the 'ABC home:Home Office' node represents an actual, physical location, the 'ABC mobile:Mobile' node represents a conceptual deployment of equipment into what is almost a *virtual* node – one modelling the idea of a 'mobile' location. Node instances have been used here (as can be seen from the underlining) since these are not nodes representing the generic idea of a 'Home Office' but represent actual instances of such a node. Of course, such a diagram could be drawn to show the typical deployment of equipment into a home office or mobile location. The construction of such a diagram is left as an exercise for the reader.

Within each node, artifact instances are used to represent the equipment deployed onto that node. Note that all the artifacts instances are typed as types of hardware that are themselves types of 'Technical Asset' which was seen on the infrastructure taxonomy as discussed in Section 4.6 on 'Class Diagrams'. Since the artifacts are ultimately all instances of 'Technical Asset', they can have values defined for the attributes of 'Technical Asset' that each inherits. This has been done for all the artifacts to show the 'Life cycle stage' that each is in. For two of the artifacts, the 'Technology option' has also been specified.

A similar example is shown in Figure 4.43, which also demonstrates some of the other notation associated with deployment diagrams.

Figure 4.43 shows the deployment of equipment (again all instances of 'Technical Asset') into the various rooms within the authors' office building. Each room is again modelled using an instance of a node, with the equipment modelled using artifact instances. The 'Library' contains no equipment and so the node is shown empty of artifacts.

For the 'Training Room' a '«deploy»' dependency is used to show that the 'Training Board:Smart Board' artifact is deployed onto the 'Training Room' node, rather than showing it by placing the artifact inside the node as has been done for the other equipment in the room. An instance of a deployment specification is used to model some of the aspects of the deployment of the 'Training Board:Smart Board'.

The 'Training Room' node also has an artifact instance with no type specified, namely 'Obi Wan'. So how is it possible to know what kind of artifact 'Obi Wan' represents? This is what the '«manifest»' dependency shows that 'Obi Wan' is a manifestation of a 'Projector'. Again, attributes have been set for artifacts to capture their 'Life cycle stage' and, in some cases, 'Technology option'.

4.11.4   Summary

Deployment diagrams show 'where to put it'; that is where to deploy system elements. They make use of 'nodes' which encapsulate the concept of a 'location' into which system elements can be deployed. Examples of nodes include other systems, organisations, rooms and geographical locations. Deployment diagrams are often heavily stereotyped and relate to other structural diagrams, in particular the component diagram.

When modelling EAs, typical views that can be modelled using deployment diagrams include:

• Infrastructure deployment views that show how infrastructure assets are deployed to business locations such as offices.

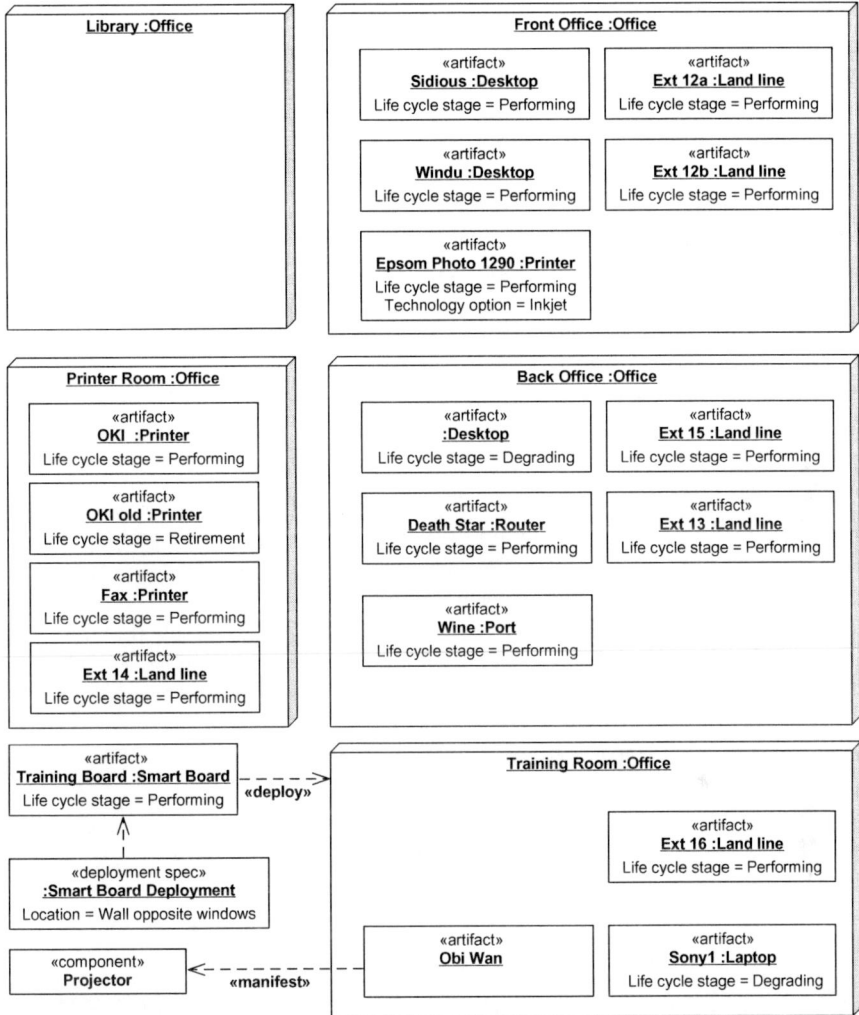

Figure 4.43 Infrastructure deployment view (office – floor 1)

The deployment diagram is the last UML structural diagram. It is now time to consider the seven UML behavioural diagrams.

4.12 State machine diagram

4.12.1 Overview

This section introduces the first of the 13 diagrams that realise a behavioural aspect of the model: the state machine diagram. State machine diagrams model the behaviour of an object, that is, they model the behaviour during the lifetime of a class. State machine diagrams model the order in which things occur and the conditions under which they occur. The 'things' in this context are, broadly speaking, activities and actions. Activities should be derived from class diagrams as they are equivalent to operations on classes. Indeed, one of the basic consistency checks that can be carried out is to ensure that any operations on a class are represented somewhere on its associated state machine diagram as activities or actions.

The most obvious question at this point is 'does every class need to have an associated state machine diagram?' The simple answer is 'no', as only classes that exhibit some form of behaviour can possibly have their behaviour defined. Some classes will not exhibit any sort of behaviour, such as data structures or database structures. The simple way to spot whether a class exhibits any behaviour is to see whether it has any operations; if a class has operations, it does something, if it does not have any operations, it does nothing. If a class does nothing, it is impossible to model the behaviour of it. Therefore, a simple rule of thumb is that any class that has one or more operation must have its behaviour defined using, for example, a state machine diagram.

4.12.2   Diagram elements

State machine diagrams are made up of two basic elements: states and transitions. These states and transitions describe the behaviour of an instance of a class over logical time. States show what is happening at any particular instance in time when an object is active. States may show when an activity is being carried out; they may even show that nothing is happening at all – that is to say that the object is waiting for something to happen. The transitions control the movement from state to state in response to triggering events and/or when the attribute of an object is equal to a particular value. A partial meta-model for state machine diagrams is given in Figure 4.44.

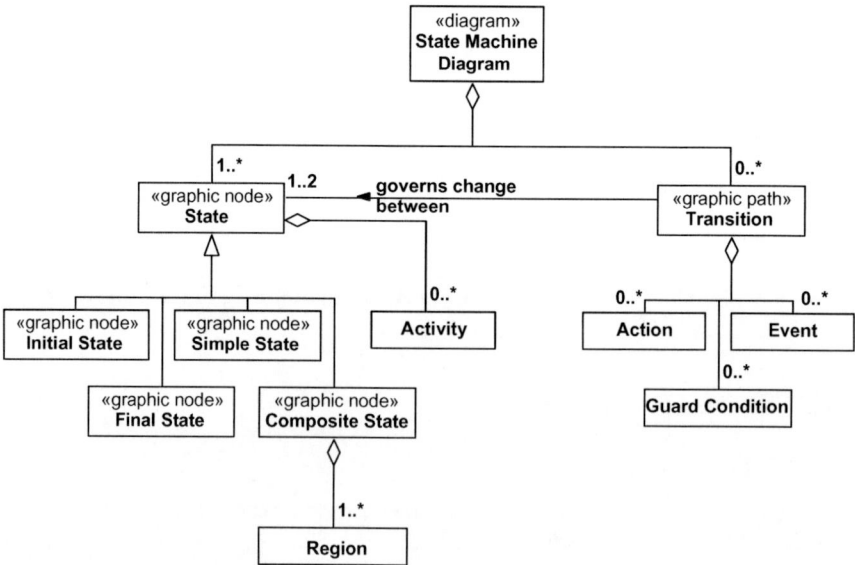

Figure 4.44   Partial meta-model for state machine diagrams

Figure 4.44 shows the partial meta-model for state machine diagrams. State machine diagrams have a very rich syntax and thus the meta-model shown here omits some detail.

From the diagram, it can be seen that a 'State Machine Diagram' is made up of one or more 'State' and zero or more 'Transition'. A 'Transition' governs change between one or two 'State'. Remember that it is possible for a transition to exit a state and then enter the same state, which makes the multiplicity one or two rather than two.

There are four types of 'State': 'Initial State', 'Final State', 'Simple State' and 'Composite State' which is made up of one or more 'Region'. A 'State' is made up of zero or more 'Activity'.

Each 'Transition' has zero or more 'Guard Condition'. A guard condition is a Boolean condition that will usually relate to the value of an attribute of the class to which the state machine relates. A guard condition must be true for the transition to take place. If there is no guard condition on a transition, then this is the same as there being a simple guard condition with the value 'true'.

A 'Transition' may also have zero or more 'Action'. An action is defined as an activity that, conceptually, is instantaneous. In reality, actions will take time to execute but the important thing is that actions are 'atomic' and non-interruptible.

Finally, a 'Transition' may have zero or more 'Event'. An event is the passing of a message, usually from one object to another, and the receipt of an event by a state machine diagram can act as a trigger on a transition. If a transition has no event specified, then it can take place as soon as any guard condition on the transition is true.

These events on transitions are sometimes called *event triggers* or *receive events*, but where do they come from? One use of the action on a transition is to generate *send events*. A send event represents the origin of a message being sent from one state machine to another. It is generally assumed that a send event is broadcast to all objects in the system and thus each of the other objects has the potential to receive and react upon receiving the message. Obviously, for each send event there must be at least one corresponding receive event in another state machine. This is one of the basic consistency checks that may be applied to different state machine diagrams to ensure that they are consistent.

Each of these diagram elements may be realised by either graphical nodes or graphical paths, as indicated by their stereotypes and are shown in Figure 4.45.

Figure 4.45 shows the main notation used on state machine diagrams. Initial and final states are represented by circles, a solid circle for an initial state and a 'bull's eye' or 'target' symbol for a final state. Simple states are indicated by 'rounded' or 'soft' boxes that contain the name of the state.

Simple states may or may not have activities associated with them that should correspond directly to operations from the class diagram. Each operation from a class *must* exist as an activity on its associated state machine and, likewise, any activities that exist on the state machine must be present as operations on the owning class. Where a state does have an associated activity it is shown in a compartment in the state, preceded by 'do/'. There are other types of activity that

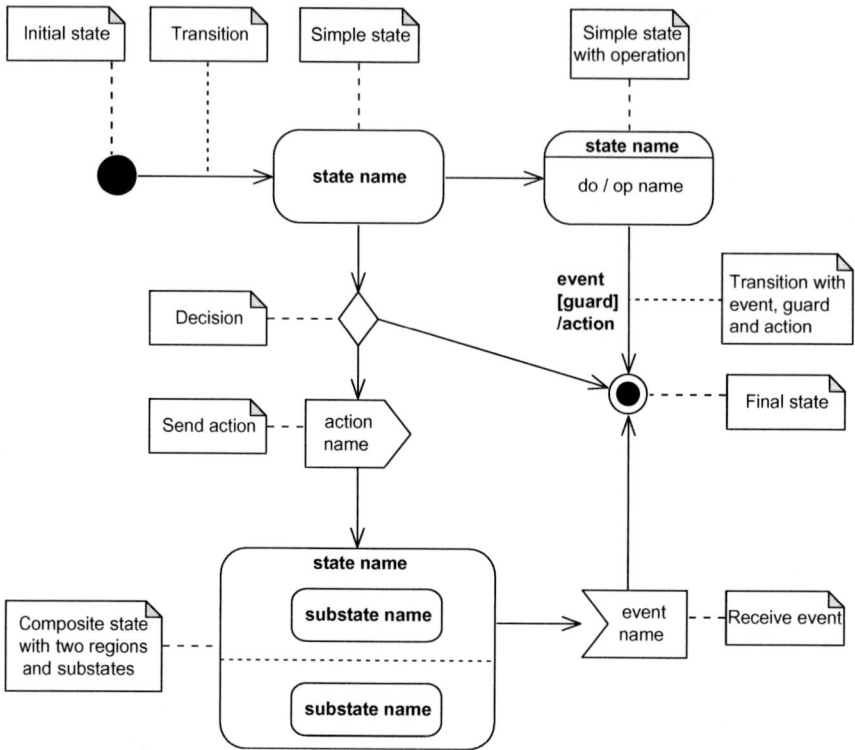

Figure 4.45   Graphical symbols for elements in a state machine diagram

can appear in a state, such as 'entry' and 'exit' activities. For information on these activity types, see References 1 and 3.

A composite state is a state with sub-states, that is, it allows small state machines to be embedded in a state. When the composite state is entered, the state machines contained inside are executed until the composite state is exited. One example of such a use is given in Section 4.12.3. A composite state may also be divided into two or more *regions*, separated by a dashed line, each of which contains mutually exclusive sub-states. In this case, the state machines in each region run separately of each other. Such a composite state is known as an *orthogonal* composite state.

The only way to go from one state to another is to cross a transition. Transitions are realised by directed lines that may have events, guard conditions and actions on them as shown earlier in the text. Transitions are uni-directional and if a return path of control is required, so too is another transition.

Where an action represents a 'send' then this can be made clear on the diagram through the use of a convex pentagon as shown earlier in the text. Similarly, if required, receive events can be emphasised through the use of a concave pentagon.

A decision, represented as a diamond, can also be used where two or more transitions from the same source state share the same triggering event (which may, of course, include the case where there is *no* such event) but differ on the guard conditions. This is shown in the diagram in Figure 4.45 where two transitions from the leftmost simple state pass through a decision, one to the final state and one to the composite state.

4.12.3   Example EA views realised using a state machine diagram

Since state machine diagrams show the states that a system element, modelled as a class, can be in and how it moves from state to state, they are very useful for modelling the life cycles of equipment and artifacts. Two example diagrams are shown in Figure 4.46.

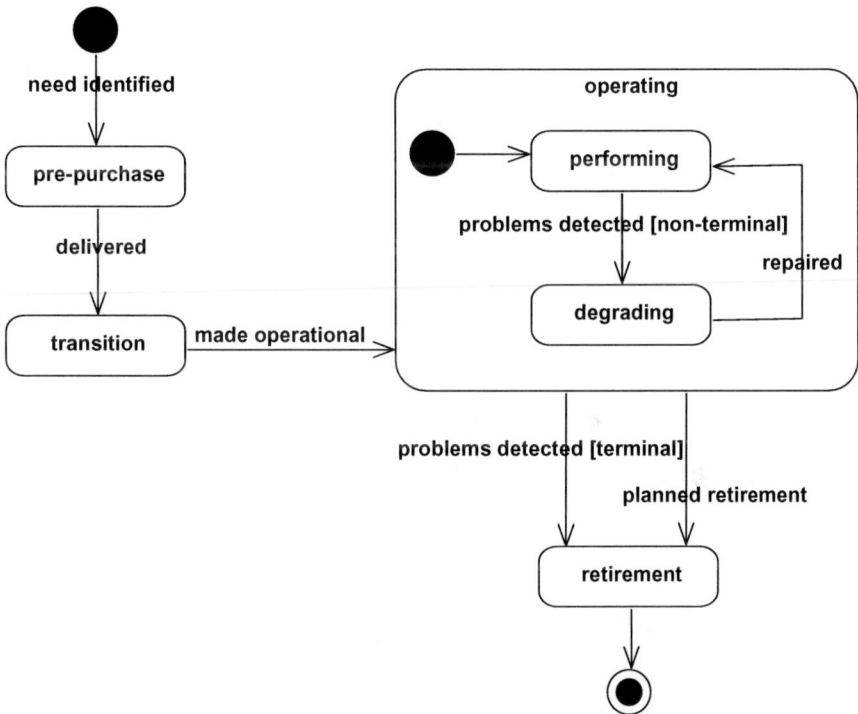

Figure 4.46   Infrastructure life cycle view (infrastructure life cycle)

Figure 4.46 shows the states that a 'Technical Asset' can be in. The 'Technical Asset' class was discussed in Section 4.6.3, where it had an attribute 'Life cycle stage' of type 'Asset Stage'. Each of the states in Figure 4.46 corresponds to one of the possible types of 'Asset Stage' (again discussed in Section 4.6 on 'Class Diagrams').

From the start state the diagram shows that once the event 'need identified' is received, the state machine moves into the 'pre-purchase' state. Once the equipment is 'delivered' the state changes to 'transition'. It then remains in this state until 'made operational' when it moves into the 'operating' state. This state is an example of a composite state, containing as it does a state machine diagram within the 'operating' state.

On entering the 'operating' state, the state machine diagram within the state is followed. The start state becomes active and a transition immediately occurs, since there is neither an event nor guard on the transition, causing the state to change to 'performing'. If the 'problems detected' event is received and they are considered non-terminal (as indicated by the guard condition), then a transition to the 'degrading' state occurs. Once the equipment is 'repaired', a transition back to 'performing' takes place. This cycle continues until one of the two things happens: either terminal problems are detected or the equipment reaches its planned retirement date, as indicated by the events 'problems detected [terminal]' and 'planned retirement'. Once this happens the state changes to 'retirement' and then onto the final state at which point the state machine diagram ends, as does the life cycle of the equipment.

Note how the 'problems detected [terminal]' and 'planned retirement' events lead from the composite 'operating' state. What this means is that they actually apply to *all* the states within the composite state, so that they apply whether in the 'performing' or 'degrading' states. Composite states are very useful for abstracting such common transitions and lead to diagrams which are much clearer than would be the case if the same transitions had to be drawn from all the states to which they apply.

The next example shows state machines used to model the states that an artifact, such as a document, goes through. It also shows where the various operations defined for such an artifact take place.

In the organisation being considered, artifacts such as documents can be in one of three states: 'creating', 'editing' or 'release'. These three states are shown in Figure 4.47.

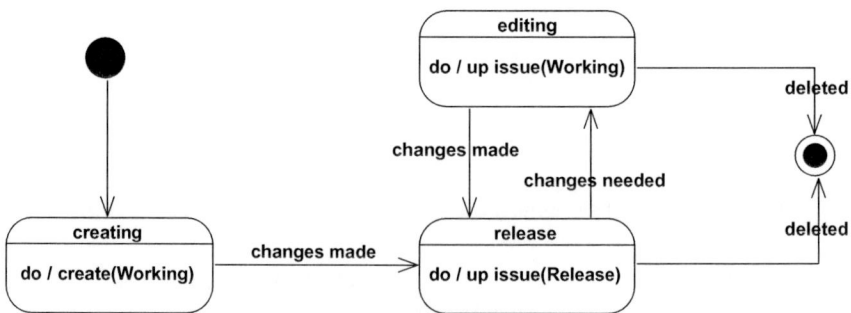

Figure 4.47   Data view (artifact life cycle)

On entering the 'creating' state, the operation 'create' is invoked with parameter 'Working'. Once the changes have been made the 'release' state is entered where the 'up issue' operation takes place with parameter 'Release'. If changes are needed, then the 'editing' state is entered where, again, the 'up issue' operation is invoked, but this time with the parameter 'Working'. The artifact cycles between these two states as changes are made until the artifact is no longer needed at which point it is deleted and the state machine exited.

To know *how* the operations of 'create' and 'editing' behave, another of the UML behavioural diagrams is needed, namely the activity diagram. These are discussed later in the text.

4.12.4   Summary

Every class with behaviour must have either a state machine or activity diagram. State machine diagrams show the internal behaviour of classes. They are related to class, interaction and activity diagrams.

When modelling EAs, typical views that can be modelled using state machine diagrams include:

* Infrastructure life cycle views that show how infrastructure assets move through their various life cycle stages
* Data views that show how artifacts move through their various life cycle stages.

Having considered how to model the behaviour within a class, the next diagram shows how to model the behaviour of an individual operation.

4.13   Activity diagram

4.13.1   Overview

This section looks at the activity diagram. Activity diagrams allow low-level modelling to be performed as compared to the other behavioural diagrams. Where interaction diagrams (covered in Section 4.15) show the behaviour between objects, and state machine diagrams show the behaviour within objects, activity diagrams may be used to model the behaviour within an operation.

The other main use for activity diagrams and one of the most useful when modelling EAs is to model processes or 'workflows'. Examples of such a use are discussed later in the text.

4.13.2   Diagram elements

The main elements of activity diagrams are shown in the diagram in Figure 4.48.

Figure 4.48 shows a partial meta-model for activity diagrams. It shows that an 'Activity Diagram' is made up of three basic elements: one or more 'Activity Node', one or more 'Activity Edge' and zero or more 'Region'. There are three main types of 'Activity Node' which are the 'Activity Invocation' and the 'Object' and 'Control Node' both of which will be discussed in more detail later in this section. The 'Activity Invocation' is where the main emphasis lies in these diagrams and it is through activity invocations that it is possible to establish traceability to the rest of the model via operations.

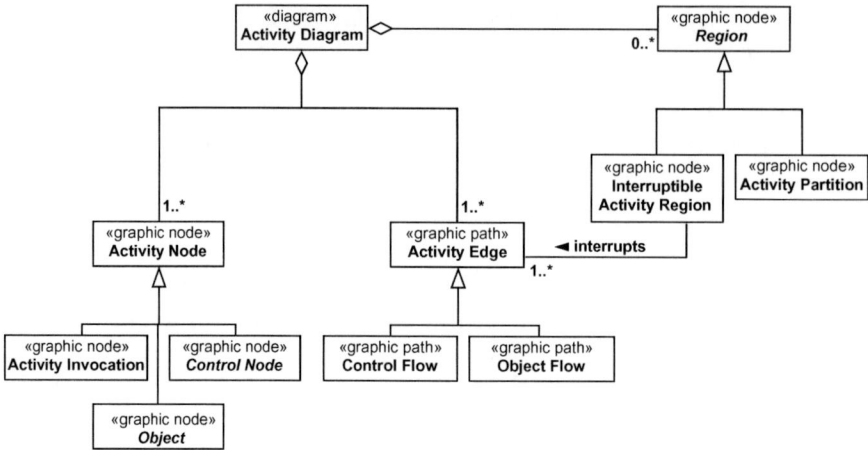

Figure 4.48   Partial meta-model for activity diagrams

The 'Activity Edge' element has two main types: 'Control Flow' and 'Object Flow'. The 'Control Flow' is used to model the flow of control through the activity diagram and the 'Object Flow' is used to model the flow of information, via the 'Object' node.

The other major element in an activity diagram in the 'Region' has two main types: the 'Interruptible Activity Region' and 'Activity Partition'. An 'Interruptible Activity Region' allows a boundary to be put into a diagram that encloses any activity invocations that may be interrupted. This is particularly powerful for software applications where it may be necessary to model different areas of the system that can be interrupted, for example, by a direct user interaction or some sort of emergency event. The 'Activity Partition' is the mechanism that is used to visualise swimlanes that allow different activity invocations to be grouped together for some reason – normally to allow allocation of responsibility to be represented.

It is worth, at this point, going into more detail with regards to control nodes and objects as there are several types of each. It should also be borne in mind that these types of control node are also applicable to the interaction overview diagram, so it is worth spending a little more space discussing the finer points of the syntax.

The diagram in Figure 4.49 shows an expanded view of the types of 'Control node' that exist in UML. Most of these go together in twos or threes so will be discussed together.

- The 'Initial Node' shows where the activity diagram starts and kicks off the diagram. Conversely, the end of the activity diagram is indicated by the 'Activity Final Node'. The 'Flow Final Node' allows a particular flow to be terminated without actually closing the diagram. For example, imagine a situation where there are two parallel control flows in a diagram and one needs to be halted whereas the other continues. In this case, a final flow node would be used as it terminates a single flow but allows the rest of the diagram to continue.

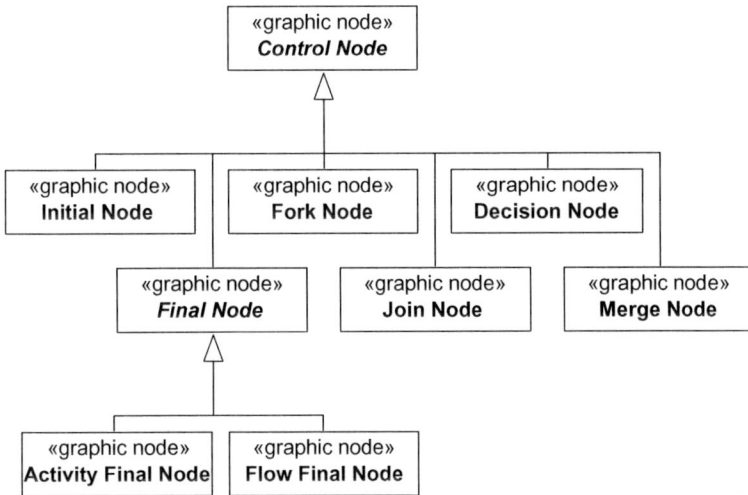

Figure 4.49   Expanded partial meta-model, focusing on 'Control Node'

- The 'Join Node' and 'Fork Node' allow the flow in a diagram to be split into several parallel paths and then rejoined at a later point in the diagram. Forks and joins use the concept of 'token passing' which basically means that whenever a flow is split into parallel flows by a fork, then imagine that each flow has been given a token. These flows can only be joined back together again when all tokens are present on the join flow. It is also possible to specify a Boolean condition on the join to create more complex rules for re-joining the flows.
- The 'Decision Node' and 'Merge Node' also complement one another nicely. A 'Decision Node' allows a flow to branch off down a particular route according to a Boolean condition, whereas a 'Merge Node' allows several flows to be merged back into a single flow.

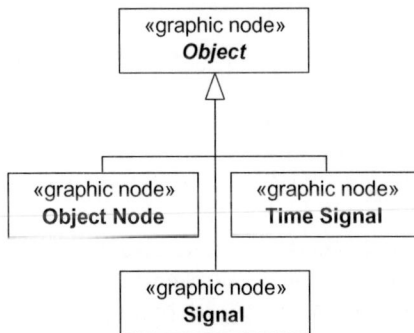

Figure 4.50   Expanded partial meta-model, focusing on 'Object'

There are three types of symbol that can be used on an activity diagram to show the flow of information carried by an 'Object Flow': the 'Object Node', the 'Signal' and the 'Time Signal', as shown in Figure 4.50. The 'Object Node' is used to represent information that has been represented elsewhere in the model by a class and which is forming and input to or an output from an activity. It is analogous in concept to the object found on an object diagram. The 'Signal' symbol is used to show signals passed in and out of the activity diagram – the same as in a state machine diagram, whereas the 'Time Signal' allows the visualisation of explicit timing events.

Each of these diagram elements may be realised by either graphical nodes or graphical paths, as indicated by their stereotypes and are illustrated in Figure 4.51.

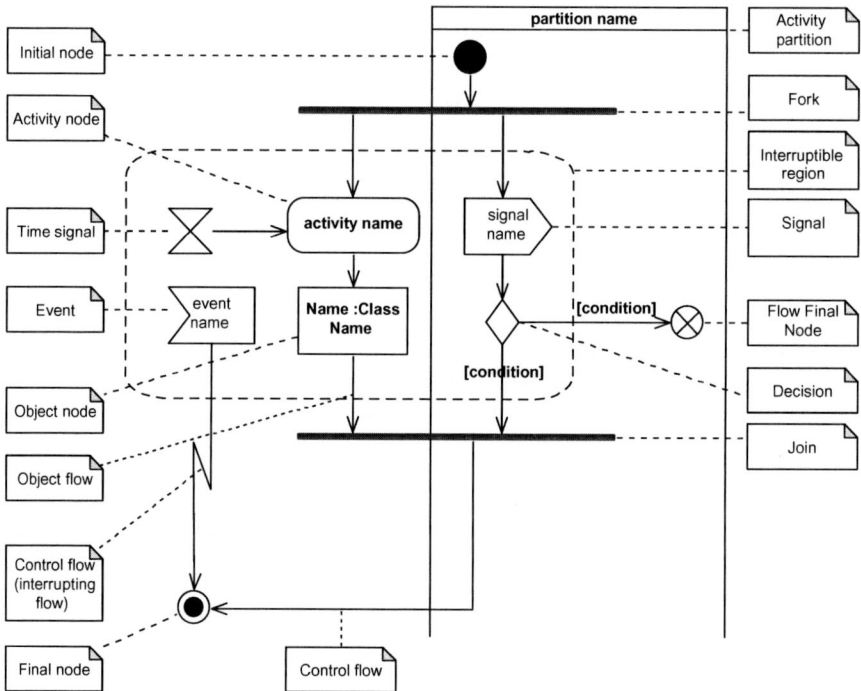

Figure 4.51   Graphical symbols for elements in an activity diagram

The diagram in Figure 4.51 shows the graphical notation for all the elements mentioned so far.

Confusingly, the object node, although essentially the same as the object on an object diagram, has a symbol that is the same as the part seen on composite structure and component diagram. There are also the two special types of object that are defined – the 'Signal' and 'Time Signal'. The 'Signal' symbol is used to show signals passed in and out of the activity diagram – the same as in a state machine diagram, whereas the 'Time signal' allows the visualisation of explicit timing events and uses an 'hour-glass' symbol.

Partitions are shown using 'swimlanes' by drawing a box or two parallel lines enclosing the relevant region. Interruptible regions are shown by a dashed soft box enclosing the portion of the diagram that can be interrupted, with a 'lightning bolt' arrow coming out of it to show where the flow goes in the event of an interruption.

Forks and joins are shown using thick lines that show the start and end of the parallel region. They can be drawn horizontally, as in Figure 4.51, or vertically.

4.13.3   Example EA views realised using an activity diagram

Two examples of activity diagrams are given in Figure 4.52. The first is the behaviour view for the course setup process, an example of a 'workflow', and the second describing how data (in this case a file-based artifact) evolves.

Figure 4.52 is the process behaviour view for the course setup process used in the authors' organisation. This process was introduced in Section 4.6 on 'Class Diagrams'. The diagram shows the ordering of the activities from the process and the flow of process artifacts, modelled as object nodes, through the process. Activity partitions (swimlanes) are used to show which stakeholder is responsible for which activities. The names in these swimlanes correspond to the relevant stakeholders shown in Figure 4.57. Note the use of square brackets on the 'Course Specification' object nodes. The text within these square brackets shows the status of the course specification, either [initial] on first creation or [updated] as it is changed by the process. Also of note are the two signals 'start "Invoice" process' and 'start "Course Delivery" process'. At these points in the activity diagram these signals are sent out to start other processes – unsurprisingly the 'Invoice' and 'Course Delivery' processes. Each of these would also be modelled on process behaviour views using activity diagrams.

Figure 4.53 shows how the status and file name of a file-based artifact change. The diagram starts by checking what the new status of the artifact is to be, and branches through a decision node depending on whether the new status is to be 'Release' or 'Working'.

If the new status is 'Release' then the internal status of the artifact is set to 'Release' and the letter 'w' removed from its filename. (In the authors' organisation a 'w' is added after the version number in the filename of any file-based artifacts.)

If the new status is 'Working' then the internal status of the artifact is set to 'Working', the version number incremented in the artifacts filename and the letter 'w' added to the filename.

Following either of these two paths through the diagram, a merge node brings the two paths together before a final decision node is used to check whether the artifact has a control sheet. If it does, then this is updated and the end of the diagram is reached. If it does not have a control sheet, then the end of the diagram is reached.

Both Figures 4.52 and 4.53 are typical uses of activity diagrams within an EA and activity diagrams form a central part of the process modelling approach used within the authors' organisation (see Reference 4 for more details).

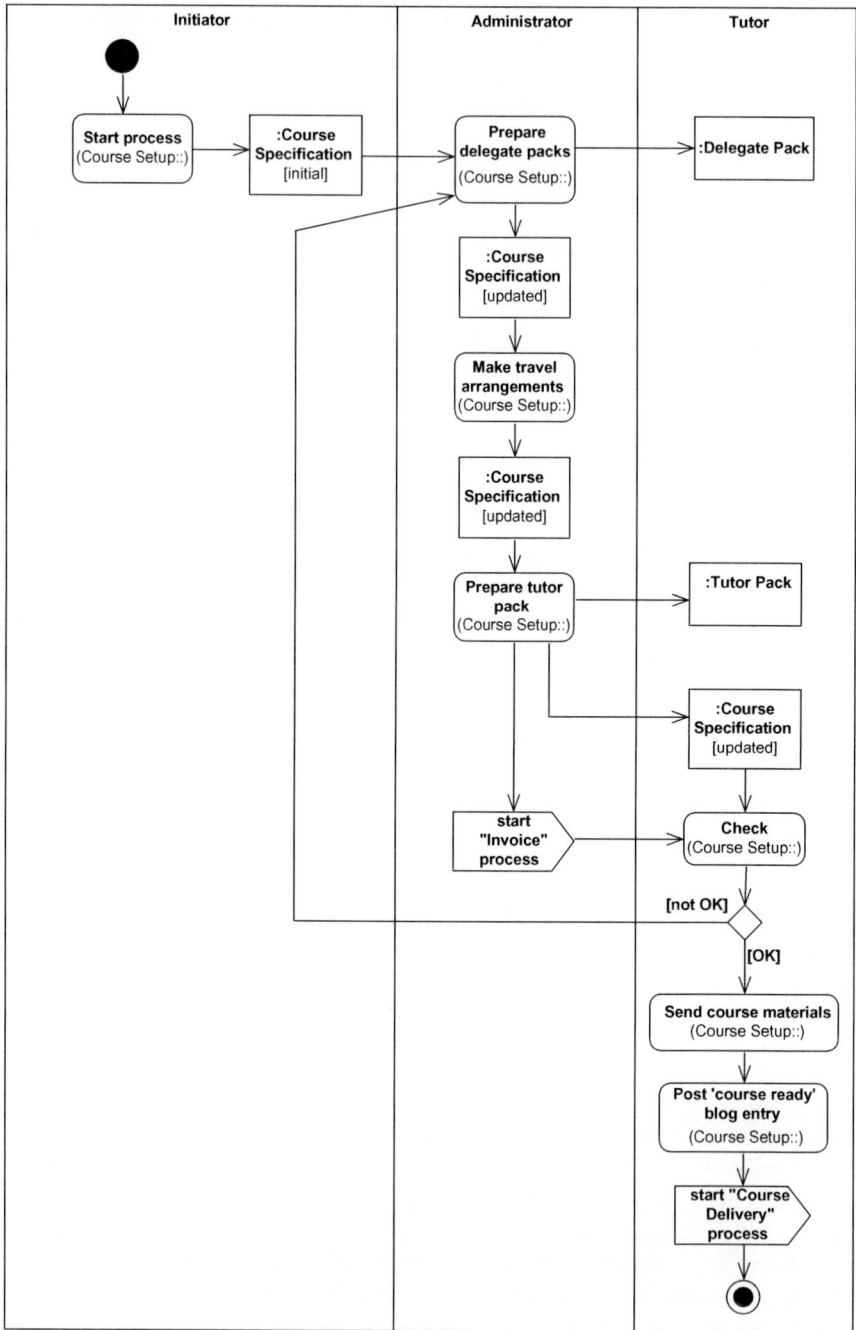

Figure 4.52   Process behaviour view (course setup)

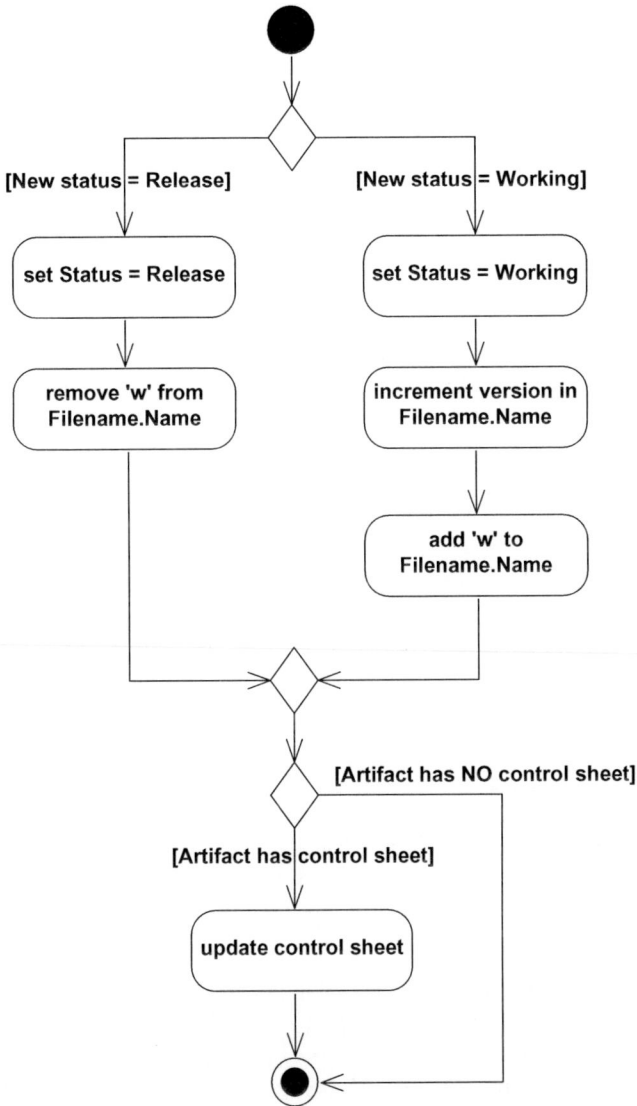

Figure 4.53   Data view (up-issue file-based artifact)

4.13.4   Summary

Activity diagrams make use of token flow concepts and simple states (activities) to model low-level behaviour such as operations of a class. They are related to class and state machine diagrams.

When modelling EAs, typical views that can be modelled using activity diagrams include:

- Process behaviour views that show how a business process is carried out.

- Data views that show version control rules for artifacts.

The activity diagram can be considered the lowest level behavioural diagram. The next diagram looks at the behaviour of a system at the highest level in terms of the required functionality.

4.14   Use case diagram

4.14.1   Overview

This section covers use case diagrams which were introduced in Chapter 3. Use case diagrams realise a behavioural aspect of the model that emphasises the functionality, rather than the control and logical timing, of the system. The use case diagram represents the highest level of abstraction that is available in the UML and it is used, primarily, to model requirements and contexts of a system. As well as the discussion in Chapter 3, use cases are covered in greater depth in Chapter 6. For this reason, this section is kept deliberately short, concentrating on the structure and notation of the diagrams.

Use case diagrams are perhaps the easiest diagram to get wrong in the UML. There are a number of reasons for this:

- The diagrams themselves look very simple, so simple in fact that they are often viewed as being a waste of time.
- It is very easy to go into too much detail on a use case model and to accidentally start analysis or design, rather than very requirements and context modelling.
- Use case diagrams are very easy to confuse with data flow diagrams as they are often perceived as being similar. This is because the symbols look the same as both use cases (in use case diagrams) and processes (in a data flow diagram) are represented by ellipses. In addition, both use cases and processes can be decomposed into lower-level elements.

With these points in mind, the remainder of this section will describe the mechanics of use case diagrams.

4.14.2   Diagram elements

Use case diagrams are composed of four basic elements: use cases, actors, relationships and a system boundary. Each use case describes a requirement that exists in the system. These requirements may be related to other requirements or actors using associations. An association describes a very high-level relationship between two diagram elements that represents some sort of communication between them.

An actor represents the role of somebody or something that somehow interacts with the system.

The system boundary is used when describing the context of a system. Many texts and tools ignore the use of the system boundary or say that it is optional without really explaining why. Think of the system boundary as the *context* of the system and its use becomes quite clear and very useful. System boundaries and contexts are discussed in more detail in Chapter 6.

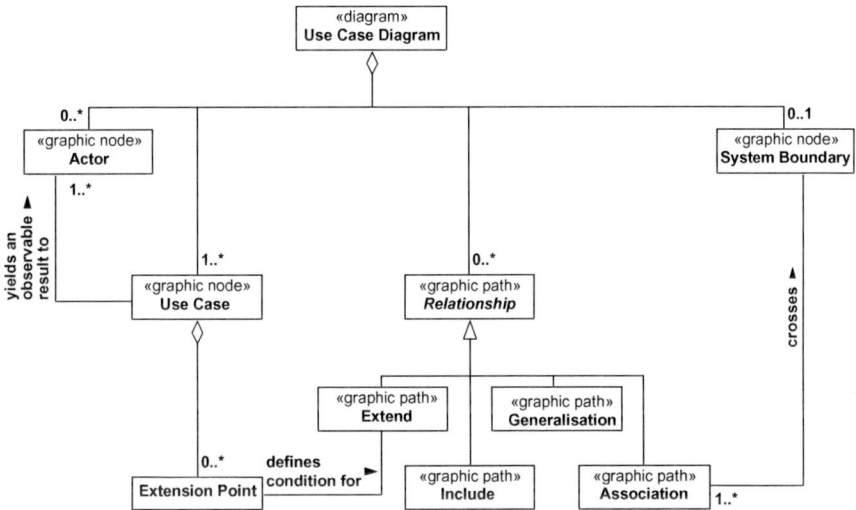

Figure 4.54 Partial meta-model for use case diagrams

Figure 4.54 shows that a 'Use Case Diagram' is made up of zero or more 'Actor', one or more 'Use Case', one or more 'Relationship' and zero or one 'System Boundary'. A 'Use case' yields an observable result to an 'Actor'.

There are four basic types of 'Relationship' which are 'Extend', 'Include', 'Generalisation' and 'Association'. An 'Association' crosses a 'System boundary' and, wherever this happens, it means that an interface must exist. The 'Extend' relationship allows atypical characteristics of a use case to be defined via an 'Extension Point' that will actually define these conditions explicitly. The 'Include' relationship allows one use case to be decomposed into other uses cases. Finally, the 'Generalisation' relationship is exactly the same as when used for class diagrams and is used to model use cases that are specialisations of a parent use case, inheriting the base functionality described by the parent use case and specialising it with additional or different functionality of their own.

Each of these diagram elements may be realised by either graphical nodes or graphical paths, as indicated by their stereotypes and are illustrated in Figure 4.55.

The use case is represented as an ellipse and the actor as a small 'stick man'. A system boundary is represented by a rectangle enclosing all the use cases, with the actors outside the rectangle. The system boundary should be named to describe the context that it represents.

Use cases are connected to actors with associations, which may also be used to relate use cases. However, using the include, extend or generalisation relationships adds more information to the model, as discussed in Chapter 3.

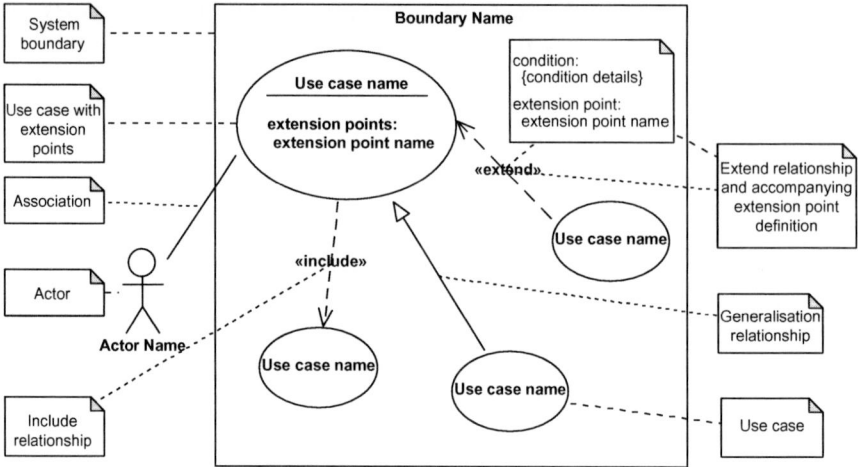

Figure 4.55   Graphical symbols for elements in a use case diagram

When using the extend relationship, the use case is annotated with a number of extension point names. These name the points in the use case where it can be extended. Every use case should have text associated with it that describes the use case. The extension point names are used as labels in this text to show where the extension takes place. In addition, the extend relationship should have text associated with it that defines the conditions under which the extension takes place and the extension points to which the extending use case apply. In Figure 4.55 this is shown as a note attached to the extend relationship.

4.14.3   Example EA views realised using a use case diagram

The main application of use case diagrams is in the modelling of requirements, as was discussed in Chapter 3 where use case diagrams were introduced to discuss behavioural modelling. Requirements are discussed in much greater detail in Chapter 6. One very important application of the use case diagram when modelling an EA is in capturing the requirements for the EA itself. This was discussed in Chapter 1. Allied to this is the capture of the requirements for the views that make up the EA. Both of these applications are discussed in more detail in Chapter 7.

Within an EA there are likely to be views that represent some aspect of the organisation that reflects a requirements view of the organisation. Two such views are given as examples in Figure 4.56.

Figure 4.56 is a use case diagram that realises the business context view of the authors' organisation. There is a system boundary, labelled 'Business Context', that shows that this use case diagram is showing some kind of *context*. Remember, not all use case diagrams are showing context information; it is the presence of the system boundary that shows that information about a particular context, or point of view, is being given.

A single stakeholder, 'Organisation', on the left-hand side of the diagram represents the organisation for which Figure 4.56 shows the business context. Other

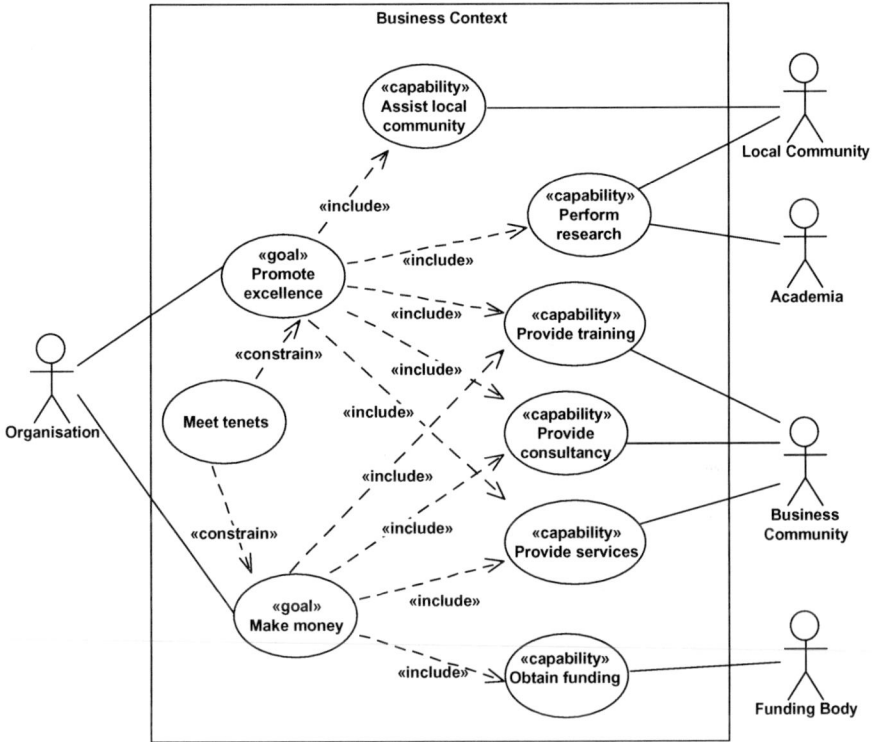

Figure 4.56 Business context view

stakeholders are shown on the right-hand side of the diagram. This layout has no intrinsic semantic meaning, it is merely a layout adopted by the authors to aid in the readability of the diagram.

It can be seen from the diagram that there are two main requirements in the organisation's business context: 'Promote excellence' and 'Make money'. These are both constrained by the requirement to 'Meet tenets' which ensures that business is carried out in a professional and ethical manner. These two requirements are broken down further into a number of other requirements using the «include» dependency to other use cases.

Note also that both 'Promote excellence' and 'Make money' are marked with the stereotype «goal». This is a stereotype defined by the authors and used to show that certain use cases represent business goals. The included use cases are all stereotyped «capability», again one defined by the authors and this time to show that a use case represents a business capability that the organisation must have to meet its business goals. The «include» dependency between the goals and capabilities makes this relationship explicit.

Figure 4.57 shows a use case diagram related to the delivery of training courses. Again it is a context diagram. This time unadorned use cases are used to model the requirements. Note the use of the «constrain» dependency to show how many of the requirements are actually constraints; rather than saying *what* has to be

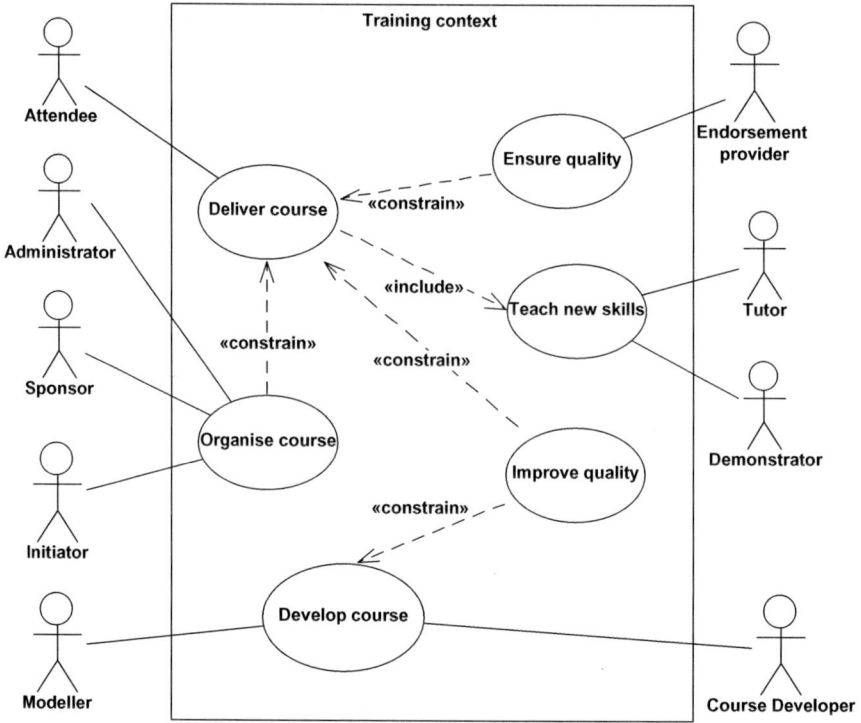

Figure 4.57   Requirements view (training course process)

done, they are, in effect, saying things about *how* it should be done. The «constrain» dependency was introduced in Chapter 3.

4.14.4   Summary

Use case diagrams are used to model requirements. They relate to class and interaction diagrams. When creating use case diagrams:

- avoid flat structures
- avoid over decomposition
- validate with scenarios.

When modelling EAs, typical views that can be modelled using use case diagrams include:

- EA requirements views that show the requirements for an EA and its associated viewpoints and views
- Requirements views for processes that show the requirements for business processes
- Business context views that show the business context for an organisation.

Having considered how to model requirements, the next section looks at diagrams that can be used to model interactions between elements and hence can be used to model *scenarios*.

4.15   Interaction diagrams

4.15.1   Introduction

This section is different from the other sections in this chapter, as *four* diagrams are being discussed rather than one. To model interactions *between* system elements, four different types of diagram can be used: sequence diagrams, communication diagrams, timing diagrams and interaction overview diagrams. All diagrams show the same information, but from slightly different viewpoints. Collectively they are often termed *interaction diagrams*. This relationship can be seen in Figure 4.58.

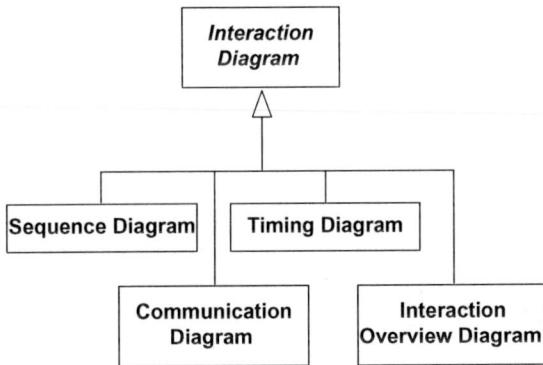

```
              ┌─────────────────┐
              │   Interaction   │
              │    Diagram      │
              └─────────────────┘
```

Figure 4.58   Types of interaction diagram

Each of the four types of diagram shows the same kind of information – how system elements interact. The main aim of any interaction diagram is to show a particular example of operation of a system, in the same way as moviemakers may draw up a storyboard. A storyboard shows the sequence of events in a film before it is made. Such storyboards in the UML are known as 'scenarios'. Scenarios highlight pertinent aspects of a particular situation and ignore all others. Each of these aspects is represented as an element known as a 'Life Line'.

A 'Life Line' represents an individual participant in an interaction, and will refer to an element from another aspect of the model, such as an instance of a class or a part. Lifelines show the type of element that they represent and can also be given a name, using the same Name:Type notation that is used for objects and parts.

Each of the four interaction diagrams will be discussed in detail later in the text.

4.15.2   *Sequence diagram*
4.15.2.1   Overview
This section introduces and discusses sequence diagrams, which realise a behavioural aspect of the model. Sequence diagrams show the high-level behaviour of a system from the *logical* timing point of view, modelling interactions between lifelines by showing the messages passed between them in logical time order. That is they show the *sequence* of messages – hence the name.

4.15.2.2   Diagram elements
Sequence diagram has a very rich syntax, much of which is outside the scope of this book. A partial meta-model for the sequence diagram is shown in Figure 4.59.

Figure 4.59 shows that a 'Sequence Diagram' is made up of zero or more 'Gate', one or more 'Message', one or more 'Life Line' and zero or more 'Interaction Occurrence'. Each lifeline in a sequence diagram has a dotted line underneath that indicates the order in which things happen (such as messages) and shows when the lifeline is active via an 'Execution Specification'. The death or termination of a lifeline is indicated by a 'Stop'. An interesting piece of syntax that is included here is the 'Interaction Occurrence' that allows, effectively, another scenario to be inserted into a sequence diagram. This means that scenarios that show repeated behaviour can be bundled into a scenario on a separate sequence diagram and then inserted at the relevant point in time into the lifeline sequence. Interaction occurrences will be seen again in Section 4.15.5 on 'Interaction Overview Diagrams'.

Another useful element here is the 'Gate' that allows a message to enter into a sequence diagram from somewhere outside the diagram. This is useful for showing the message that invokes, or kicks off a particular interaction without specifying exactly where it has come from (although this must be specified at some point in the model).

The element 'Event Occurrence' shows when a message occurs on the lifeline. It has no notation, but is represented by the intersection of a message arrow and a lifeline. A 'Message' may be either an 'Asynchronous Message' or a synchronous message modelled as a pair of 'Call' and 'Reply' messages.

Each of these diagram elements is realised by either graphical nodes or graphical paths, as indicated by their stereotypes and are illustrated in Figure 4.60.

The diagram in Figure 4.60 shows the graphical notation used in sequence diagrams. The main symbol here is the lifeline with the dotted line underneath it that represents the life of the lifeline. It is from such lifelines that all the behaviour of the interaction is shown via message between the lifelines. The interaction occurrence is a frame, with the keyword 'ref' in the top left corner and the name of the referenced diagram in the body of the frame. Conceptually, when the sequence diagram enters the interaction occurrence, the scenario referenced is inserted in that part of the diagram.

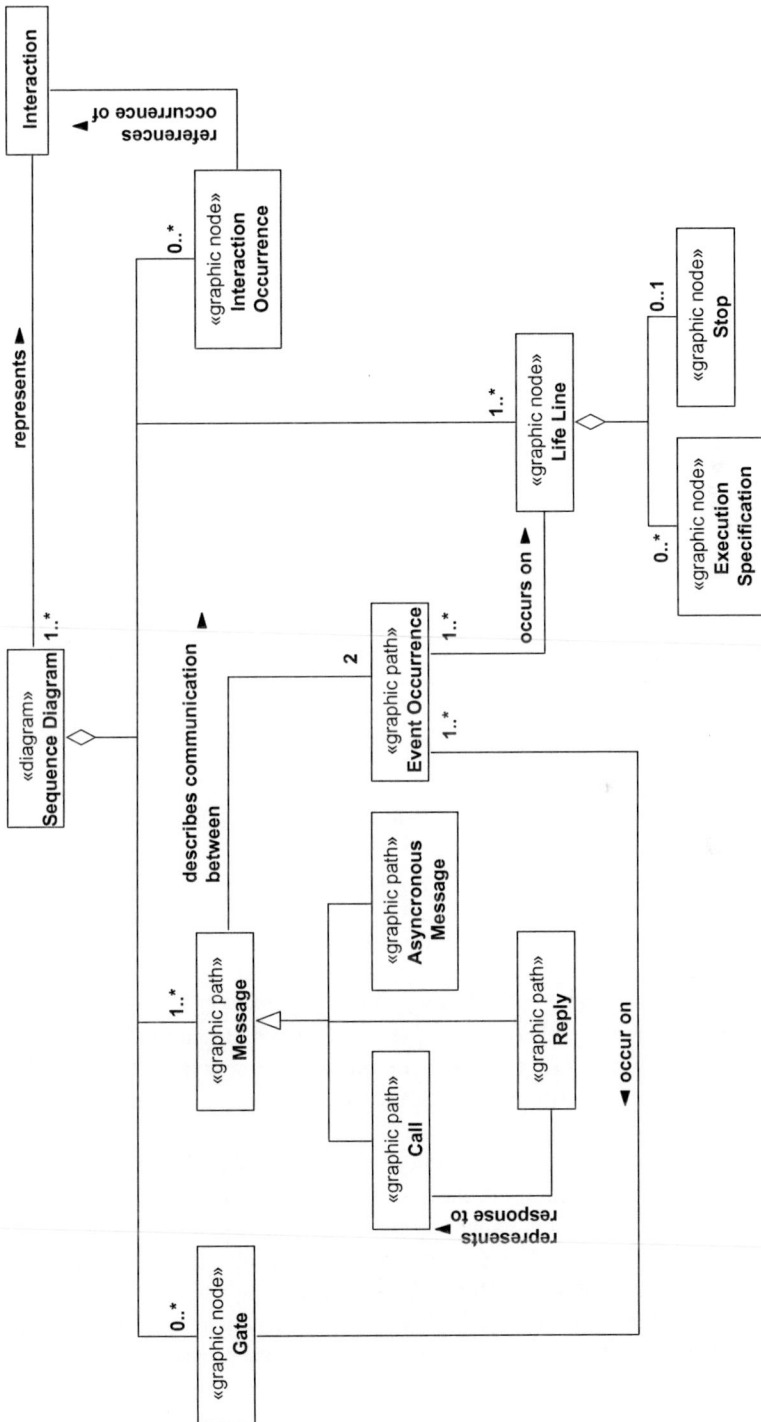

Figure 4.59   Partial meta-model for sequence diagrams

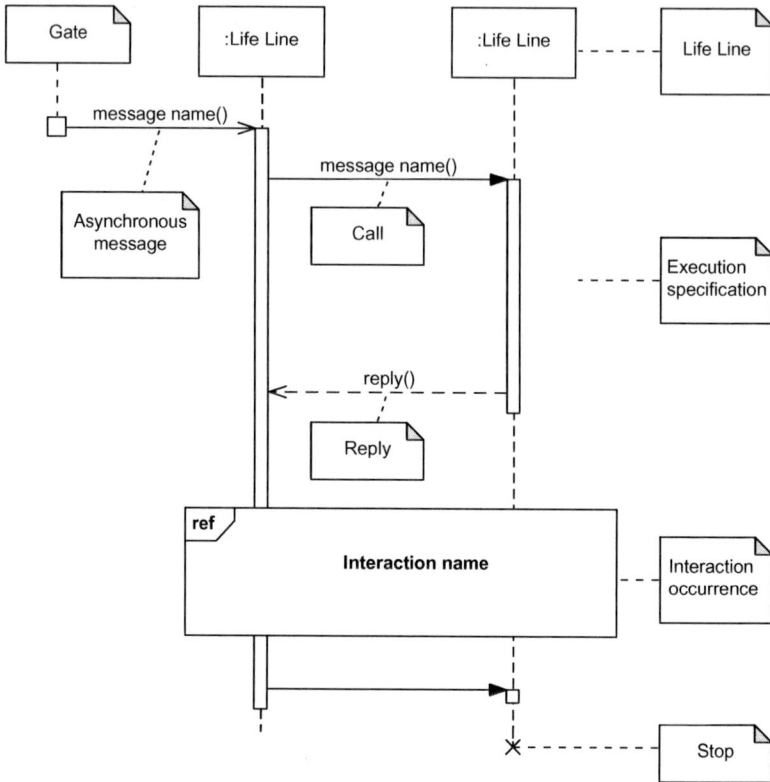

Figure 4.60   Graphical symbols for elements in a sequence diagram

There is much more that can be done with sequence diagrams, such as the modelling of timing constraints, looping and parallel behaviour. The reader is directed to References 1 and 3 for more information.

4.15.2.3   Example EA views realised using a sequence diagram

Given their use in modelling scenarios, sequence diagrams are particularly suited, when modelling an EA, in representing the *capability* of an organisation. That is in showing sequences of organisational processes that can be run in defined orders to deliver a certain capability. They are also useful for providing information on how items of infrastructure should be configured and operated to fulfil a particular operational scenario. Examples of both kinds of use are given in Figure 4.61.

Figure 4.61 defines one such 'capability definition view' which, in this case, is for the delivery of training courses using three organisational processes each represented by a lifeline: 'Course Setup', 'Course Delivery' and 'Course Follow-up'. Each of these lifelines corresponds to a process that should be defined elsewhere in the EA. Part of the definition of the 'Course Setup' process has been seen earlier in Sections 4.6 and 4.13 on 'Class Diagrams' and 'Activity Diagrams', respectively.

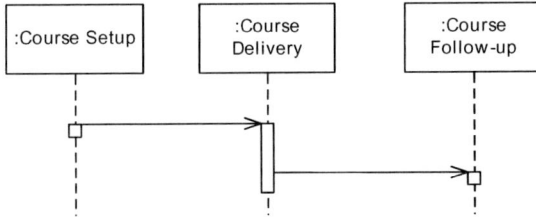

Figure 4.61   Capability definition view (training course)

A similar capability definition view, this time for proposal generation, is given in Figure 4.62.

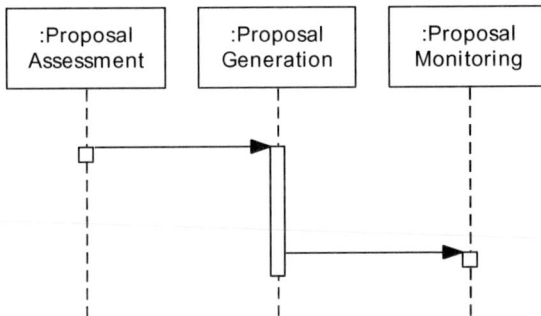

Figure 4.62   Capability definition view (proposal generation)

Again the diagram shows how a number of processes can be sequenced to deliver a stated capability. The question to ask when generating such diagrams is 'Do the processes exist to deliver a stated capability and what order should they be run in?'. If all the necessary processes do *not* exist then the organisation does *not* have that capability and the organisational processes will need revisiting.

The two examples seen so far have been very simple, unnamed messages showing the sequence of interactions and no complicated syntax such as self-calls, looping or parallelism. These could, of course, be added to these diagrams if needed. An example of a sequence diagram that shows more of the syntax in use is given in Figure 4.63.

Figure 4.63 shows a scenario that shows how a course tutor interacts with certain infrastructure equipment (in this case a laptop and projector) when delivering a course. It shows the tutor turning on the laptop and then the laptop interacting with the projector (via the video() message) while, in parallel, the tutor interacts with the laptop. The looping and parallel behaviour are shown by the frames with the words 'loop' and 'par' in the top left corner. These are examples of so-called *combined fragments*, details of which can be found in References 1 and 3.

While Figure 4.63 is a somewhat artificial example, similar sequence diagrams are very useful when complex equipment has to be used in a number of complex

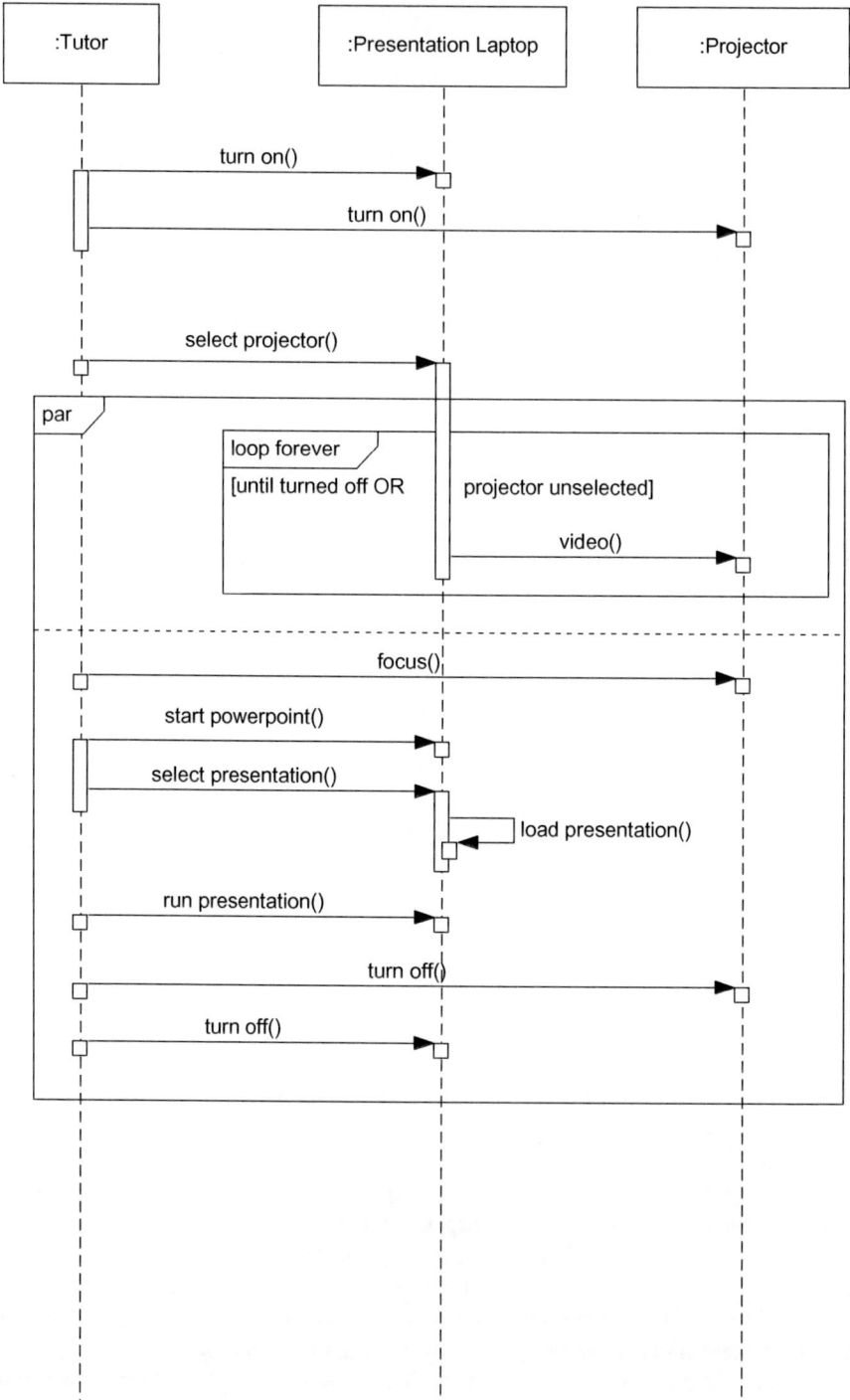

Figure 4.63   Infrastructure configuration view (use of technical assets for presentation)

scenarios. They can form useful visual guidelines to operating infrastructure and can be included in any text-based operating instructions to aid understanding.

4.15.3   Communication diagram
4.15.3.1   Overview
This section introduces and discusses communication diagrams. Communication diagrams realise a behavioural aspect of the model of a system. A communication diagram models interactions between lifelines in a system. The emphasis of a communication diagram is on the organisational layout of the diagram elements on the page. This can be very powerful as, quite often, people will like to assign conceptual meaning to where a particular diagram element lies on a page. For example, some people like to show the flow of control going from left to right, whereas others prefer top-to-bottom. Another possibility is to keep geographically located similar elements on the same part of the page, which can aid comprehension of a problem.

Communication diagrams are closely related to sequence diagrams which were discussed in Section 4.15.2. Indeed, the information shown by both these types of interaction diagram is essentially the same, but from a slightly different point of view and the scenario on a communication diagram can be represented by an equivalent sequence diagram. The main difference between a communication diagram and a sequence diagram is that communication diagrams show the high-level behaviour of a system from an organisational point of view, whereas sequence diagrams show the high-level behaviour of a system from the logical timing point of view.

4.15.3.2   Diagram elements
The partial meta-model for the communication diagram is shown in Figure 4.64.

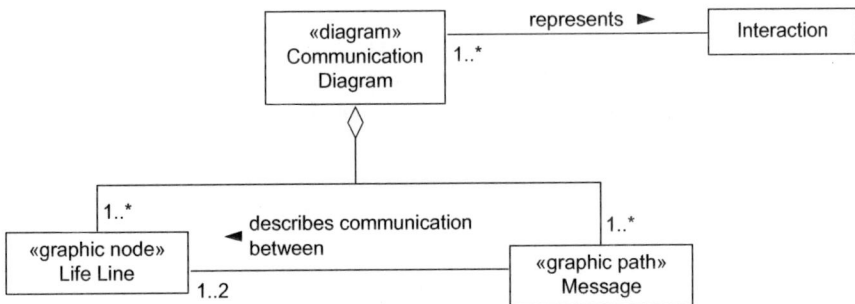

Figure 4.64   Partial meta-model for communication diagrams

Figure 4.64 shows a partial meta-model for communication diagrams. It can be seen that the 'Communication Diagram' is made up of one or more 'Life Line' and one or more 'Message'. Each 'Message' describes communication between one or two 'Life Line'. Also, one or more 'Communication diagram' represents an 'Interaction'.

Each of these diagram elements may be realised by either graphical nodes or graphical paths, as indicated by their stereotypes and are illustrated in Figure 4.65.

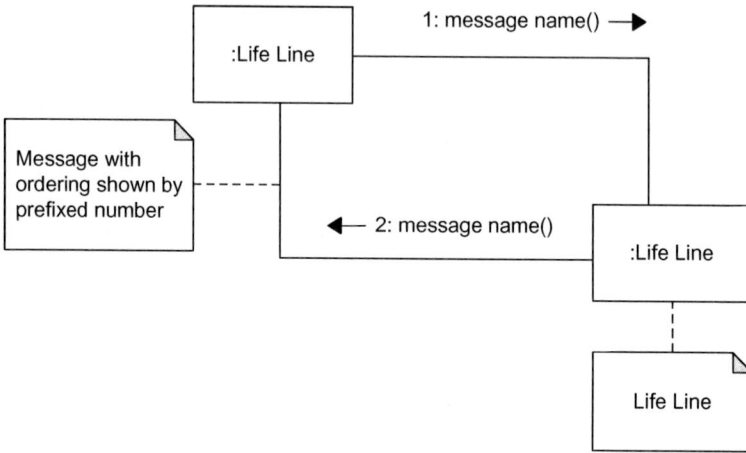

Figure 4.65   Graphical symbols for elements in a communication diagram

Given the rather simple meta-model for communication diagrams, the notation used is also very simple. Lifelines are shown as rectangles and messages as solid lines. The name of the message, along with any parameters, is shown next to the line. A small arrow is used to show the direction of the message and the message name is prefixed with a number to show the time-ordering of the message.

4.15.3.3   Example EA views realised using a communication diagram

Given their relationship with sequence diagrams, communication diagrams tend to be used for much the same EA views as sequence diagrams. The authors tend to prefer sequence diagrams rather than communication diagram when there is a choice between the two. For this reason, the two examples given in Figure 4.66 are simply the communication diagram equivalents of the two sequence diagrams used to realise the capability definition views in Section 4.15.2.3.

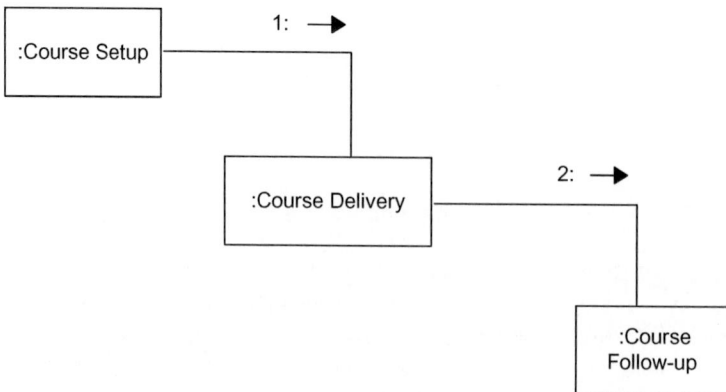

Figure 4.66   Capability definition view (training course)

Figure 4.66 shows the capability definition view for the training course capability. Again, lifelines are used to represent the three processes involved in delivering this capability. They have been offset vertically from each other to give an indication of progression through time, but could equally have been arranged vertically, horizontally or indeed, in any spatial layout, since the positioning of lifelines on a communication diagram has no semantic significance. The numbered messages between the lifelines show the order that the processes have to be run to deliver the capability.

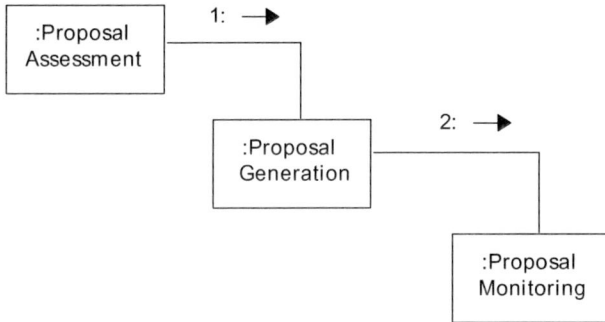

Figure 4.67   Capability definition view (proposal generation)

Figure 4.67 shows the capability definition view for the proposal generation capability and the same comments given for Figure 4.66 apply.

4.15.4   Timing diagram

4.15.4.1   Overview

Timing diagrams are intended to bridge the gap between UML and the many real-time approaches that exist in the modelling world. The world of real-time systems modelling is a large one and has been the subject of many debates for many years. Several UML diagrams now allow the inclusion of real-time information, such as the state machine diagram and the sequence diagram, but there is now a single diagram that is dedicated to realising timing aspects of interaction, the timing diagram.

The timing diagram allows timing information to be added to interactions and allows two main visual views of the timing behaviour – one based on general timing values and one based on states and condition on a time line. Since the UML includes neither process nor methodology, any real-time modelling methodology should be able to be applied to UML without having to tailor the diagram elements. For information regarding real-time modelling techniques see Reference 6. As with the other interaction diagrams, a timing diagram models a specific scenario or class of scenarios.

4.15.4.2   Diagram elements

The timing diagram allows timing information to be included as part of the UML model at the scenario or interaction level. The basic elements of the interaction diagram are still present but, this time, new elements have been introduced to allow real-time modelling. The graphical notation for timing diagrams is shown in the partial meta-model in Figure 4.68.

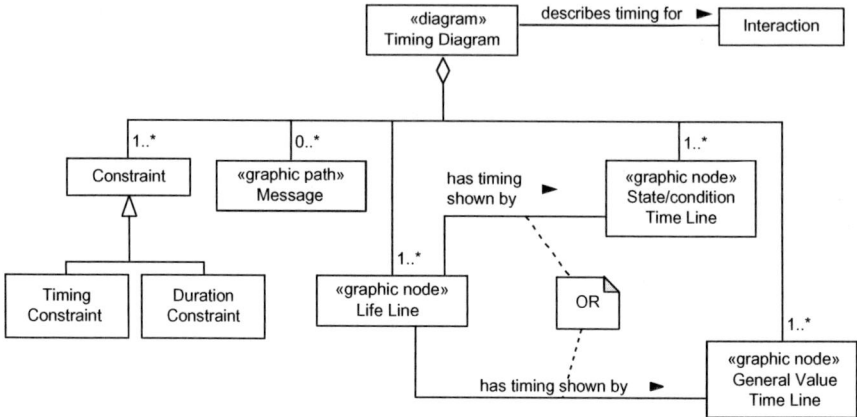

Figure 4.68   Partial meta-model for timing diagrams

The diagram in Figure 4.68 shows a partial meta-model for the timing diagram. A 'Timing Diagram' is made up of one or more 'Life Line', zero or more 'Message', one or more 'Constraint', one or more 'State/condition Time Line' and one or more 'General Value Time Line'. Each 'Life Line' has timing shown *either* by a 'State/condition Time Line' *or* by a 'General Value Time Line'.

The 'State/condition Time Line' allows an emphasis to be put on the timing of the states of the system, whereas the 'General Value Time Line' allows the emphasis to be put on the actual timing values. Time can be shown in two ways by the inclusion of a 'Constraint' that can be either a 'Timing Constraint' or a 'Duration Constraint'.

Where a diagram contains more than one 'Life Line', a 'Message' can be used to show communication between each 'Life Line'.

The graphical notation used on the timing diagram can be seen in Figure 4.69.

The diagram in Figure 4.69, which is itself a timing diagram, shows the graphical notation used. On timing diagrams, several lifelines may be shown on a single diagram, so individual lifelines are simply referenced using text on the left-hand side of each timeline, flipped by 90° to make the diagram more compact. The diagram shows three such lifelines. The bottom two are simply named, whereas the top one also shows the *type* of the element that the lifeline relates to. This will normally be the name of a class.

The two lifelines at the top of the diagram use the 'State/condition Time Line' notation. This shows what most people will associate with a generic timing diagram – a line that goes from left to right as time increases and that changes level according to value. In this case, the values refer to states (check for consistency with state machine diagrams).

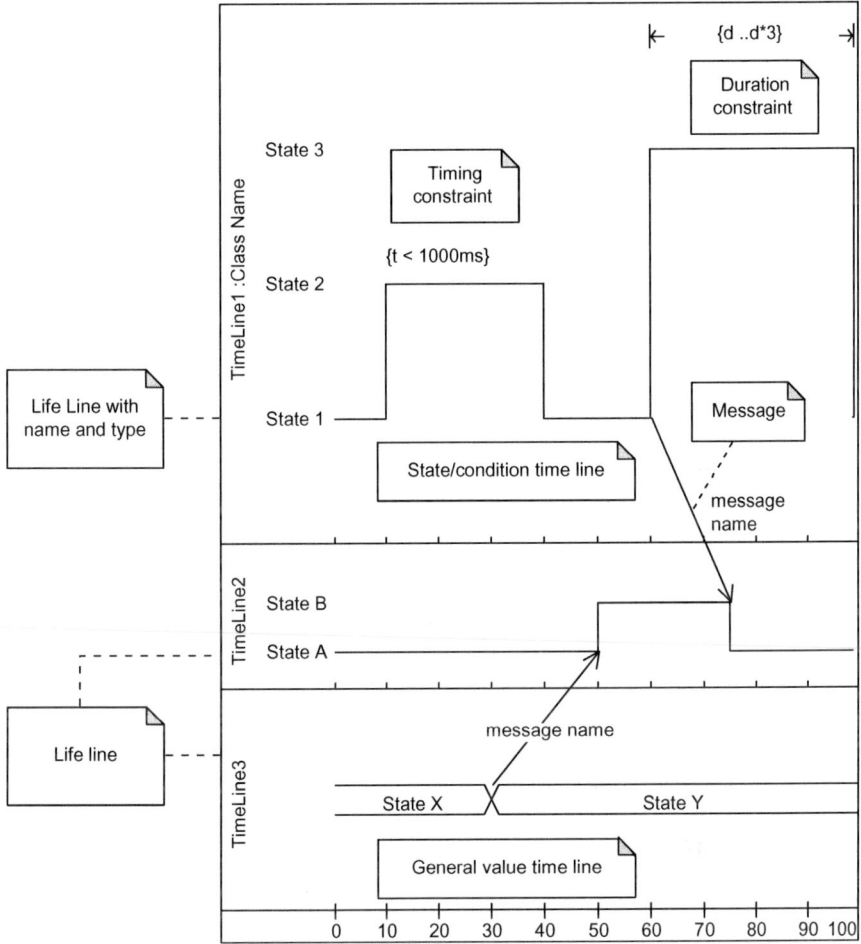

Figure 4.69 Graphical symbols for elements in a timing diagram

Another way to show the same information visually is by using the 'General Value Time Line' that shows, again, time going from left to right, but in this case there are no separate levels to indicate state, but blocks of time that have the state name written inside. The lifeline at the bottom of the diagram is an example of the use of the 'General Value Time Line' notation.

As well as showing time on the scale at the bottom of the diagram, it may also be represented by showing basic timing constraints associated with the length of the timeline. These constraints may either be in explicit time using the 'Timing Constraint' or in terms of durations, using the 'Duration Constraint'.

Message leaving one lifeline at a specified time and arriving at another lifeline, again at a specified time, can also be added to the diagram to capture the interactions between the various system elements whose lifelines are shown.

4.15.4.3   Example EA views realised using a timing diagram

Like the other interaction diagrams, the timing diagram is used to show *scenarios*. However, the timing diagram is closely related to the state machine diagram as it shows scenarios based on change of state. Two examples are given in Figure 4.70 that show scenarios for system elements whose state machine diagrams were discussed in Section 4.12.

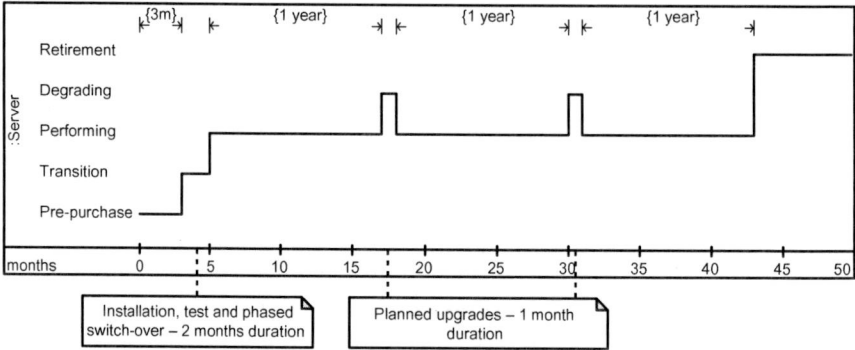

Figure 4.70   Infrastructure life cycle view (planned server life cycle)

Figure 4.70 shows a timing diagram for the planned life cycle of a server. The state machine diagram for the server was discussed in Figure 4.46. The states of the server life cycle are shown on the left-hand side of the diagram, with a timescale in months shown at the bottom. The lifeline in the body of the diagram and the associated duration constraints running along the top of the diagram show that the server is in 'Pre-purchase' for three months. Following this, two months are spent in 'Transition' while the server is installed, tested and switched over, as shown in the note. The server is then 'Performing' for three years, with a single month at the end of years one and two in the 'Degrading' state while the server undergoes planned upgrades, again as indicated by the note. Finally, at the end of the third year of the 'Performing' state, the server moves into the 'Retirement' state.

Scenarios modelled using timing diagrams can be particularly useful for gap analysis such as ensuring continuity of service or availability of infrastructure, as shown in Figure 4.71.

In Figure 4.71, an additional lifeline compartment has been added for a 'Server' identified as 'Old server'. The original, anonymous 'Server' has been renamed 'New server' and its lifeline is the same as in Figure 4.70.

The diagram shows that 'Old server' transitions from the 'Performing' to 'Retirement' state at the same time as 'New server' enters the 'Transition' state. This means that, according to the diagram, there will be a two-month period with no server in the 'Performing' state. That is the diagram shows that if the retirement of 'Old server' and purchase of 'New server' take place according to the scenario modelled, there will be a capability gap of two months and so the purchase of 'New server' needs to be brought forward and/or the retirement of 'Old server' put back to close the gap.

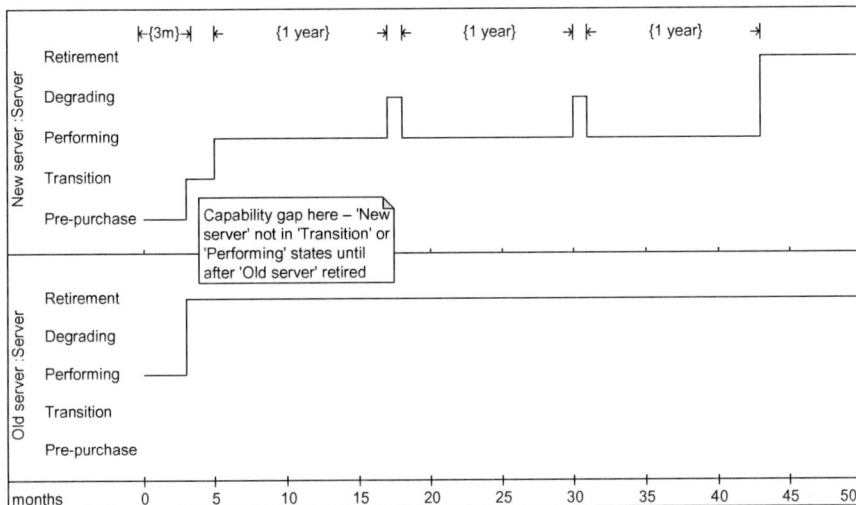

Figure 4.71   Infrastructure life cycle view (planned server life cycle showing capability gap)

The final example, in Figures 4.72 and 4.73, shows the use of timing diagrams for modelling the planned life cycle of a process artifact, such as a proposal.

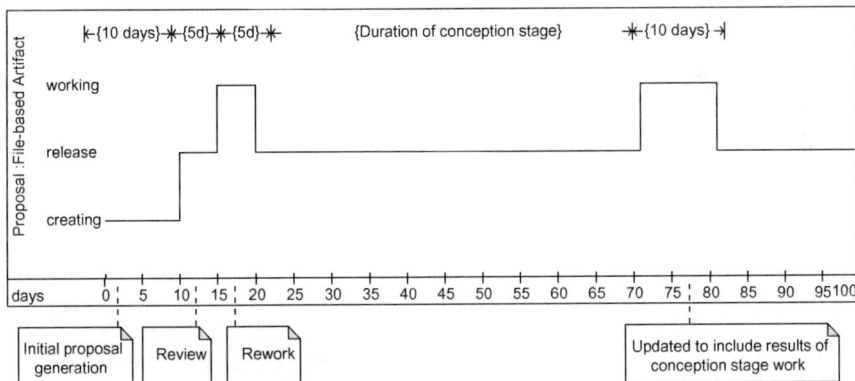

Figure 4.72   Data view (proposal life cycle)

Figure 4.72 shows a typical scenario for the life cycle of a 'Proposal' which is an example of a 'File-based Artifact'. The state machine diagram associated with such artifacts was discussed in Section 4.12.3. The diagram shows the 'Proposal' in the 'creating' state for 10 days, followed by 5 days in the 'release' state while it is reviewed. Following the review it enters the 'working' state for 5 days during which time it is reworked. It remains in the 'release' state for 'Duration of conception stage' after which it re-enters the 'working' state for 10 days while it is updated with results of the conception stage work, before returning to the 'release' state.

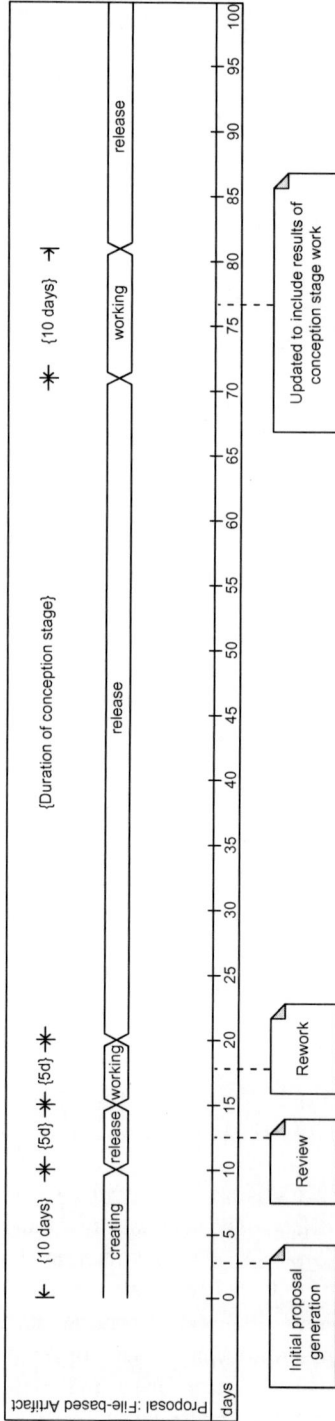

Figure 4.73 Data view (proposal life cycle – value lifeline version)

Having seen examples of timing diagrams represented using the 'state/condition time line' notation, what does one look like represented using the 'general value time line' notation? Figure 4.73 gives an example.

Figure 4.73 is a 'general value time line' equivalent of the 'state/condition time line' example seen in Figure 4.72. There is no semantic difference in meaning between the two diagrams, just an alternative notation. As a matter of personal preference, the authors prefer the 'state/condition time line' notation as it makes the transitions graphically more explicit.

4.15.5   Interaction overview diagram

4.15.5.1   Overview

The fourth type of interaction diagram to be discussed is the interaction overview diagram. Interaction overview diagrams are used to assemble complex behaviours from simple (or simpler) scenarios. For example, it may be that one scenario covers the initialisation of a system whereas there are three main modes of operation. Although this is easy to model in the UML by creating four different scenarios, it is often difficult to get an idea of the 'bigger picture' of the overall operation of the system. In fact, quite often people will use an activity diagram incorrectly to explain the high-level operation of a system as the paths in an activity diagram (decisions, control forks, joins, etc.) lend themselves to showing an overall behaviour. The interaction overview diagram provides the functionality of the paths of an activity diagram but at a high level, where the nodes represent entire interactions presenting a high-level, complex operation of the system. In fact, it is possible to include an interaction that is realised by any of the four interaction diagrams – even an interaction overview diagram.

4.15.5.2   Diagram elements

The interaction overview diagram looks, at first appearance, rather like an activity diagram. Indeed, it has similar syntax to an activity diagram with regards to the graphical paths and some graphical nodes but, instead of activities, the basic graphical node in the interaction overview diagram is the interaction occurrence. A partial meta-model for the interaction overview diagram is shown in Figure 4.74.

The diagram in Figure 4.74 shows the partial meta-model for the interaction overview diagram. Note the similarities to the activity diagram meta-model that has been discussed in Section 4.13.2. The diagram is made up of one or more 'Interaction Occurrence', one or more 'Control Node' and one or more 'Activity Edge'. There are a number of types of 'Control Node', not shown in this diagram. They are the same as those found on the activity diagram and are shown in Figure 4.49. The 'Activity Edge' has two types: 'Control Flow' and 'Object Flow'. The symbols for these elements are shown in Figure 4.75.

Figure 4.75 shows the graphical representation of elements in an interaction diagram. Note how the symbols for the interaction occurrence are the same as those on the sequence diagram, whereas the rest of the symbols look like the activity diagram symbols.

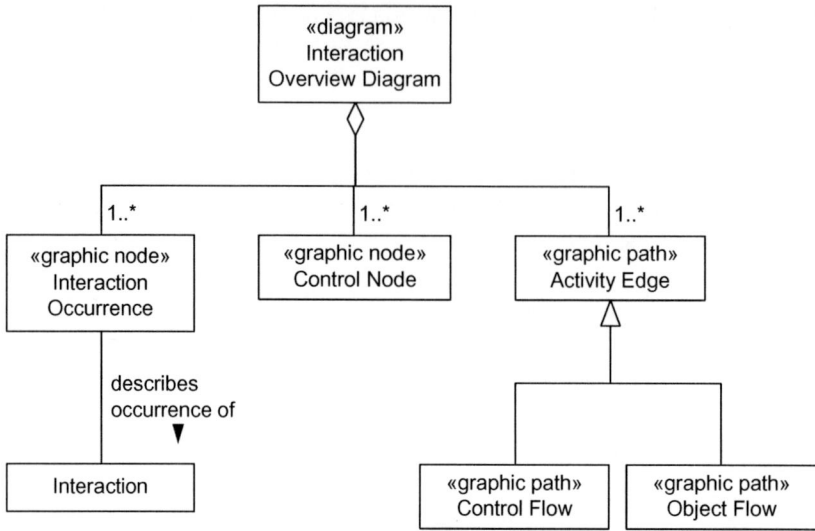

Figure 4.74   Partial meta-model for interaction overview diagrams

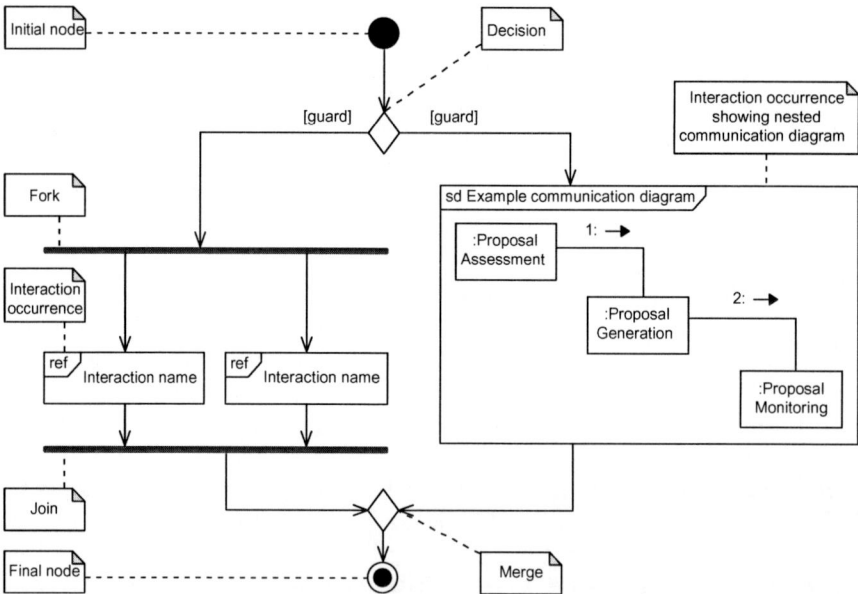

Figure 4.75   Graphical symbols for elements in an interaction overview diagram

4.15.5.3   Example EA views realised using an interaction overview diagram

Because the interaction overview diagram can be used to represent high-level scenarios that are made up of smaller scenarios (which can be modelled using any of the four interaction diagrams), it is particularly useful, when modelling an EA, for representing *programmes of work*. Two examples of such a use of the interaction overview diagram follow.

Figure 4.76 shows a 'Programme View' from the EA of the authors' organisation. It depicts a programme consisting of the generation of a proposal followed by the conduction of a competency assessment. A region is then entered in which mentoring and delivery of a training course are optionally carried out in parallel. Following this a further competency assessment is conducted.

Each of the items of work to be carried out is represented as a *reference* interaction occurrence. That is each interaction occurrence frame *refers* to another interaction diagram (sequence, communication, timing or interaction overview diagram) defined elsewhere in the EA. The full name referenced shows that each of these is defined in a 'Capability Definition View', again one of the view types defined in the authors' organisational EA. The 'Proposal Generation' and 'Training Course' capability definition views have been seen earlier in Sections 4.15.2.3 and 4.15.3.3, where they were modelled as both sequence and communication diagrams.

Note that Figure 4.76 links programmes of work carried out by an organisation to its capabilities as modelled in the referenced capability definition views. These, in turn, link organisational capabilities through to organisational processes, as discussed in Sections 4.15.2.3 and 4.15.3.3. So, through modelling and the creation of appropriate EA views, it is possible to ensure that an organisation has the processes in place to deliver the capabilities it needs to deliver the programmes of work it is engaged in, and in a traceable and consistent manner.

However, since Figure 4.76 only references the capability definition views; it is not possible to tell what they contain without looking at their diagrams. One way to avoid having to do this is by using interaction occurrences that contain a *nested* copy of the diagram they represent. An example can be seen in Figure 4.77.

Figure 4.77 again shows a programme of work, this time a much simpler one consisting of a training course followed by mentoring. While the interaction occurrence for mentoring is a reference to the 'Capability Definition View – Mentoring' diagram, the interaction occurrence for the 'Capability Definition View – Training Course' diagram shows a *nested* depiction of the contents of the diagram (which is the same diagram as seen in Figure 4.61). This allows the contents of the interaction occurrence to be seen explicitly in Figure 4.77.

But which approach, referencing or nesting, is best? Like much in modelling, the somewhat unhelpful answer is 'it depends'. It is important that a diagram be fit for purpose, presenting the information it needs to without overwhelming the viewer. If all the references in Figure 4.76 were expanded into nested diagrams much more information would be presented on the diagram but, depending on the contents of the nested diagrams, perhaps leading to a diagram that is too cluttered.

Figure 4.77, a much simpler interaction overview diagram than Figure 4.76, is a perfect candidate for the use of nesting and the 'Capability Definition View – Mentoring' interaction occurrence could be replaced with a nested version without unduly increasing the complexity of the diagram. There are no hard and fast rules about this. The modeller should try different modelling possibilities and choose the one he thinks fit.

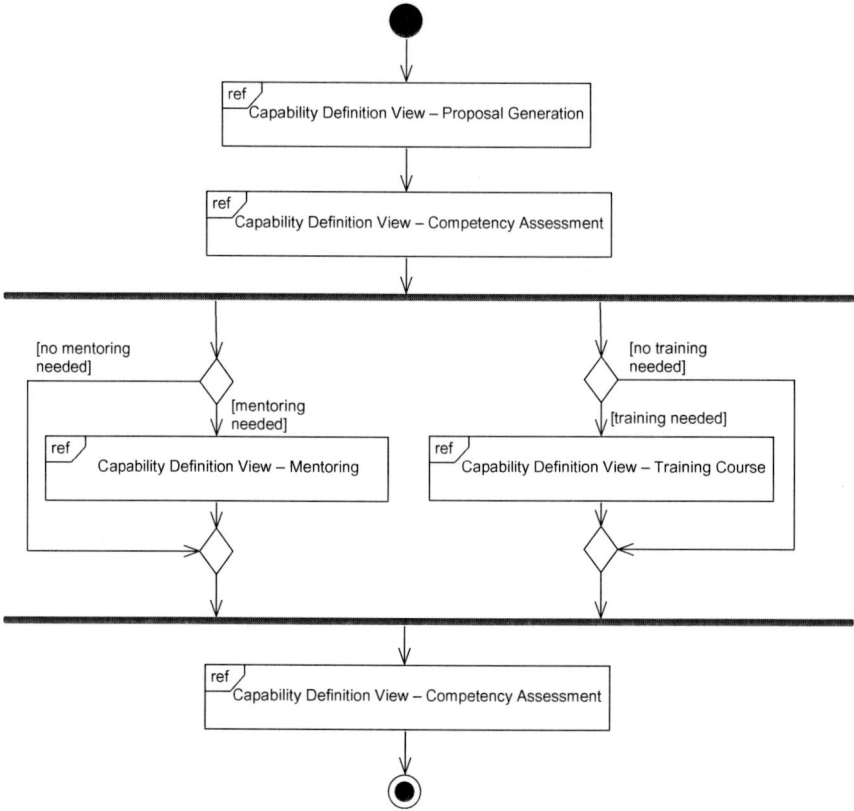

Figure 4.76   Programme view (proposal leading to assessment, mentoring and training)

4.15.6   Summary

Interaction diagrams are related to all other diagrams and show scenarios:

- By organisation – communication diagrams
- By logical timing – sequence diagrams
- By time – timing diagrams
- By arrangement – interaction overview diagrams

When modelling EAs, typical views that can be modelled using interaction diagrams include:

- Capability definition views that show how business processes can be put together to deliver organisational capability
- Infrastructure configuration views that show how infrastructure should be set up and used
- Data view that show how artifact life cycles change over time
- Infrastructure life cycle views that show how infrastructure asset life cycles change over time

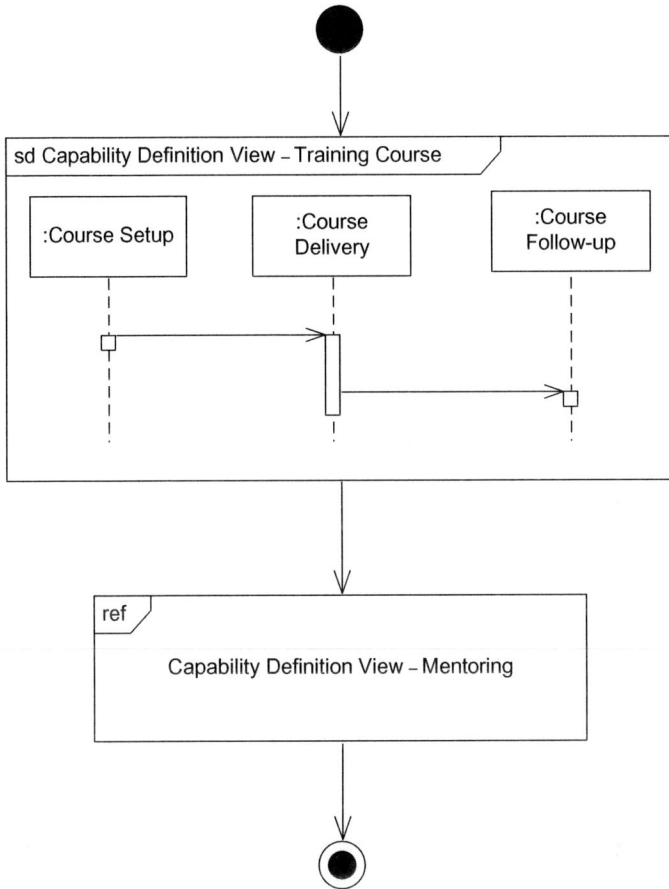

Figure 4.77   Programme view (training course followed by mentoring)

- Programme views that show the ways that programmes of work are to be carried out.

The four interaction diagrams give the enterprise architect a rich and varied syntax and different ways of representing scenarios. As with all modelling, the type of interaction diagram to use will be guided both by how the scenario is best represented to meet the requirements of a particular view and also, to some extent, by the personal preferences of the modeller.

References

1. Booch, G., Rumbaugh, J. & Jacobson, I. *The Unified Modeling Language User Guide.* 2nd edn. Boston, MA: Addison-Wesley; 2005.
2. Fowler, M. *UML Distilled.* 3rd edn. Boston, MA: Addison-Wesley; 2004.

3. Rumbaugh, J., Jacobson, I. & Booch, G. *The Unified Modeling Language Reference Manual*. 2nd edn. Boston, MA: Addison-Wesley; 2004.
4. Holt, J. *A Pragmatic Guide to Business Process Modelling*. 2nd edn. Swindon: The British Computer Society; 2009.
5. Holt, J. *UML for Systems Engineering – Watching the Wheels*. 2nd edn. London: IEE Publishing; 2004 (reprinted IET Publishing; 2007).
6. Douglass, B.P. *Real-time UML*. 3rd edn. Boston, MA: Addison-Wesley; 2004.

Chapter 5

Essential elements for EA

Now concentrate this time, Dougal. These are very small – those are far away.

Father Ted Crilly

5.1 Introduction

This chapter looks at some of the essential elements that make up any enterprise architecture (EA). It has already been discussed that no single approach to EA will fit all businesses and situations but there are, however, certain common elements that occur in every framework or approach to EA. This chapter looks at these key elements and discusses why each is important. As well as these key elements, certain key themes also emerge which will also be discussed.

All of these will be summarised in the EA meta-model that will be introduced in this chapter.

5.1.1 The three themes

The three themes that emerge when considering any type of EA modelling are: requirements, process and structure. In terms of where to start looking at these three themes, they each feed into and have an impact on one another, so there is no natural start place. Bearing this in mind, the remainder of this chapter discusses each key theme, in no particular order.

5.2 EA structure

Any and every EA must have a structure. The structure defines what the conceptual hierarchy of elements in the EA are and what the ontology is.

5.2.1 The EA ontology

5.2.1.1 Introduction to the ontology

An *ontology* is a rigorous and exhaustive representation of a set of knowledge that defines all the key elements and the relationships between them. An ontology is far more than a dictionary and actually helps to identify and define the key concepts and the relationships between them. In the world of EA, the ontology is key to everything and forms the very heart of the EA.

The ontology is arguably the single most important artefact for any EA. The ontology forms the cornerstone of the EA and provides the basis for each and every view in the EA. An effective ontology is what will transform the EA from a collection of pictures into a powerful and true model that reflects the business in a realistic way.

An example of ontology is shown in Figure 5.1.

There is no single ontology that will apply to every type of business, as each business will have its own terminology and concepts and, even where businesses exist that may share a common language, there will be differences in the business goals and, hence, the emphasis of the business.

The example of ontology shown here is a generic one that, although not directly applicable to a business, is a good start point to get people thinking about the EA. It is recommended that this ontology is used as a way to get the creative juices flowing when it comes to generating an ontology. Indeed, many of the concepts that appear here will appear in many businesses, albeit under different names and maybe defined in a different way.

5.2.1.2   Business goals as a start point

As a start point for this discussion, let us consider the nature of the business itself, in terms of the business goals and the capabilities of the business. This may be seen as a logical start point if you are involved at a senior level of the business. Every business will have business goals and every business will have capabilities, although in many cases, these will not be formalised in any way. If your business does not have them formalised then this may be a good start point for your EA. If your business does have them formalised, then pay attention anyway, as this is very important.

The diagram in Figure 5.2 shows the simple concepts of 'Business Goal' and 'Capability'. The diagram also shows that these two are actually related together in the sense that one or more 'Capability' realises one or more 'Business Goal'.

A large part of the value of an ontology is to define a single set of concepts in terms of identifying the elements that make up the business, their definition and the relationships between them. This single diagram, with some added definitions, achieves this.

- The elements are identified as 'Business Goal' and 'Capability'.
- The elements in the ontology have their inter-relationships defined by identifying various relationships between them on the diagram, such as associations, dependencies, etc.
- Each element will have a text description associated with it. This text description will define exactly what is meant by the concept that is represented by the element and be consistent with the terminology (first point in this list) and the relationships (second point in this list).

  For this example, the concepts were defined as follows:

- *'A business goal represents one of the high-level business needs of the company. A set of business goals should describe the raison d'etre of the organisation and should be able to be summarised in a few sentences in a clear and*

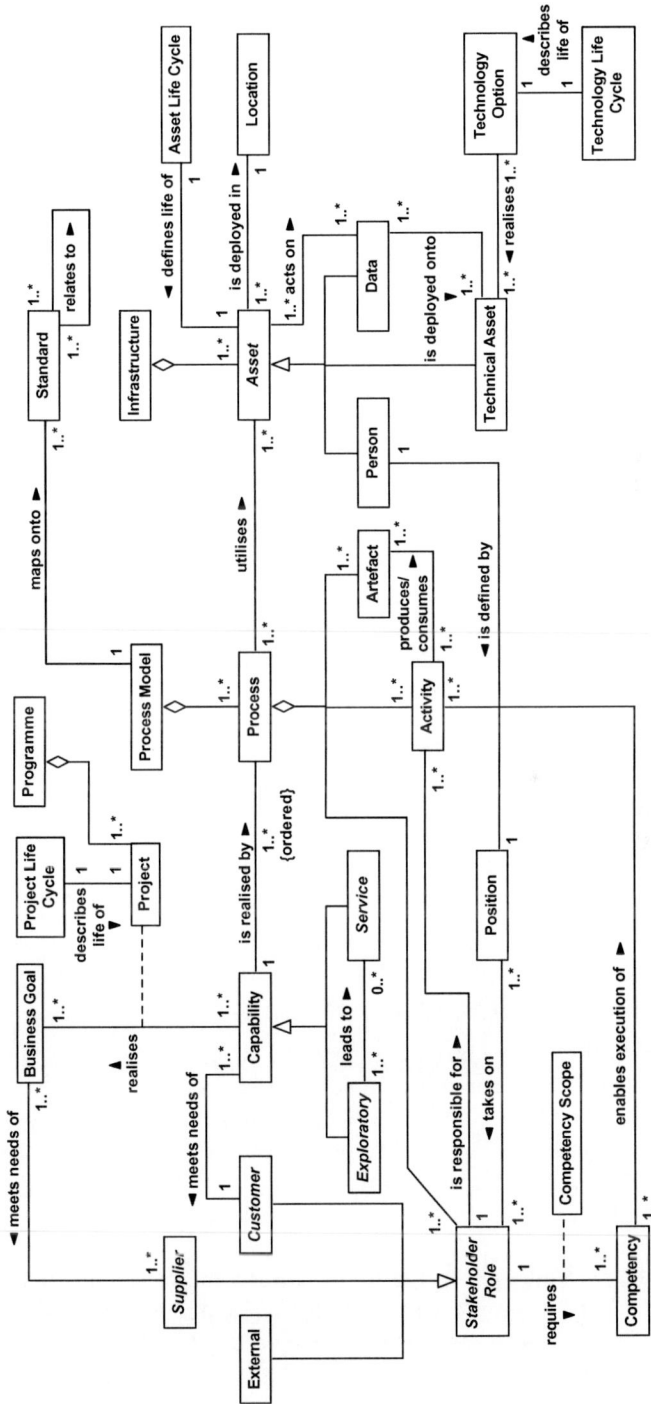

Figure 5.1 Example ontology

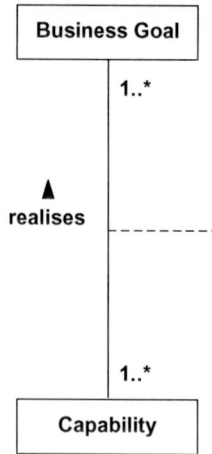

Figure 5.2   Example partial ontology starting with business goals

concise manner. It is essential that the business goals of the organisation are communicated to all people in the company.'
- '*A business goal is realised by a number of organisational capabilities that reflect what abilities the company has.*'
- '*Capability describes the ability of the organisation to carry out business activities. Capability is realised through process – that is to say that any capability may be described by identifying and defining the execution of a set of processes.*'

The next step is to expand these concepts to apply to the wider business. In this example, there are a few questions that may spring to mind:
- How do the capabilities realise the business goals, exactly?
- What are the capabilities that exist?
- Who, or what, benefits from the goals and capabilities?

By answering these questions and others like them, it is possible to start to expand the ontology. These questions are neither imaginary nor rhetorical but are fundamental questions that need to be answered to understand the business. If you cannot answer the questions, then find someone who can or thinks that they can. Leave yourself quite a bit of time, however, as it is surprising how many people *think* that they understand the business, until the ontology is staring them in the face.

Consider the first question in the list – how do the capabilities realise the business goals, exactly? For this example, the answer is 'through projects'. What do we know about projects? (another question) – they each have their own project life cycle and they each form part of a programme. This information can now be added to the ontology and the ontology starts to grow, as shown in Figure 5.3.

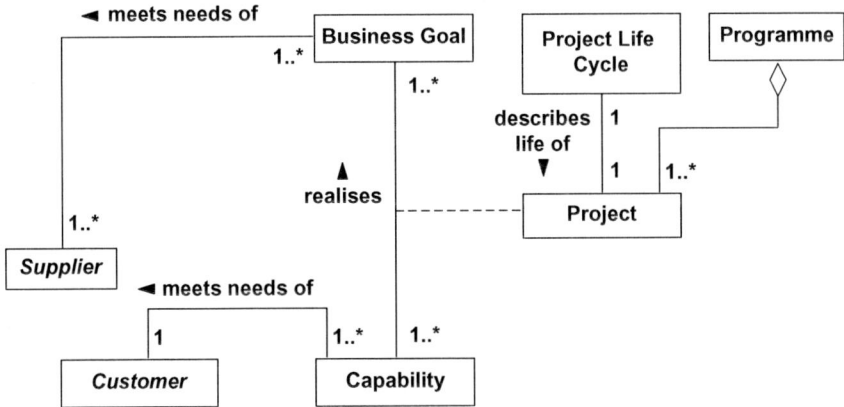

Figure 5.3   Expanded ontology

In exactly the same way as before, each concept may now be defined and its definition added into the model:

- 'A project realises a number of capabilities in order to meet the business goals of the organisation. A number of projects may be grouped together into a programme.'
- 'A programme identifies a number of projects that are related in some way. An example of this may be a programme that is specific to a key customer. For example, a single customer may require a number of training courses, plus mentoring and consultancy, so all these projects would be grouped into a single programme. This could also be when developing a new product, such as a training course, a number of workshops may be held along with some public speaking at conferences to test the water.'
- 'The customer stakeholder role is a general classification for all roles that exist outside the organisation that the EA is being defined for and that revive or use some sort of product or service that is provided by the organisation.'
- 'The supplier stakeholder role is a general classification for all roles that exist outside the organisation but that are not customers. Typically the organisation will have no control over these roles at all and will include roles such as: standards bodies, standards, policing bodies, etc.'

Moving on to the next question in the list – what are the capabilities that exist? Well, there are many capabilities that exist in the organisation and these may be grouped into two broad groups: 'Exploratory' and 'Services'.

5.2.2   Other start points

There is no reason why the definition of the EA needs to start with business goals and capabilities. Using the same example, three other start points will be considered: the competencies, the assets and the processes.

5.2.2.1   Starting with competency

It may be that the main emphasis of the business is related to its staff and their associated skills. It may also be that the information that is known about the business is mainly concerned with the staff. It may be that the EA is being started from the point of view of a human resources department. There could be any number of reasons why you may want to start thinking about competencies as a start point. In the example shown here, there are a few concepts that need to be defined initially – those of people, positions, stakeholder roles and the associated competencies. For this example, these have been defined in Figure 5.4.

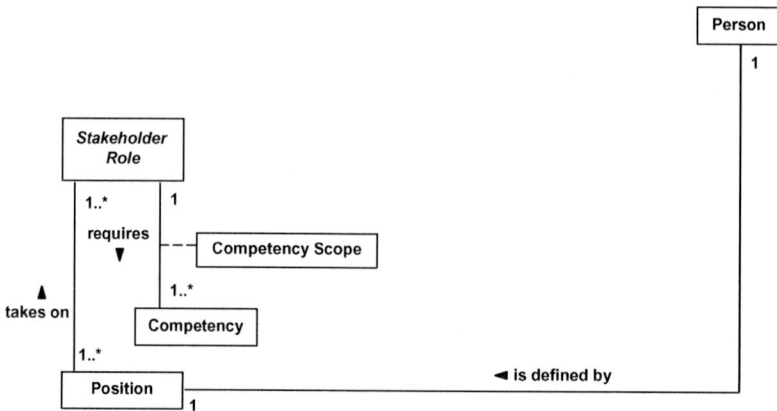

Figure 5.4   Example ontology with competencies start point

Rather than go through the same steps as before (which are the same), let us assume that the questions have been answered, but let us now question what is in this partial ontology.

The first question that springs to mind, and one that comes up every time people are considered is exactly what are the differences between the various terms? In the example, these terms are defined as follows:

- '*A stakeholder role describes the role of a person, place or thing that has an interest in the EA. Note that a stakeholder role is not necessarily associated with a person.*'
- '*A competency describes the ability of an individual and relates to a number of competency indicators that reflect skills.*'
- '*A position defines a person within the organisation. The position itself will have relationships with other positions, such as reporting and supporting relationships. A position is defined by a number of roles that is associated with each.*'
- '*A competency scope describes a number of competencies and the level that each needs to be held at for each stakeholder role. Each competency will be identified and a source reference provided for each, for example, which*

standard or best-practice source the competency has been drawn from. Along with each competency will be a level that this competency needs to be held at for the stakeholder roles. The aggregation of all these competencies and role forms the competency profile and a single profile is defined for each stakeholder role.'

- *'A person is an individual employee of the organisation and is regarded as an asset of the company. A person is defined by their position within the organisation.'*

This works well for the example, but does this work for you? Making the assumption that all organisations will have people in them, is this how they are defined in your organisation? Are people assigned a single 'Position' as is the case here, or is it possible for a single person to have multiple positions? How are these positions defined? In this case, a position is defined by associating one or more 'Role' with it but, again, does this fit for your organisation?

Another important aspect of this part of the EA is related to the term 'Stakeholder Role'. This term has been used elsewhere in the ontology. In fact, the initial start point for the example was concerned with the business goals and the capabilities and it was seen that each was related to different stakeholder roles. Consistency now becomes very important, as the same terms are now being used in different parts of the ontology and it is essential that they are consistent with one another so that the different parts of the business can communicate with one another and harmonise.

These are just a few of the questions that may come to mind but this is one of the reasons why an ontology is so important – an ontology provides the means to question what is known (or believed to be known) in the business. An ontology will promote and encourage discussion amongst people in the business so that they can obtain a consensus.

5.2.2.2 Starting with capability

To some businesses, the capabilities that they possess define both their internal abilities and also what they can potentially sell to their customers, hence, this is a valid start point for the ontology.

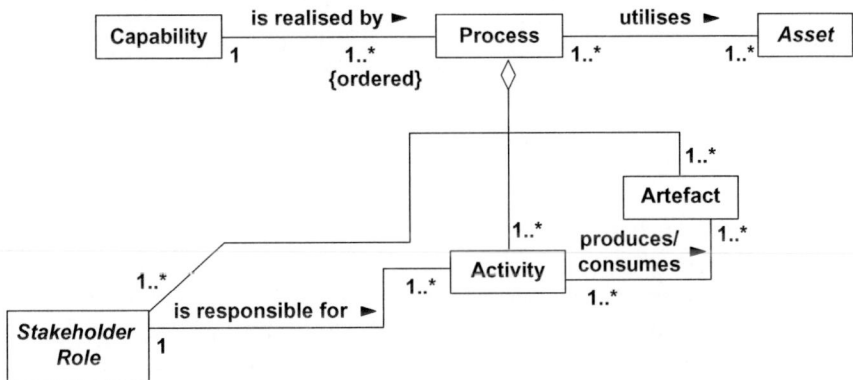

Figure 5.5   Example ontology with capability as a start point

In the example shown in Figure 5.5, the main focus is on 'Capability' and, in particular, the concept of a 'Process'. The definitions for these terms are as follows:

- *'Capability describes the ability of the organisation to carry out business activities. Capability is realised through process – that is to say that any capability may be described by identifying and defining the execution of a set of processes.'*
- *'A process describes an approach to doing something and is defined by its: artefacts, activities and responsibility. All organisational processes should be traceable back to source best-practice standards. The process also describes the fundamental driver for all organisational capabilities, and also the driver behind the staff competencies.'*
- *'An artefact is the work product that is produced or consumed by an activity and forms an integral part of a process. An artefact is tangible, for example, a document, a blog entry, a piece of software, hardware, etc. An artefact may be generated internally to a process or may come from outside the process. The artefacts for a process are explored in more detail in the company process model.'*
- *'A stakeholder role describes the role of a person, place or thing that has an interest in the EA. Note that a stakeholder role is not necessarily associated with a person.'*
- *'An activity is a unit of behaviour that is carried out during a process. Each activity will produce and/or consume a number of artefacts. A stakeholder's role is responsible for each activity. The activities for a particular process are explored more in the company process model.'*

Again, look at the definitions of these terms – do you agree with them? I do not, how would you show them differently? Also, are the definitions shown here consistent with the definitions provided earlier in the ontology?

The importance of the process has already been discussed in this book as it forms the basis for everything that the business can do. It is the process that forms the heart of any quality system and the process that is assessed or audited during any sort of quality exercise.

This part of the ontology uses concepts that have been used elsewhere and hence the need for consistency arises once more. Remember, it is this consistency that provides the rigour for the ontology, and that the ontology forms the backbone of the views and the consistency between them, hence, of the entire EA.

5.2.2.3   Starting with infrastructure

The infrastructure of an organisation may be chosen as a valid start point for the ontology, particularly if the business is IT-focussed or is a pre-existing business.

The diagram in Figure 5.6 shows how the 'Infrastructure' is made up of a number of 'Asset' and that there are three different types of 'Asset': 'Person', 'Data' and 'Technical Asset'. Notice here how two different types of life cycle are introduced – the 'Asset Life Cycle' and the 'Technology Life Cycle'. Again, the

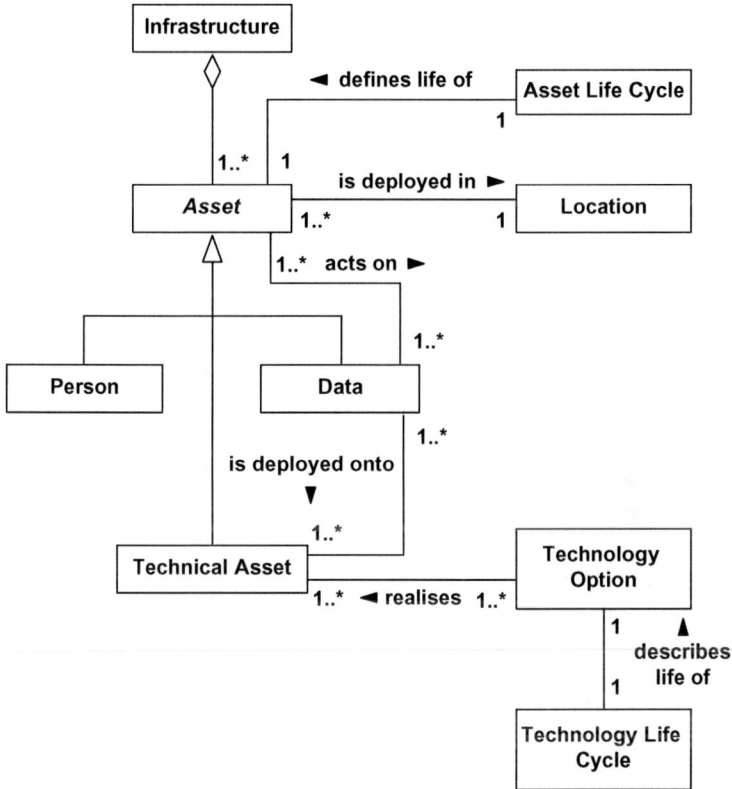

Figure 5.6   Example ontology with infrastructure as the start point

meaning of these will be specific to each business, but are they relevant for you and your business? If not, why not?

These terms are defined as follows:

- '*An asset is the generic name for something that holds value to the company. The three types of asset that exist are "Data", "Person" and "Technical asset". The term asset refers to the concept of an asset and, hence, has no instances (an abstract class).*'
- '*Technical asset is any type of asset that is not a person and that is owned and used by the organisation.*'
- '*Data is the generic term for any information that has any meaning or value to the organisation. Data may range from electronic data that is held on a database to hard-copy data, such as letters, log books, etc.*'
- '*The technology option describes a type of technology that may be used to realise a particular technical asset. For example, a network may be realised using copper-wired, fibre-optic or wireless technologies.*'
- '*The life cycle that will be applied to all assets in the enterprise. This describes the life of an asset from pre-purchase to retirement.*'

Assets are no doubt key to any business, and this can often form a large part of the views. In many EAs, the emphasis is very much on assets, especially IT-focussed EAs where the computers, applications and services are the main focus.

5.2.3   Consistency

Consistency is the key to a successful model. Diagrams without consistency are pictures, whereas diagrams with consistency form a model. When it comes to EAs, it is a model that is required, not a set of pictures.

Notice how, as the ontology for the EA grew, the different parts of it began to overlap. For example, the term 'Stakeholder Role' was used when looking at the business goals as a start point, when considering people and also when considering processes. It is essential that the definition for each term, in this case 'Stakeholder Role', is consistent with one another. If the model is correct and the definitions are based directly on the model, then the consistency of terminology is automatic. In fact, the definitions should form part of the model and not be seen as being separate.

Another advantage of embedding the definitions as an inherent part of the model is that it is then possible to automatically generate a glossary of terms with a few rather useful features:

- All terms used will be real terms and will be relevant. Many glossaries provide terms that are never actually used or are not relevant. This is often the case when glossaries have been cut-and-pasted from other projects or documents which, unfortunately, is all-too-common in real life.
- The glossary will have coverage across the whole enterprise. The previous point in this list made the case that it is easy to see glossaries that have terms that are not relevant. Complementary to this is the fact that all relevant terms must be defined in the glossary, or that the terms cover the whole enterprise. Again, with a model-based approach this is guaranteed.

Consistency will form the cornerstone of this book and it will be discussed in many sections.

5.2.4   Getting it wrong

Very often, people are worried about getting something wrong in the ontology. The simple answer is 'don't be'. The ontology is essential to a successful EA and getting it right is very important. However, it is impossible to get the model right initially and getting it wrong is often a very good first step. This may sound counter-intuitive, but it is far easier for people to critique a diagram than it is to critique a blank sheet of paper. When trying to understand something for the first time, people want to be able to 'think out loud' and this will almost always involve trying out ideas that are incorrect.

Remember, the goal is to end up with a model that is correct. This will not happen overnight and will be a continuously evolving process. The same holds true for the start point of the EA. Which is the best start point? The answer is that 'it depends'. What must be stressed, however, is that the start point is just that – a place to begin thinking from. Don't get too bogged down with where to start, just start where you think you understand the most about the business.

5.3   The EA hierarchy

There will always be several levels of abstraction in the hierarchy that makes up the structure of the EA. Although there is no definitive number for the levels that will apply to every EA, three levels of abstraction seem to fit with many frameworks and approaches (this will be discussed more in Chapter 8).

The diagram in Figure 5.7 shows a high-level representation of the structural breakdown of key EA concepts, and will be discussed in more detail later in the text.

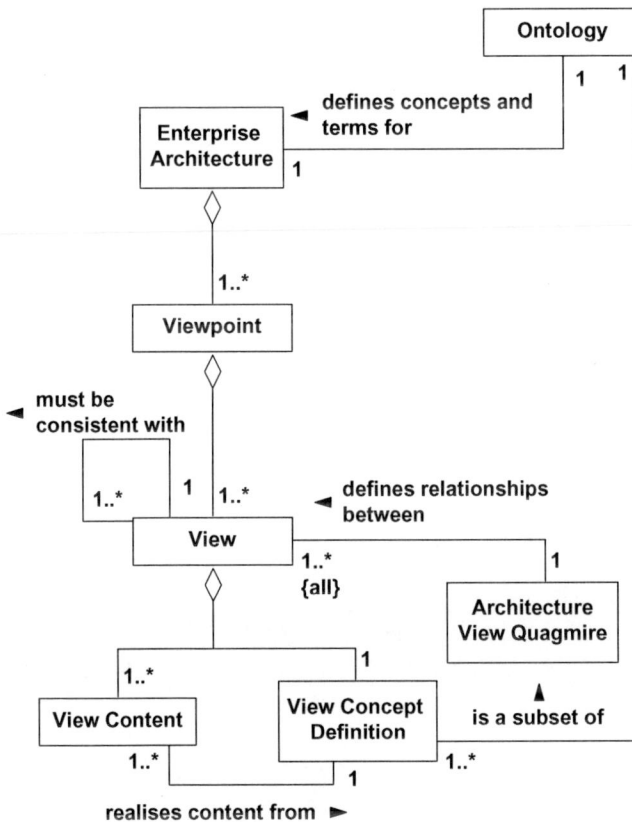

Figure 5.7   The EA hierarchy

The top level is relatively straightforward and can be given the generic label of 'Enterprise Architecture'. This represents the entirety of the EA and will exist for every business. As has been discussed in the previous section, the 'Ontology' defines the terms and concepts for the 'EA'.

The next level down usually describes a grouping of views, which will be referred to here as the 'Viewpoint'. A 'Viewpoint', at its simplest, is a collection of views that has some sort of common connection. The 'Enterprise Architecture' will be made up of one or more 'Viewpoint' and this number is typically quite low (usually under 10).

The next level down is usually the view level, which will be referred to here as 'View'. A 'View' represents a single image of a small part of the overall EA. Each 'Viewpoint' will be made up of one or more 'View'. The view itself must be defined and populated, which leads to there being two essential elements to each view – the 'View Concept Definition' and the 'View Content'.

The 'View Content Definition' is an expanded subset of the ontology that defines elements that appear on that view. The ontology represents all the key concepts on the business, whereas the 'View Content Definition' is concerned with a small subset of these concepts – sometimes, one, two, three, four or more (but usually a low number), and considers them in more detail. For example, a single concept may be broken down into more detail or may be given a number of attributes to describe it.

The diagram in Figure 5.8 shows an example of view concept definition. As can be seen here, this diagram is simply a subset of the overall ontology, but with more detail on it.

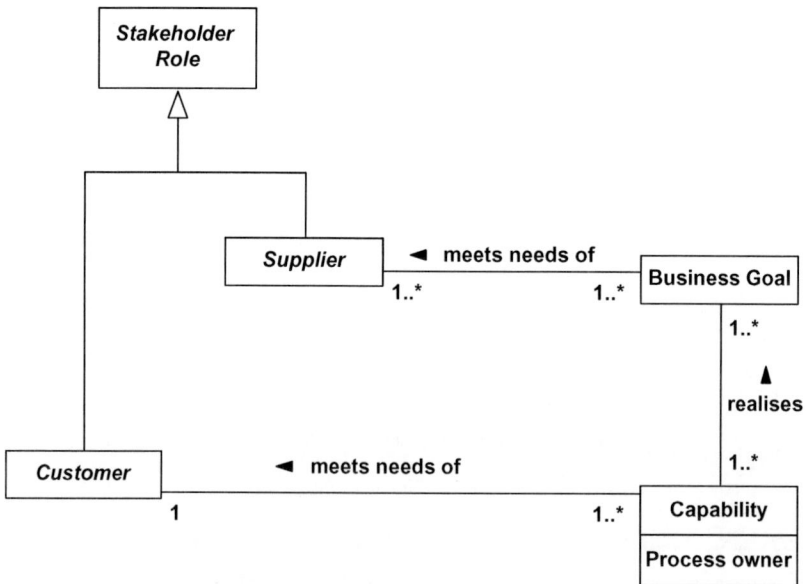

Figure 5.8   Example view concept definition

This particular view is concerned with looking at how the business goals and organisational capabilities relate together. The 'View Content Definition' will look at these two elements in more detail and specify more information about them – in this case each capability has a 'Process owner' associated with it, which would be defined here.

The view concept definition will *always* be modelled using a class diagram, when using Unified Modelling Language (UML) as the preferred modelling language.

This example is quite a simple one and will be discussed in more detail in Chapter 7.

The 'View Content' is the actual populated views themselves. Each of these views may be thought of as instantiating the information in the 'View Content Definition'. Common sense dictates that there must be a view concept definition before any view contents are generated and this is certainly true both theoretically and in many cases in practice. However, sometimes, it may be desirable to reverse engineer's number of views and abstract the view concept definition from them. This may occur when there is a legacy EA in place, when an existing EA is being analysed or after brainstorming what needs to be in a view by generating the view content.

The diagram in Figure 5.9 shows an example of a view content or, to put it another way, the actual view.

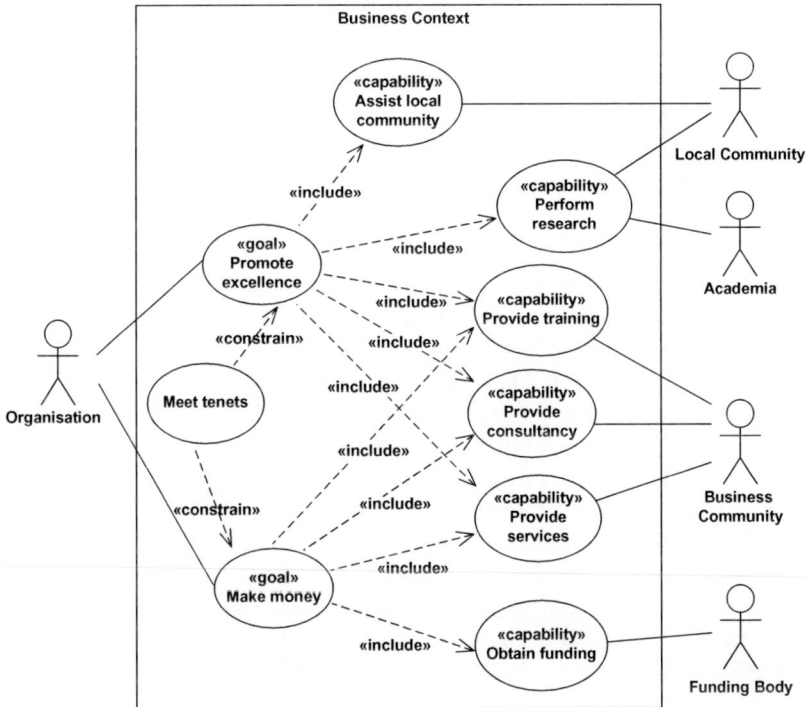

Figure 5.9   Example view content

The view content here is based on the view concept definition shown in Figure 5.8 with capabilities and business goals shown as stereotypes. Notice how each element in the view concept definition (and, hence, the ontology) is realised here as elements in the use case diagram. There is no single diagram that should be used for a view content and any or any combination of diagrams may be used to realise each view. The key here is to ensure the consistency of the views, and that is what the view concept definitions (and, hence, the ontology) enforce.

There is another aspect of each view that must be defined, that of the requirements for each view, but this will be discussed in more detail in the next section.

When a number of views have been defined, it is important to get a feel for the complexity of the number of views and the relationships between them. This is where the concept of the 'Architecture View Quagmire' comes in. The term *quagmire* is used here to represent a big sticky mess and is deliberately chosen as a word that implies complexity. This is a term that was coined in the engineering world by Sarah Sheard [1] in her world-renowned standard quagmire.

Continuing with the example that has been introduced in this chapter, Figure 5.10 shows an example of quagmire. As with all the examples, this is just one possible way that the quagmire may turn out and will not necessarily be an accurate representation of your particular business. There should be, however, enough general features in the diagram to be able to relate to the discussion.

The diagram in Figure 5.10 shows a high-level quagmire. Most people's initial thoughts on seeing such a view are 'what a mess'. And they would be right. The diagram here is deliberately complex as it goes some way to show just how complex the whole EA is. The diagram here is a relatively simple quagmire and only has four viewpoints and around twenty views, and only *some* of the relationships are shown. Another point to bear in mind here is that each element on the diagram represents the generic view, each of which may have many, many diagrams beneath it to realise that view.

It can be seen from the diagram that four viewpoints have been identified:

- Business Strategy Viewpoint. This viewpoint is aimed at understanding the nature of the business as whole – what its goals are, what the roles are, how the people fit in and so on.
- Operational Viewpoint. This viewpoint is aimed at understanding the operational activities that are current in the organisation. This will include current programmes, projects and so on. At the moment, this view is sparsely populated.
- Capability Viewpoint. The capability viewpoint is primarily concerned with the capabilities and competencies of the business. The capabilities refer to the abilities of the organisation and are defined in terms of their processes, whereas the competencies refer to the abilities of individuals. This viewpoint will also include some views concerned with standards and best-practice models.
- Technical Infrastructure Viewpoint. The technical infrastructure views are the ones that are concerned with assets of the business, where they are deployed, where they are in their life cycles and so on. These are the views that people often think of when they hear the term 'EA'.

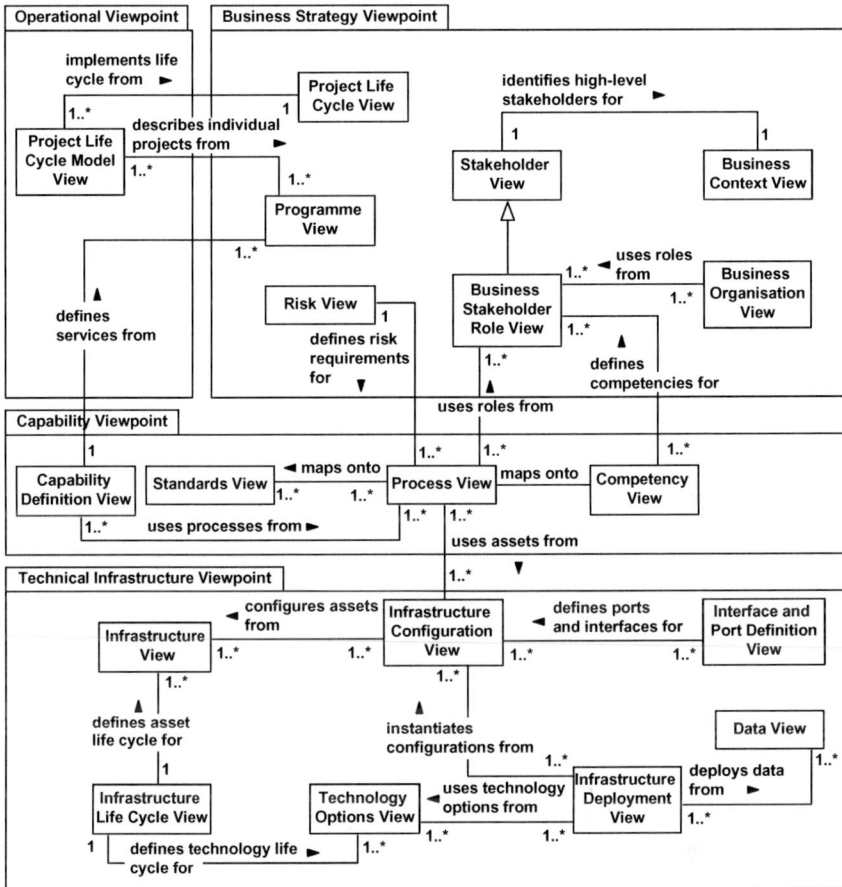

Figure 5.10   Example view quagmire

Each viewpoint is realised by a package in this diagram with their associated views being realised by classes. In practical terms, the quagmire is usually updated as and when new views are created, rather than identifying each view in the quagmire and then defining each. There is nothing wrong with this approach, although in reality the quagmire is usually a live artefact.

5.4   Requirements for EA

5.4.1   Introduction

The second of the three major EA themes is that of requirements. The requirements for the EA exist at all levels of the structure that were discussed in the previous section and may also exist in the form of a best-practice set of requirements.

```
        ┌─────────────────┐
        │  EA Business    │
        │  Requirements   │
        │      Set        │
        └─────────────────┘
              ▲  │ 1
        satisfies │
                  │ 1
        ┌─────────────────┐
        │  EA Definition  │
        │  Requirement    │
        │      Set        │
        └─────────────────┘
              ▲  │ 1
        is derived │
           from    │ 1..*
        ┌─────────────────┐
        │   Viewpoint     │
        │  Requirements   │
        │      Set        │
        └─────────────────┘
              ▲  │ 1
        is derived │
           from    │ 0..1
        ┌─────────────────┐
        │     View        │
        │  Requirements   │
        │      Set        │
        └─────────────────┘
```

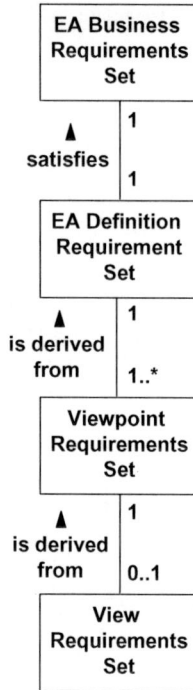

Figure 5.11   The hierarchy of requirements

The diagram in Figure 5.11 shows a simple hierarchy of requirements sets. There is an obvious parallel between the requirements sets here and the hierarchy that was introduced in the previous section. This will be explored in more detail when the concept of the EA meta-model is introduced later in this chapter.

All of the requirements sets are realised using use case diagrams when UML is the preferred modelling notation. The approach to creating and understanding the use case diagrams is described in Chapters 4 and 6, and this section assumes that knowledge.

These various types of requirements are discussed in more detail later in the text.

The EA business requirements set: It is possible to generate a generic set of requirements for all EAs but this needs heavy tailoring to make it realistic for any specific business. Having said that, however, this generic set of requirements can be a useful start point when considering why you need an EA in the first place. For the purposes of this book, this generic requirements set will be referred to as the 'EA Business Requirements Set', an example of which is shown in Figure 5.12.

The diagram in Figure 5.12 shows the generic EA requirements business set that will be used for this book.

Each of the requirements shown here is represented at a high level and could be applied to almost any business. Whether these requirements are relevant to a

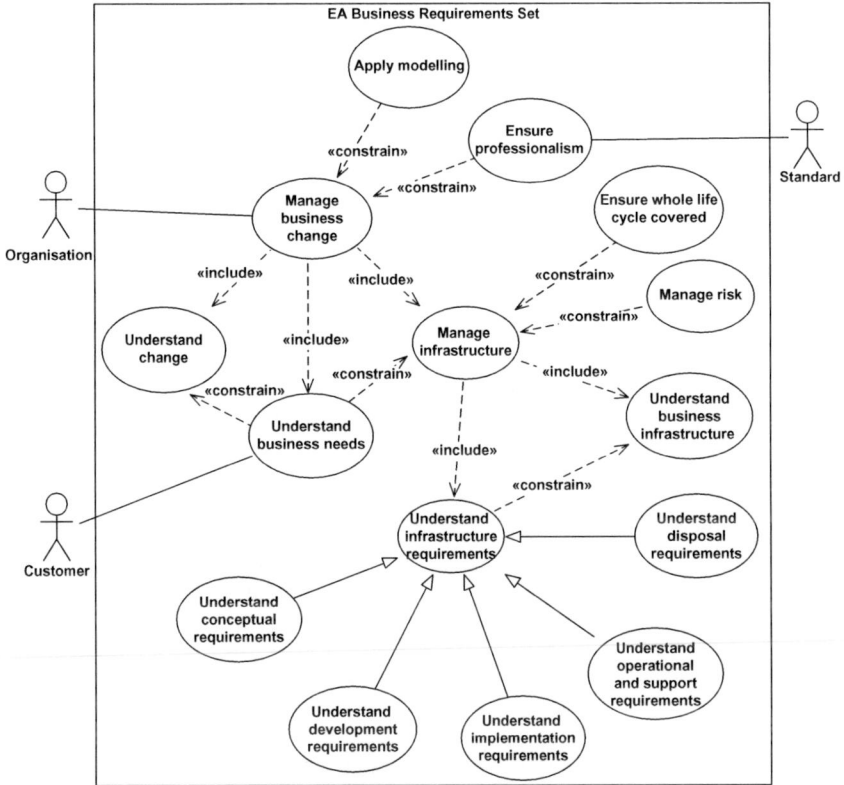

Figure 5.12 Generic EA business requirements set

particular business, or how these requirements may be realised will be completely dependent on the business.

A diagram such as this may be used as a basis for the actual business EA, but bear in mind that this is for guidance only and is not carved in stone. In the context of this book, this set of requirements formed the basis for discussion in Chapter 1.

The next level down in the requirements hierarchy is the 'EA Definition Requirements Set' that defines the requirements for the EA being produced. It is essential that a set of requirements is generated for the actual business that needs the EA defined. This is referred to as the 'EA Definition Requirements Set'. This may be based on the generic 'EA Business Requirements Set' as described earlier in the text, or may be generated using a blank-sheet approach. One of these will be required for each EA that is generated, or one per business.

The diagram in Figure 5.13 shows an example of 'EA Definition Requirements Set'. This set of requirements is fundamental to the success of the EA and the question must be asked 'why do you want an EA?' The answers to this could be

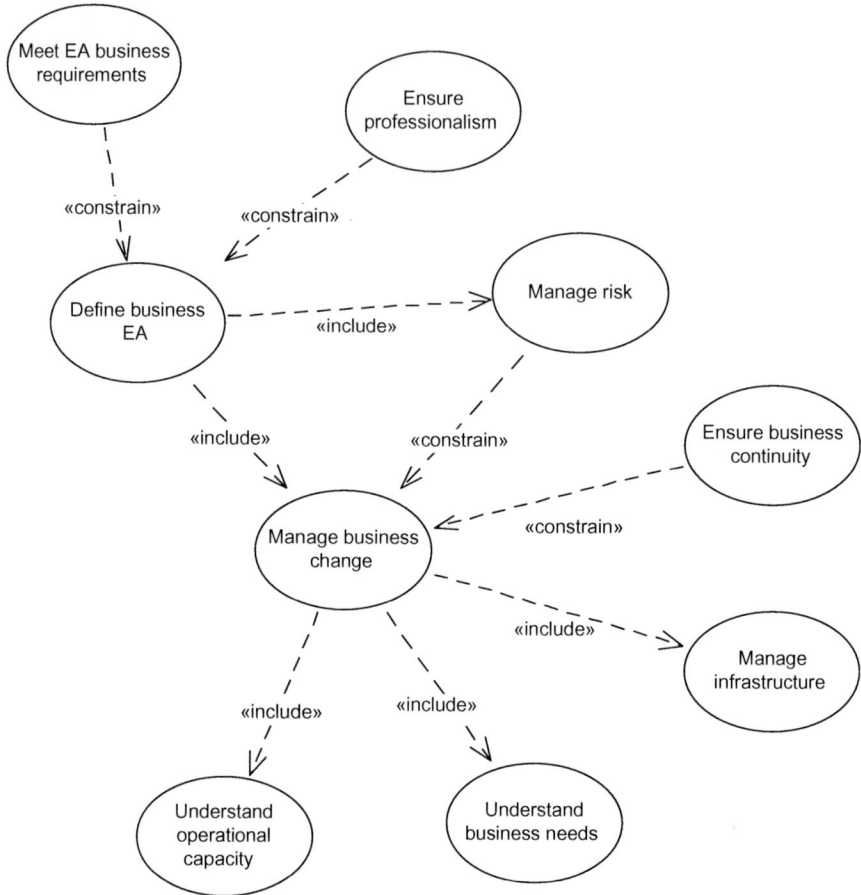

Figure 5.13   Example EA definition requirements set

many and varied and this was discussed in Chapter 1. Is the main requirement is to manage and predict future business? Is it to merge several organisations? Is it to understand an existing organisation? There is no off-the-shelf answer to this question as every business is different.

The next level down in the hierarchy is the 'Viewpoint Requirements Set'. Each viewpoint from the structure needs its own requirements set, which is known as the 'Viewpoint Requirements Set'. This must be derived from the 'EA definition requirements set' and should describe the reason why each viewpoint is required. The combination of all the viewpoints' requirements sets should meet the requirements of the 'EA Definition Requirements Set'. One 'EA Definition Requirements Set' will be required for each viewpoint in the EA.

The diagram in Figure 5.14 shows the requirements set for the 'Business Strategy Viewpoint'. The requirements here describe the overall need for the viewpoint, the main aim of which is to 'Understand business needs'. The other requirements

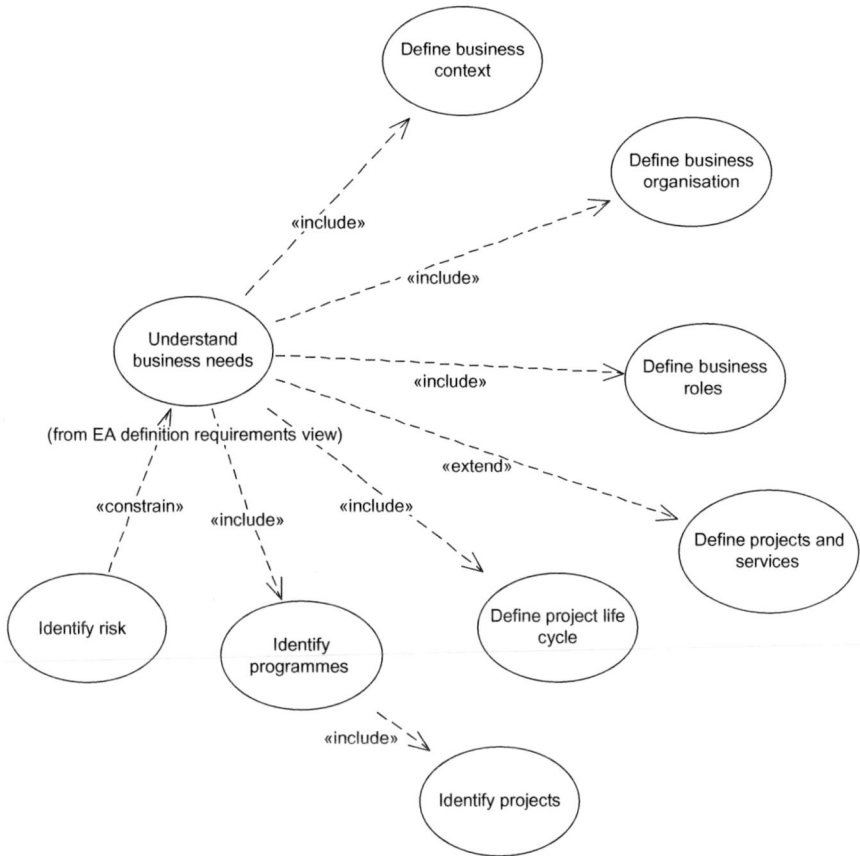

Figure 5.14   Example viewpoint requirements set

that are shown as inclusions and constraints on the top-level requirement will clearly be dependent on the organisation. The set of secondary requirements shown here should have some synergy with most businesses.

It is the role of the combination of all the views to meet these high-level requirements, which leads on to the 'View Requirements Set'. Each individual view must have its own reason for its existence defined and justified, which is achieved through defining a 'View Requirements Set'. One of these will be required for each view in the EA.

The diagram shown in Figure 5.15 shows the requirements for an individual view, in this case the 'Business Context View'. Again, the requirements shown here reflect what is needed from the view.

It now becomes important to compare these requirements with the information contained in the 'View' from the EA hierarchy. Notice that the information described in the 'View Concept Definition' should allow all of these requirements to be met, and that the information contained in the 'View Content' must actually

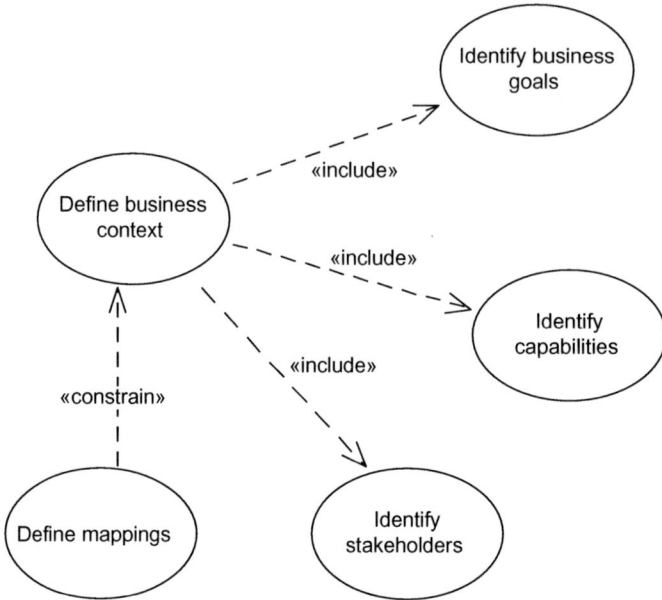

Figure 5.15   Example view requirements set

satisfy these requirements. Again, bear in mind that there may be any number of actual views that may need to be considered as a group that meet the requirements shown here.

5.5   Organisational process

5.5.1   Introduction

It has been mentioned previously that there is a lot of misunderstanding when it comes to EAs. One of the most common is that everything is about views. Although it is true that views form the heart of any EA, it is essential that people have the appropriate capabilities and competencies to be able to create, build and maintain an effective EA.

The essential part of realising the capability to develop an EA is to have an appropriate and effective process model in place.

There is potential for a lot of confusion at this point as it is possible to get into a conceptual chicken-and-egg situation. It is essential to have processes in place to develop the EA, yet the process model itself will form part of the EA.

The simple answer to this conundrum is to think of the whole EA as a continuously evolving living entity. It is simply not possible to develop an EA in a linear fashion, taking a single start point and then progressing forwards until the EA is complete. The whole process of EA development is highly iterative and therefore, it may be that processes are developed before, after or even during the development of the EA.

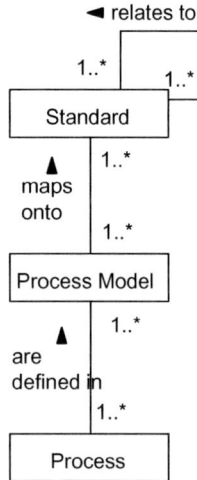

Figure 5.16   Organisational process

The diagram shown in Figure 5.16 illustrates the concept of having an organisational process model and each 'Process' is defined in the 'Process Model'. Any 'Process' model should map onto one or more 'Standard'. This is important from a quality point of view and to ensure that best practice is being followed. The use of standards also makes it easier to demonstrate the company's capabilities to any third party.

The process model will contain all the processes that describe what the organisation can do. Some of these processes must relate to the development, management and maintenance of the organisational EA. In many cases, if the whole concept of EA is new to the organisation, then these processes may not actually exist. This is not necessarily a huge problem as, from a practical point of view, processes are often developed in parallel with new capabilities. Clearly, it is a good idea if there is a starting point for the processes, such as a best-practice model or learning from the way that other people have developed their EAs. Such best-practice models may be very useful, for example, the information in this book or a standard, such as TOGAF.

In many cases, some existing process may be tailored to fit EA development. Any systems development processes may be applied to the development of an EA as, after all, an EA is a system. Therefore, a more generic systems engineering standard, such as ISO 15288, may be used as a starting point for a set of EA development processes. Any established systems engineering process model will contain processes that relate to: requirements engineering, analysis, design, implementation, verification validation and so on.

5.6   Bringing it all together – the EA meta-model

5.6.1   Introducing the EA meta-model

All of the information discussed so far in this chapter may be combined to form a single, coherent image of the essential elements of any EA. Each has been introduced and discussed, but part of this discussion has been to re-enforce the point that consistency is key to everything that we do in an EA. The meta-model brings the three main themes of the EA together and shows the relationships between them.

The diagram shown in Figure 5.17 shows the EA meta-model. This shows essentially the three themes out together with relationships between them.

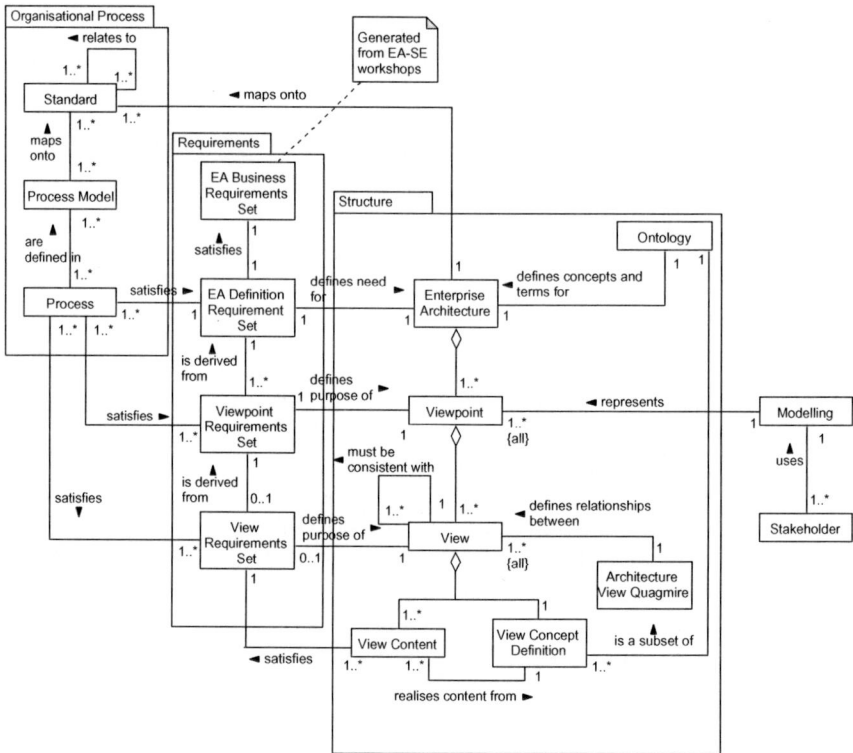

Figure 5.17   The EA meta-model

The diagram uses packages to group the different diagram elements into the three themes. The main relationships show that the 'Requirements' package generally defines the purpose or need for the 'Structure', and that the 'Organisational Process' satisfies the 'Requirements'.

Another key relationship here is shown between 'Enterprise Architecture' and 'Standard' that shows the need for the EA to map onto standards and best-practice models. An overview of some of the most popular and widely used ones can be found in Chapter 8.

5.6.2   Realisation of the meta-model through modelling

This book uses the UML as its modelling notation. As a quick summary, the following rules should be used to determine which diagrams should be used to realise each element of the meta-model.

- All requirements views will be realised using UML use case diagrams. These will be supported by class diagrams for any structural aspects and interaction diagrams to analyse scenarios. For advanced requirements views, parametric diagrams (from SysML) may be used for formal validation.
- The ontology will be realised using UML class diagrams. The overall ontology should try to be limited to a single-page diagram but, where this is not possible, the ontology may be spread over a number of diagrams. The concept definition views which are, in essence, lower-level views of the ontology will also be realised using UML class diagrams. It should be possible to paste all of the concept definition views together to form a complete ontology. Of course, in practice, this is rarely desirable or practical.
- The quagmire will be generated using a UML class diagram. This will be a standard class diagram with classes representing individual views and packages representing viewpoints.
- The view content. Any single diagram, or combination of diagrams, may potentially be used to realise each view. Also, any graphical, tabular or text notation may be used. In the context of this book, the notation used is UML and SysML.

A full description of how to use the meta-model and its elements to develop, analyse or maintain an EA will be discussed in detail in Chapter 7.

5.7 Conclusions

This chapter has introduced the basic elements that are essential for developing an EA. This may be summarised by the following key points:

- The structure that considers the ontology of the EA and the hierarchy of its views and groupings of views.
- The requirements that must be considered at all levels of the EA.
- The process that allows the EA to be generated and also forms part of the EA.

These three themes are brought together in the meta-model, along with the realisation of the views through effective modelling.

Understanding these three themes, the meta-model and modelling are really key to understanding and hence developing an EA. The rest of this book will focus on realising each part of the meta-model. To support this, a case study will be presented and a number of existing frameworks will be looked at that are compatible with this meta-model.

Reference

1. Sheard, S. *The frameworks quagmire, a brief look*. Proceedings of the Seventh Annual International Symposium of the International Council on Systems Engineering, Los Angeles, CA, INCOSE; 1997.

Chapter 6

Requirements modelling for EAs

If you want a guarantee, buy a toaster.

Clint Eastwood

6.1 Introduction

This chapter provides a simple overview of the world of requirements engineering with a specific focus on enterprise architecture (EA). A simple process for identifying and analysing requirements is provided for guidance.

6.2 Background

When engineering any kind of system, it is essential that the requirements for those systems are well understood. An EA can be considered as a system and, therefore, all the established and well-proven techniques for system development can be applied. Although there are many different methodologies and approaches to systems development, they all have one thing in common – requirements. Any approach or best-practice model worth its salt will state an explicit need to both understand and manage the requirements for a system effectively.

6.3 The need for requirements

To understand the requirements for a system, it is not enough to simply state the needs of a group of users, but it is necessary to engineer the requirements of all relevant stakeholders.

Requirements engineering is therefore essential for a number of reasons:

- Systems approach. All systems approaches identify a need to understand the requirements properly. This relates to all types of systems whether they are technical, social, financial or whatever.
- Quality. There are many definitions of quality but the two that will be considered here are both from the International Standards Organisation (ISO). This first definition, which is arguably the most common definition of quality used in the world is: 'fitness for purpose'. Fitness for purpose means that the system does what it is supposed to do or, to put it another way, the systems satisfies its

original requirements. The second definition that will be cited here is also from ISO, and is: 'conformance to requirements' – no explanation needed.

- Requirements drive the project. Every aspect of the project should be traceable back to the source requirements. The requirements should drive everything that is done in the project and if they are not, then some serious questions need to be asked.
- Benchmark for acceptance. Acceptance testing – the tests which provide the customer with the confidence that the system is fit for purpose – are based solely on requirements. Acceptance tests are neither based on the design nor on the implementation techniques that are applied (unless they are constraints) but are based entirely on the requirements set for the system. Therefore, if the requirements are not fully understood, how on earth can the final system be accepted?
- For increased confidence. One of the least tangible, yet most powerful benefits of applying an effective systems approach is one of confidence. When the requirements of the system are understood, the system can be demonstrated and accepted. When the requirements are understood, they can be agreed by the customer somewhere in the initial, or conceptual stage of a project. This confidence refers to the confidence of both the customer and the supplier sides of the relationships. In other words, the confidence of all the stakeholders will be increased. Although difficult to measure, confidence is an immensely valuable attribute for any relationship.

The points raised here make the case for understanding requirements. To understand the requirements, it is necessary to engineer them and this gives rise to the discipline known as 'requirements engineering'. An effective approach to requirements engineering will result in a concise, consistent and lucid definition of the requirements of any system and will yield the following benefits.

- Increased probability of optimum solution. If the requirements for any system are unknown or badly defined, then there is no way that the system under development can meet them. There is also no way that the system can be validated, as validation is based solely on the requirements. In the context of an EA, consider the EA as the system under development.
- Full traceability. It is important that any aspect of the system can be traced back to its source requirement. Not only is traceability essential for effective verification and validation of the system, but it is also a crucial part of quality assurance.
- Requirements that are independent of the solution. A good set of requirements should be independent of any specific solution. In the real world, this is rarely completely achievable as there will almost always be some aspect of the requirements where the solution, part of the solution or the technology used by the solution has already been decided. When and where this does occur, such requirements are considered to be 'constraints' as they will limit, in some way, how that requirement may be realised. In some cases this may refer to a solution or partial solution. In others, there may be a quality constraint, such as meeting a particular standard or following a specific process. Otherwise, the constraint may come from a specific technology or approach being adopted on

the development. There are, of course, many more types of constraints that exist but this brief list should provide an insight to the kind of requirements that may be considered as constraints.

This brief list just provides an overview of good reasons to perform effective requirements engineering. Requirements engineering is an entire subject matter in itself, so this chapter can only hope to provide a very high-level view of the rationale behind requirements engineering (see References 1–4).

From a systems engineering point of view, getting the requirements right is crucial. From the point of view of this book, there are five main aspects of getting it right, which are:

Capture. It is important that an initial set of requirements can be captured in some way, whether this is by someone producing an initial requirements specification, or whether the requirements need to be extracted from somewhere.

Specification. By the term *specification* here we mean to state specific features of the requirements in an unambiguous manner. This is very important but is only useful when it is done alongside the other four items in this list. As will be discussed later, specifying individual requirements, although necessary, is only a small part of the overall requirements engineering.

Analysis. By the term *analysis* we mean *understanding*. By the term understanding, we do not mean understanding the sentence that describes the requirement or the individual words, but true understanding as to the nature of the requirement, where it came from, how important it is, how it can be tested and so on.

Organisation. The requirements themselves must be organised in some way. This may include grouping the requirements into related categories, defining different contexts, relating requirements together and so on.

Management. Once the requirements have been analysed, organised and specified, it is important that they can be managed effectively. Requirements form a complex, living entity that will evolve over time and, hence, they must be properly controlled. Invariably, this will be made easier by the use of tools, whether it is within a modelling tool or whether a requirements-specific tool is used.

The requirements engineering must be carried out within the context of a project life cycle and it is usual for this to happen close to the beginning of a project. Any life cycle will be made up of a number of stages, or phases, one of which will represent the first stage in a project, and have a name like: 'conception', 'initial', 'requirements', 'inception' or whatever. It should be remembered, however, that the requirements set is a living entity and, as such, it will evolve and change as the project progresses through its life cycle. It is crucial, therefore, that the requirements set is managed and that it can be re-visited at different points in the project to validate that the project is being developed correctly.

6.3.1 Requirements capture

There are many and varied techniques for obtaining requirements. In many organisations, this may be straightforward as they may be presented with an initial requirements set in the form of a document. In other cases, however, it may be that there are no formal requirements at all and that the requirements are inside people's heads. There is no definitive approach to capturing requirements as it will depend on the nature of the business, the application, project, etc., but there are a number of basic techniques that can be used to assist with the capture. This list includes, but is not limited to the following:

Interviews. A good way to capture requirements is to talk to people. This may be as simple as an informal conversation with a stakeholder, or as complex as a dedicated meeting where all relevant stakeholders are present and a formal process is followed to extract the requirements.

Business requirements. Understanding an organisation's business requirements can provide a valuable insight into what requirements for a particular project may exist. All projects within an organisation must contribute to the business requirements of that business, otherwise why does the project exist?

Maintenance feedback. In the situation where a system is a new version of, or is closely related to an existing system, then comments and observations from people who are users of that system can prove to be invaluable sources for requirements capture.

Working in the target environment. One of the basic problems with trying to understand requirements is trying to establish a rapport with the stakeholders. This can be very difficult if, for example, there is no common domain knowledge shared between the stakeholders. Working in a target environment provides real value with regards to capturing domain knowledge and also can help to build a relationship with the stakeholder.

User groups. When a system has a large base of users, many organisations will organise user groups and even user conferences to better understand the way their system are being used.

Formal studies. Journals, conference proceedings, trade magazines and so on, are all great sources for requirements for some systems. Caution must be exercised, however, as some formal studies may not be as neutral or unbiased as they first appear. Looking at formal studies must be treated as a serious piece of research, even if it is a small one. Also, do not believe everything that is on the Internet!

Prototypes. Very often stakeholders know what they want but do not know how to articulate their thoughts and ideas. Providing a prototype can give an end user a clear, visual indication of what the final system may look like.

User modification. If an end user modifies a system, it means that the system does not meet all of their requirements. If this is a key client, or if more than one end user modifies the system in the same way, then this new user-created 'feature' can become a new requirement for the system.

The focus of this chapter is not requirements capture; therefore this section is kept deliberately brief.

6.4   Types of requirements

This section looks at some of the different types of requirement that exist. There is no definitive list of different types of requirement, but there are some basic generic types that exist in most organisations.

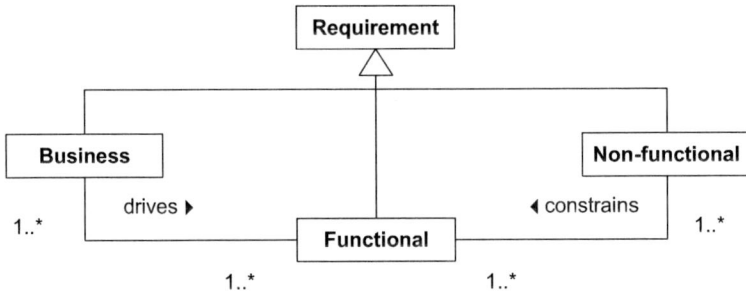

Figure 6.1   Different types of requirement

The diagram in Figure 6.1 shows that there are three types of 'Requirements': 'Business' requirement, 'Functional' requirement and 'Non-functional' requirement.

A 'Business' requirement is a high-level requirement that encapsulates, in a concise manner, one single requirement that describes what the business is setting out to do. Business requirements drive the organisation and everything that is done in the organisation should be traceable, either directly or indirectly, back to the business requirements.

Business requirements represent the fundamental nature of the business and may be based on the following:

- Strategy, such as technical, expansion and planning for change strategies.
- Markets, such as current and future.
- Mission, the business requirements should reflect the overall mission of the business. In some cases, where the organisation has an explicit mission statement, it may be desirable to represent the mission as a business requirement. Mission statements can be very useful and very powerful when used appropriately and when they are based in the real world. Unfortunately, mission statements generally have become the butt of many jokes in business. This is a reputation that is on the large, well deserved, as people will write any sort of nonsense, laminate it, attach it to a wall and call it a mission statement.

One point that should emerge from the concept of a business requirement is that they are fundamental to understanding a business and, therefore, form a key view, or group of views, within the company EA. As will be seen later on in this book, business requirements, business contexts, stakeholders and so on will form part of the EA case study in Chapter 7.

The concept of a 'Functional' requirement is one that is mainly intended when people use the generic term 'requirement' or 'user requirement'. A functional requirement is one that has some sort of perceivable impact on a stakeholder. Functional requirements often have verbs that imply some sort of string activity, such as 'produce', 'perform', 'provide' and so on.

To many people, the main focus of a requirements exercise will be to capture the functional requirements and only the functional requirements. Functional requirements must be analysed in conjunction with the stakeholders and the non-functional requirements to provide a complete picture of the requirements and their context.

The 'Non-functional' requirements, or constraints, in a system represent any requirement that will limit or constrain another requirement in some way. As has already been discussed, examples of non-functional requirements or constraints include: quality requirements, implementation requirements, solution-specific requirements, etc.

There is a lot of difference of opinion over which is the more important – functional or non-functional requirements. At the end of the day, this will be application or project dependent. In some projects, the function requirements may be very straightforward but there may be many very complex constraints that apply to them. Conversely, the system may have many complex functional requirements yet have few constraints. Whichever type of requirement is considered the more important is irrelevant and can be perceived as a waste of time and effort, but what is absolutely crucial is that the two of them are considered together. In many cases, functional and non-functional requirements are separated out and treated independently and, in some situations, dealt with using different teams of people. It is essential that functional and non-functional requirements are related to each other and this is one of the key aspects of requirements modelling that is discussed in this chapter.

It is important to be able to differentiate between the different types of requirement and looking through a list of generic requirements and simply asking which of the three broad types of requirements classifies each one can be a very worthwhile exercise. In many cases, the answer will be clear but try to do the same exercise with more than one person in the room; particularly if each person is a different stakeholder in the system. It has been discussed that each stakeholder may potentially have a different set of requirement from each other, but they may also interpret the same requirement in a different way, depending on their role.

In the situation where everyone agrees on the requirement classification, all is well and good. However, in some cases there will be a difference of opinion. In many of these cases it will indicate that:

- the requirement is very ambiguous and means something completely different to each stakeholder or
- there are two separate types of requirement that exist.

As well as classifying requirements, it is also necessary to define or specify each requirement.

6.5   Defining individual requirements

It is important that each individual requirement is described in a consistent and accurate way. However, just having a requirement described in such a way is not enough – it is just as important that the relationships between different requirements and between requirements and stakeholders is also understood. As a general rule, the relationships between the requirements will be established by the modelling of the requirements and the definition of each individual; requirement will be established by specifying each requirement.

It is usual to identify a number of features, or attributes for each requirement. Although there is no definitive set of these attributes, there are some common, best-practice attributes that will occur in most approaches. For example, the SysML suggests two attributes (called 'properties' in SysML) that must be defined as an absolute minimum: the identifier and the description. In reality, there should be more than these two, but they are intended as a start point only and the SysML specification recommends that more are defined. Some examples of attributes that may be considered are shown in Figure 6.2.

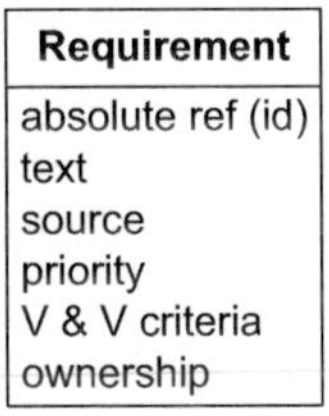

Requirement
absolute ref (id)
text
source
priority
V & V criteria
ownership

Figure 6.2   Properties of a requirement

The diagram in Figure 6.2 shows the concept of a requirement represented graphically as a class (the rectangle) and the properties of that requirement are shown as a list in a second box (attributes). This forms the specification of a requirement that should be:

- Owned. Every requirement should have the concept of 'ownership'. What this actually means in reality is that a stakeholder role should be assigned to each requirement to indicate the ownership of it.
- Well described (unambiguous). Each requirement will have a 'text' field associated with it that will form the description of it. This should be an unambiguous text description that should be kept concise and accurate.
- Able to be verified and validated. Every requirement must have a description of its 'V & V' criteria. For the purposes of this book, *verification* is defined as making sure that something works, whereas *validation* is defined as making sure that something does what it is supposed to do. It is essential that both verification and validation can be applied to each requirement.
- Prioritised. Each requirement must have a 'priority' defined. For example, it may be decided that each requirement may be set at one of three levels, such as *essential, desirable* and *bells and whistles*. In the event that not all require-ments can be met or those compromises have to be made, then clearly it makes sense to implement each requirement based on its priority.

- Traceable to and from. Each requirement must have its own 'absolute reference (id)'. It is essential that full traceability can be established from each requirement to any part of the project or system, or vice versa. Also, it should be borne in mind that requirements will invariably change during the lifetime of a project. In some cases this may be a minor change but, in others, the final specification of a requirement may be unrecognisable from its first draft.
- Have an identifiable source stakeholder. Each requirement must have a 'source' so that it can be established where the requirement originated from. This should be one of the project stakeholders, which will provide consistency with the stakeholder view. This is important as in many cases there will be questions and queries concerning individual requirements and it then becomes essential to know who to ask concerning the requirement. Also, this provides a handle on requirements creep, as it makes clear which stakeholder needs to provide the validation that the requirement is properly understood and that it can be demonstrated that it can be met.

Over all, each requirement must be managed and controlled and it is by identifying and specifying these requirements that this can be achieved. In projects with a high degree of complexity, requirements management tools will often be employed. These tools can be very powerful and, indeed, essential on real projects, but it must be remembered exactly what the tool can and cannot do. It is an all-to-common mistake to confuse the management of the requirements with the modelling of the requirements, which are two very different things. Both are essential, but it is important not to confuse the two.

6.6   Stakeholders

One of the most important concepts to understand when dealing with requirements is that of the stakeholder. The whole concept of contexts, that is essential for any sort of requirements engineering, is solely dependent on stakeholders for its basic definition.

The basic definition of a stakeholder is shown in Figure 6.3.

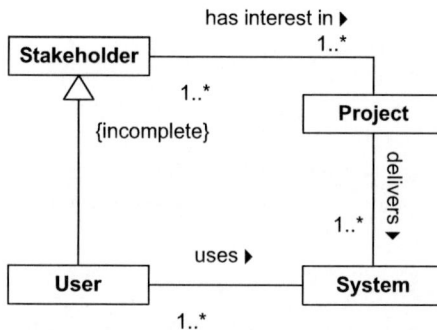

Figure 6.3   Definition of a stakeholder

The diagram in Figure 6.3 shows that a 'Stakeholder' has an interest in one or more 'Project'. The 'Project' itself delivers one or more 'System'. A 'User' is a special type of 'Stakeholder'.

The important thing to understand here is that a stakeholder defines the *role* of a person or thing that has an interest in a project. In many cases, the name associated with the role will turn out to be a person, but in many other cases, this will not be so.

A user is defined as a special type of stakeholder and this point is emphasised here due to the fact that many people use the awful term 'user requirements' when, in reality, they actually mean 'stakeholder requirements'. To understand this properly, consider the simple stakeholder view shown in Figure 6.4.

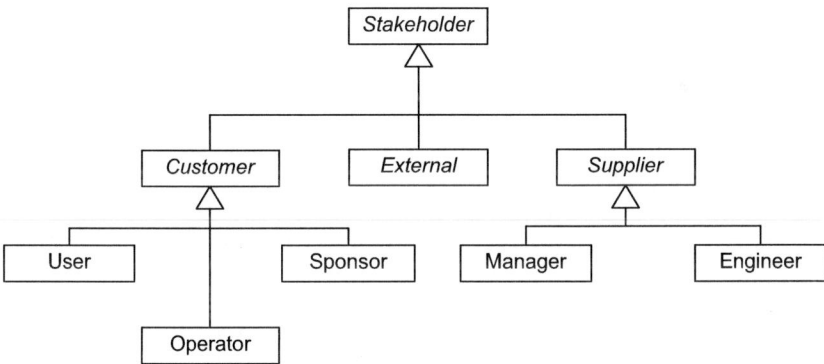

Figure 6.4   A simple stakeholder view

The diagram in Figure 6.4 shows a simple classification hierarchy, or 'taxonomy' of different types of stakeholders. Notice that the first level of the taxonomy shows that stakeholders can be divided into three main categories:

1. 'Customer' that describes all roles that may make use of the system or service or that the supplier needs to keep satisfied. In many cases, the supplier may have some influence over the customer and be in a position to discuss issues and agree compromises with them.
2. 'External' that describes the roles that must be satisfied by the supplier, but that cannot be negotiated with in any way. In other words, the supplier has no influence on external stakeholder roles.
3. 'Supplier' that describe all the roles that are involved with the development and delivery of the product or service.

Each of the stakeholder roles will have one or more names associated with it that describe who or what realises this rule.

To discuss the nature of these roles, consider the example of a passenger airline.

For the 'Customer' stakeholder roles:

- The 'User' role will be realised by any number of passengers who are the end users of the airline. In almost all cases, there will be a list of names that can be specified to realise a single role. In other words, a single stakeholder role is not limited to a single name and may have any number of names associated with it to realise that role.
- The 'Operator' role will encompass all the employees or associates of the airline, ranging from ticket sales, to the pilot and stewards, to the air-traffic controllers. Again, this is an example of many names that will realise a single role. Notice here that the role does not imply in any way how the role is realised. For example, the role of ticket sales may be realised by a person (or people) or by an automated system. The stakeholder role does not care how it is realised and is only concerned with the definition of the role.
- The 'Sponsor' role will represent all the people or businesses that have a financial stake in the airline enterprise. Again, this will be realised by many names in reality. Notice here, however, that some of the names may represent organisations or businesses, rather than individual names.

This makes the case quite nicely for a single stakeholder role having any number of names associated with it. It is also possible, however, to have a single person that takes on any number of roles. Imagine a person who is a pilot for their main job. When working, this person takes on the role of a pilot, which will be a type of 'Operator'. When the person is not working, they may go on holiday and they may travel on an aeroplane. In this situation, the same person that usually takes on the role of pilot (when working) will take on the role of passenger (which will be a special type of 'User'). Also, that person may have shares in the company, which means that the same person will sometimes take the role of shareholder, which will be a type of 'Sponsor'. In this example, it is possible for a single person to take on multiple roles, which is why it is essential to avoid individual or company names when it comes to specifying stakeholder roles.

For external roles:

- The 'Law' role will include all legal roles that may exist. Examples of this role include: individual piece of legislation, treaties or agreements, national or international laws or any industry-specific mandatory requirements. This will be realised by all the laws and legislation that apply to the world of air travel.
- The 'Standard' role will encompass all the standards that may apply to the airline. This will range from international standards, to country-specific standards, to industry standards, right down to in-house processes, guidelines and work instructions.

Notice in the example here that none of the roles discussed for this section are realised by people, but are 'things'. In some cases these things may be pieces of paper (documents) or may even be virtual documents (such as work instructions on the Internet, etc.).

For supplier stakeholder roles:

- The 'Manager' roles will be realised by all the managers involved in the project. This will include, for example, project managers, operational managers, configuration managers, etc.
- The 'Engineer' role will be realised by all the engineers involved in the project, such as software engineers, hardware engineers, electrical engineers, mechanical engineers, etc.

In the example provided here, almost all of these roles will be taken by actual people rather than things.

It is important that the various stakeholder roles involved with the project can be identified properly and accurately as the requirements will differ for each stakeholder and they may even conflict with other stakeholder's requirements. To put it another way, each stakeholder has, potentially, its own individual set of requirements. A set of requirements from a particular stakeholders point of view is known as a 'context', which must be understood for any effective requirements engineering.

6.7 Context modelling

Context modelling is a concept that is fundamental to requirements engineering, yet one that is often glossed over or, more worryingly, not considered at all. Understanding the context of a system is essential for understanding the requirements.

A context may be thought of, when using modelling, as the highest level view of the requirements of a system. The context identifies the boundary of the system and separates the outside world from the capabilities or requirements of the system. Everything inside the system boundary is represented as a requirements, or capability of the system. These should be functional elements and should consist of verb-constructs. Everything outside the system boundary may be thought of as an external system, person or anything that represents the roles of something that has an interest in the system. These are often referred to as 'enabling systems'.

Each requirement inside the system boundary must have some sort of relationship with an enabling system. By this, it is meant that the requirement must yield some sort of observable result to an enabling system. This may be a direct relationship, between the requirements to the enabling system, or it may be an indirect relationship that is traceable through several requirements that are closely related together. For example, if a single requirement is made up of several other, lower-level requirements, then it is enough to say that the higher-level requirement is related to an enabling system and then there is no need to state a specific relationship between its child requirements and the enabling system.

Each time one of these relationships exists, then the relationship must cross the system boundary. Each time the system boundary is crossed then a system interface is identified. This is a good way to identify the high-level system interfaces using a context.

Using the modelling techniques in this book, a context is visualised using a use case diagram that will consist of use cases (requirements), a boundary (system boundary) and actors (enabling systems). These use cases may then be analysed in terms of their patterns and structures to provide a well-balanced context.

Of course, once a context exists, then this is only the start point. The context may then be analysed using 'scenarios'. A scenario is a sequence of events or actions that achieve a particular goal and may be thought of as 'instances' or 'examples' of requirements. Any requirements will, therefore, have a number of scenarios associated with it and this is one of the most powerful ways to analyse requirements.

The previous description sums up the mechanics of creating a diagram to describe a context but the most important point, and the one that is very often missed off or ignored is that *a context must be described from a particular point of view.* Any stakeholder in the system will, potentially, have a different point of view on the same system and this is what the context encapsulates. To illustrate this point, consider again the example of a passenger airline system. There are many stakeholders involved with the passenger airline system, but let us discuss just a few here:

- The business context. What is the business all about? The bottom-line answer here is probably that it is all about making money. Part of this requirement is going to involve trying to get people to pay as much as possible whilst reducing the costs of running the airline.
- The end users, or passengers. Most passengers will want comfort, lots of food and drink, entertainment and a speedy flight but all for as little money as possible. Already, this conflicts with some of the business requirements. If the business wants to reduce running costs, then food, drink and entertainment will be the first things looked at. Likewise, will the business care less about comfort if more passengers can be squeezed onto the flight?
- Other airlines. Competitors will also have their own context, but what is it? Clearly, understanding a competitor's business context will allow us to look at our own business context and to optimise it.
- Subsystems. A context need not just be a stakeholder, but may be subsystem of the overall system, or a system in a larger system of systems. The engine control system, for example, is probably not too concerned with passengers, but with the pilot or the auto-pilot system. Again, each subsystem will potentially have its own context.

The point to be stressed here is that any system can be looked at from a number of points of view (contexts) and that, invariably, there will be conflicts between these different points of view. To look at a system from only a single point of view is quite simply folly.

To describe and analyse a context, it is important to start to apply modelling techniques. The next section looks at the two main diagrams that are used for modelling requirements, the use case diagram (Unified Modelling Language (UML) and SysML) and the requirements diagram (SysML only).

6.8 Modelling requirements

6.8.1 Introduction

To model effectively, it is crucial to have a standardised modelling notation. In this book, the preferred notation is the UML with some extensions using SysML.

Both UML and SysML have diagram for modelling requirements, each of which will be discussed in this section.

6.8.2 The requirements diagram

Anybody familiar with the SysML (systems engineering modelling language – see Reference 3 for more details) may be aware of a new type of diagram that is used for modelling requirements called the 'requirements diagram'. The 'requirements diagram' is essentially a class diagram that uses a stereotype of a class named 'requirement' and that specifies a number of special attributes and relationship types. This diagram is used mainly as an aid to documenting and managing requirements as opposed to understanding the context of a system.

Requirements diagrams are very useful for the following listed processes.

Forming the basis of a bridge between the model and text-based requirements. For example, the source requirements for a project are often held in a text-based repository, which must be maintained. The model may sit alongside this and it is important that the two can be traced between. In this situation, the requirements diagram is very useful as it can potentially be automatically generated (tool permitting) and be used as great reference point for use cases, scenarios, etc.

Tracing between different parts of the model. It is often desirable to trace between different parts of the model and to know which parts satisfy which requirements. For example, a single requirement may map onto a use case diagram, or a single use case. It is important to understand this relationship. Also, it may be that a number of scenarios are associated with a single requirement, or that part of a design is used to satisfy the requirement. In all these cases, the requirements diagram may be used.

Tracing between test cases and requirements. Whether this is done visually using scenarios, state machine diagram or activity diagrams, it is important to understand the relationships back to the source requirements. The requirements diagram may also trace to code, if test are being automatically generated.

The diagram in Figure 6.5 shows an example of a requirements diagram.

The diagram shown in Figure 6.5 shows how requirements may be represented in a hierarchical fashion, and that may have been auto-generated between a modelling tool and a requirements management tool. This could then form the start point of traceability to the rest of the model. Notice how a number of attributes have been defined that help to describe each requirement. Although in standard SysML, there are only two basic attributes (properties in SysML) defined, these will always be more defined in a real-life project and these will almost always be captured in the requirements management tool.

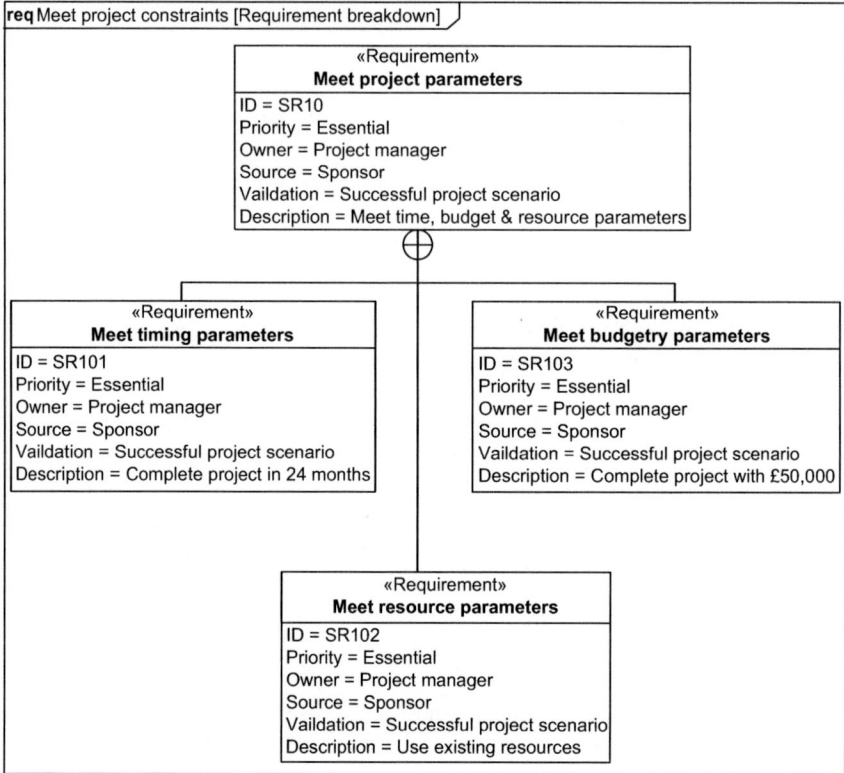

Figure 6.5   Example requirements diagram showing requirements hierarchy

The next example shows how the requirements from a requirements diagram may be used to illustrate traceability.

The diagram in Figure 6.6 shows how the requirements diagram can be used to show traceability between system elements. At the top of the diagram, a use case is shown as tracing to a requirement using the «trace» relationship. On the right-hand side of the diagram, a block diagram (a SysML construct similar to a class diagram in UML) is shown as satisfying two requirements. Also, note the use of notes to show the rationale of a relationship and an alternate for showing traceability with a note.

6.8.3   The use case diagram

When using the UML the most common diagram to use for modelling requirements is the use case diagram. An overview of the use case diagram can be found in Chapter 4, but a brief refresher will be provided here of the syntax and a more in-depth discussion on the use of use case diagram will be provided.

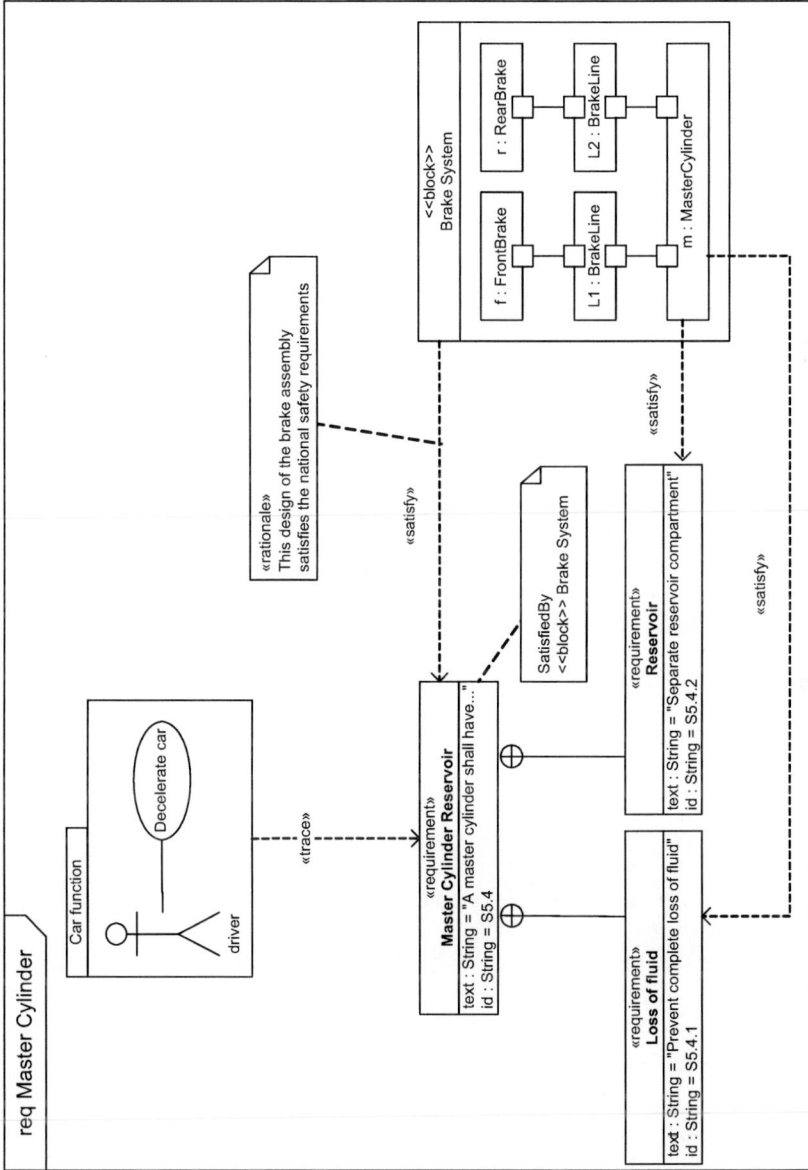

Figure 6.6 Example requirements diagram showing requirements traceability

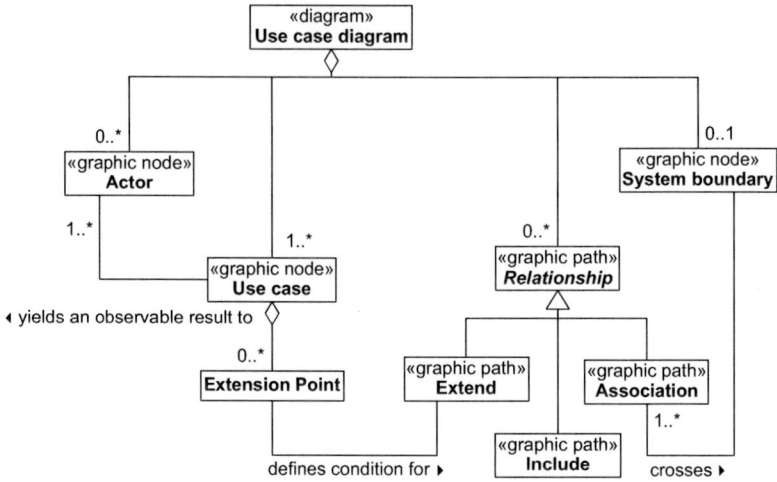

Figure 6.7   Use case diagram meta-model

The basic syntax of the use case diagram is shown in Figure 6.7.

The diagram shown in Figure 6.7 shows an extract from the UML meta-model concerning the use case diagram (see Chapter 4 for more details).

The diagram in Figure 6.8 shows the basic set of symbols that is used for use case diagrams. The symbols may be summarised as follows:

- Use case. A use case is used to represent a requirement, capability or goal, depending on the context. Use cases should be verb-constructs and describe, at a very high level, what the needs of the system are from a particular point of view.
- Actor. An actor represents a stakeholder or enabling systems that is outside the boundary of the system. Actors should be noun-constructs.
- Association. An association describes a relationship between a use case and an actor that identifies some sort of interaction between the two and also identifies a system boundary.
- Include. The «include» relationship describes a requirement that is always part of another requirement.
- Extend. The «extend» relationship describes a requirement that is sometimes part of another requirement, dependent on a condition described at an extension point.

For a full description of use case diagrams, see Chapter 4.

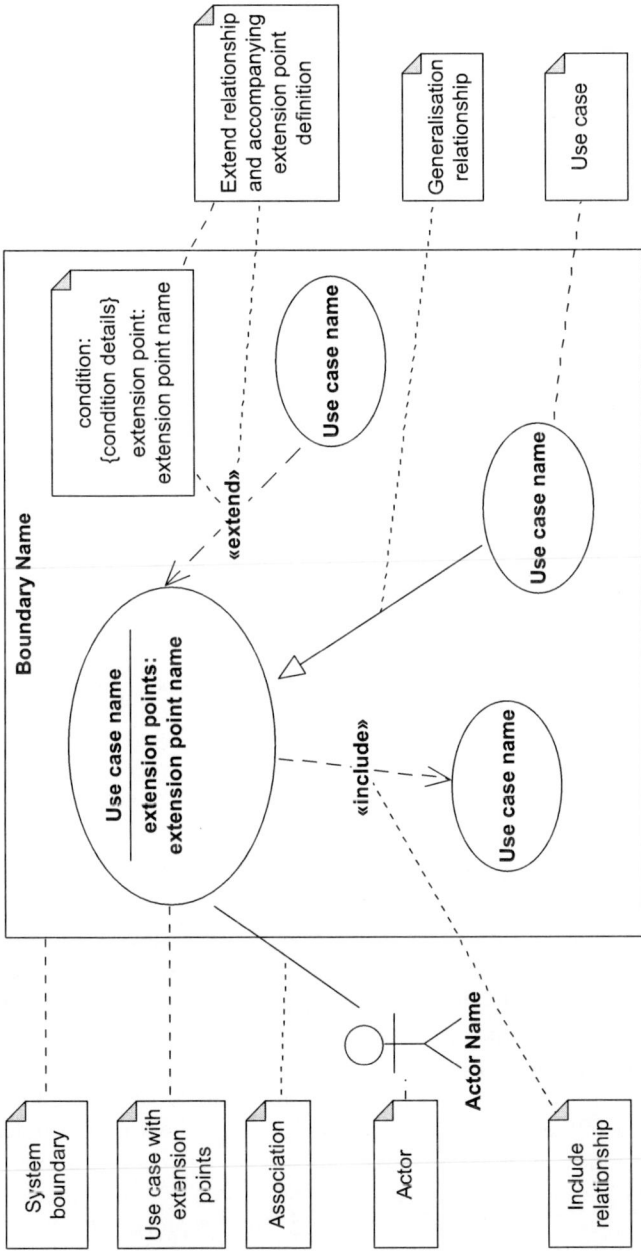

Figure 6.8 Symbols for a UML use case diagram

6.9   Example requirements modelling

6.9.1   Introduction

This section uses the UML use case diagram to realise the concepts of requirements engineering that have been introduced and discussed so far in this chapter. This section also introduces a very simple requirements process that may be used as a basis for requirements engineering.

6.9.2   The requirements process

This section introduces a simple requirements process that may be used as a basis for a requirements engineering exercise. The process presented here is deliberately simple but contains all the key elements that make up a good requirements process and, to that end, the process is fully traceable back to best-practice standards.

A good process should be well defined and its use should be repeatable, consistent and flexible. The structure of a generic process is shown in the diagram in Figure 6.9.

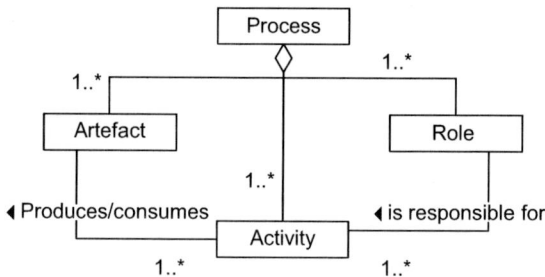

Figure 6.9   Structure of a generic process

From the diagram in Figure 6.9, it can be seen that any process is made up of three main elements:

- One or more 'Artefact'. An artefact is defined here as anything that is produced or consumed by a process. In reality, this may be a document, code, information, material, speech, etc. It is important that the artefacts for a process are identified and well understood and, where possible, their structure should be defined using templates and example formatting.
- One or more 'Activity'. An activity is defined here as something that has to be done as part of the process. This may be some sort of manual activity, such as someone filling in data, pressing a button or walking across a room. Equally, the activity may be automated, such as executing code, processing data, sending an email or whatever. For a good, flexible process, the activity should be defined in such a way that it is implementation-independent.
- One or more 'Stakeholder Role'. A stakeholder role is the same as a stakeholder that has been introduced already in this chapter. In the case of the process, the stakeholder is used to assign responsibilities of activities in the process. This is represented graphically using swimlanes in an activity diagram.

The process itself will be introduced and described and example artefacts will be shown for each activity in the process.

6.9.3   Process overview

The behaviour of the requirements process can be seen in Figure 6.10.

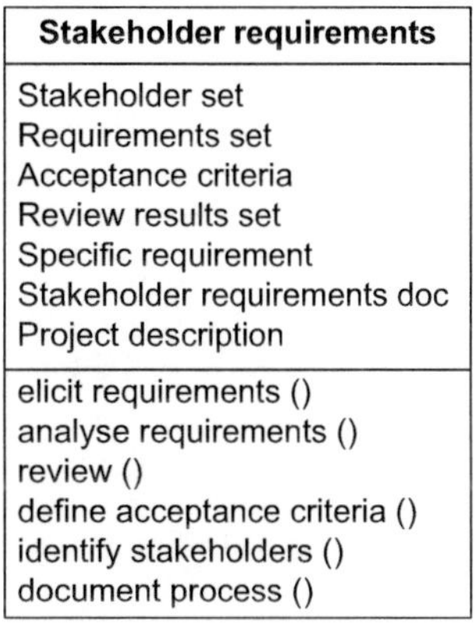

Stakeholder requirements
Stakeholder set
Requirements set
Acceptance criteria
Review results set
Specific requirement
Stakeholder requirements doc
Project description
elicit requirements ()
analyse requirements ()
review ()
define acceptance criteria ()
identify stakeholders ()
document process ()

Figure 6.10   Generic requirements process

The diagram in Figure 6.10 shows the process represented as a simple class. The artefacts of the process are shown as attributes on the class and the activities are shown as operations on the class.

The artefacts are defined as follows:

- 'Stakeholder set'. The stakeholder set identifies all relevant stakeholders for the requirements. As discussed elsewhere, these stakeholders may be anything that represents the role of a person, organisation, thing, standards, etc.
- 'Requirements set'. The requirements set identifies all the immediately known or captured requirements for the system.
- 'Acceptance criteria'. It is essential to be able to demonstrate to the customer that each of the requirements has been met. This is the purpose of the 'Acceptance criteria'. The acceptance criteria must be based solely on the requirements and defines how the customer will accept whether or not the work has met the original requirements.
- 'Review results set'. The 'review results set' is the formal output of the review. This may be as informal as a set of notes in a log book, or may be formal as in the case where minutes may be captured, action points identified, action plans defined, etc. Clearly, this will depend on the complexity of the project or work.
- 'Specific requirement'. The 'Specific requirement' is the detailed description of each individual requirement.
- 'Stakeholder requirements document'. This is the formal write up of all the process artefacts and is the final deliverable.
- 'Project description'. This is the initial description of the work or project and will form the basis of everything that is done on the project.

All of these artefacts will evolve over time. For example, the 'Requirements set' may start off as a simple list but will evolve into a number of diagrams that form part of the overall model.

The activities are defined as follows:

- 'elicit requirements'. This activity describes how to capture the requirements from the source information.
- 'analyse requirements'. This activity describes how to take each requirement and then understand it fully. This will include some level of modelling.
- 'review'. This activity looks at the artefacts that have been generated by the process and judges whether or not they are acceptable and up to standard.
- 'define acceptance criteria'. This activity describes how to define the basis of customer acceptance in the form of acceptance criteria.
- 'identify stakeholders'. This activity describes how to take the initial source information and identify the relevant stakeholders for the project.
- 'document process'. This activity documents all the artefacts for the entire process.

The exact way that each of these activities is carried out will depend on any guidelines, methodologies or other information specific to the project, however, an example of how these may be performed is provided in the next section.

6.10   Executing the process

6.10.1   Overview of the process execution

This section looks at executing the simple process that was outlined previously. The artefacts and activities have been described at a high level, but nothing has been said so far concerning how these activities are carried out and what the artefacts may look like.

The basic activity flow of the process is shown in the diagram in Figure 6.11.

The basic behaviour of the requirements process is shown in Figure 6.11. The diagram shows the order in which the activities are executed and where the artefacts are produced and consumed by each activity. The swimlanes in the diagram show the responsibility for each of the activities and relates back to stakeholder roles.

6.10.2   Elicit requirements

The elicit requirements activity is concerned with capturing the initial 'Requirements set' and, for the sake of this example, assume that a meeting has been held where a number of project stakeholders have defined a set of basic requirements.

In this example, the main purpose is to try to identify requirements related to a set of business views for the EA. The initial set of requirements is shown in the following list:

- Define business context. This will involve looking at the basic business requirements of the organisation.

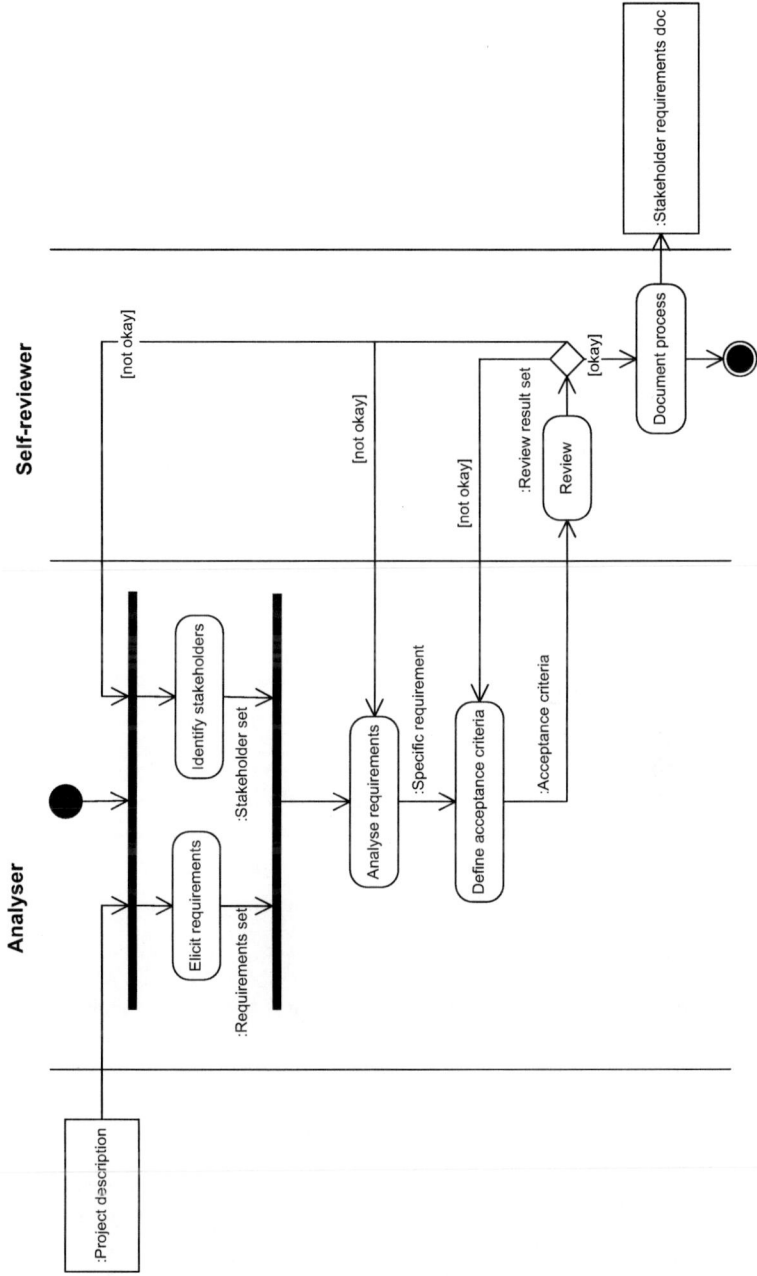

Figure 6.11   Behaviour of a generic requirements process

- Define business organisation. This involves defining the main organisational chart for the business.
- Define business roles. This involves looking at the role that exist in the business.
- Define projects and services. This involves stating what services and projects the business offers.
- Define project life cycle. This is related to projects and will help in project and programme management.
- Identify programmes. This involves looking at all the major programmes in the business.
- Identify risks. Identify the risks associated with the business.

This list is incomplete and quite ambiguous as it stands, but is typical of what may be generated from such a meeting.

6.10.3   Identify stakeholders

In a similar fashion, and at the same meeting, a set of stakeholders was also identified. These are as follows:

- Business Manager. The role responsible for managing new and existing business in the organisation.
- CEO. The Chief Executive Officer.
- Programme Manager. The role responsible for managing one or more programmes in the organisation.
- Project Manager. The role responsible for managing one or more projects within a programme.

Again, this is an initial list and will, in all probability, change. For example, are all of these stakeholders actually playing roles? One common mistake is to confuse job titles with roles – has this been done here?

6.10.4   Analyse requirements

The main aim of this activity is to truly understand the requirements and stakeholders in the form of a context and to specify each individual requirement.

From a modelling point of view, this will involve the following steps:

1. Draw a use case for each requirement. This will result in a diagram full of ellipses.
2. Draw a large rectangle around the use cases to show the system boundary.
3. Draw on an actor for each stakeholder. This will result in a number of stick people being added around the outside of the diagram.
4. Consider each use case, and then decide which actor or actors have an interest in it. Draw a line to show the associations between use cases and actors. This will result in a large, messy diagram.

5. Rationalise the diagram by applying the following simple rules:
   - Are there any use cases that are not associated with actors? If so, this indicates that either there is an actor missing, an association missing or that the use case is not required.
   - Are there any actors that are not associated with use cases? If so, this indicates that either there is a use case missing, an association missing or that the actor is not required.
   - Are there any use cases that are associated with the same set of actors? If so, this probably indicates that the actors are strongly related and that they can be abstracted into a higher-level actor to simplify the diagram. The detail may be shown on stakeholder view using a class diagram.
   - Are there any actors that are associated with the same set of use cases? If so, this probably indicates that the use cases are strongly related and that they can be abstracted into a higher-level use case to simplify the diagram. The detail may be shown on a decomposed use case diagram.

6. Identify relationships between the use cases. Consider if any use cases are part of other use case (using «include»), if any use cases are sometimes part of other use cases (using «extend») or whether any use cases constrain other use cases (using «constrain»).

By applying these rules it is possible to produce a diagram as shown in Figure 6.12.

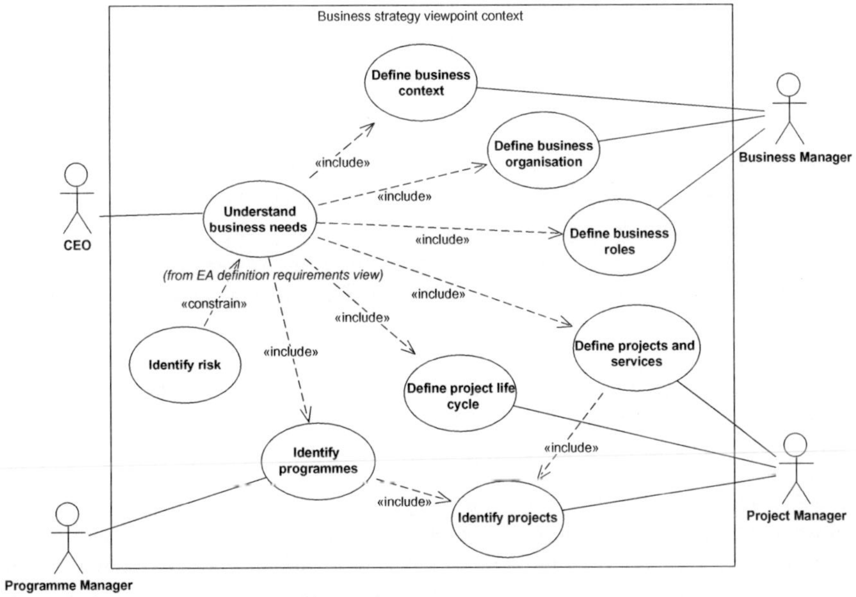

Figure 6.12   Example context

The diagram in Figure 6.12 shows a set of requirements and stakeholders that form a context. Notice that some new requirements have been derived during the analysis activity:

- 'Understand business needs'. This high-level requirement was not in the original list but it was felt that it summed up the whole set of requirements neatly.
- 'Identify projects'. This was identified as a common requirement as part of both 'Identify programmes' and 'Define projects and services'.

In reality, generating this diagram will take a lot of time and effort and will involve several iterations around the process. Part of the benefit of the modelling is that it forces you to think about what you are doing. When looking at a list of items, a common mistake is to read each item, understand and then to make the assumption that because each item is understood individually, then the totality of the requirements is also understood. It is essential to identify and understand the complexity that manifests through relationships between requirements, rather than assuming this knowledge.

The modelling provides the overall understanding of the requirements, their relationships and the complexity of the model, but this must still be augmented by specifying each requirement individually, as shown in Figure 6.2. Using the modelling techniques in this book, this may be achieved by using the requirement diagram, as shown in Figures 6.5 and 6.6, or by documenting each use case. In reality, the specification of each requirement, whether by requirement diagram or use case, will be controlled using a tool.

6.10.5   Define acceptance criteria

If a requirement cannot be tested, then it is not a requirement. The key point here is that once a customer has accepted a requirement for a system, then it is crucial that it can be demonstrated that the requirement has been met. This is where acceptance testing comes in. The acceptance test demonstrates to the customer that the requirement has been met so it makes sense to think about this during the requirements process, whilst the requirements are being understood, then waiting for the delivery of the system.

Using modelling, it is possible to demonstrate that a use case can be met by defining and investigating 'scenarios'. In modelling terms, a scenario is defined as an instance of a use case, or a specific example of how a use case may be met. Scenarios, therefore, are ideal for providing the basis for acceptance testing and have the added benefit of being a powerful analysis tool for use cases. Scenarios are discussed in more detail in Chapter 4.

6.10.6   Review

The review activity takes all the artefacts from the process and assesses them in some way. The review may be very formal, completely informal or anywhere in between. Most processes will have an element of reviewing or checking at some point to ensure that the process artefacts are fit for purpose.

6.10.7   Document process

This activity is concerned with documenting the process. This may be a manual documentation where the artefacts are taken and then described and documented or, when modelling correctly, they may be automatically generated. One of the benefits of modelling is that, when performed correctly, much of the documentation can be generated at the push of a button. Of course, this will be dependent on the capabilities of the tool that is being used to implement the modelling.

6.11   Conclusions

This chapter has introduced the concept of requirements modelling at a very high level. Unlike other aspects of modelling, there is an entire chapter devoted to requirements modelling and remember that this is still just a very high-level discussion on requirements. The reason why requirements are being emphasised so much is that they are so important to an effective EA. In the previous chapter it was shown that knowing 'why' at each level of the structure of the EA was essential for an effective EA and it is the requirements that allow this to occur.

References

1. Alexander, I. & Stevens, R. *Writing Better Requirements*. London: Addison Wesley; 2002.
2. Alexander, I. & BeusDukic, L. *Discovering Requirements – How to Specify Products and Services*. Chichester: John Wiley and Sons; 2009.
3. Holt, J. & Perry, S. *SysML for Systems Engineering*. London: IET Publishing; 2008.
4. Holt, J. *UML for Systems Engineering – Watching the Wheels*. 2nd edn. London: IEE Publishing; 2005 (reprinted IET Publishing).

Chapter 7
Enterprise architecture case study

I don't want someone shoving his views down my throat, unless they're covered in a crunchy candy shell.

Stephen Colbert, The Colbert Report, 2 May 2006

7.1   Introduction

Chapter 1 introduced the concepts behind enterprise architectures (EAs), namely the *requirements* for an EA, that of the EA *meta-model* and *ontology*, and *viewpoints* and *views*.

The diagrams in Chapter 1 were taken from a real organisational EA. The organisation is the world's largest independent supplier of industrial-grade, collaborative modelling tools for complex, mission-critical systems and software. As well as supplying modelling tools, the organisation also provides tool-independent training and consultancy in EAs, architectural frameworks, modelling and systems engineering. The authors developed the EA for this part of the organisation.

This chapter shows how the EA was developed and will show, through the discussion of a number of real views from the EA, how the various concepts relate together in practice.

7.2   The meta-model

The starting point for the creation of an EA is the *meta-model*. This was introduced and described in Chapter 1 and is reproduced in Figure 7.1.

Before starting to develop an EA it is essential to understand *why* it is to be developed. That is the *requirements* for the EA must be established. Figure 7.1 highlights the two key requirements sets that must be defined and understood. The 'EA Definition Requirements Set' must be defined for the organisation and should be based on (and must satisfy) the generic 'EA Business Requirements Set' and the actual business drivers for the organisation.

The generic 'EA Business Requirements Set' was introduced in Chapter 1 and the high-level requirements are reproduced in Figure 7.2.

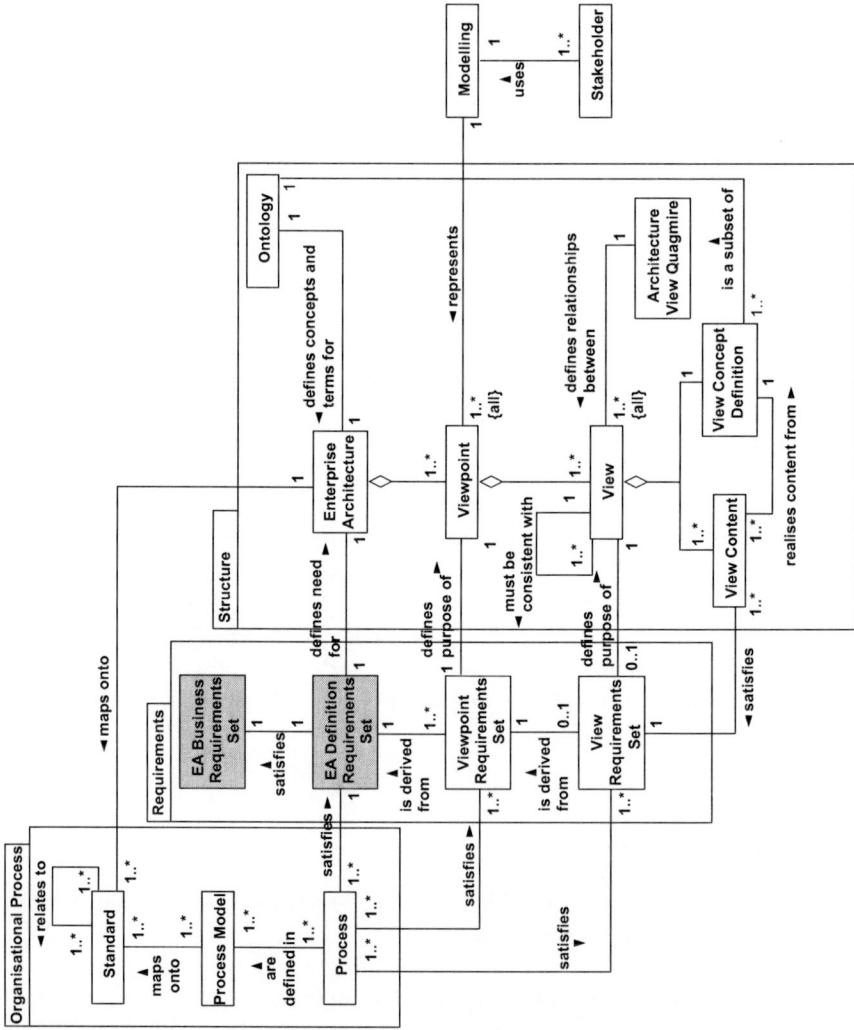

Figure 7.1 *The EA meta-model – requirements sets highlighted*

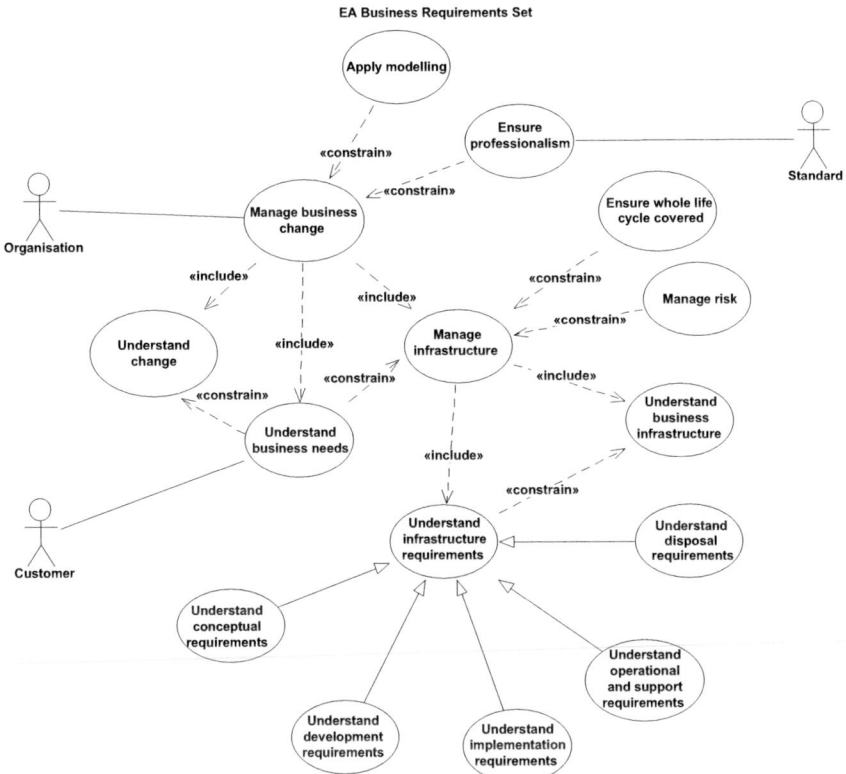

Figure 7.2   EA Business Requirements Set – high-level requirements

Using the 'EA Business Requirements Set' and the business drivers for their organisation, the authors defined the 'EA Definition Requirements Set' for their organisational EA. Modelling of requirements is discussed in Chapter 6. The 'EA Definition Requirements Set' is shown in Figure 7.3.

The main driver to our requirement to 'Define business EA' was the need to 'Manage business change' and 'Manage risk' (which itself constrains the way that business change is managed). In defining an EA for the business we also wanted to 'Meet EA business requirements' (i.e. develop an EA that meets the 'EA Business Requirements Set' shown earlier and which represent best practice as determined by the EA-SE project as discussed in Chapter 1). In addition, any EA produced should allow the organisation to 'Ensure professionalism' by addressing issues such as staff competency.

To manage business change, the key requirements were identified as 'Understand business needs', 'Understand operational capacity' and 'Manage infrastructure'. This last requirement is one of the main drivers for many EAs in which the emphasis is often placed on the information systems used by the organisation (an approach discussed in Chapter 1). For the organisation under consideration,

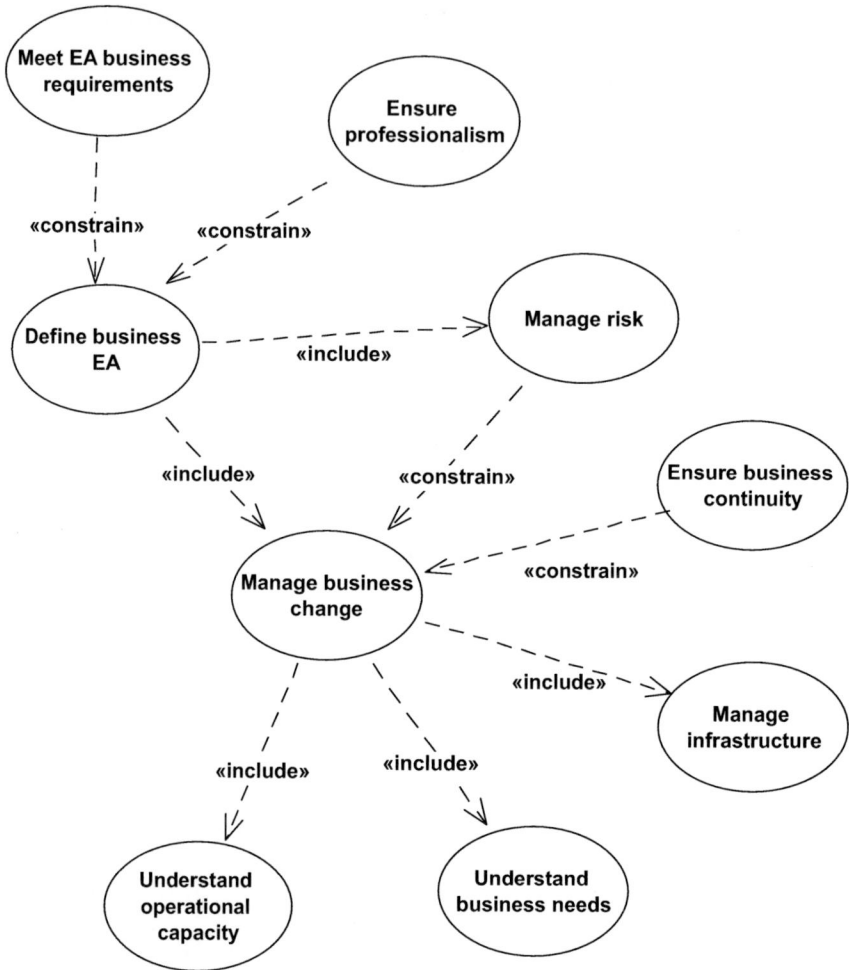

Figure 7.3   EA Definition Requirements Set

while this requirement is important, it is not the main driver for the need for an EA. Finally, any business change must take place in such a way as to 'Ensure business continuity' and the EA must capture information that helps to ensure any change programme undertaken by the organisation does not result in business failure.

7.3   The ontology

Having established the requirements for the EA, the next step is to develop the *ontology* for the organisation.

As discussed in Chapter 1, the ontology describes the terminology, concepts and common language specific to the organisation. The ontology is more than just a list of concepts and terms; an essential part of the ontology is the *relationships* between the concepts.

The ontology should be based on existing organisational structures, capabilities, responsibilities, processes, standards and infrastructure. Developing the ontology is neither a quick nor an easy process and it is almost impossible to get right immediately. It may require a number of iterations to develop and will need the input from a range of interested parties. Attempting to develop an ontology single handedly is almost impossible, except in the smallest of organisations.

The organisational ontology was introduced in Chapter 1 and is reproduced in Figure 7.4.

The ontology in Figure 7.4 contains the key organisational concepts and relationships and covers such key areas as *programmes* and *projects*, *business goals* and *capabilities*, *processes* and *standards*, organisational *infrastructure* made up of different kinds of *assets* (including *persons* as well as *data* and *technical assets*), the *stakeholders* that have an interest in the work done by the organisation and the *positions* taken by the people working for the organisation.

The ontology defines the main concepts and terms that are used in the views that comprise the EA. The use of the ontology in developing the views is discussed in Section 7.5.

7.4 Initial viewpoints

Having established the ontology, the next stage in the development of the EA is to identify an initial set of *viewpoints*. This corresponds to the highlighted classes in the meta-model in Figure 7.5.

Each viewpoint should be defined and should be accompanied by a 'Viewpoint Requirements Set'. The viewpoints are simply groupings of *views* that present information on the enterprise, each view contributing to the requirements in a viewpoint's 'Viewpoint Requirements Set'.

The initial viewpoints that were defined are shown in Figure 7.6.

Figure 7.6 shows the four viewpoints that were defined for the organisation: the 'Operational Viewpoint', 'Business Strategy Viewpoint', 'Capability Viewpoint' and 'Technical Infrastructure Viewpoint'. Since each viewpoint is, in effect, just a container for related views, packages have been used to represent the viewpoints.

Each of these viewpoints is intended to contain views that realise one or more of the requirements from the 'EA Definition Requirement Set' discussed in Section 7.2.

- The 'Operational Viewpoint' will contain views that realise the 'Understand operational capacity' requirement.
- The 'Business Strategy Viewpoint' will contain views that realise the 'Manage risk', 'Understand business needs' and 'Understand operational capacity' requirements.

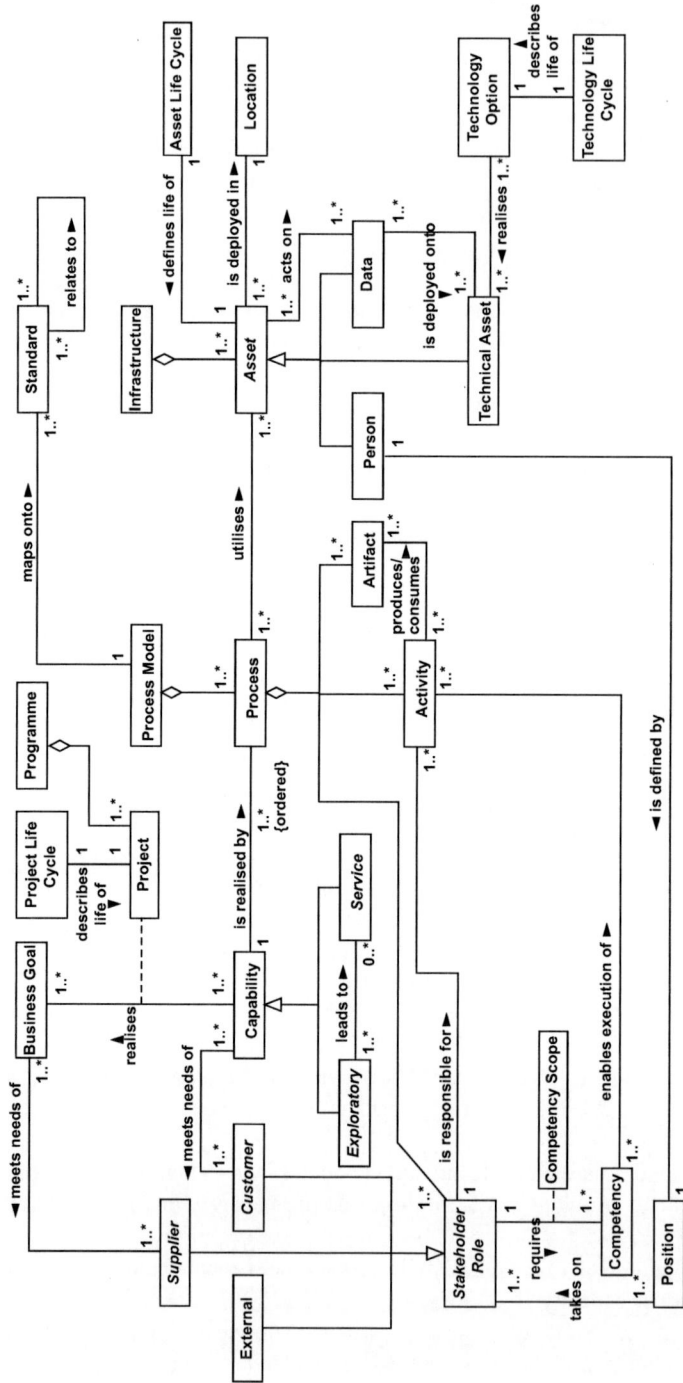

Figure 7.4 The EA ontology

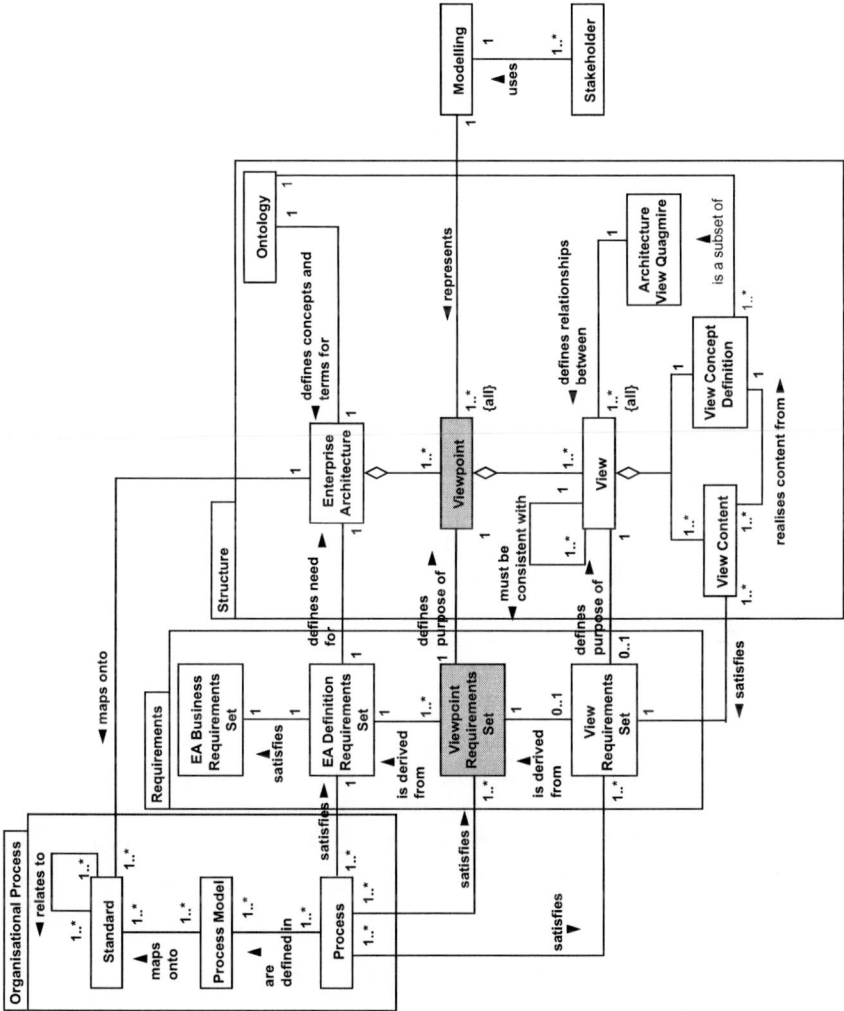

Figure 7.5 The EA meta-model – viewpoints highlighted

Operational Viewpoint	Business Strategy Viewpoint

Capability Viewpoint

Technical Infrastructure Viewpoint

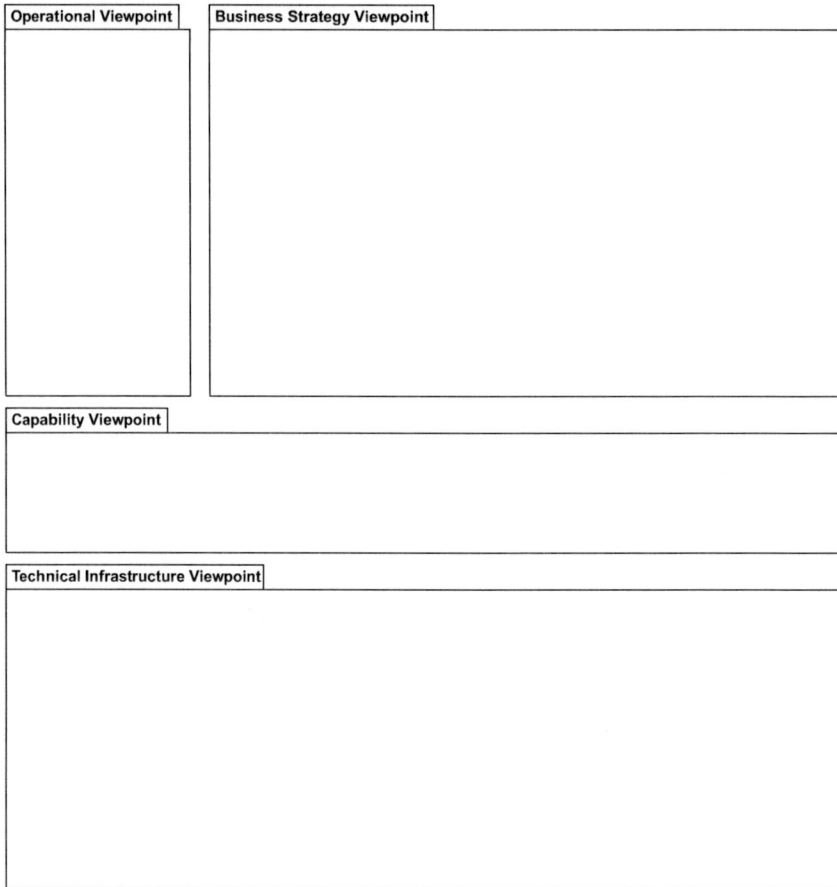

Figure 7.6   Initial viewpoints

- The 'Capability Viewpoint' will contain views that realise the 'Ensure professionalism' and 'Ensure business continuity' requirements.
- The 'Technical Infrastructure Viewpoint' will contain views that realise the 'Manage infrastructure' requirement.

Note that these viewpoints fit the chosen organisation but may not be suitable for all.

As stated earlier in the text, each viewpoint will have an accompanying 'Viewpoint Requirements Set' which is derived from the 'EA Definition Requirements Set'. The 'Viewpoint Requirements Set' for the 'Business Strategy Viewpoint' is shown in Figure 7.7.

The main requirement for the viewpoint is to enable the organisation to 'Understand business needs'. To do this, the viewpoint must contain views that allow the organisation to understand the context in which it operates, its organisation and the business roles in the organisation ('Define business context', 'Define

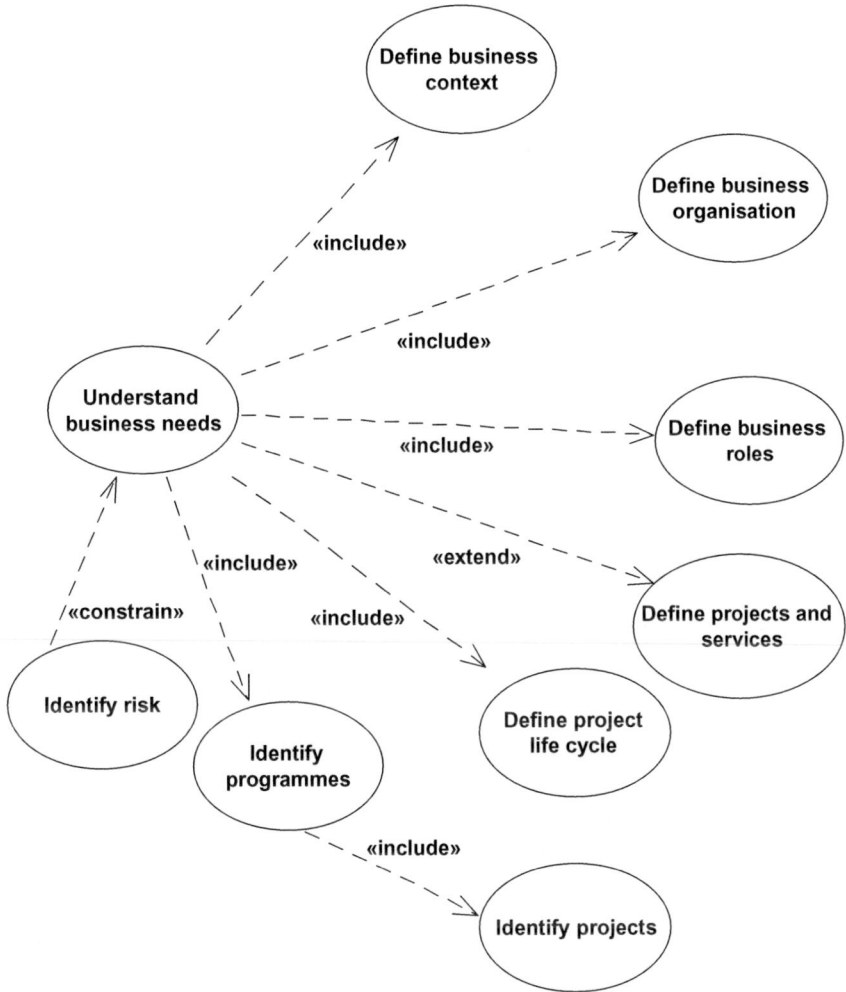

Figure 7.7   Viewpoint Requirements Set for the Business Strategy Viewpoint

business organisation' and 'Define business roles'). The projects and services that an organisation undertakes, the life cycles followed by the projects and the way projects are organised into programmes all need to be understood ('Define projects and services', 'Define project life cycle', 'Identify programmes' and 'Identify projects'). Finally, it is important for the organisation to be able to identify and understand the risk in all that it does (Identify risk).

The requirements for a particular viewpoint will typically be gathered using a number of different approaches including, but not limited to:

- interviews with stakeholders
- consideration of business requirements

- requirements workshops
- looking at requirements for EAs for comparable organisations.

With the viewpoints and their requirements defined, it is time to start developing the views that make up the heart of the EA. This is discussed in the next section.

7.5   Generating views

The problem with many EAs is that the views they contain often do not address the needs of the organisation. Having views in an EA because they seemed like a good idea at the time leads to an architecture that is often inconsistent, unwieldy and costly to maintain.

Key to the successful generation of views are the meta-model elements highlighted in Figure 7.8.

Before creating a 'View' in the EA it is essential to understand why it is needed. This is done by generating the 'View Requirements Set', derived from the 'Viewpoint Requirements Set' that the 'View' will belong to, and which defines the purpose of the 'View'.

Next the definition of the 'View' is created, that is the 'View Concept Definition'. This takes the relevant elements from the 'Ontology', expanding them as necessary, to define the elements and concepts that the 'View' will represent.

Based on the 'View Concept Definition', the actual view is created and populated in a 'View Content'. This is a realisation of the 'View Concept Definition', which may be a diagram (using a notation such as Unified Modelling Language (UML) or SysML), text (such as tabular information) or any representation that is appropriate to represent the concepts defined in the 'View Concept Definition'. It should be noted here that a single 'View' may be realised by one or more 'View Content'. It is wrong to assume that a 'View' only has a single representation.

Finally, with the 'View' defined and populated it should be added to the 'Architecture View Quagmire'. This is a diagram that, when complete, shows all the views in the EA and how they are related to each other, grouped by viewpoint. As views are defined and created, the quagmire will become more complex as the views and relationships are added. Often, early in the construction of the EA, it is not possible to add the relationships to the quagmire as the related views may not have yet been defined. Nonetheless it is essential that the relevant relations are added to the quagmire once the related views have been defined and added.

The quagmire is often missing from EAs, but it is key to understand the relationships between the views and is one of the key diagrams for ensuring consistency and coverage of the architecture.

The rest of this section will illustrate the approach described earlier for four views, one from each of the four viewpoints described in Section 7.4.

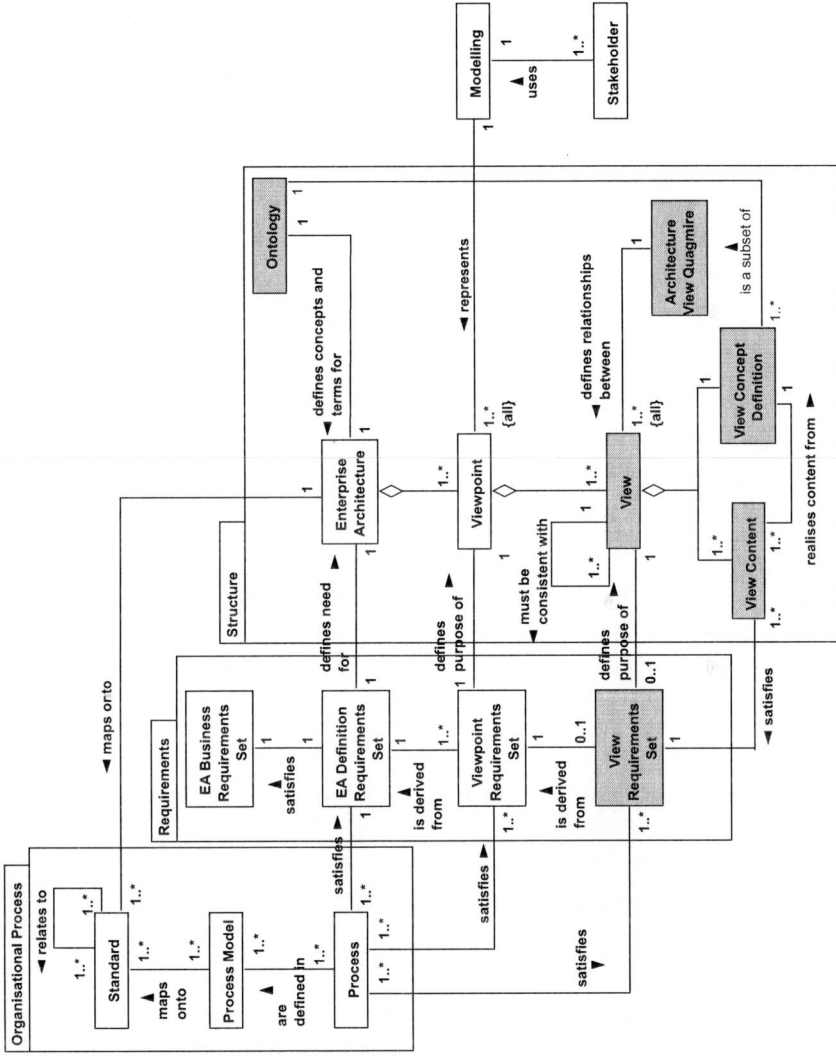

Figure 7.8 The EA meta-model – view elements highlighted

7.5.1   *The business context view*

Every organisation works within a *business context* which establishes the highest level requirements for that organisation – typically the goals and capabilities of the organisation, together with the stakeholders involved. The view that captures this context is the 'Business Context View'.

7.5.1.1   View requirements

The 'View Requirements Set' for the *Business Context View* is given in Figure 7.9.

The main requirement for this view is to 'Define business context'. To define the business context it is necessary to identify the *goals* of the business (Identify business goals), the *capabilities* that the business has (Identify capabilities), how these capabilities contribute to the attainment of its business goals (Define mappings) and the *stakeholders* involved (Identify stakeholders).

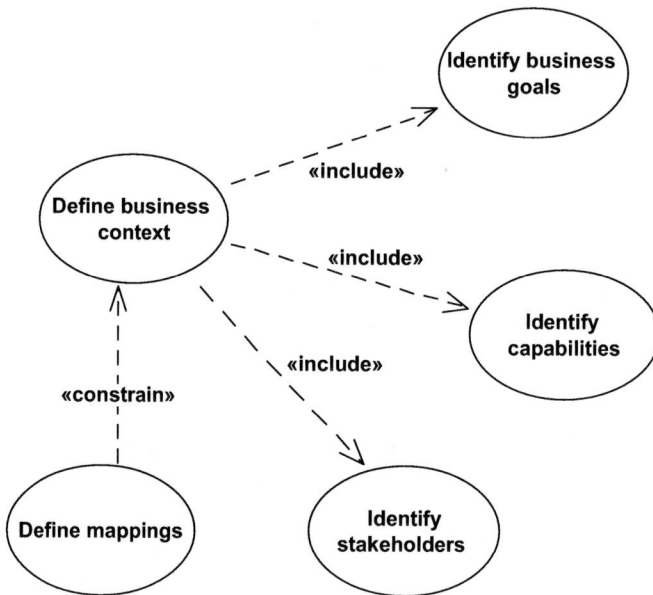

Figure 7.9   Business Context View – View Requirements Set

7.5.1.2   View concept definition

Having defined the requirements for the view, the relevant elements from the ontology were identified, as shown highlighted in the diagram in Figure 7.10.

The key elements to be represented in *Business Context View* are highlighted in Figure 7.10. These are 'Stakeholder Role', 'Customer' and 'Supplier', 'Capability' and 'Business Goal'.

These elements were expanded on the 'View Concept Definition', shown in Figure 7.11, to define all the elements to appear on realisations of the *Business Context View*.

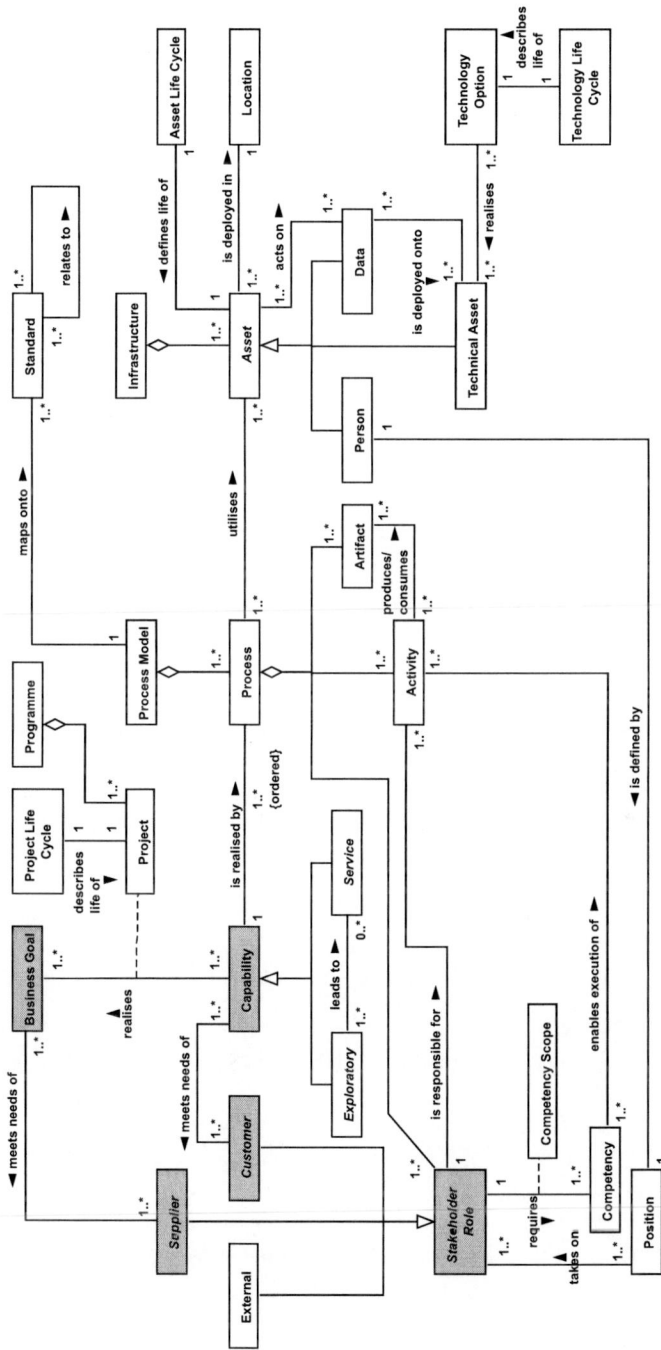

Figure 7.10 Business Context View – the ontology highlighted

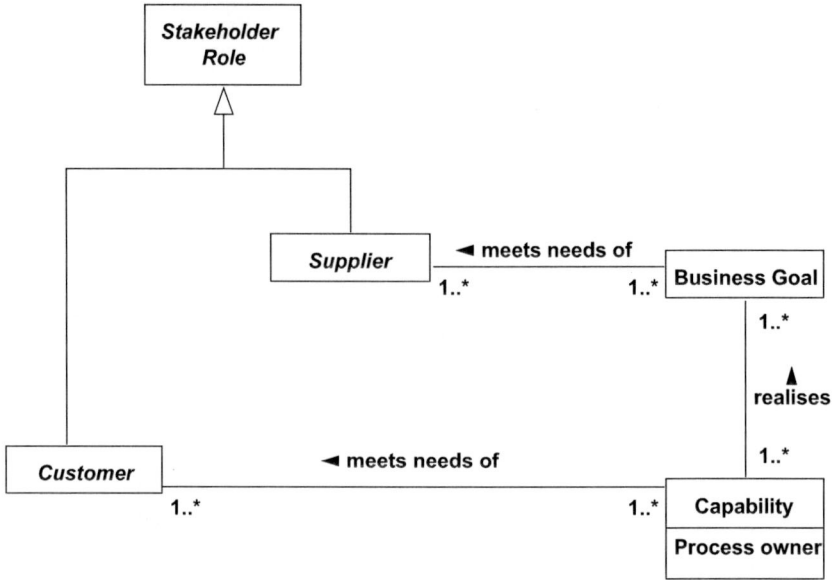

Figure 7.11   Business Context View – View Concept Definition

The 'View Concept Definition' for the *Business Context View* shows that the view must show a number of 'Business Goal' and 'Capability' for the organisation, together with which 'Capability' realise which 'Business Goal'. A 'Capability' may also have a 'Process owner' identified, showing the person within the organisation responsible for the organisational processes that deliver the capability.

A number of 'Stakeholder Role' are also to be shown specifically the 'Customer' and 'Supplier' roles. The view must show which 'Capability' meet the needs of which 'Customer' and which 'Business Goal' meet the needs of which 'Supplier'.

7.5.1.3   View content

The *Business Context View* is realised by a UML (or SysML) use case diagram, as shown in Figure 7.12.

The diagram shows that the two main goals of the organisation are 'Promote excellence' and 'Make money'. Note the use of the «goal» stereotype to indicate that these use cases represent goals. These two goals are constrained by the need to 'Meet tenets' – that is by the need to meet the professional tenets of the organisation. The stakeholder 'Organisation' is related to these two goals as shown in the diagram.

Each of these goals is realised by a number of capabilities. The capabilities are modelled as use cases stereotyped «capability» and «include» dependencies are used to show which capabilities realise which goals.

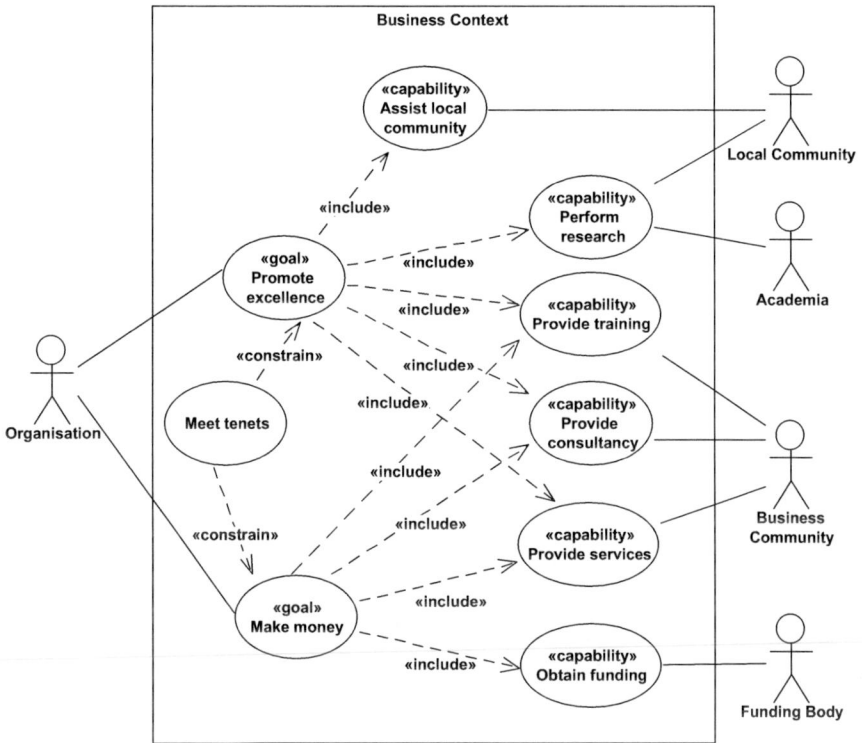

Figure 7.12   Business Context View – View Content

The goal 'Promote excellence' is realised by the capabilities:

- 'Assist local community' – primarily helping to teach engineering to children in local schools. The involved stakeholder is 'Local Community'.
- 'Perform research' – carrying out research into areas such as systems engineering, UML, SysML, process modelling, EAs and competency assessment. The stakeholders involved are 'Local Community' (again, primarily local schools) and 'Academia'.
- 'Provide training' – delivery of training courses in areas such as systems engineering, UML, SysML, process modelling, EAs and competency assessment to the 'Business Community'.
- 'Provide consultancy' – provision of consultancy in areas such as systems engineering, UML, SysML, process modelling, EAs and competency assessment to the 'Business Community'.
- 'Provide services' – provision of services, such as UML and SysML modelling, competency assessments, artefact reviews, to the 'Business Community'.

The goal 'Make money' is also realised by the capabilities 'Provide training', 'Provide consultancy' and 'Provide services' as described earlier in the text. In addition, it is realised by the capability 'Obtain funding' through the stakeholder

'Funding body', for example, applying for business development grants through regional development organisation.

7.5.1.4   Populating the quagmire

With the *Business Context View* defined, it is added to the evolving quagmire. This is in Figure 7.13 with the *Business Context View* highlighted.

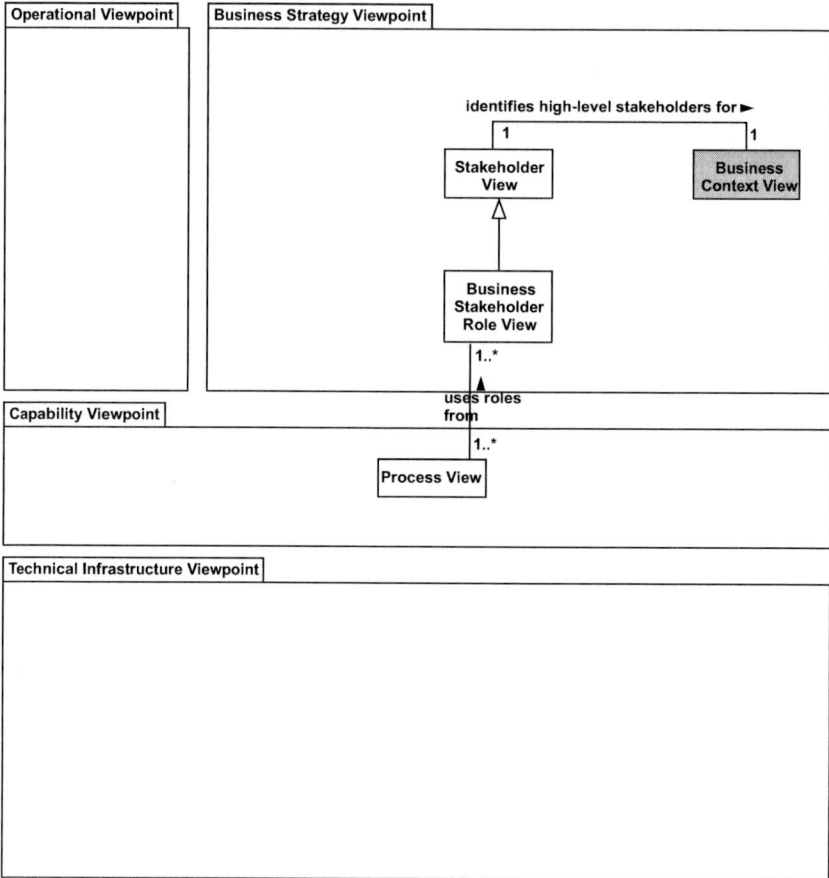

Figure 7.13   Architecture View Quagmire – Business Context View added

At this point it is possible to begin thinking about other views that may be required. Looking at the 'View Concept Definition' for the *Business Context View* we see that the view shows stakeholders and that process owners may also be shown. This suggests that views are needed to show stakeholders and processes. These additional views are shown in the diagram in Figure 7.13, together with the relevant relationships between them.

When developing the EA these views would be good candidates for con-sideration next. That is not to say that each of these views need to be completely defined and populated in order, but that at the least the requirements for these views could be defined and some thought given to the definition of these views. This in turn would, through the 'View Concept Definition' for each view, suggest additional views needed in the EA.

This illustrates an important point, namely the *iterative* nature of developing an EA: work on one view may indicate additional views that are required to maintain consistency across the architecture. Similarly, work on one view may result in changes being needed for other views that have already been defined. Thus the enterprise architect must be prepared to move from view to view, developing and refining iteratively, rather than hoping to complete a view before moving on to the next.

7.5.2   The competency view

In order for an organisation to be able to deliver its capabilities (see Section 7.5.1, *Business Context View*) it must have staff with the necessary *competencies* for roles involved in the delivery of each capability. For this reason a *Competency View* was considered essential as part of the organisation's EA.

7.5.2.1   View requirements

The 'View Requirements Set' for the *Competency View* is shown in Figure 7.14.

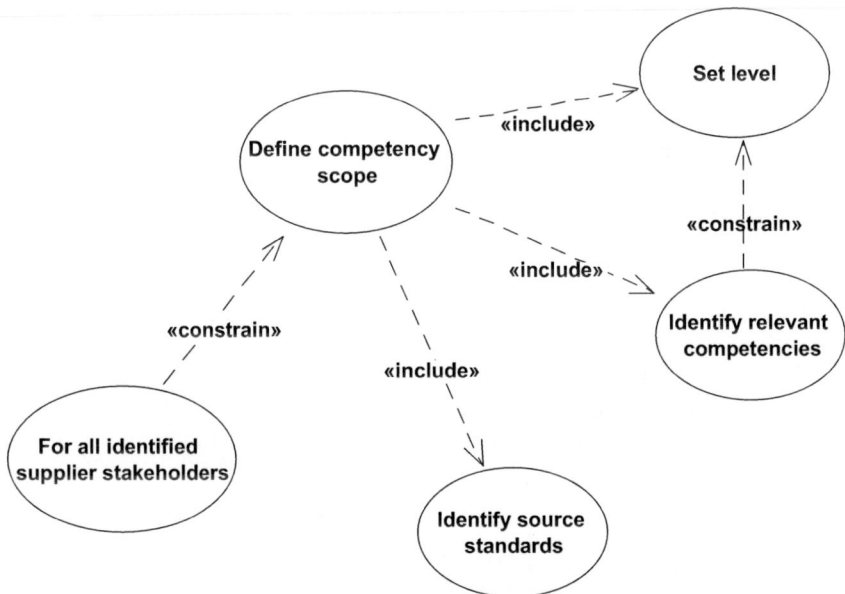

Figure 7.14   Competency View – View Requirements Set

The main requirement for this view is to 'Define competency scope' for the organisation. Such competency scopes must be defined 'For all identified supplier stakeholders' and must show the relevant competencies needed by each stakeholder (Identify relevant competencies) and the level at which each competency is to be held by that stakeholder (Set level). In addition, the source standard from which each competency is taken must also be identified (Identify source standards).

7.5.2.2 View concept definition

Having defined the requirements for the view, the relevant ontology elements were identified as highlighted on Figure 7.15.

The key elements to be represented in the *Competency View* are shown highlighted, namely 'Competency' and 'Competency Scope'. These were used as the basis of the 'View Concept Definition' where the concepts that need to appear on the realisations of the *Competency View* are defined. The 'View Concept Definition' is shown in the diagram in Figure 7.16.

The 'View Concept Definition' for the *Competency View* greatly expands the concepts surrounding competency from those appearing on the ontology, where only 'Competency' and 'Competency Scope' are shown. The diagram in Figure 7.16 shows the high-level 'View Concept Definition'.

Each 'Competency' is made up of one or more 'Indicator'. These indicators are the *concepts* that must be demonstrated to be considered as holding the competency. Each 'Competency' is held at a 'Level' which can be 'Awareness', 'Support', 'Lead' or 'Expert' in that competency.

Competencies are used in a 'Competency Scope' which defines the competencies, required levels and source standards for each competency that is needed by an organisation 'Role' (modelled as an attribute of the 'Competency Scope'). Rather than a competency scope and the relevant competencies being directly related, they are linked via one or more 'Competency Reference' that uses attributes to hold the name, required level and source standard for a given competency in a given scope.

Competencies are also grouped. The 'Competency Framework' represents the overall organisational competency framework and is mapped on to one or more 'Competency Framework' (representing a *standard* that defines a competency framework, for example, the INCOSE Systems Engineering Competencies Framework). The 'Competency Framework' is made up of three 'Competency Type' which in turn are made up of one or more 'Competency Area' which group one or more similar 'Competency'.

The three types of competency are shown in the diagram in Figure 7.17.

The three 'Competency Type' are as follows:

- 'Skill' – technical skills such as UML modelling and process modelling, and soft skills such as writing and public speaking.
- 'Domain Knowledge' – knowledge relating to the domain in which the person being assessed for competency works.
- 'Systems Knowledge' – competencies relating to the field of systems engineering, such as system concepts, selecting preferred solutions and life cycle process definition.

It should be noted here that while, in the organisational EA under discussion, the basic concepts of 'Competency' and 'Competency Scope' are expanded in

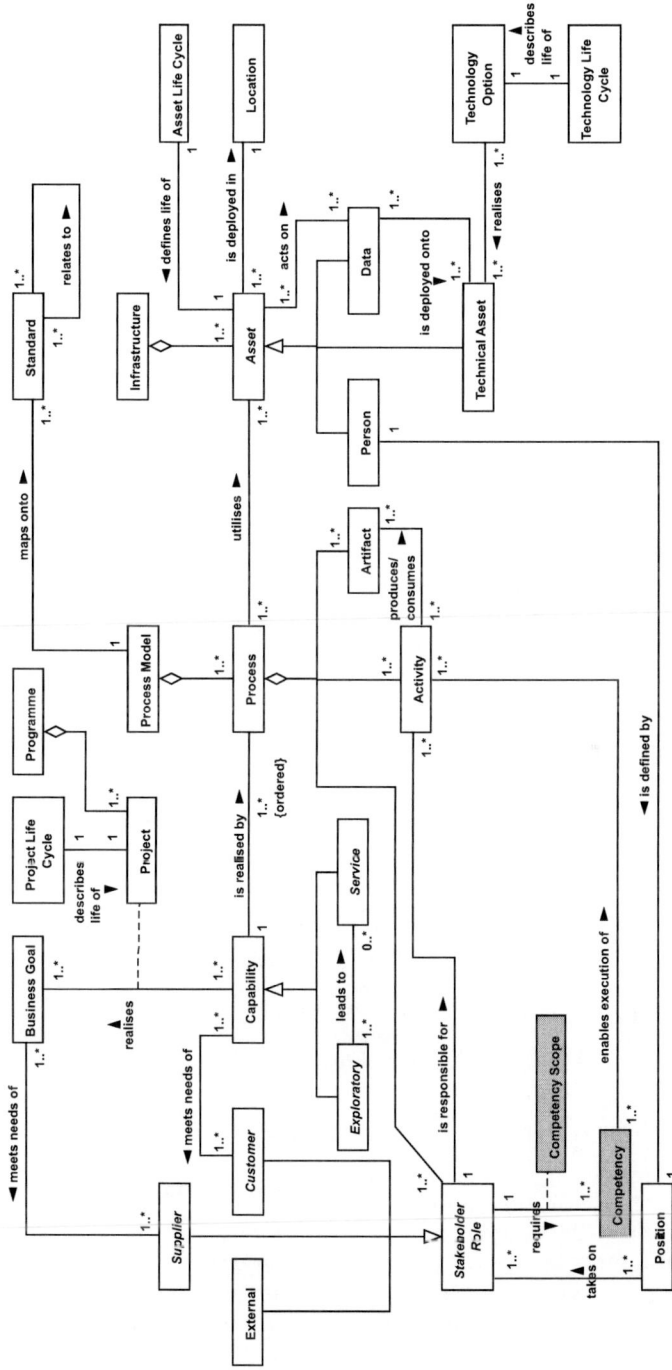

Figure 7.15 Competency View – the ontology highlighted

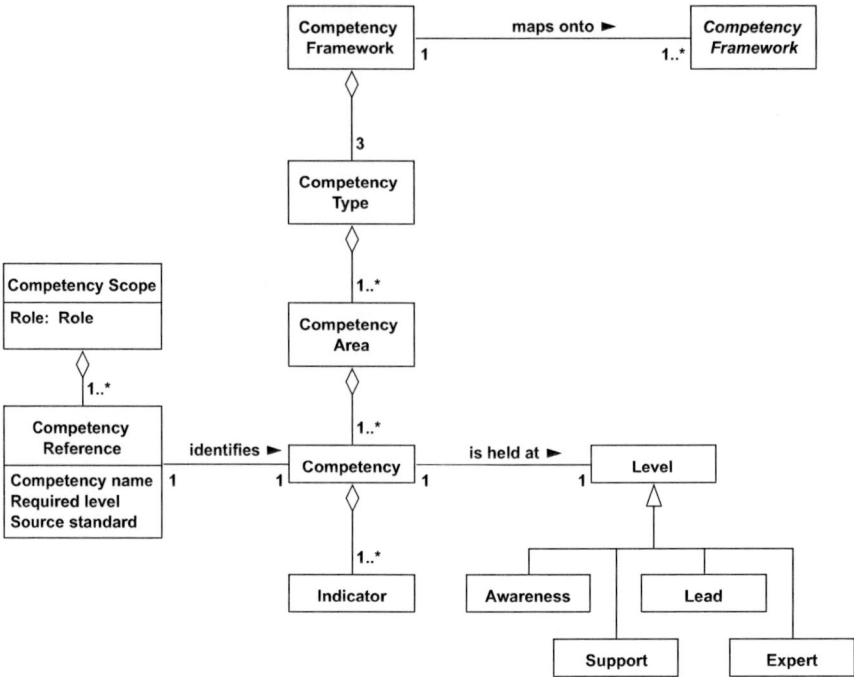

Figure 7.16   Competency View – View Concept Definition – High-Level

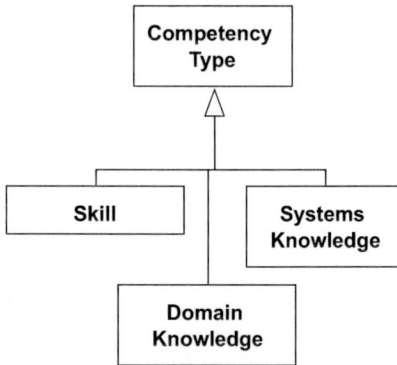

Figure 7.17   Competency View – View Concept Definition – Competency Type

detail in the 'View Concept Definition' and supporting diagrams (only one of which is shown here, the diagram in Figure 7.17 showing 'Competency Type', and which are considered to be part of the view definition), it would be possible to define additional views that show this extra information. That is the 'View Concept Definition' and supporting diagrams in Figures 7.16 and 7.17 would be simplified and expanded from a single *Competency View* into a number of related competency views. This is left as an exercise for the reader.

7.5.2.3 View content

The *Competency View* is realised as a number of UML object diagrams, one diagram per supplier stakeholder role. One such diagram is given in Figure 7.18.

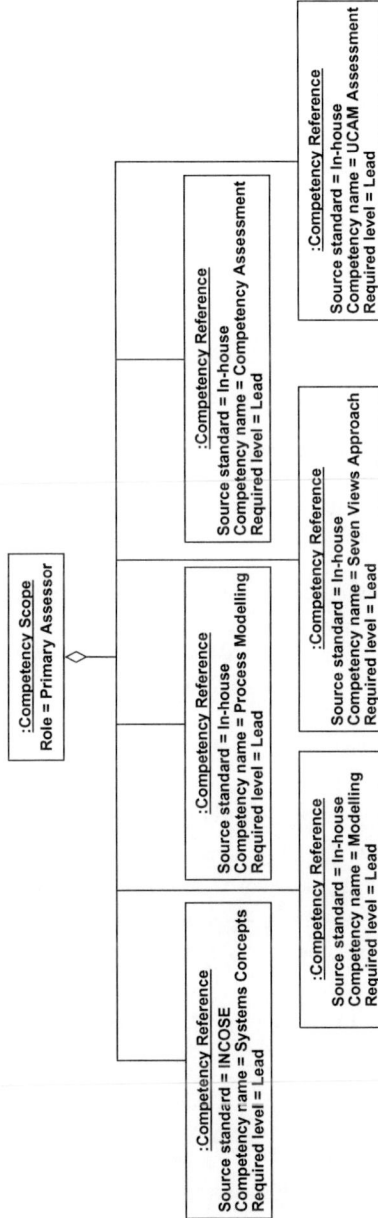

Figure 7.18 *Competency View – Primary Assessor – View Content*

The diagram shows the competencies for the role of 'Primary Assessor' as indicated by the value assigned to the 'Role' attribute in the 'Competency Scope' object.

Each competency is modelled as a 'Competency Reference' object with the attributes assigned the relevant values for the competency name, required level and source standard.

As can be seen, the Primary Assessor role requires six competencies, all to be held at the 'Lead' level. One of these (the 'System Concepts' competency) is defined in the INCOSE competency standard (the INCOSE Systems Engineering Competencies Framework). All the others are from the organisations own competency framework (represented as 'In-house' in the diagram).

7.5.2.4   Populating the quagmire

With the *Competency View* defined, it is added to the evolving quagmire. This is shown in Figure 7.19.

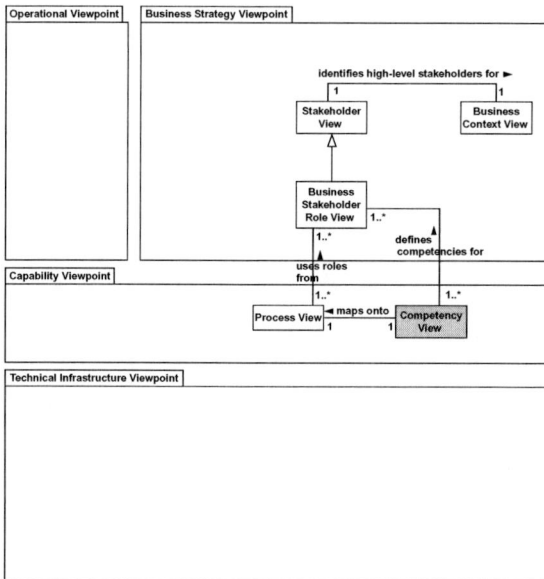

Figure 7.19   Architecture View Quagmire – Competency View added

Again, the *Competency View* is highlighted and any other views and relations shown as discussed in Section 7.5.

7.5.3   The project life cycle model view

Every project carried out by the organisation goes through a project life cycle. A view was needed that defined the life cycles of these projects. This view is called the 'Project Life Cycle View'.

7.5.3.1   View requirements

The 'View Requirements Set' for the *Project Life Cycle Model View* is given in Figure 7.20.

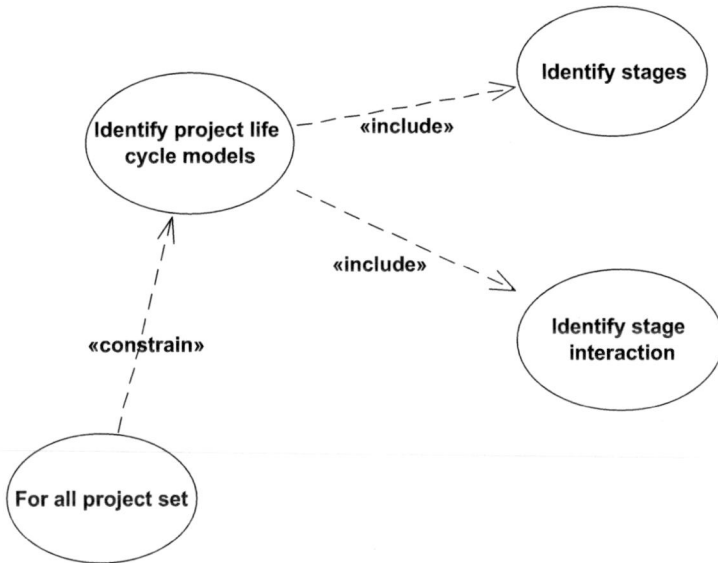

Figure 7.20   Project Life Cycle Model – View Requirements Set

The main requirement for this view is to 'Identify project life cycle models'. Life cycle models need to be identified for all projects carried out by the organisation (the 'For all project set' requirement). As part of identifying the project life cycle models, the view must also 'Identify stages' and 'Identify stage interaction' (i.e. how a project moves from one stage to another).

7.5.3.2   View concept definition

With the requirements for the view defined, the relevant elements from the ontology were identified. They are shown highlighted on the ontology diagram in Figure 7.21.

The highlighted elements on the ontology identify the key elements to be represented in the *Project Life Cycle Model View*, in this case the 'Project Life Cycle' and the 'Project'. These elements were then expanded on the 'View Concept Definition' to define all the elements to appear on the realisations of the view. This is shown in Figure 7.22.

The 'View Concept Definition' for the *Project Life Cycle Model View* shows that this view must show a 'Project Life Cycle' that describes the life of a 'Project'.

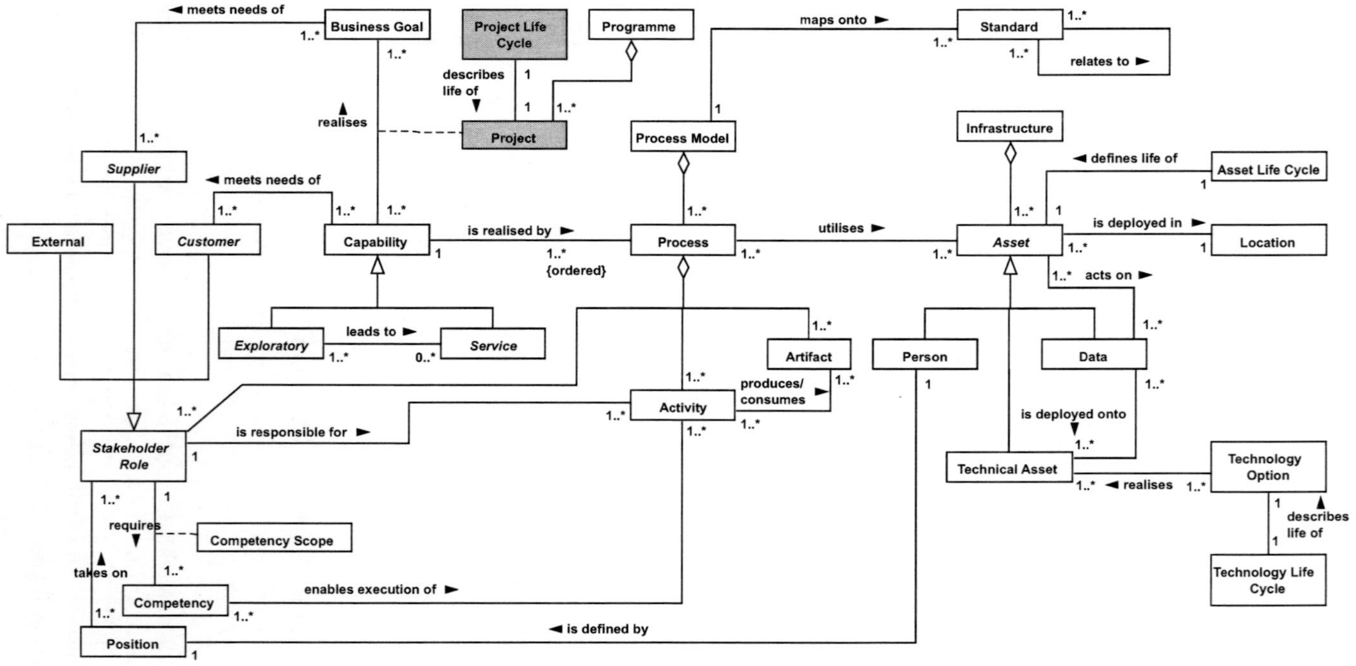

Figure 7.21   Project Life Cycle Model View – the ontology highlighted

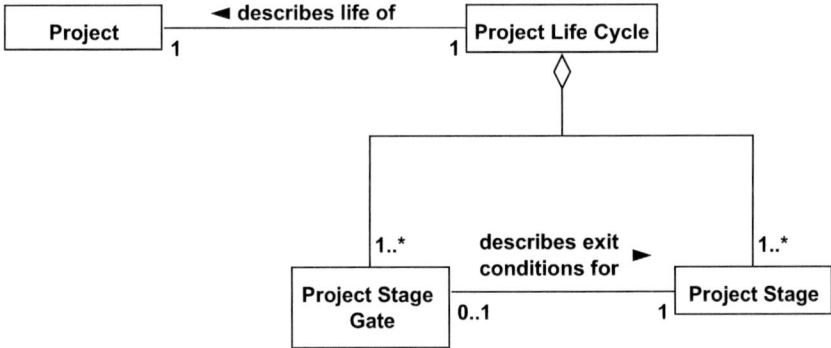

Figure 7.22   Project Life Cycle Model View – View Concept Definition

The 'Project Life Cycle' is made up of one or more 'Project Stage' and one or more 'Project Stage Gate' that describes the exit conditions for the 'Project Stage'.

It is worth noting here that this view shows the *Project Life Cycle Model*. That is its realisations should be *behavioural* diagrams that show the life cycle model for a given project that is the stages of an actual project and the way the project moves from one stage to another. In the full EA there is a related *structural* view, the *Project Life Cycle View*, that defines the project stages and gates that can apply to *any* project.

7.5.3.3   View content

The *Project Life Cycle Model View* is realised by a number of UML (or SysML) sequence diagrams, one diagram per project undertaken by the organisation. One such diagram is given in Figure 7.23.

The diagram shows the project life cycle model for a typical workshop as carried out by the organisation. It can be seen that the project went through five stages: 'Concept', 'Development', 'Construction', 'Operations' and 'Retirement'. As discussed earlier in the text, these stages are actually defined in another view (the Project Life Cycle View).

Such diagrams form part of the input to the organisational project planning process. The sequence diagram in Figure 7.23 is annotated with timing information to indicate the duration of each stage. Notes are used to show the criteria that must be met to exit the gate at the end of one stage for transition to the next stage.

7.5.3.4   Populating the quagmire

With the *Project Life Cycle Model View* defined, it is added to the evolving quagmire. This is shown in Figure 7.24.

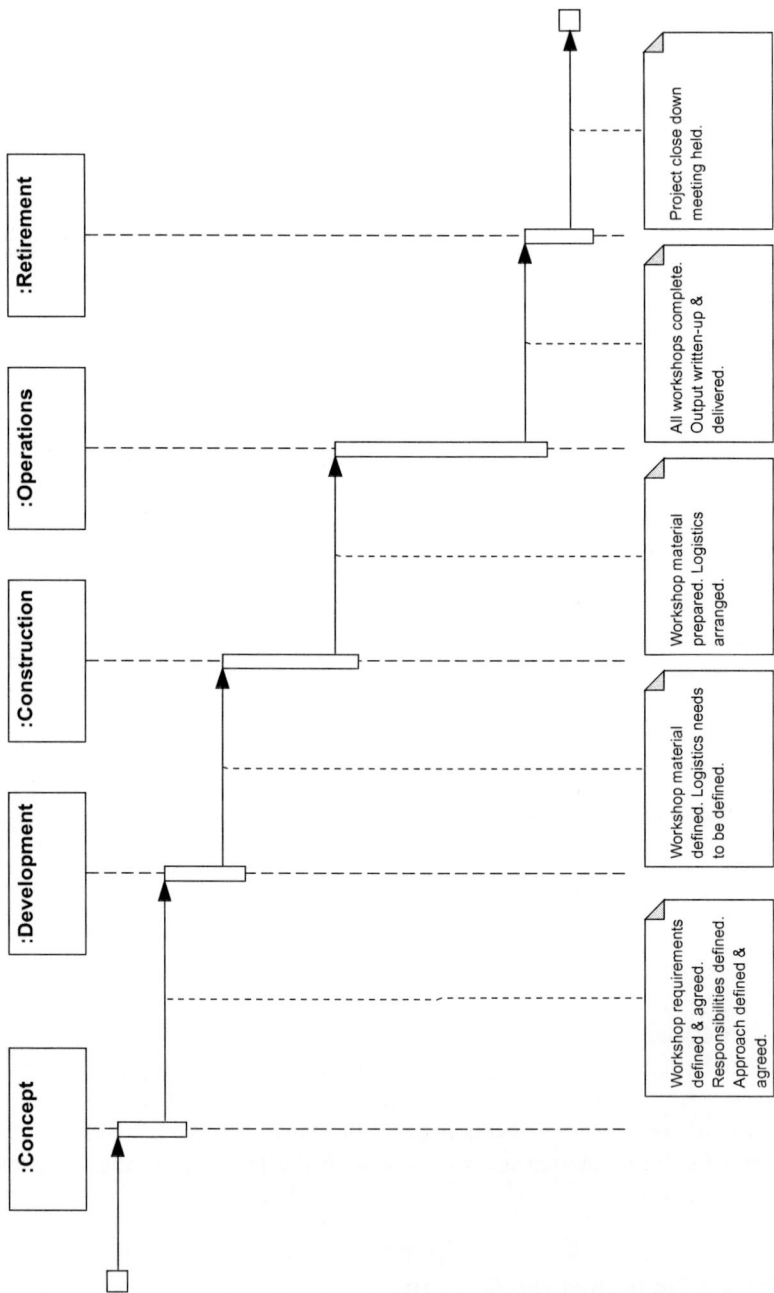

Figure 7.23   Project Life Cycle Model – Workshops – View Content

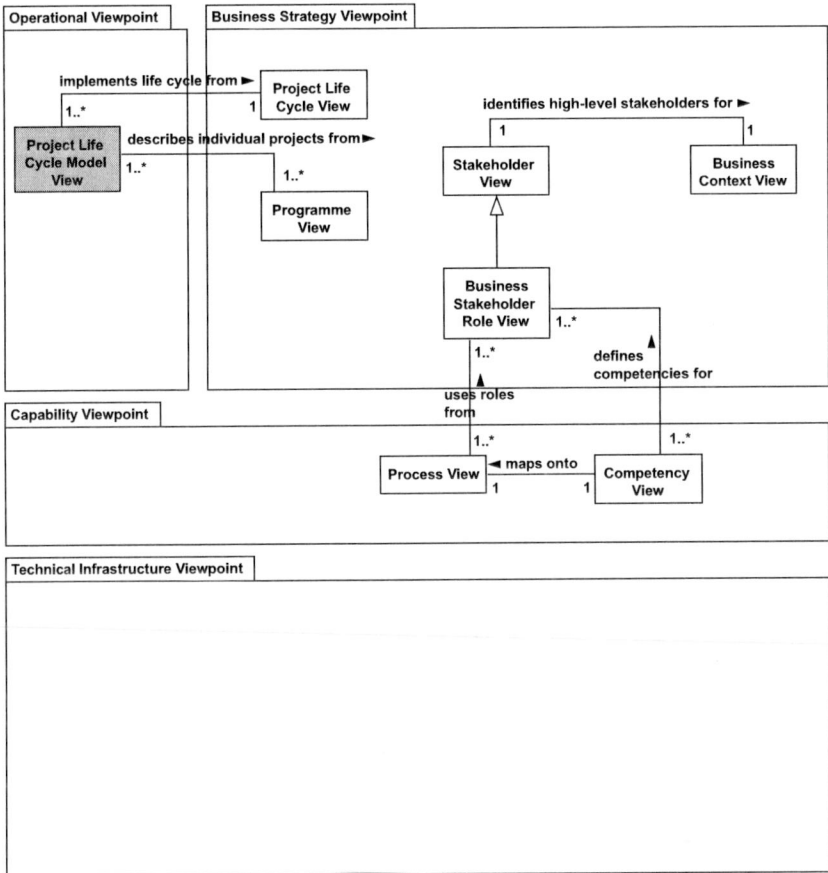

Figure 7.24   Architecture View Quagmire – Project Life Cycle Model View added

The *Project Life Cycle Model View* is shown highlighted. As with the *Business Context View* described in Section 7.5.1, the definition of the *Project Life Cycle Model View* suggests additional views, namely the *Project Life Cycle View* and the *Programme View*. These are also shown on the quagmire.

7.5.4   The infrastructure life cycle view

To help manage organisational infrastructure, a view was needed that defined the life cycles of the assets that make up the organisation's infrastructure. This view is called the 'Infrastructure Life Cycle View'.

7.5.4.1   View requirements set

The 'View Requirements Set' for the *Infrastructure Life Cycle View* is given in Figure 7.25.

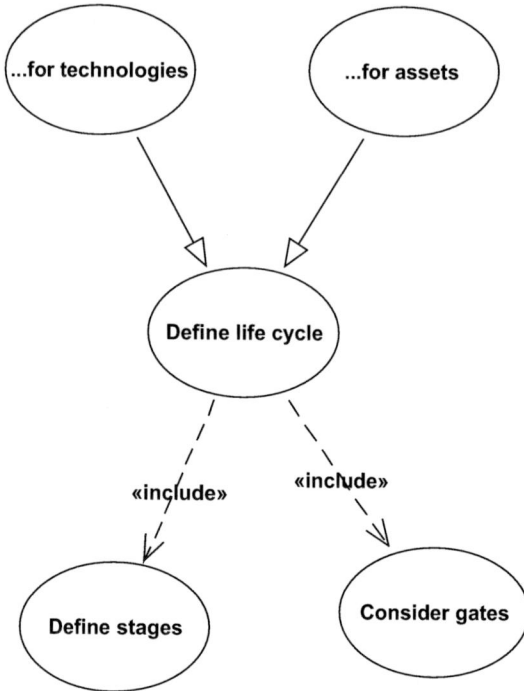

Figure 7.25   Infrastructure Life Cycle View – View Requirements Set

The main requirement for this view is to 'Define life cycle'. This has to be done for both the assets and the technologies that make up the organisation's infrastructure. As part of defining the life cycles for assets and technologies, it is important to be able to 'Define stages' relevant to the life cycle and also to 'Consider gates' that may be need to govern transition from one stage to another.

7.5.4.2   View concept definition

With the requirements for the view defined, the relevant elements from the ontology were identified. They are shown highlighted in the ontology diagram in Figure 7.26.

The highlighted elements on the ontology identify the key elements to be represented in the *Infrastructure Life Cycle View,* in this case the 'Asset Life Cycle' and the 'Technology Life Cycle'. These elements were then expanded on the 'View Concept Definition' to define all the elements to appear on the realisations of the view. This is shown in Figure 7.27.

The 'View Concept Definition' for the *Infrastructure Life Cycle View* shows that this view must show an 'Asset Life Cycle' made up of one or more 'Asset Stage' and a 'Technology Life Cycle' made up of one or more 'Technology Stage'.

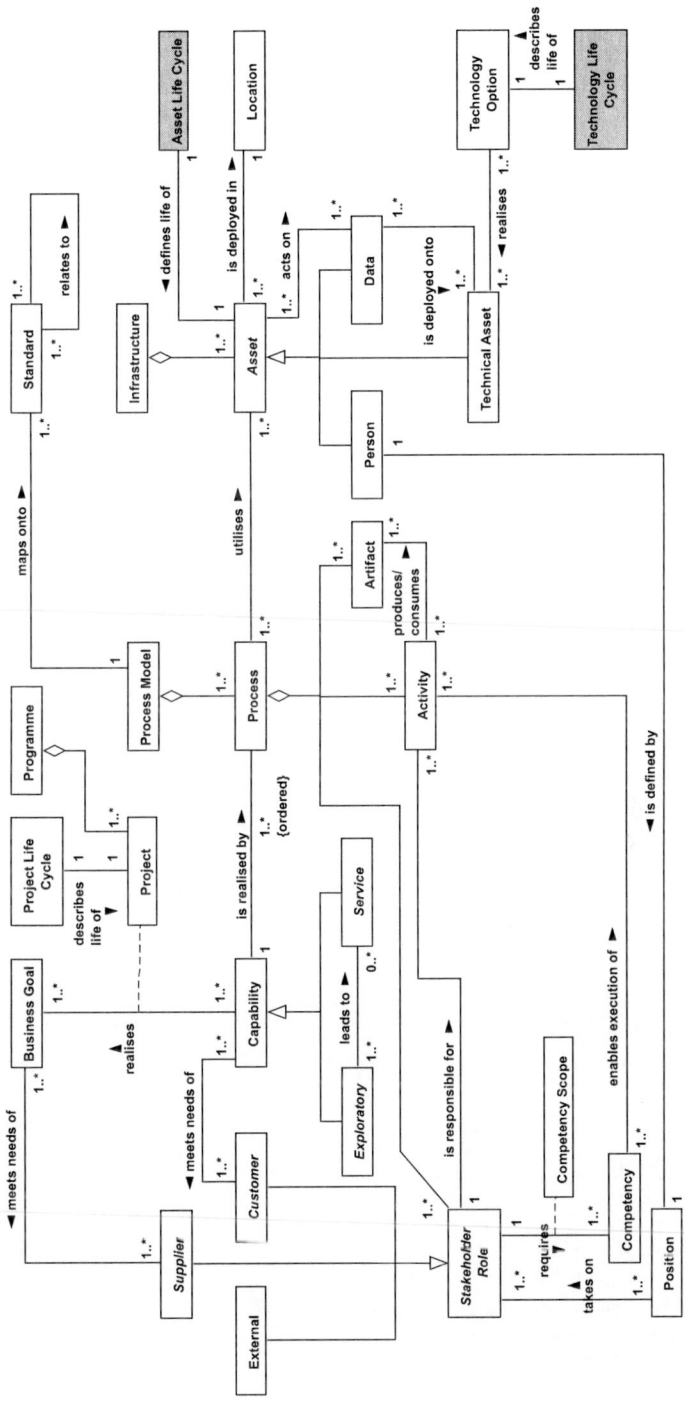

Figure 7.26 Infrastructure Life Cycle View – the ontology highlighted

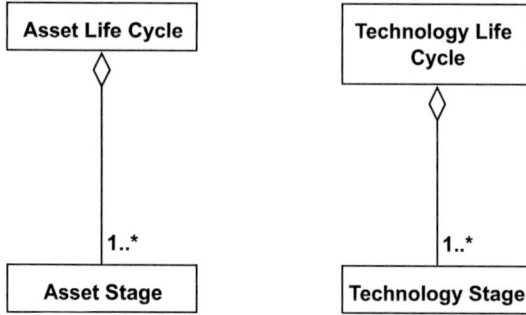

Figure 7.27   Infrastructure Life Cycle – View Concept Definition

There are a number of points to note here. They are as follows:

- As currently defined, the view does not say anything about 'gates'. That is the requirement 'Consider gates' from the 'View Requirements Set' is yet to be addressed by the view.
- Since a view can have a number of realisations, the definition does *not* imply that both asset and technology life cycles need to appear on the same diagram (or even the same type of diagram). The architect may put both life cycles on the same diagram should he so wish, but this is not a requirement of the definition.

The addition of 'gates' to the definition is left as an exercise for the reader.

7.5.4.3   View content

The *Infrastructure Life Cycle View* is actually realised (at the time of writing) by three diagrams. Two of them are given in Figure 7.28.

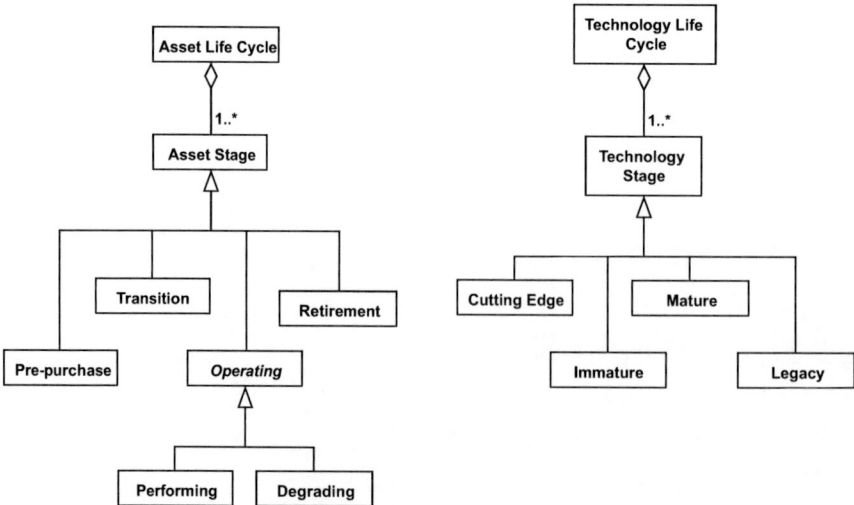

Figure 7.28   Infrastructure Life Cycle View – View Content

The diagram in Figure 7.28 defines the stages that make up both the 'Asset Life Cycle' and the 'Technology Life Cycle'. As discussed in Section 7.5.4.2 this diagram *could* have been split into two, one diagram for the 'Asset Life Cycle' and one for the 'Technology Life Cycle'. Given the relative simplicity of the diagram, this was felt to be unnecessary. However, once the definition of the view is extended to include 'gates', as it should be to fully meet the 'View Requirements Set', it may be necessary to split this diagram.

While this diagram defines the stages applicable to the asset and technology life cycles, it is purely structural. That is it says nothing about how these stages are related or sequenced. For this reason two behavioural diagrams (state machine diagrams) were also created for this view: one for the asset life cycle and one for the technology life cycle. The diagram for the asset life cycle is given in Figure 7.29.

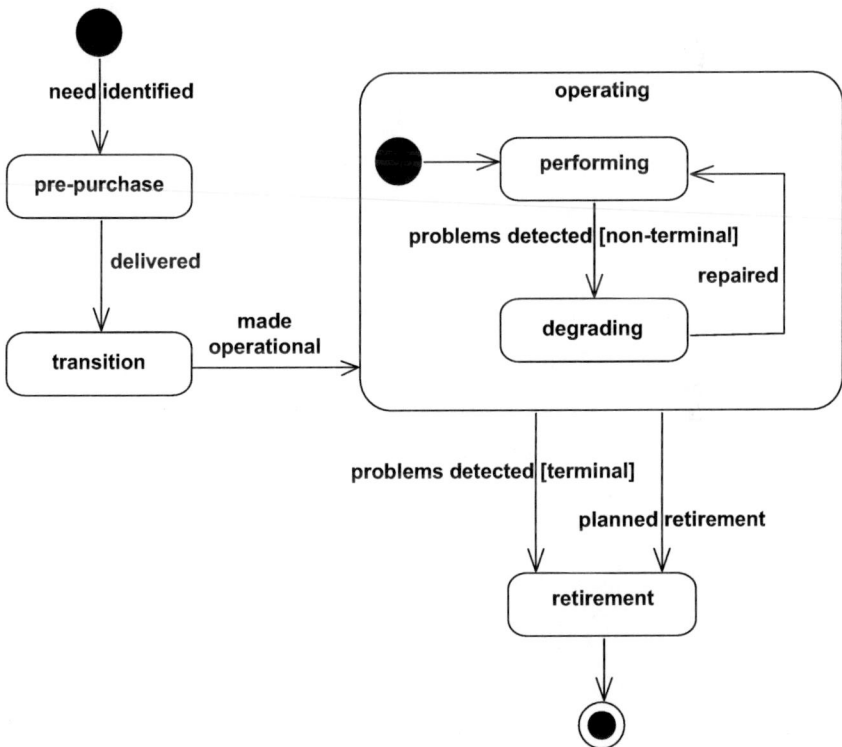

Figure 7.29   Infrastructure Life Cycle (Assets) – View Content

This state machine diagram shows how the life cycle stages for an asset are related and how an asset transitions from one life cycle stage to another.

Each life cycle stage from Figure 7.28 is represented as a state, with the 'Operating' stage and its two sub-types ('Performing' and 'Degrading') being represented by a composite state with two sub-states.

These two diagrams form an input to the organisational asset register. Every asset in the asset register has its current life cycle stage recorded (i.e. whether it is in pre-purchase, transition, performing, degrading or in retirement). For operating assets, their planned retirement dates are also recorded to enable forward planning of infrastructure needs.

7.5.4.4   Populating the quagmire

With the *Infrastructure Life Cycle View* defined, it is added to the evolving quagmire. This is shown in Figure 7.30.

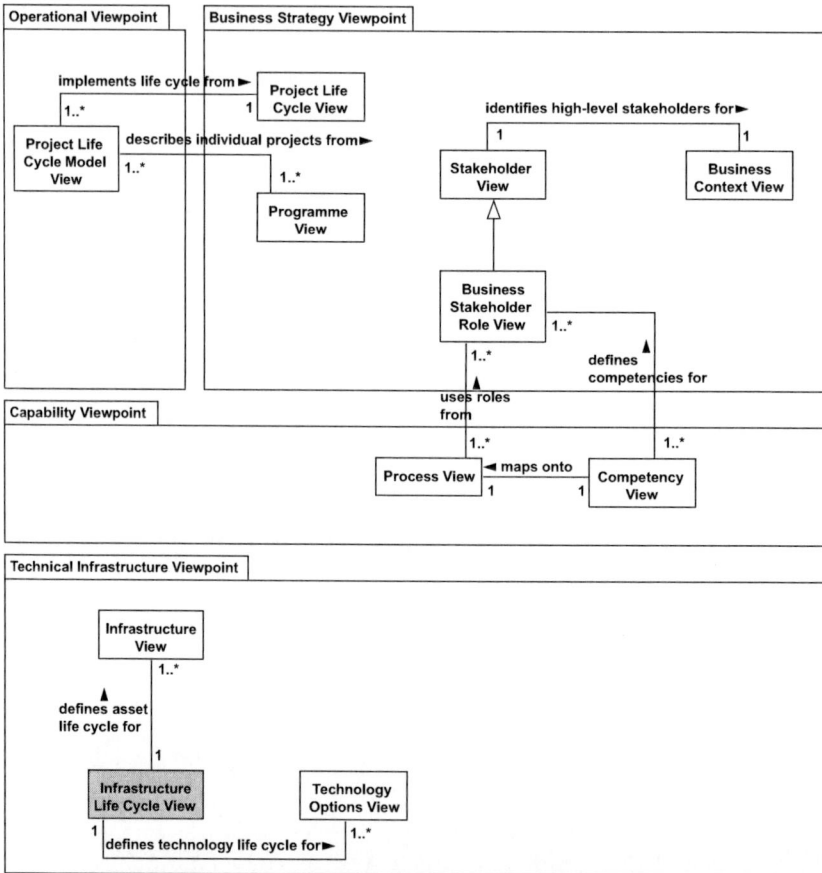

Figure 7.30   Architecture View Quagmire – Infrastructure Life Cycle View added

The *Infrastructure Life Cycle View* is shown highlighted. Again, the definition of the view suggests additional views, namely the *Infrastructure View* and the *Technology Options View*. These are also shown on the quagmire.

7.6 The complete architecture view quagmire

Figure 7.31 shows the completed 'Architecture View Quagmire' for the organisation.

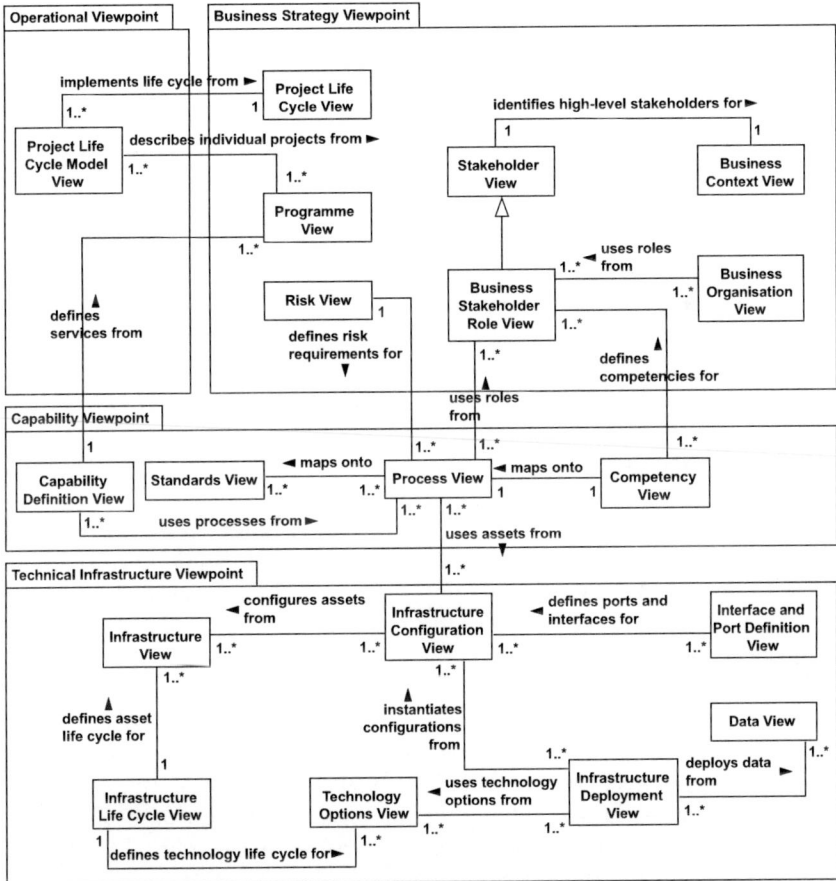

Figure 7.31 The Architectural View Quagmire – complete

The diagram shows every view in the EA, grouped into their viewpoints. The relationships between the views are also shown and help to ensure consistency of the EA.

For example, consider the 'Process View' and the 'Business Stakeholder Role View'. The quagmire shows that the 'Process View' *uses roles from* the 'Business Stakeholder Role View'. This means that any role appearing on the realisations of the 'Process View' *must* also appear on a realisation of the 'Business Stakeholder Role View'. Similar consistency checks apply to the other related view.

Again it must be stressed here that one view does not mean only one representation. Each view can have multiple realisations. For example, in the EA that this case study discusses the 'Competency View' is currently realised by eight UML object diagrams (one example of which was given in Section 7.5.2.3). Each of these diagrams corresponds to the competencies for one of the roles from the 'Business Stakeholder Role View'.

Also, it is important to understand that an EA is an evolving entity that has to be maintained and developed throughout its lifetime. Again, looking at the 'Competency View', this currently has diagrams defining competencies for eight roles. However, the 'Business Stakeholder Role View' defines more than eight roles. While the EA is *consistent*, since each of the 'Competency View' diagrams does define competencies for a role from the 'Business Stakeholder Role View', the architecture is still *incomplete* since not all the roles have competencies defined. A similar situation holds with some of the other views. This is to be expected. As the architecture is refined and maintained, with more and more realisations of views created, it will become more and more complete – at least until new views are defined!

7.7   Conclusions

Developing an EA is neither a trivial nor quick undertaking. Before starting out on the development of an EA it is vital to understand *why* it is being developed. What are the requirements for the EA? In the terms used in the meta-model discussed earlier in the text this corresponds to the establishment of the 'EA Business Requirements Set' and the 'EA Definition Requirements Set'.

Having established the need for and the requirements of the EA, many organisations make the mistake of attempting to generate views immediately. This is doomed to failure without two other elements of the architecture being in place. First, the ontology needs to be defined (at least to a level that captures enough concepts and relationships to allow thought to be given to the views). Second, the viewpoints that the EA will contain should be considered. These force the architect into thinking about the kinds of information that the EA will contain, since each viewpoint will contain related views. The 'Viewpoint Requirements Set' needs to be defined that gives the requirements for the viewpoints.

With the viewpoints defined (not all of which need to be defined at this point) thought can be given to the views that make up a viewpoint. Again, many EAs fail at this point because the views are generated with little thought to *why* the view is needed and *what* it is to contain. That is the 'View Requirements Set' and the 'View Concept Definition' elements of the meta-model are often neglected or, more often, completely omitted. It is these two elements that enable the architect to understand the information to be included in the view and to make sure that the view thus created is consistent with both the ontology and other views. Too often EAs are created at great cost which are nothing more than a collection of unrelated, inconsistent pictures generated seemingly out of thin air. Consistency should be the watchword of any enterprise architect.

The example given in this chapter and the discussion earlier all suggest a linear approach to the development of an EA. The reality will be very different, and is usually a much more iterative approach. When developing the EA discussed in this book the authors did *not* define all the viewpoints, then define and populate each view one by one. One or two viewpoints were defined and some views in each defined and populated. This lead to the realisation that additional views were needed, which may have belonged to an undefined viewpoint. This was then defined before moving back on to the views. And so on, moving from views to viewpoints to the ontology (as changes to it were discovered) through the various requirements sets and possible representations of views, each time resulting in a more complete, more consistent EA. A process that is still continuing.

Chapter 8
Example Frameworks

Most people are other people. Their thoughts are someone else's opinions, their lives a mimicry, their passions a quotation.

Oscar Wilde

8.1 Introduction

This chapter looks at some of the more widely used architectural frameworks that exist today. There are literally hundreds of frameworks and it would clearly be impossible to provide any sort of full comparison here. A small selection of frameworks will be discussed at a high level, and comments will be made on their use and suitability for different applications. Even if the frameworks do not apply directly to your industry, the principles on which they are based are generic ones and therefore there will be some aspects that probably will relate to most industries. The frameworks were chosen due to their popularity and widespread use, and their inclusion in this chapter does not certainly imply in any way that they are somehow necessarily superior to any architectural frameworks.

An architectural framework will specify a number of views and viewpoints that it is deemed necessary to produce to meet the requirements of that framework. It is important that the reason why the framework exists and, hence, its intended use is considered before one is adopted blindly – remember the old woman who swallowed a fly from Chapter 1. Also, it has to be borne in mind that a framework does not necessarily advise on how the views should be derived, but simply state what views should be derived and what sort of information each should contain. There are some frameworks that are not frameworks as such and are actually methodologies or processes that help you create frameworks, such as TOGAF, that is discussed in this chapter.

8.2 The Zachman Framework

8.2.1 Background

The Zachman Framework is a framework for enterprise architecture (EA). The Zachman Framework is one of the oldest and most mature frameworks and is certainly one of the most widely used in industry today.

The framework itself takes the form of a simple matrix, comprising rows and columns with intersecting cells that describe aspects of an entity. Usually there are 36 cells as the matrix usually has six rows and always has six columns.

Zachman derived the framework from the world of classical (building) architecture and, hence, the names of the views and the perspectives relate to the terminology of architecture.

8.2.2   Description

The basic ontology of the Zachman Framework can be seen in the diagram in Figure 8.1.

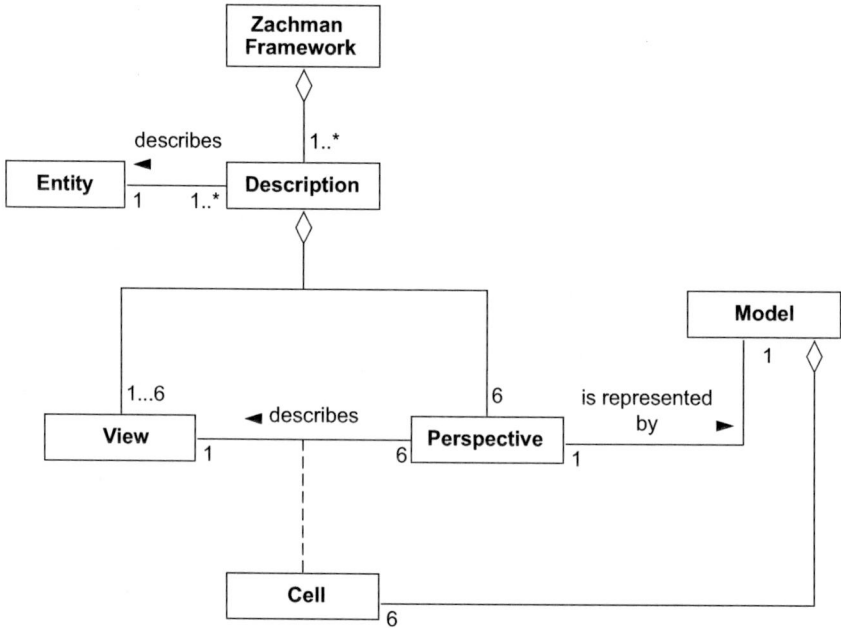

Figure 8.1   Overview of the Zachman Framework

The 'Zachman Framework' is made up of a 'Description' that can be created to describe any type of 'Entity'. These entities may literally be anything from abstract concepts to concrete systems, although the entities are usually enterprises or information systems.

This 'Description' is made up of a set of between one and six 'View' and a set of six 'Perspective'. Each 'View' is represented by a row on the matrix and each 'Perspective' is represented by a column on the matrix. For each 'View' there is a set of six 'Perspective'.

The intersection of each row and column on the matrix is a 'Cell' and the set of cells for each 'View' go to make up the 'Model' that represents the 'Perspective'.

The set of views is clearly defined and is expanded upon in the next diagram in Figure 8.2.

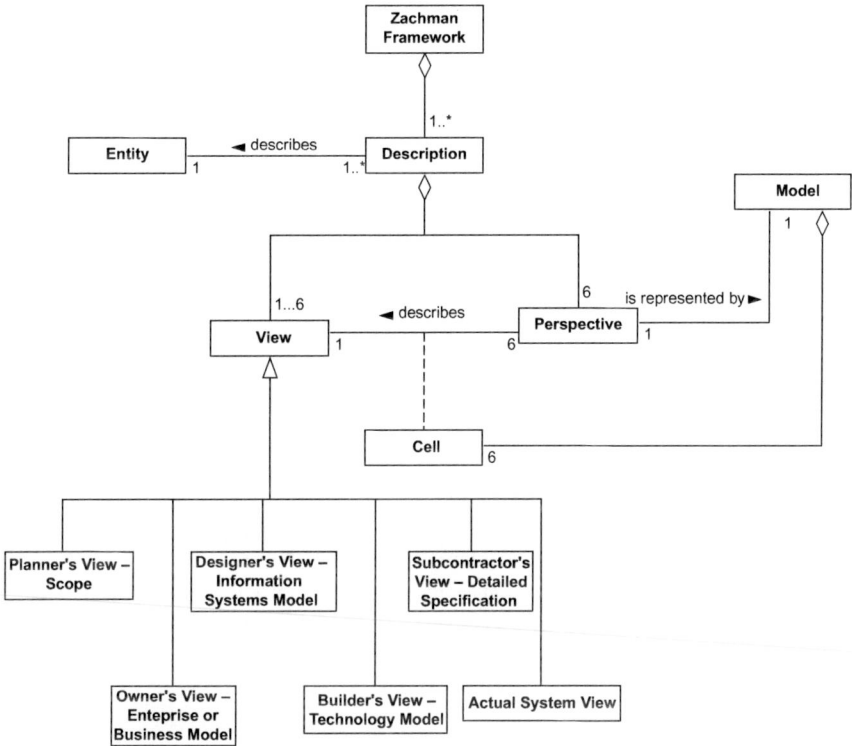

Figure 8.2   The Zachman Framework with a focus on views

From the diagram in Figure 8.2, it can be seen that there are six types of view:

- Planner's View – Scope. This may be thought of as an executive summary for the project. This will include aspects such as the overall size, cost, relationship to the environment, etc. This will help to define the scope and the context of the project.
- Owner's View – Enterprise or Business Model. This view represents the architect's plans that show a high-level view of the system from the owner's point of view. This will include the business entities such as processes that need to be understood to use the system properly.
- Designer's View – Information Systems Model. This represents the interpretation of the owners' views into something that can be used by the designers. This will usually be more technically detailed view such as data structures, behavioural, partitioning, etc.
- Builder's View – Technology Model. This view contains the same information as in the designer's view, but from the builder's point of view. Therefore, the emphasis will be on implementation issues and constraints such as tools, technologies, building materials, etc.

- Subcontractor's View – Detailed Specification. This could be the detailed designs that are given to the builders or programming team that are derived from the builder's view. In the case of off-the-shelf components, this would be the full specification for the systems or subsystems that are required. This view will also include any configuration, build and deployment information that is required.
- Actual System View. The actual systems that are being developed or modelled.

Not all of these views need to be defined, although it is usual to use all six. For each of these views, however, it is essential that all six perspectives are generated. These perspectives are shown in Figure 8.3.

The perspectives in the Zachman Framework are defined as follows:

- Data Description – What? This is a classic structural view that shows the main elements and the relationships between them.
- Function Description – How? This is a behavioural view that describes how each of the elements functions and also how they function together.
- Network Description – Where? This view shows the deployment aspects of the system elements and any dependencies between them.
- People Description – Who? This view shows the people involved in the view.
- Time Description – When? This view shows any temporal, or timing, aspects of the system.
- Motivation Description – Why? This view provides the basic rational or requirements for the view.

Both the views and the perspectives exist in the Zachman Framework and are constrained by a number of rules that describe how the views relate to one another. These rules are shown in Figure 8.4.

The Zachman Framework has seven basic rules that constrain the way the views and perspectives may be generated, and are described as follows:

- Rule #1 – The columns have no order. The columns, which represent the perspectives, have no particular order. For example, just because the 'motivation description' is last in the list, it does not mean that it is either created after the other perspectives or that it has less of a priority. The number of perspectives must always be six, and this cannot be reduced or increased in number.
- Rule #2 – Each column has its own model. Each perspective has its own model, and this model will be represented by any number of diagrams, description or other artefacts. Each perspective may also have its own meta-model that describes the structure of the model.
- Rule #3 – Each model is unique. Each model for the perspectives must be unique. It must be remembered that each model will have relationships with other models and must be consistent with other models.
- Rule #4 – Each row describes a unique perspective. Each of the rows represents a view of the systems from a particular point of view. Although there are usually six rows, there is no reason why there cannot be more or fewer of these

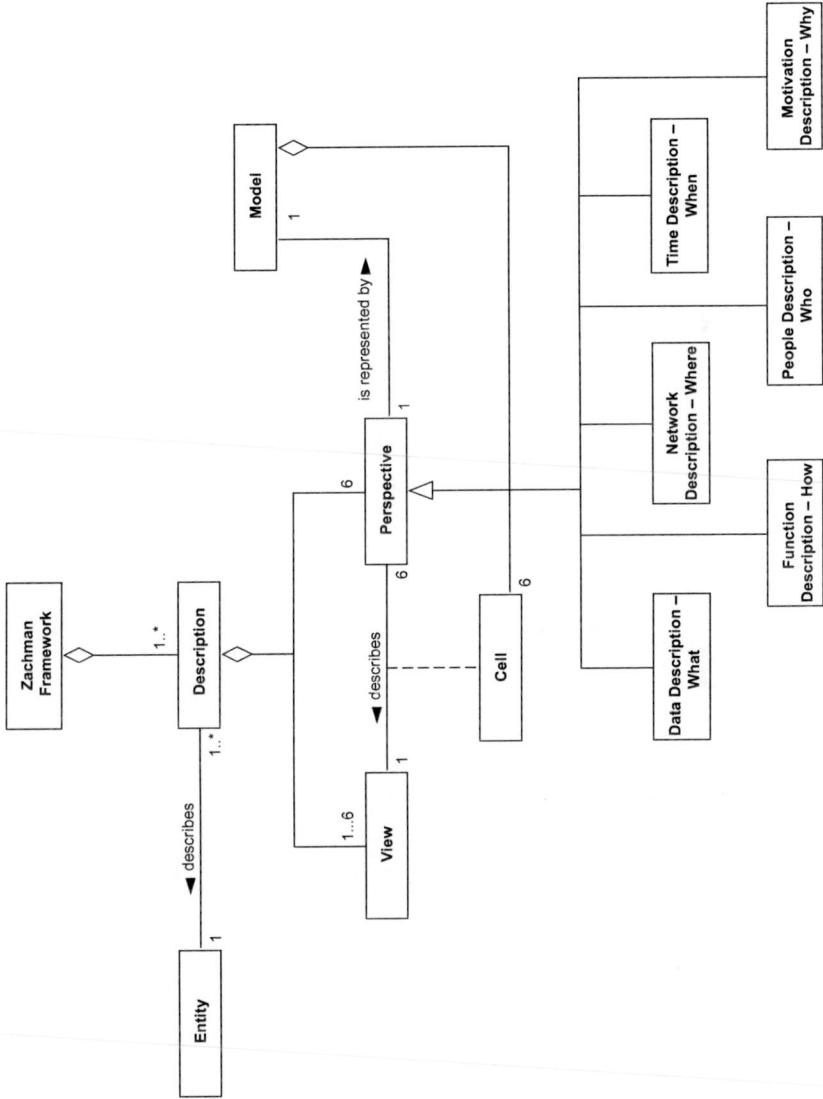

Figure 8.3 *The Zachman Framework with a focus on perspectives*

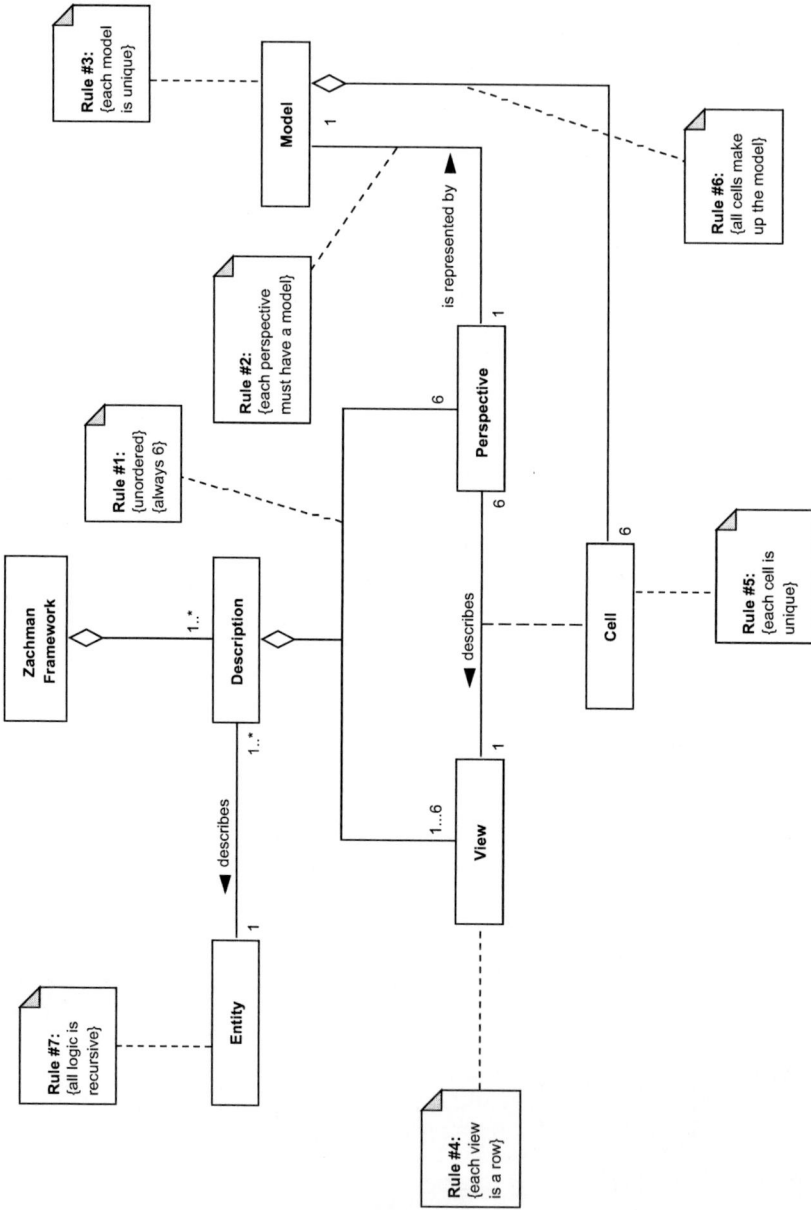

Figure 8.4   The Zachman Framework with a focus on rules

rows depending on the number of views identified. It is also usual for the views to be hierarchical in some way, so the first row represents the highest level view and the sixth (or lowest) represents the lowest level of abstraction.

- Rule #5 – Each cell is unique. If each model is unique (rule #3) and each row describes a unique perspective (rule #4), then each of the cells should also be unique.
- Rule #6 – All cells combine to form a model. To have a complete model for any particular perspective, each of the models and, hence, cells, for that row must be present. Therefore, the combination of all of the cells in a specific row forms the model for that perspective.
- Rule #7 – The logic is recursive. The logical structure of the framework and its models applies to all instances of the entity that is being modelled.

8.2.3 Discussion

The Zachman Framework is arguably the most widely used framework in existence. It is a pioneering framework that has been a direct influence on all the other frameworks mentioned in this chapter. The Zachman Framework has been used and implemented predominantly in the ICT world. The framework itself is very flexible as each of the cells on the matrix may be realised by anything from a simple statement or list to an entire model. Also, not all the cells need to be used, which makes the framework highly scalable. As a result of this flexibility and scalability, it is important that the rationale for each cell is fully understood, as the matrix, as it stands, does not dictate usage of the view, but what sort of information it should contain. Therefore, if one wanted to create a framework specific for a particular industry, the Zachman Framework would be an excellent start point and the relevant cells could be tailored to represent specific views in a bespoke framework.

8.3 Defence-based architectural frameworks

8.3.1 Introduction

One of the industries that use architecture frameworks extensively is the defence industry. Even if you do not work in the defence industry (or find it abhorrent), there is a lot that can be learned by examining some of the existing frameworks.

Many frameworks exist in the defence industry, three of which are very closely related: MODAF, DoDAF and NAF. Each of these will be discussed at a high level and then a further model will be considered – that of the Unified Profile for DoDAF and MODAF (one of the industry's finest moments, an abbreviation made up almost entirely of other abbreviations and acronyms).

8.3.2 Misuse of defence-based architectural frameworks

All of the frameworks discussed in this section are very often misused and applied in a completely incorrect working context. All of these frameworks have been designed with a specific use in mind, which is to improve the efficiency and effectiveness of the defence acquisition process. The defence industry is one where acquisition is essential to the successful realisation of its key objectives – to defend a particular nation, or group of nations. Bearing in mind the severity of the potential consequences of getting this wrong, it is no surprise that the sheer amount of effort that goes into ensuring that acquisition runs smoothly is enormous.

Each of these frameworks is intended to be used in a similar way, by defining views in several main categories. In all cases there are two generic categories of views that apply to all the others, which are the general descriptive views (known as 'All' views) and the standards definition views (known as the 'Technical'-type views). The other categories cover:

- The identification of programmes and projects within the organisation.
- The identification and definition of key capabilities that are required by the organisation.
- The definition of the operational elements, in terms of structure and behaviour, which are required to realise these capabilities. These elements are non-solution specific and allow the possibility of a variety of solutions to be evaluated.
- The definition of solution elements, such as systems and services that represent real-life elements that meet the needs of the operational elements.

These views are used to improve the acquisition of systems to enable capabilities. These frameworks are *neither* development architectures *nor* methodologies. Unfortunately, many people mistakenly use such frameworks as a basis for their development activities that will inevitably end in disaster. There is a strong relationship between the artefacts produced by a good development process and the information required to generate these views, but they are not the same and, indeed, the information required by the architectural frameworks is a fraction of the information required by and development process. With this in mind, several defence architectural frameworks are now described and discussed.

8.3.3   MODAF

8.3.3.1   Introduction

The Ministry of Defence Architectural Framework (MODAF) is the UK Government's specification for architectural frameworks for the defence industry. The framework itself is owned, managed and configured by the UK Ministry of Defence (MOD) and its documented specification is available in the public domain.

The MODAF takes both DoDAF and Zachman as two of its main influences. MODAF, however, describes more viewpoints and views than DoDAF, although it has a similar scope.

Key to any of these architectural frameworks is their underlying meta-model which, with MODAF, is specified using the Unified Modelling Language (UML). Unfortunately, the meta-model itself is very detailed and highly impenetrable and several attempts to simply it (such as the now-abandoned Enterprise Reference Model) have not really helped matters. Indeed, in the latest version of MODAF there is a high-level meta-model description that uses its own UML-like notation and that is massively inconsistent with itself – see the MODAF source documentation and apply basic modelling analysis to it [1].

The official definition of MODAF is as follows:

> MODAF: The MOD Architectural Framework (MODAF) is an enabler for managing complexity. It provides a specification of how to represent an integrated model of an enterprise, from the operational/business aspects to the Systems that provide capability, with appropriate Standards and programmatic aspects. It assists in managing complexity by providing a logical, standardised way to present and integrate models of the enterprise. By covering both the operational and technical aspects across the enterprise, MODAF-compliant Architectures enable all communities of interest to gain the essential common understanding that will be required to deliver the benefits to be derived from Network Enabled Capability (NEC). MODAF provides a rigorous method for understanding, analysing, and specifying: Capabilities, Systems, Systems of Systems (SoS), Organisational Structures and Business Processes. It is intended to facilitate the successful delivery of NEC. The key benefits that MODAF delivers are improvements to the specification and implementation of interoperability between Systems. MODAF supports a wide variety of MOD processes, including: capability management, acquisition and sustainment.

As with many defence-related things, this definition is not terribly clear and in some parts is clearly wrong (for example, 'MODAF provides a rigorous method for understanding, analysing, and specifying ...' – no it doesn't!).

The definition on an architectural framework used in MODAF is far more palatable and makes a lot more sense.

> Architectural Framework: An Architectural Framework (AF) is a specification of how to organise and present architectural models. Because Enterprise Architecture is such an all-encompassing discipline, and because the enterprises it describes are often large, it can result in very complex models. To manage this complexity, an AF defines a standard set of model categories (called "Views") which each have a specific purpose. These views are often categorised by the domain they cover – e.g. operational/business, technical, etc. – which are known in MODAF as Viewpoints.

Bearing this definition in mind, MODAF is intended to be used to improve the acquisition process and has now been mandated on all network-enabled capability (NEC) projects.

8.3.3.2 The MODAF viewpoints and views

The MODAF specification identifies seven viewpoints that are required to make up the full architectural framework. These are shown graphically in Figure 8.5 and are described in more detail in subsequent sections.

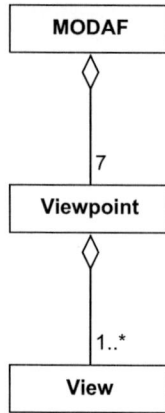

Figure 8.5   MODAF overview

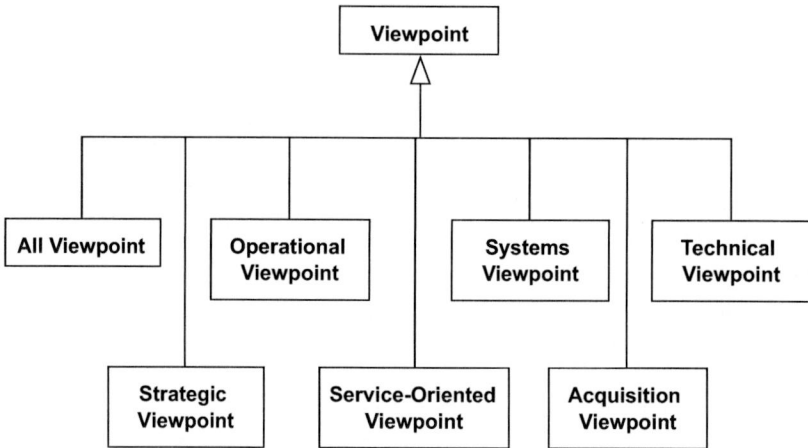

Figure 8.6   The MODAF viewpoints

The MODAF is made up of seven 'Viewpoint', each of which is made up of one or more 'View'. These viewpoints are simply collections of views and serve to group views that are used for similar purposes. The viewpoints are defined as follows.

The seven viewpoints are shown in the diagram in Figure 8.6 and are described as follows:

The 'All Views' viewpoint is created to define the generic, high-level information that applies to all the other viewpoints. This will define key information, such as:

- The scope of the architecture that is being defined by the architectural framework.
- The purpose of the architecture that is being defined by the architectural frameworks.
- A set of intended users and the views that will be generated. This is very important as, usually, not all the MODAF views will exist in a particular

framework. The number of views, what they are and how they are used will be dependent on the intended users of the framework. For example, a framework may consist of some strategic views and some operational views, and then this information may be used as part of the acquisition cycle as part of an invitation to tender. Organisations who intend to submit proposal for the tender may then be invited to respond (in part) by providing a set of system views that meet the operational elements defined in the operational views.

- The environment in which the architecture will be deployed may be identified or described here to provide some context.
- A defined set of terms in some sort of dictionary or ontology that must be used in the framework.

Clearly, this viewpoint will exist for all architectural frameworks.

The acquisition viewpoint is used to identify programmes and projects that are relevant to the framework and that will be executed to deliver the capabilities that have been identified in the strategy views. As well as the projects and programmes themselves, the relationships, timing requirements and dependencies between them are also identified. The views are intended to be closely coupled with the MoD's acquisition cycle, although no formal relationship between the views and the acquisition artefacts is defined. This is clearly something that does need to be defined.

The strategic viewpoint defines views that support the analysis and optimisation of military capability. The intention is to capture long-term missions, goals and visions, and to define what capabilities are required to realise them. The capabilities, once identified, can then be described and the relationships and dependencies between them defined. These views may be used for high-level analysis, such as capability gap analysis as well as being used as part of the acquisition process itself for defining the capabilities that must be delivered by the acquired systems and services.

The operational viewpoint contains views that describe the operational elements required to meet the capabilities defined in the strategic views. This is achieved by considering a number of high-level scenarios, and then defining what sort of elements, such as generic operational nodes and operational activities exist in the scenarios. The operational views are solution-independent and do not describe an actual solution. These views are used primarily of part of tendering where they will be made available to supplier organisations and form the basis of evaluating the system views that are provided as the supplier's proposed solution.

The system viewpoint contains views that relate directly to the solution that is being offered to meet the required capabilities that have been identified in the strategic views and expanded upon in the operational views. Therefore, there is a very strong relationship between the system viewpoint and the operational viewpoint. The system views describe the actual systems, their interconnections and their use. This will also include performance characteristics and may even specify protocols that must be used for particular communications. The system views, however, do constitute the design for the solutions; they represent a specification of what the systems are, how they work together and how they meet the required capability.

Ultimately, it is the combination of the system views and the service views (described next) that present the solutions offered by a particular vendor and form the basis for the acquisition decision.

The service-oriented viewpoint contains views that allow the solution to be described in terms of its services. This allows a solution to be specified as a complete service-oriented architecture where desirable. The service-oriented views are very similar to the system views and, indeed, it is the composition of these two viewpoints that form the solution to the required capability and form the basis for acquisition decision.

The technical viewpoint contains two views that allow all the relevant standards to be defined. This is split into two categories: current standards and predicted/future standards. Standards are an essential part of any architecture and it should be borne in mind that any number of standards may be applied to any element in the architecture.

The diagram here shows the high-level relationships between the different viewpoints.

Trying to remember what all the viewpoints are and how they fit together can be confusing and difficult, so visualise the viewpoints as in Figure 8.7 with five core viewpoints and two satellite ones, and then apply the following:

• The 'All Viewpoint' relates to the five core viewpoints and defines the terms and concepts used in each one.

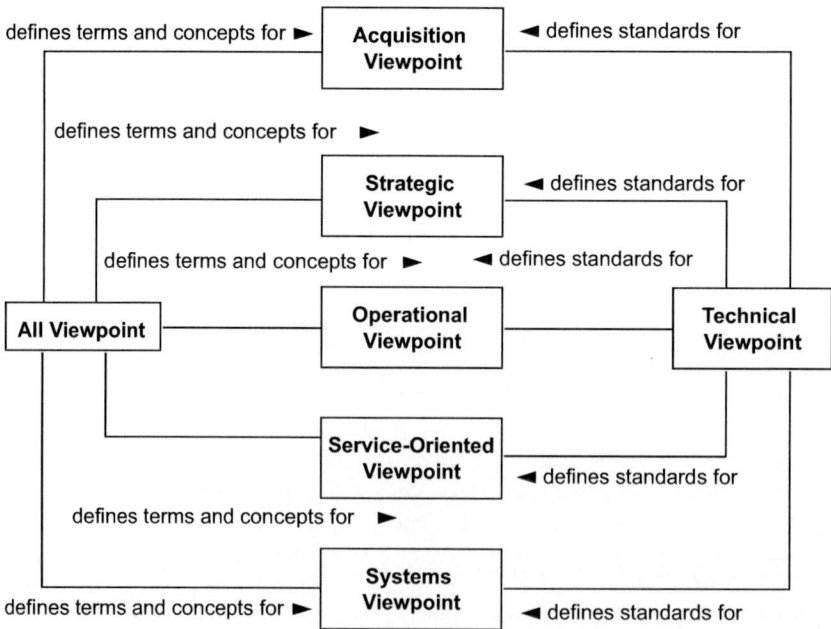

Figure 8.7   Overview of the seven viewpoints and their inter-relationships

- The 'Technical Viewpoint' defines the standards for the five core viewpoints.
- The 'Acquisition Viewpoint' identifies and defines projects and programmes.
- The 'Strategic Viewpoint' identifies and defines the required capabilities – what is needed.
- The 'Operational Viewpoint' analyses these capabilities and describes the operational elements required to satisfy them.
- The 'System Viewpoint' and 'Service-Oriented Viewpoint' allow potential solutions to be described that realise the operational elements and, hence, satisfy the required capabilities.

The viewpoints required will vary depending on who needs what information and what stage of the acquisition cycle is being considered.

Each of these views is described in some detail in the specification, with examples provided of how the views can be visualised. However, there are many different techniques used to realise each view, which is understandable as MODAF does not want to be too proscriptive, but this does lead to a lot of confusion and does not help the whole issue of trying to improve communication between stakeholders when everyone is using different notations. Also, there is no single example provided for all views – many examples are provided that change on a view-by-view basis, so it is difficult to see the consistency between views.

8.3.3.3 Discussion

MODAF is a very powerful framework that has a lot of application in the defence industry and the wider world. MODAF does have its own problems, such as inconsistencies in the meta-model and its lack of consistency with presenting view visualisations, but these can be overcome with some effort.

As these problems lead to a lack of consistency with visualisation of views, hence there is a knock-on effect with regard to tool implementation with different tool vendors implementing MODAF in different ways.

One possible solution to these problems is to adopt a set of guidelines for implementation, such as the UPDM, described later in this section.

8.3.4 DoDAF

8.3.4.1 Background

The Department of Defense Architectural Framework was first published in August of 2003, but did exist previously in the form of the C4ISR Architectural Framework (Command, Control, Communications, Computers, Intelligence, Surveillance and Reconnaissance) in the 1990s.

DoDAF has been a prime reference for both MODAF and NAF and is the most mature of the defence-based architectural frameworks. The latest version, at the time of publication, was in May of 2009 with the release of version 1.5 [2]. This version of DoDAF consists of three major parts: Volume 1: Manager's guide (117 pages), Volume 2, Architect's guide (284 pages) and Volume 3, Developer's guide (13 pages!). DoDAF defines itself as:

(DoDAF) serves as the overarching, comprehensive framework and conceptual model enabling the development of architectures to facilitate the ability of Department of Defense (DoD) managers at all levels to make key decisions more effectively through organized information sharing across the Department, Joint Capability Areas (JCAs), Mission, Component, and Program boundaries. The DoDAF serves as one of the principal pillars supporting the DoD Chief Information Officer (CIO) in his responsibilities for development and maintenance of architectures required under the Clinger-Cohen Act. It also reflects guidance from the Office of Management and Budget (OMB) Circular A-130, and other Departmental directives and instructions. This version of the Framework provides extensive guidance on the development of architectures supporting the adoption and execution of Net-centric services within the Department.

This rather verbose description boils down to being very similar to the other two frameworks discussed in this section.

8.3.4.2   Description

The basic structure and terminology used in the DoDAF is shown in the diagram in Figure 8.8. Note that the structure is the same as that of MODAF even though the terms used are different.

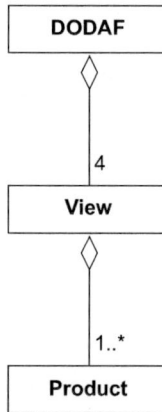

Figure 8.8   DoDAF overview

The diagram shown in Figure 8.1 shows that DoDAF is made up of four 'View', each of which is made up of a number of 'Product'. The four types of view that are defined are described in the following section.

The diagram in Figure 8.9 shows that there are four types of 'View' in DoDAF, which are as follows:

- The 'All View' that describes the general information associated with the architecture.

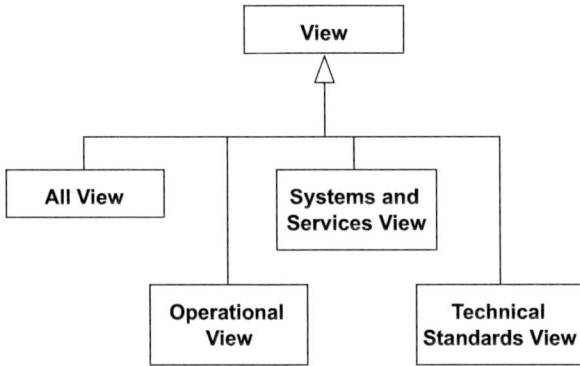

Figure 8.9   The DoDAF views

- The 'Operational View' that describes the operational elements in the architecture such as operational nodes and activities that are required.
- The 'Systems and Services View' that describes the solutions that realise the operational elements described in the operational view.
- The 'Technical View' that defines standards for all the architecture.

There are clear similarities between these views and the viewpoints that are described in MODAF and, due to the duplication of concepts, the descriptions here are kept deliberately brief.

The relationships between these views are shown in the diagram in Figure 8.10.

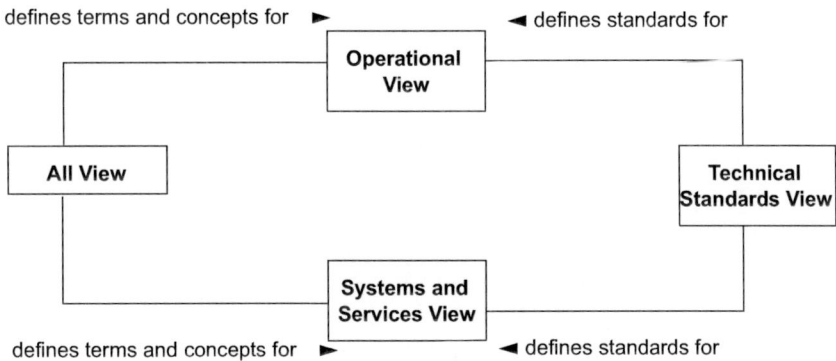

Figure 8.10   Relationships between views

The diagram in Figure 8.10 shows the relationships between the views in DoDAF. It can be seen that the 'All View' defines the terms and concepts for the 'Operational' and 'Systems and Services Views'. Likewise the 'Technical Standards View' also applies to both the 'Operational View' and the 'Systems and Services View' by defining their standards.

8.3.4.3   Discussion

The DoDAF bears a startling resemblance to MODAF, which is not surprising as DoDAF was the starting point for MODAF. The main difference between the two is that MODAF has added more views, but with a new, updated version of DoDAF imminent at the time of publishing this book, this is set to change.

DoDAF is arguably the most mature of all the defence-based architectural frameworks and, as such, has a wealth of experience and lessons learned that will be used as inputs to the new version. Although the content is not yet confirmed, it is strongly suspected that DoDAF will increase the number of its views to bring it more in line with MODAF and NAF.

8.3.5   NAF

8.3.5.1   Background

The NATO (North Atlantic Treaty Organisation) architectural framework (NAF). Version 3 of the NAF weighs in at a mind-numbing 882 pages! The whole specification is made up of an executive summary, seven main chapters and three annexes that describe all aspects of the NAF [3].

Initial versions of NAF were based mainly on DoDAF, but version 3 is based on both DoDAF and MODAF as well as experiences gained from many other countries.

8.3.5.2   Description

The structure of NAF is shown in the diagram in Figure 8.11.

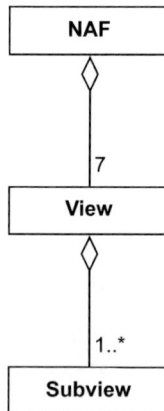

Figure 8.11   Overview of NAF concepts

The diagram in Figure 8.11 shows that the 'NAF' is made up of seven 'View', each of which is made up of a one or more 'Subview'. A 'View' here is defined as a set of subviews that are grouped by purpose. There are a number of 'main' subviews per view, but some of these main subviews have several parts that make up the view. Sometimes these parts are denoted by an additional letter, such as 'NOV-6a', whereas some others are not further denoted.

The seven views may be expanded directly from this diagram, as shown in Figure 8.12.

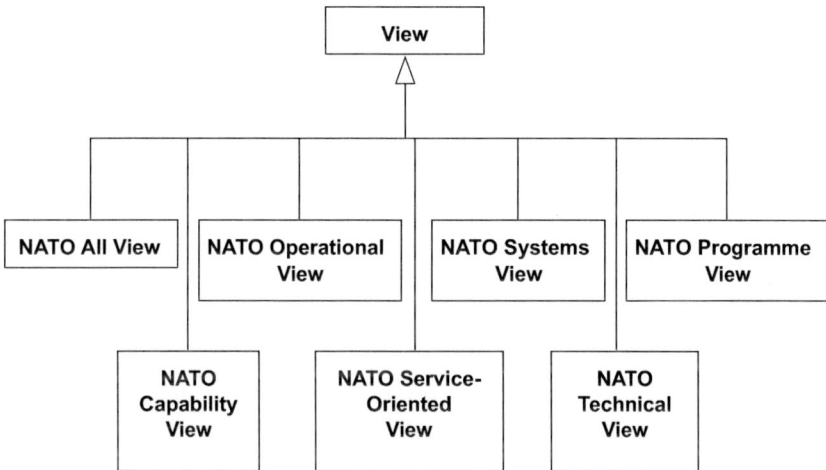

Figure 8.12   The seven views

The seven views in the NAF are:

- NAV, the NATO All View. The NAV consists of three main subviews that describe the overarching aspects of architectures that apply to all views in the NAF.
- NCV, the NATO Capability View. The NCV consists of seven main subviews, and captures the essential elements of NATO's strategic vision and concepts and NATO's capability planning process.
- NOV, the NATO Operational View. The NOV consists of seven subviews and describes the tasks and activities, operational elements and information exchanges required to accomplish NATO missions.
- NSOV, the NATO Service-Oriented View. The NSOV consists of five sub-views and describes the services needed to directly support the operational domain described in the NOVs.
- NSV, the NATO Systems View. The NSV consists of 12 main subviews and describes the systems and interconnections required to directly support the operational domain.
- NTV, the NATO Technical View. The NTV consists of three main subviews and describes the technical implementation guidelines upon which engineering specifications are based.
- NPV, the NATO Programme View. The NPV consists of two main subviews and describes the relationships between NATO capability requirements and the various programmes and projects that are implemented in the programmes.

Due to the similarity between NAF and MODAF, the descriptions here are kept deliberately brief.

The basic relationships between the seven views are captured in the diagram in Figure 8.13.

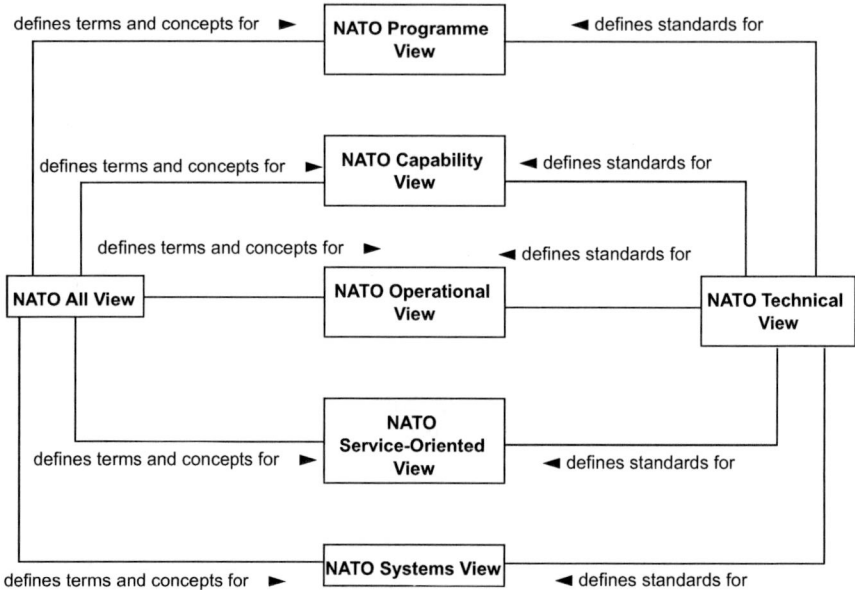

Figure 8.13   Relationships between the seven views

The diagram in Figure 8.13 is almost identical to the one shown in Figure 8.7 and all the same points apply. Note that the only differences between the two are that:

- The NAF views all have the word 'NATO' in front of them and, hence, the extra letter 'N' in their abbreviations.
- What is called the 'Acquisition Viewpoint' in MODAF is named the 'Programme View' in NAF – a far more sensible and intuitive name.
- What is called the 'Strategic Viewpoint' in MODAF is named the 'Capability View' in NAF – a far more sensible and intuitive name.

This only goes to show how similar the frameworks are.

8.3.5.3   Discussion

The NAF is almost identical to MODAF and, hence, very similar to DoDAF. All three of these frameworks are very similar, although they each use slightly different terminology. This difference in terminology can be seen by comparing the information in Figures 8.5, 8.8 and 8.11 and can be summarised in Table 8.1.

As can be seen in Table 8.1, there are several key concepts that are common to all three of the frameworks but they do use different terms. Care must be taken,

Table 8.1   Comparison of terminology between frameworks

MODAF	DoDAF	NAF
Viewpoint	View	View
View	Product	Subview
All Viewpoint	All View	NATO All View
Acquisition Viewpoint	–	NATO Programme View
Strategic Viewpoint	–	NATO Capability View
Operational Viewpoint	Operational View	NATO Operational View
Systems Viewpoint	Systems and Services View	NATO Systems View
Service-Oriented Viewpoint	Systems and Services View	NATO Service-Oriented View
Technical Viewpoint	Technical Standards View	NATO Technical View

however, as the term 'View' actually means different things depending on which framework it refers to.

8.3.6   UPDM

8.3.6.1   Background

One of the main goals of all three of the defence-related architectural frameworks is to enable some form of NEC. This is a great idea in theory, but there are some key issues that must be addressed before this can be achieved:

- Consistency of each architectural framework. It has been discussed in this book that it is key to get the underlying meta-model and ontology consistent and correct before an effective architecture can be realised. To date, there have been some problems with inconsistency of the information presented as part of the specifications for these frameworks. As such, there is a certain amount of work involved to realise their associated views successfully.
- Visualisation of views. Each of the framework descriptions tries to be a generic as possible to avoid being proscriptive, whilst trying to be as detailed as possible so as to make the framework meaningful. This is no mean feat and the two requirements are themselves contradictory. For example, MODAF will make several recommendations of various notations that may be used to visualise each view, but surely this goes against the fundamental need to a common language?
- Working between the frameworks. Working between nations is becoming an increasingly important requirement. Imagine the situation where the United States and the United Kingdom are working together, bearing in mind that both are members of NATO. Which framework should each nation use? Clearly there is a need for a common communication mechanism that can be used between the various frameworks and nations.

The Unified Profile for DoDAF and MODAF sets out to address these issues.

8.3.6.2   Description

The UPDM started life as the 'UML Profile for DoDAF and MODAF' but has since been renamed the 'Unified Profile for DoDAF and MODAF' [4]. The UPDM is *not* an architectural framework but is a profile of UML and SysML that can be used to visualise many of the views in MODAF and DoDAF. The key thing to remember about the UPDM is that it is really a set of guidelines on exactly how to visualise each view to achieve consistency and, hence, interoperability between the frameworks. The UPDM takes each view or subview, or product, depending on the framework, and states exactly how that view must be realised.

8.3.6.3   Discussion

The UPDM is unusual in that it is not a framework, but a profile. As such it should really be viewed as a set of guidelines or rules on how to visualise each view. This is an excellent idea in theory as it means that, when implemented correctly, it is possible to achieve true interoperability between the various nations and the frameworks that they adopt. On the other hand, it can be argued that the UPDM is too restrictive and, therefore, not a good way to implement any of the frameworks.

8.3.7   TOGAF

8.3.7.1   Background

The Open Group Architectural Framework (TOGAF) is described as being 'the *de facto* global standard for assisting in the acceptance, production, use and maintenance of architectures'. Grand words, indeed, but TOGAF does have an incredible track record for defining architectures when applied correctly. This final qualifier is carefully chosen as many people will cite TOGAF as a source for their EA but do not actually follow it properly [5].

8.3.7.2   Description

TOGAF describes an approach to manage and control the development and delivery of an EA. The key constructs involved with TOGAF are shown in the diagram in Figure 8.14.

The main aim of TOGAF is to develop an 'Enterprise Architecture' that fulfils the 'Need' (both the 'Business Need' and 'Information Need') of the organisation. The EA is made up of four 'Architecture Domain', which are as follows:

- The 'Business Architecture'. This is the business strategy, organisation and key business process information that describes the business. The business architecture not only defines each of these elements, but also the relationships between them.
- The 'Applications Architecture'. This is the major logical grouping of capabilities needed to support the architecture.
- The 'Data Architecture'. This forms the structure of an organisation's logical and physical data assets and resources.
- The 'Technical Architecture'. This is the description of the architecture that is to be produced, often referred to as the 'future architecture'. Usually, a number of technical architectures will exist that may then be evaluated before one is finally implemented.

The Architecture Development Method, or ADM, is the formal approach that is described by TOGAF to manage and control the development of architectures.

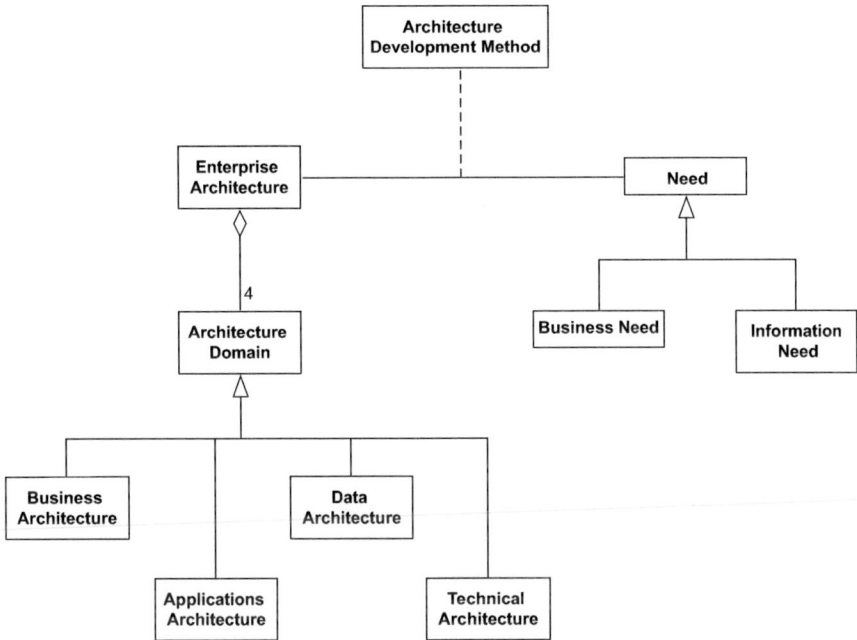

Figure 8.14   TOGAF structural concepts

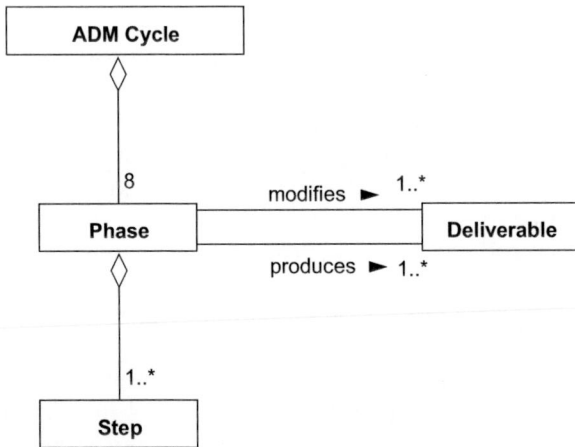

Figure 8.15   The Architecture Development Method (ADM) structure

The diagram in Figure 8.15 shows that the 'ADM Cycle' is made up of eight 'Phase'. Each of these phases is made up of one or more 'Step' and modifies and produces one or more 'Deliverable'. The phases themselves are shown in the next diagram in Figure 8.16.

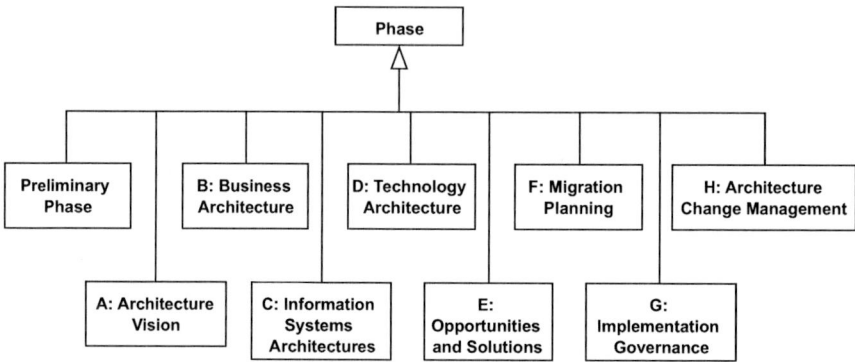

Figure 8.16   The ADM phases

The diagram in Figure 8.16 shows the eight phases that make up the ADM cycle. The first thing that stands out here is that there are nine phases and not eight, as described in the documentation. This is because there is an initial phase, known as the 'Preliminary Phase' that is not included in the general list of eight phases.

- The *preliminary phase* is executed once and is intended to set up the whole project. This includes ensuring that buy-in is obtained from all relevant stakeholders defining any high-level architectural principles that will be applied throughout the project. Any processes, standards, methodologies and specific techniques that will be employed are identified at this point, so that it can be ensured that there are sufficient competencies in place. The basic scope and context of the architecture are defined, along with validation criteria and any associated process that will be used to ensure that the architecture meets its stated goals. All roles and responsibilities are also stated at this point. From an EA point of view, this is very interesting as all this information will be used to form views in the EA itself.
- Phase A is named 'Architectural Vision', and is primarily concerned with defining the high-level requirements of the architectural and getting the formal go-ahead for the architectural work approved. This will include the business requirements (such as business goals, business principles and business drivers) and the constraints that will impact these requirements. The scope and main components of the baseline architecture are also defined at this point. The baseline architecture here refers to existing architecture when the current Phase A begins. In the case that the preliminary phase has just been run, there will

be no architecture as such. The main stakeholders are identified at this point and their requirements defined.

- Phase B is named the 'Business Architecture' phase. The business architecture is the first of the four architecture domains, as shown in Figure 8.14, which should be defined as it drives the remaining three phases. The business architecture describes the product or service strategy (in terms of organisation, function, process, information and deployment) based on the architectural vision that was generated during Phase A. As a general architectural principle, re-use is explored here to optimise the system development and the choice of tools may also be looked at.
- Phase C is known as the 'Information Systems' phase and is concerned with developing the information and/or application architectural domains. These are the second and third domains that were identified in Figure 8.14 and will be based on the business architecture developed during Phase B. The scope of Phase C is limited to the IT-related processes and the non-IT processes that are directly related to IT (support processes).
- Phase D is known as the 'Technology Architecture'. The aim of the technology architecture is to provide a complete description of the logical software and hardware capabilities that are used to support the information and application architectures. The technology architecture forms the basis of the implementation work.
- Phase E is known as the 'Opportunities and Solutions' phase. The main aim of Phase E is to plan the implementation of the architecture by looking at various solutions that may meet the requirements or any other opportunities that may be applicable. For example, decisions may be made here to decide whether to develop a solution or to go for a COTS (commercial off-the-shelf) approach to realising the components of the architecture. This phase will also decide the resources and budgets to be used, along with identifying the high-level work packages or projects required to realise the architecture.
- Phase F is known as the 'Migration and Planning' phase. This phase is concerned with sorting the various projects or work packages associated with the architecture into some sort of order. This will depend on the priorities assigned to each project or work package and the dependencies between them. This will result in the production of a detailed implementation and migration plan.
- Phase G is known as the 'Implementation Governance' phase. It is during this phase that the actual projects are executed and this phase is concerned primarily with coordinating and managing these projects, to ensure that they deliver the architecture.
- Phase H is known as the 'Architecture Change Management' phase. This phase ensures that any changes to the architecture are managed and controlled in an effective manner. This phase effectively implements a change management process that applies to the architecture.

These phases are executed in a continuous cycle, with the start point for a new architecture being the preliminary phase and then each of the phases, A through H, executed in a number of cycles. It should be noted here that the emphasis with TOGAF is very much based on the management or developing an architecture, rather than the actual development. This can be seen clearly in Phase G, where the development work is going on in parallel with the phase itself.

Each stage is described in terms of its objectives, the approach to be adopted, the inputs and outputs to the phase and the steps involved with delivering the phase.

8.3.7.3   Discussion

The term 'framework' is somewhat of a misnomer when it comes to TOGAF. TOGAF itself is not actually an architectural framework but, rather, a set of phases and associated processes in the form of the ADM that will enable an EA to be created for an organisation. TOGAF does not define any particular views (although it does hint strongly at some) but focuses on how to manage the development and delivery of the architecture. This is an important point as the TOGAF is effectively a management-based approach and, hence, focuses largely on management and planning, rather than the actual development of the architecture and its views.

8.4   Conclusions

This chapter has introduced and discussed, at a high level, some of the most prevalent architecture frameworks and related technologies being used in the world today. Although this is not intended to be an exhaustive list of frameworks, nor the most in-depth, the intention is to provide an overview of the sort of information that is out there in the public domain being used on real projects.

One point that emerges from these descriptions is that some of the frameworks are true architectural frameworks, whereas others are not really. TOGAF is really focussed on the process of developing and maintaining a framework, rather than being a framework itself, and the UPDM is a profile that provides guidance on realising framework views.

The basic structure of any framework is one of views and their groupings, along with a rationale for why each view should exist and how it should be used. This, in essence, is the meta-model that is presented in this book.

- The frameworks themselves, such as the defence-based architecture frameworks, may be thought of as the structure and requirements of the meta-model.
- Process-related descriptions, such as TOGAF, may be thought of as the process and requirements aspects of the meta-model.
- Profiles and visualisation guidance, such as UPDM, may be thought of as enabling the modelling aspect of the meta-model.

Any, all or none of these sources may be used in reality and all are compatible with the meta-model approach on this book. The important thing to remember is that even if none of the information here is directly relevant for your business, there are aspects of it that will be and this can all be learned from.

References

1. The Ministry of Defence Architectural Framework, 2007. Available from http://www.mod.uk/modaf.
2. DoDAF Architectural Framework, version 1.5, 2007. Available from http://cio-nii.defense.gov/docs.
3. NATO Architectural Framework version 3, 2007. Available from http://www.nhqc3s.nato.int/ARCHITECTURE/_docs/NAF_v3/ANNEX1.pdf.
4. Unified profile for the Department of Defense Architectural Framework (DoDAF) and the Ministry of Defence Architectural Framework (MODAF), 2008. Available from http://syseng.omg.org/UPDM.htm.
5. The Open Group Architectural Framework (TOGAF), version 9. Available from http://www.opengroup.org/architecture/togaf9-doc/arch/ [Accessed 17 Feb 2010].

Appendix A
Summary of key elements

The two most common elements in the universe are Hydrogen and stupidity.

Harlan Ellison (1934–)

A.1   Introduction

Appendix A provides a summary of the key enterprise architecture (EA) concepts:

- Enterprise Architecture Meta-Model
- Enterprise Architecture Business Requirements Set
- Generic EA Ontology
- An Example EA View Quagmire

This appendix does *not* add further information to that found in the body of the book, but is intended to provide a single summary section of the noted diagrams. See Chapters 1, 5 and 7 for a discussion of each diagram.

A.2   Enterprise architecture meta-model

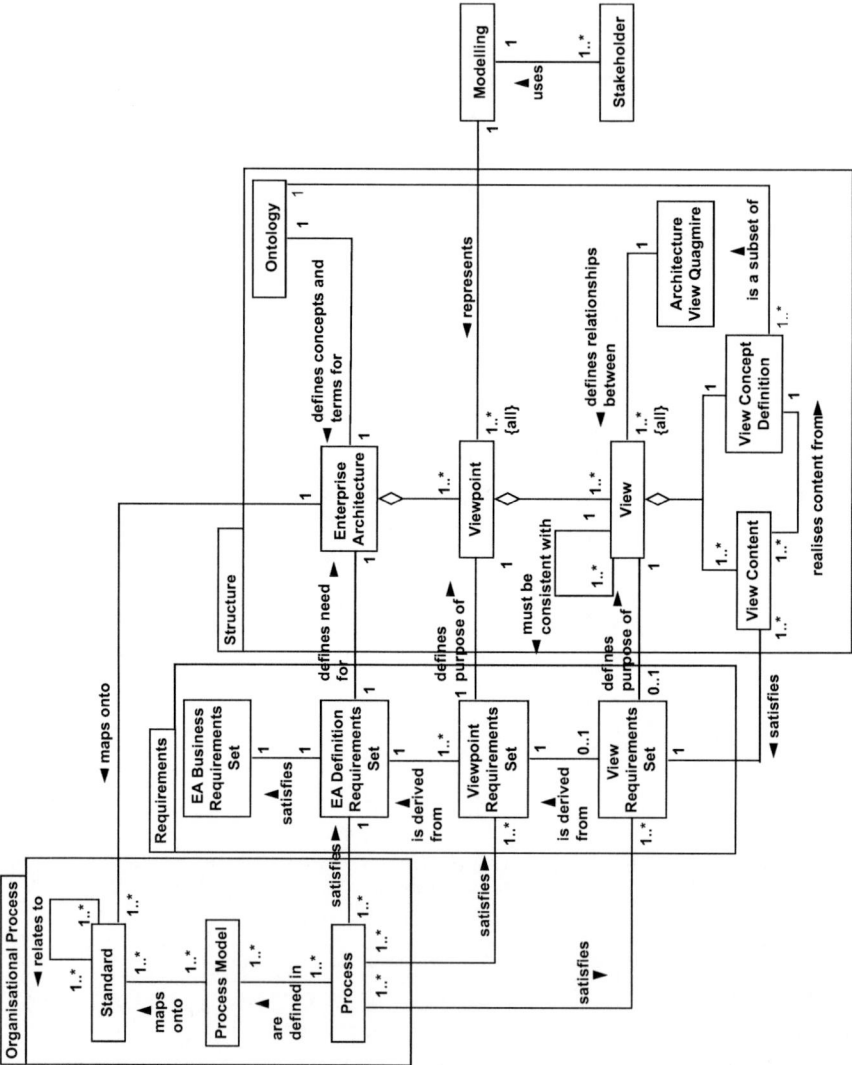

Figure A.1   The enterprise architecture meta-model

A.3 Enterprise architecture business requirements set

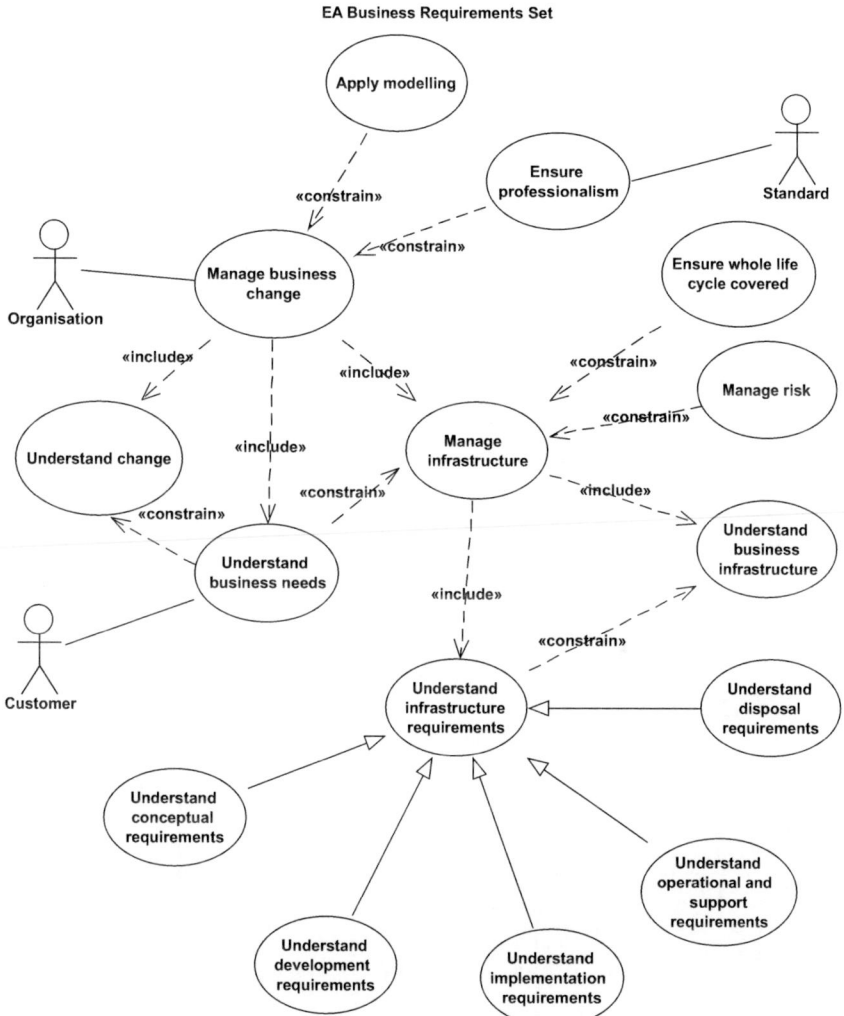

Figure A.2 EA business requirements set – high-level requirements

A.4   A generic EA ontology

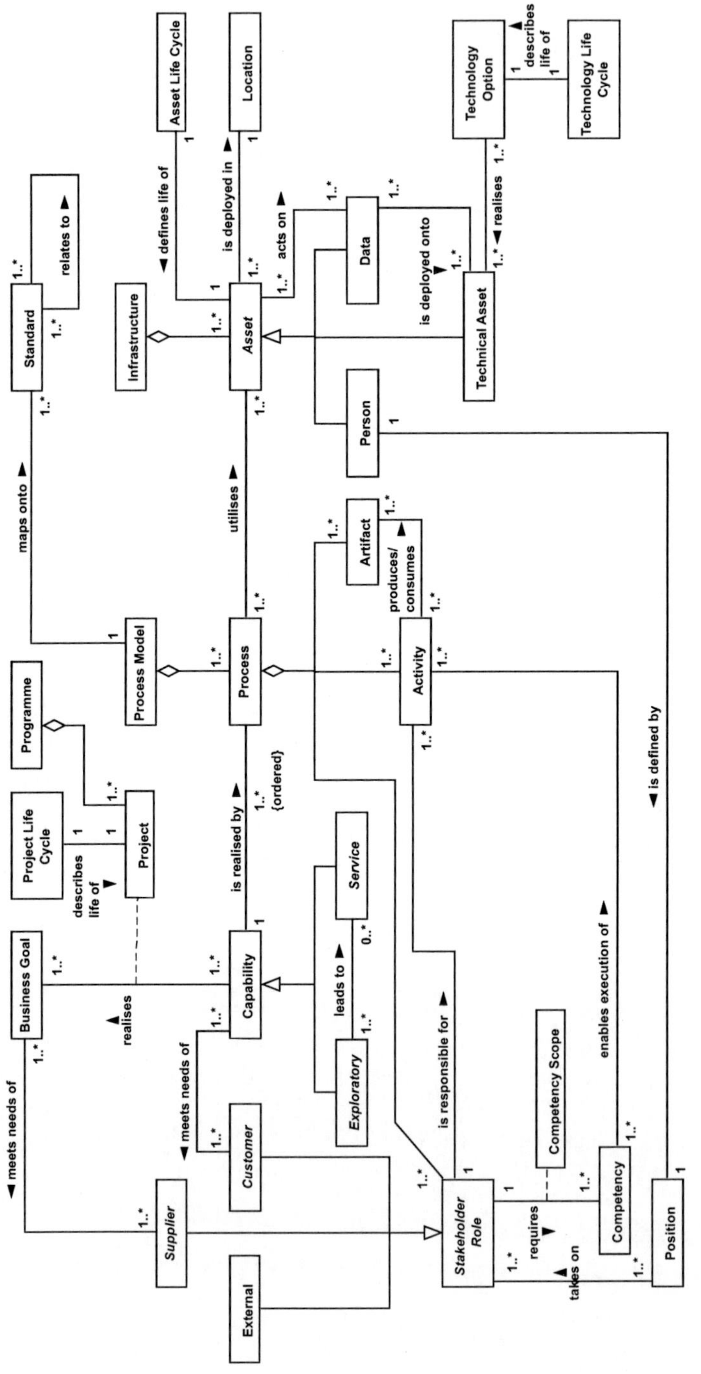

Figure A.3   A generic EA ontology

A.5   An example EA view quagmire

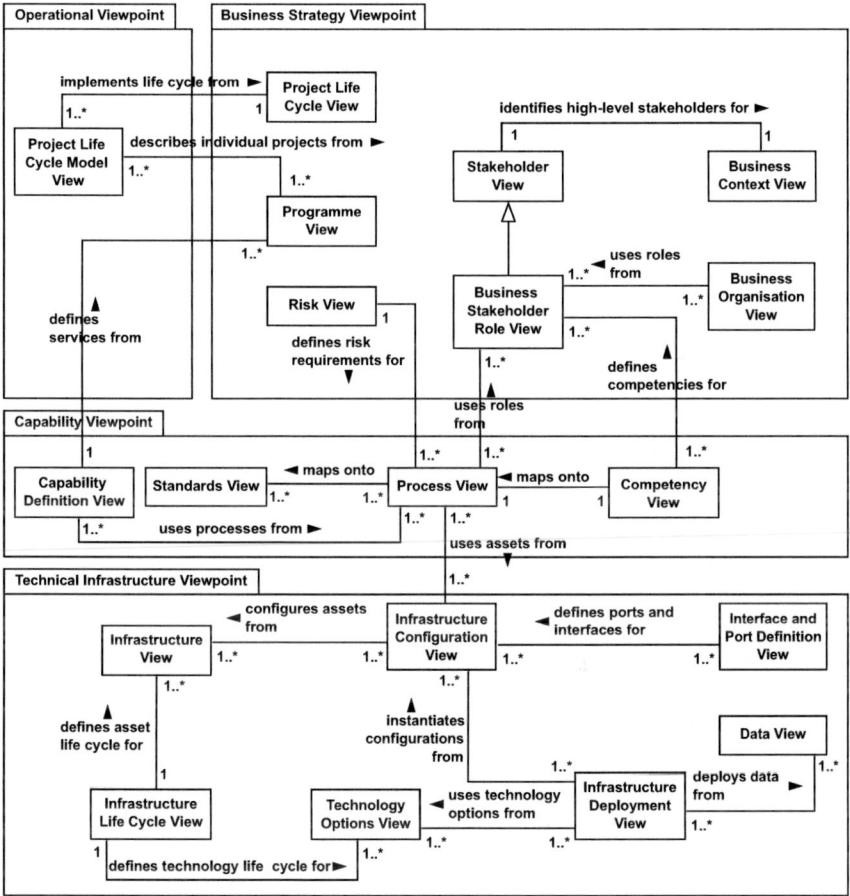

Figure A.4   An example EA view quagmire

Appendix B

Summary of notation

To summarize: it is a well-known fact that those people who must want to rule people are, *ipso facto*, those least suited to do it. To summarize the summary: anyone who is capable of getting themselves made President should on no account be allowed to do the job. To summarize the summary of the summary: people are a problem.

Douglas Adams (1952–2001), The Restaurant at the End of the
Universe

B.1   Introduction

Appendix B provides a summary of the meta-model and notation diagrams for Unified Modelling Language (UML) and SysML that are used in Chapter 4. For each of the 13 UML diagram types, grouped into structural and behavioural diagrams, three diagrams are given:

- A partial meta-model for that diagram type.
- The notation used on that diagram type.
- An example of that diagram type.

This appendix does *not* add further information to that found in Chapter 4, but is intended to provide a single summary section of the noted diagrams. See Chapter 4 for a discussion of each diagram.

B.2   Structural diagrams

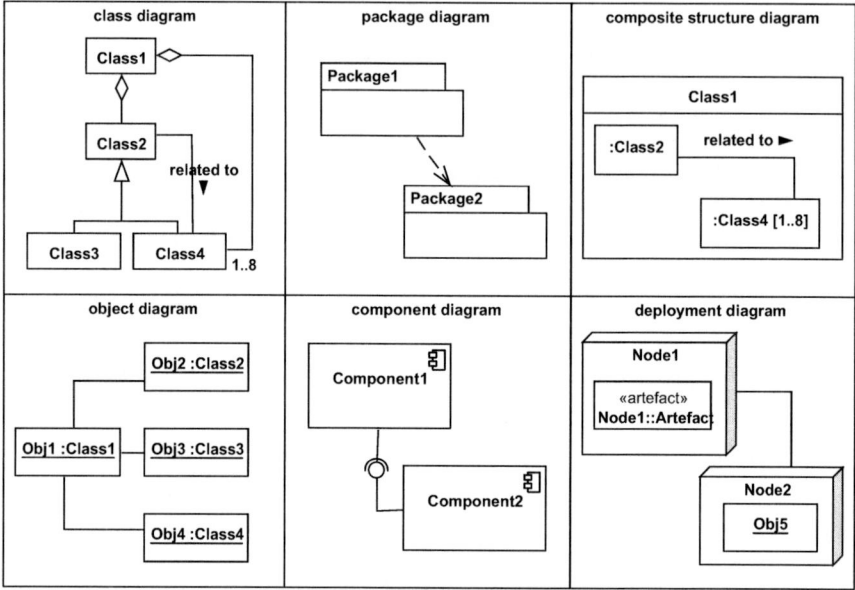

Figure B.1   Summary of structural diagrams

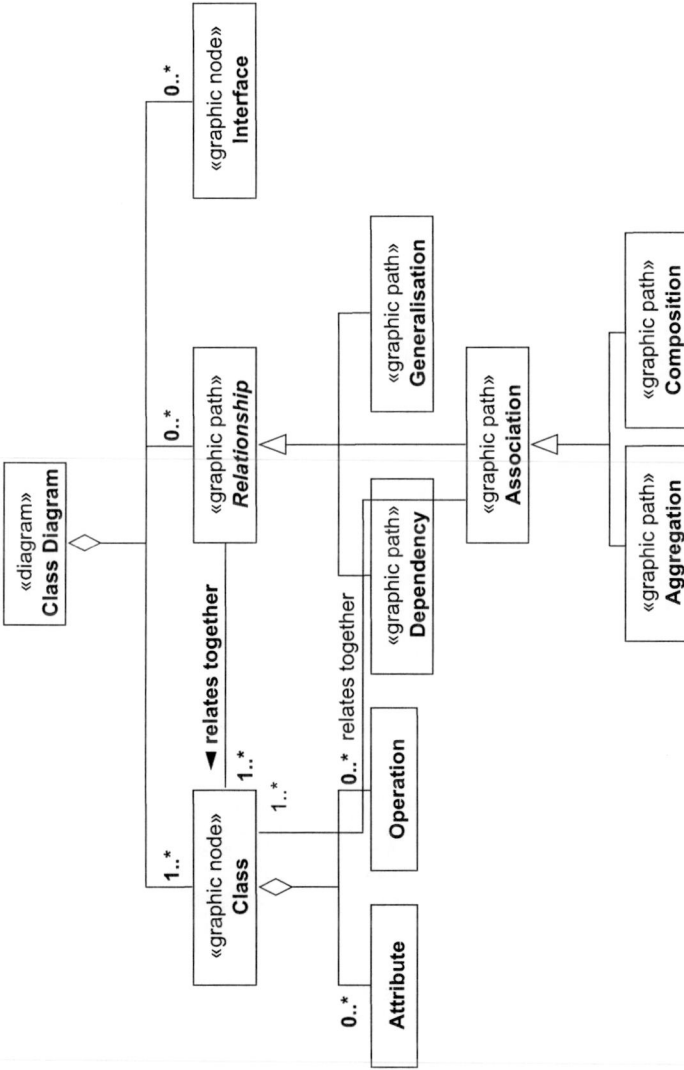

Figure B.2   Partial meta-mode for class diagrams

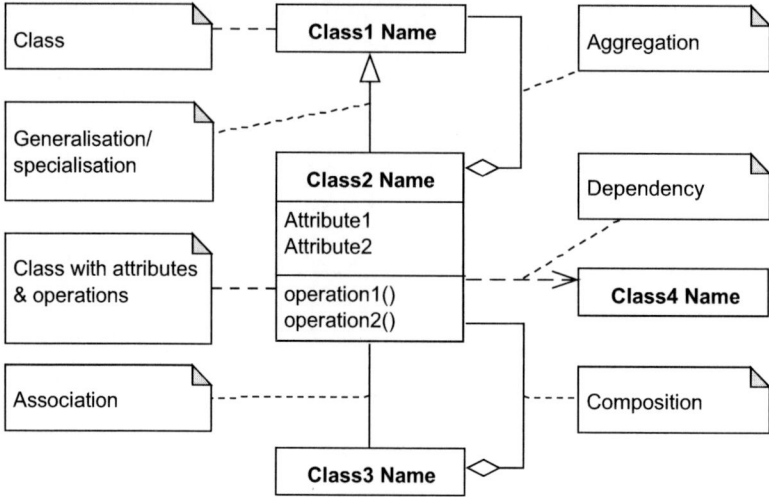

Figure B.3   Graphical symbols for elements in a class diagram

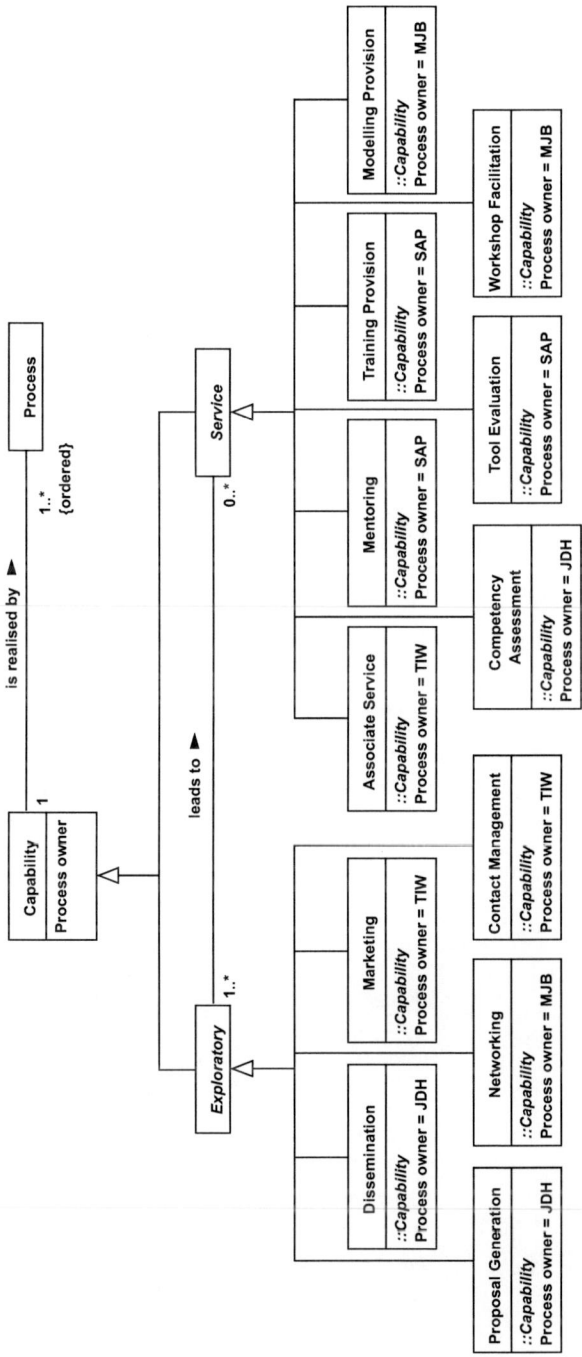

Figure B.4 Example class diagram

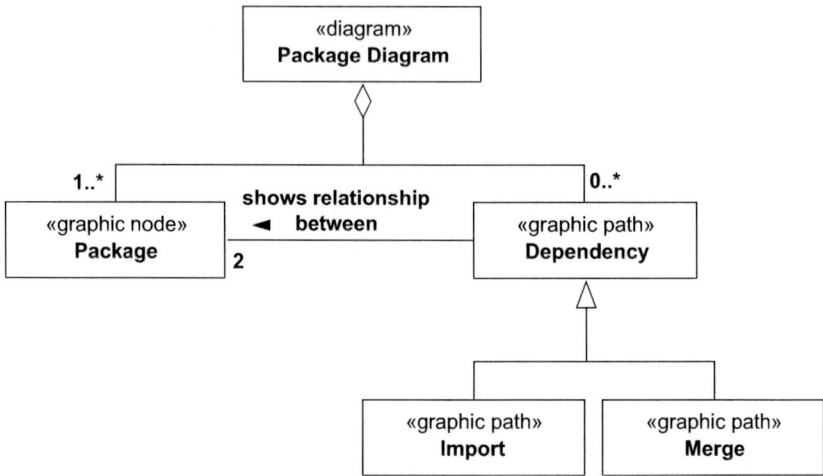

Figure B.5   Partial meta-model for package diagrams

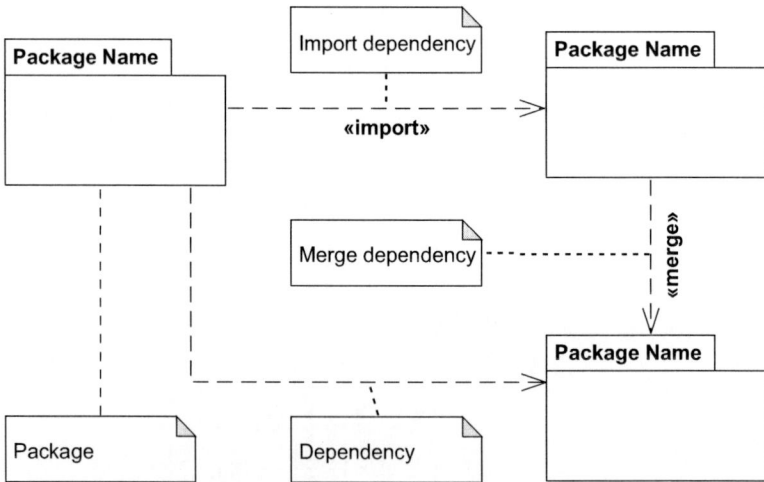

Figure B.6   Graphical symbols for elements in a package diagram

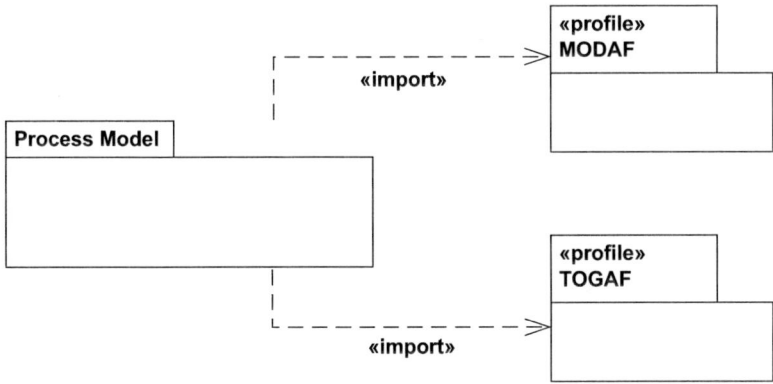

Figure B.7   Example package diagram

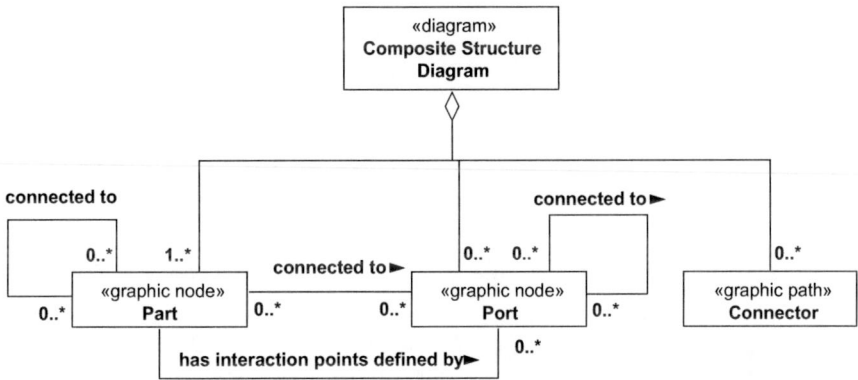

Figure B.8   Partial meta-model for composite structure diagram

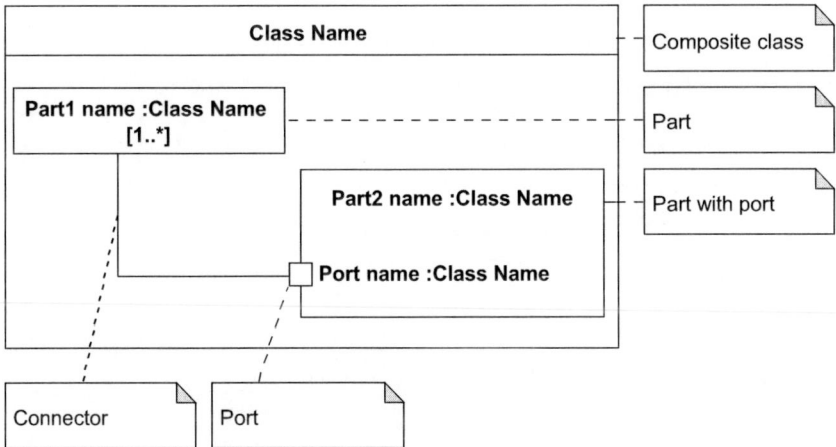

Figure B.9   Graphical symbols for elements in a composite structure diagram

EA Course Material :Delegate Pack

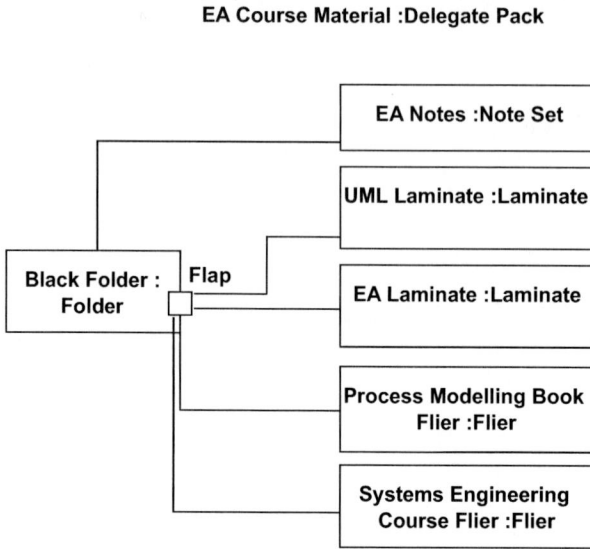

Figure B.10   Example composite structure diagram

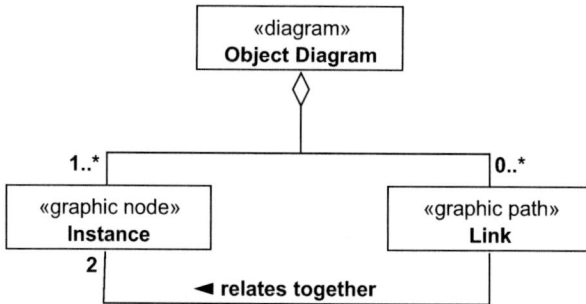

Figure B.11   Partial meta-model for object diagrams

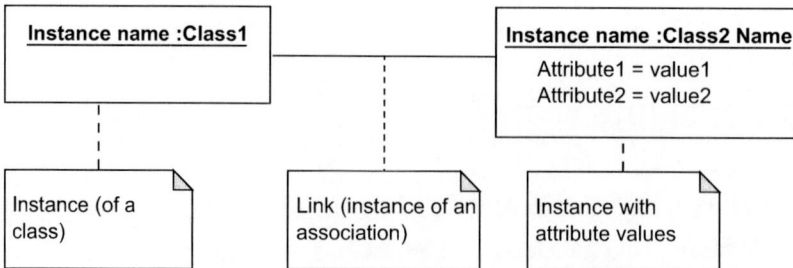

Figure B.12   Graphical symbols for elements in an object diagram

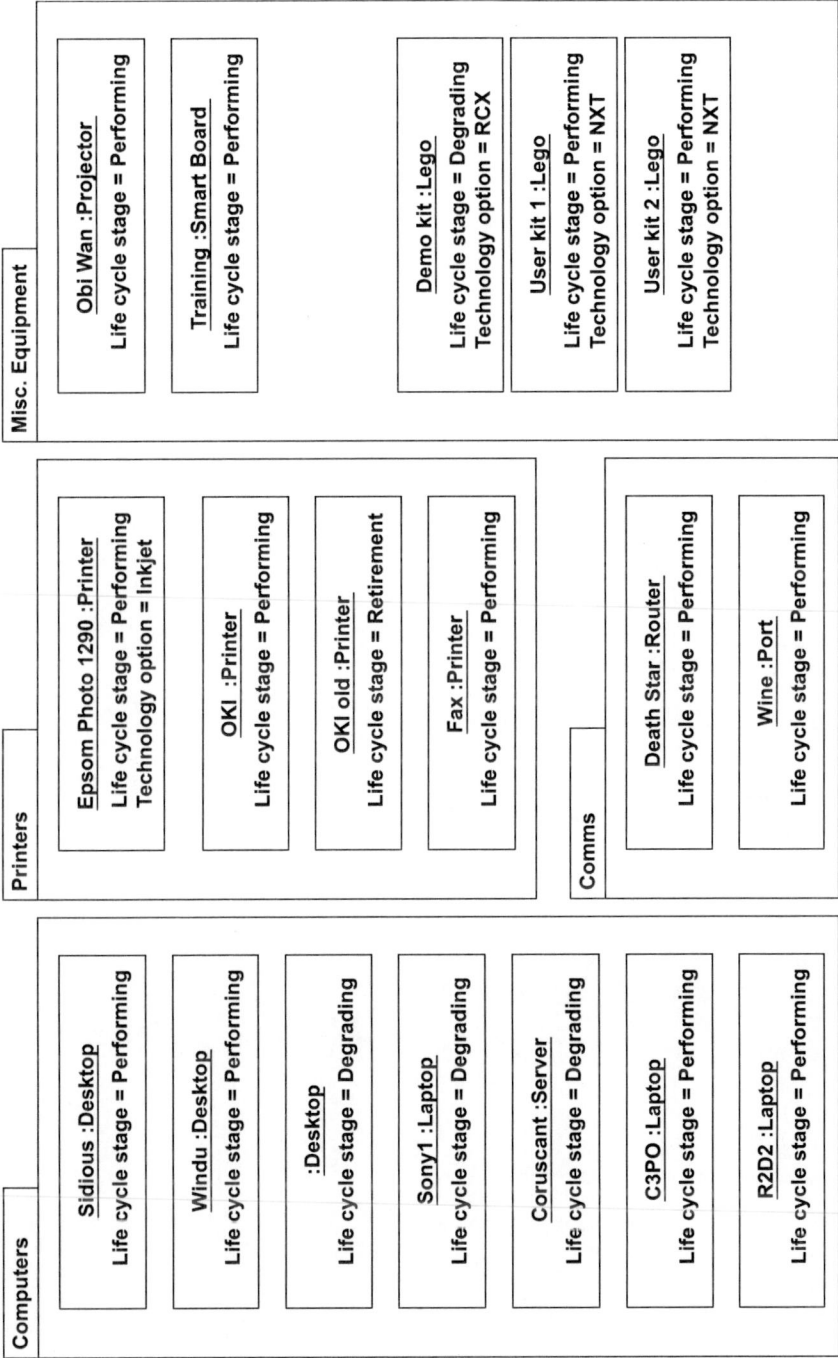

Figure B.13   Example object diagram

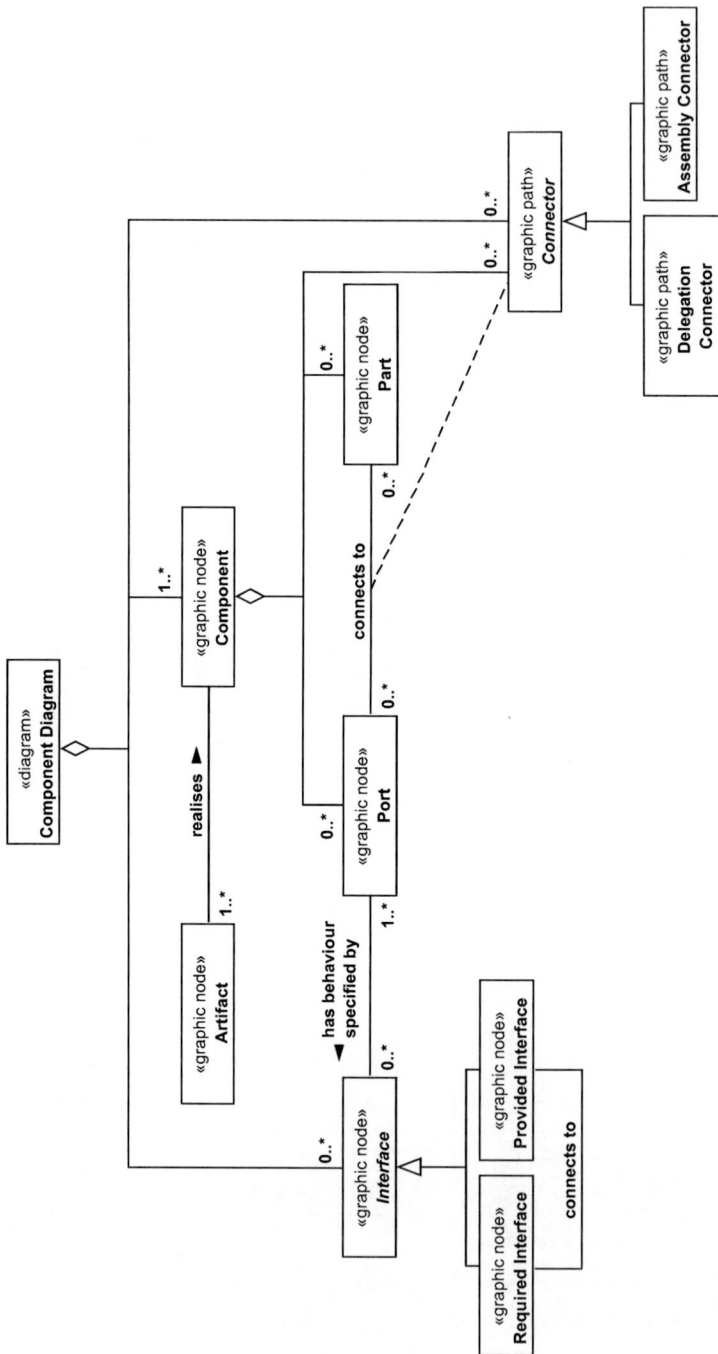

Figure B.14   Partial meta-model for component diagrams

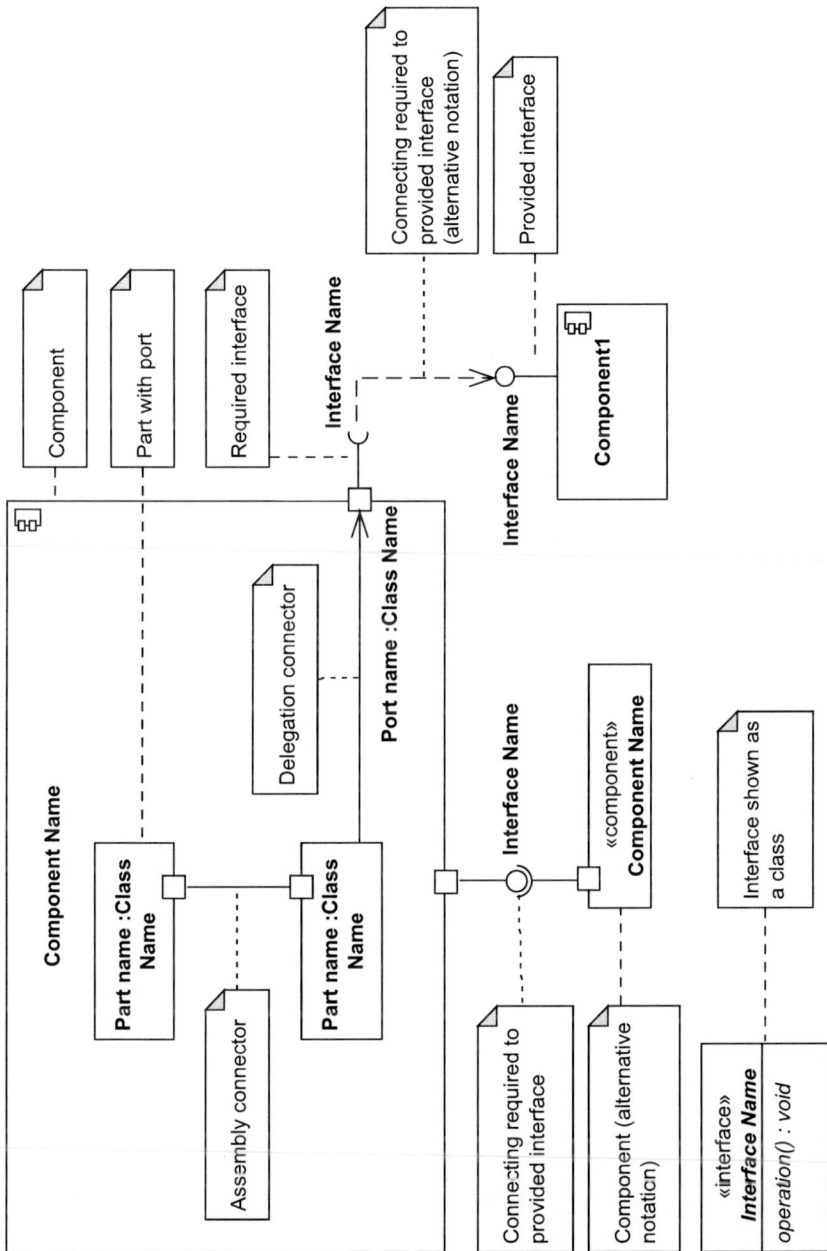

Figure B.15 Graphical symbols for elements in a component diagram

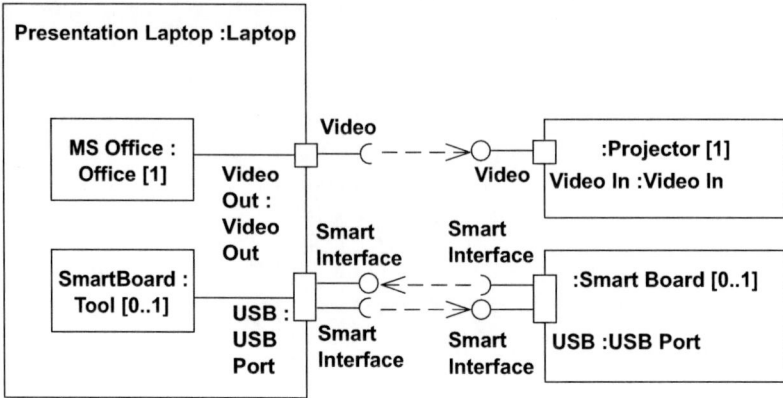

Figure B.16   Example component diagram

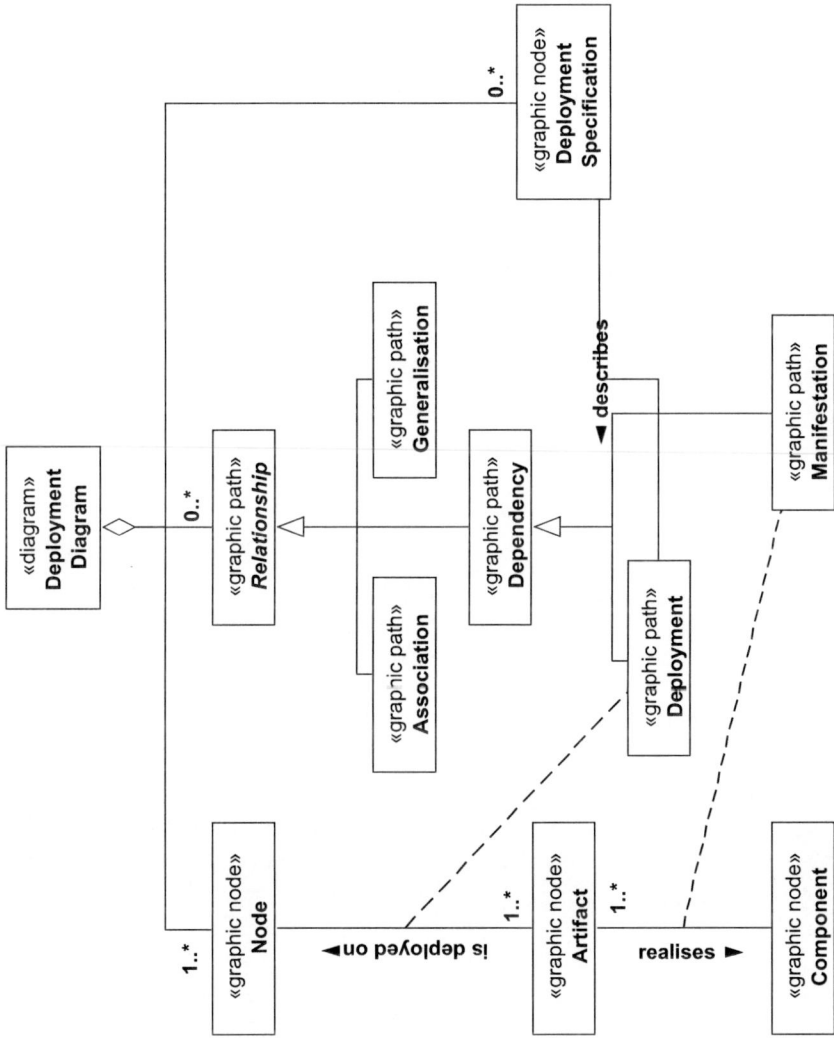

Figure B.17 Partial meta-model for deployment diagrams

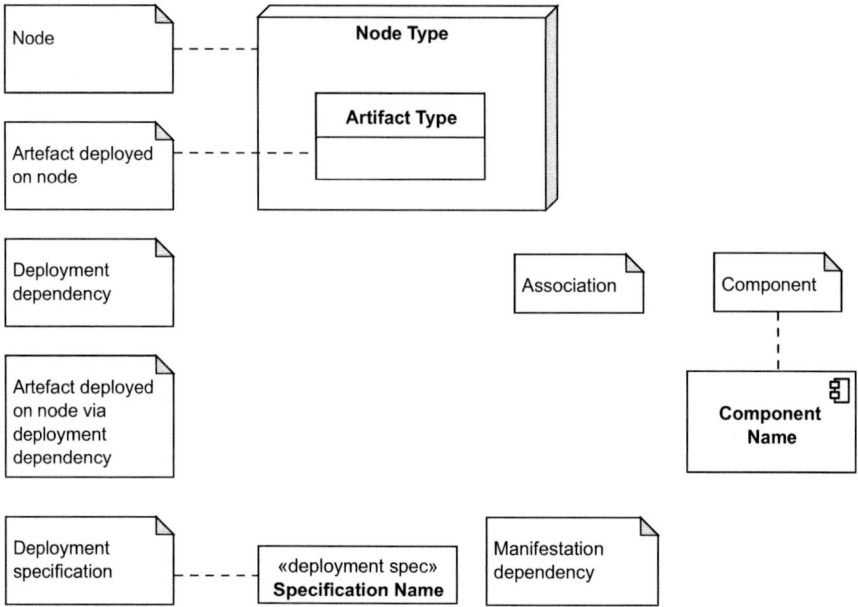

Figure B.18   Graphical symbols for elements in a deployment diagram

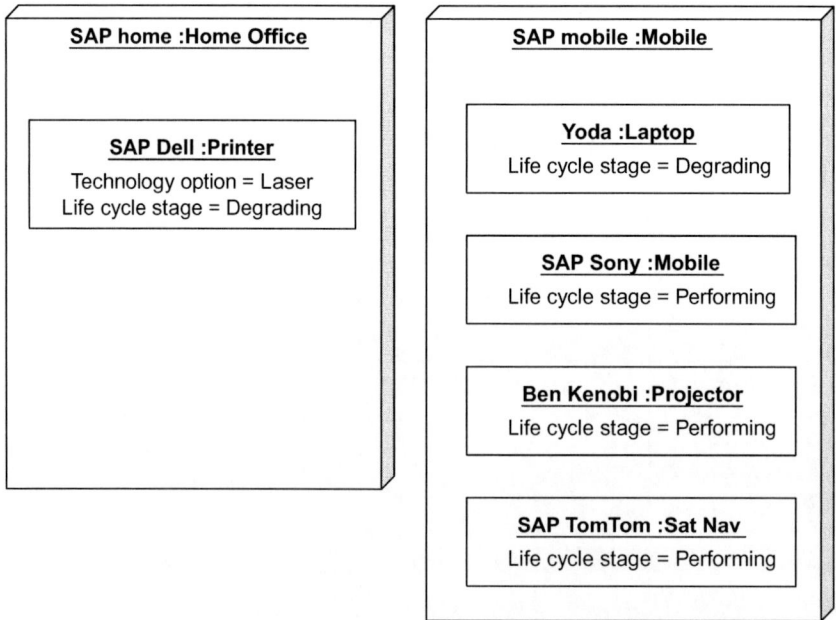

Figure B.19   Example deployment diagram

B.3 Behavioural diagrams

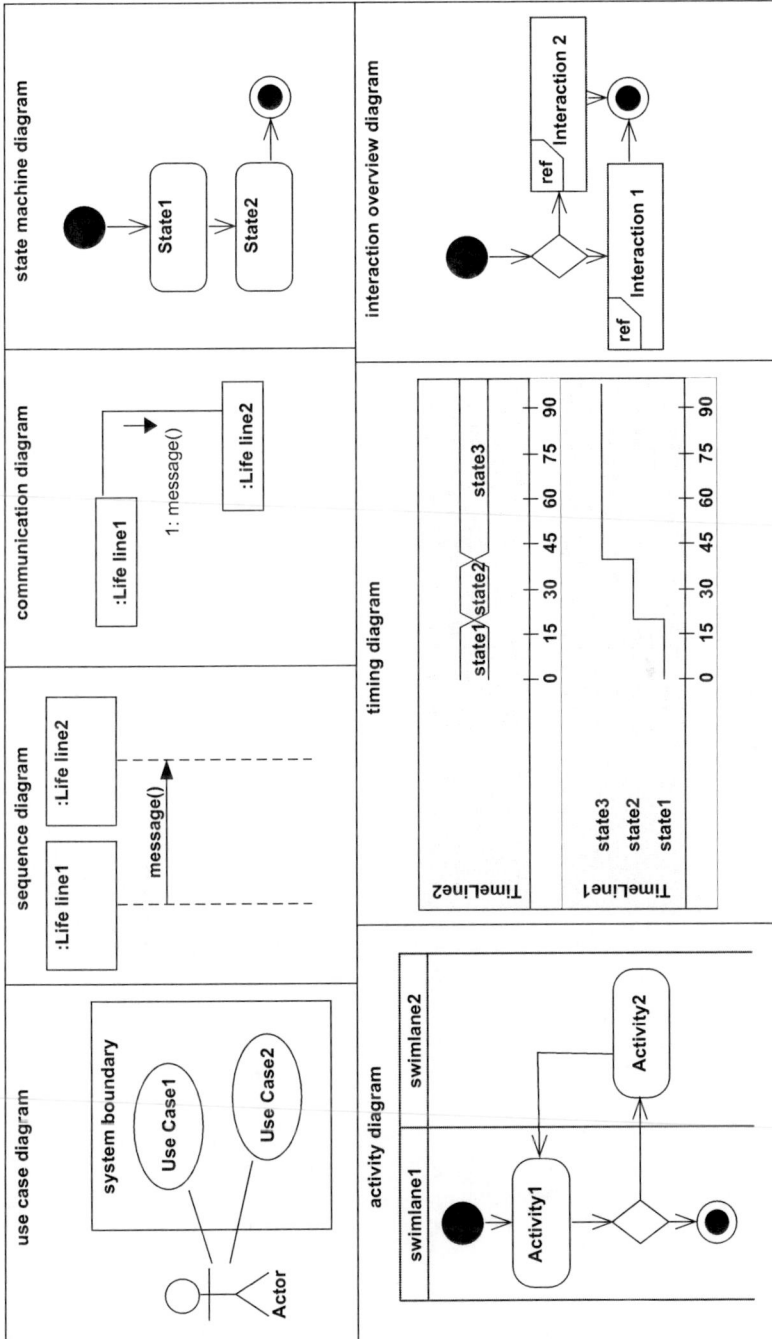

Figure B.20 Summary of behavioural diagrams

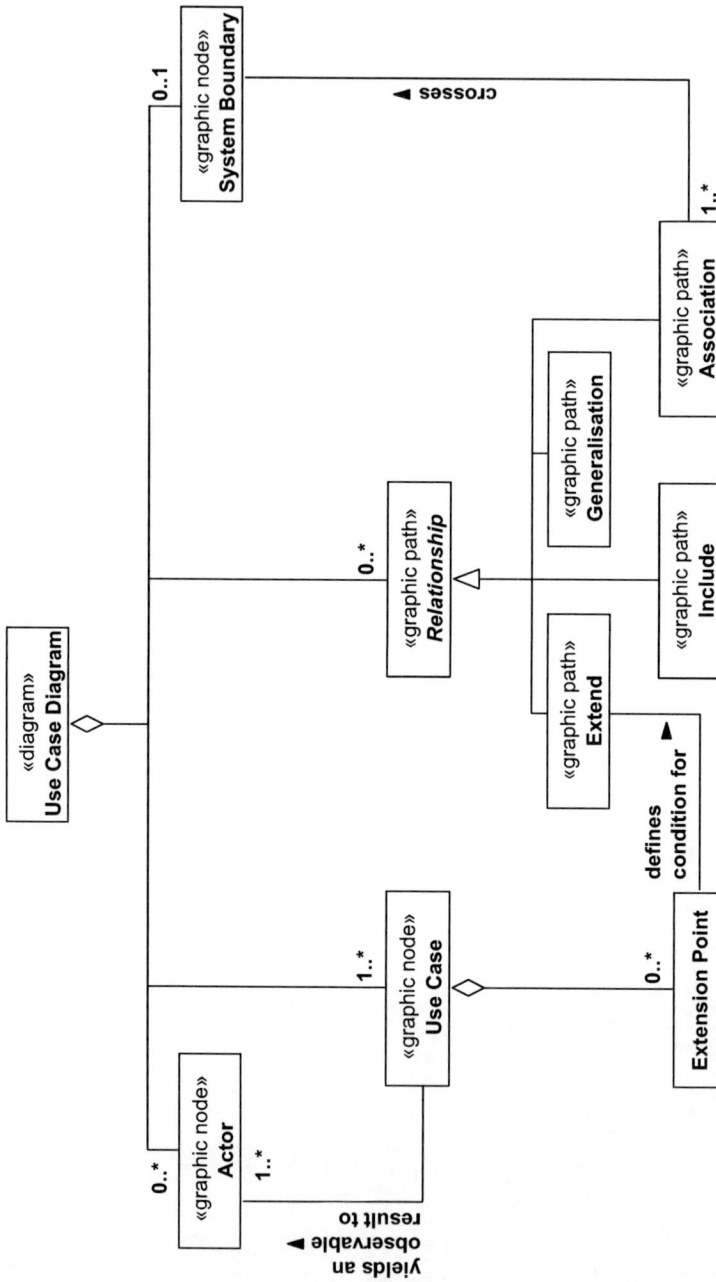

Figure B.21 Partial meta-model for use case diagrams

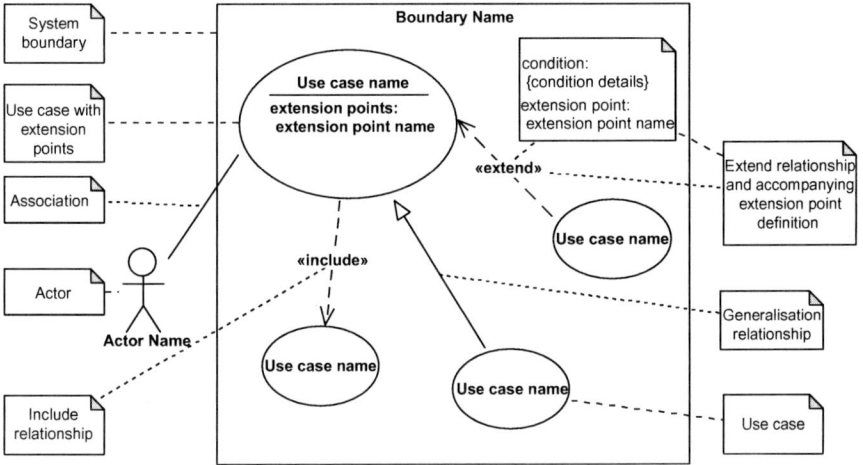

Figure B.22   Graphical symbols for elements in a use case diagram

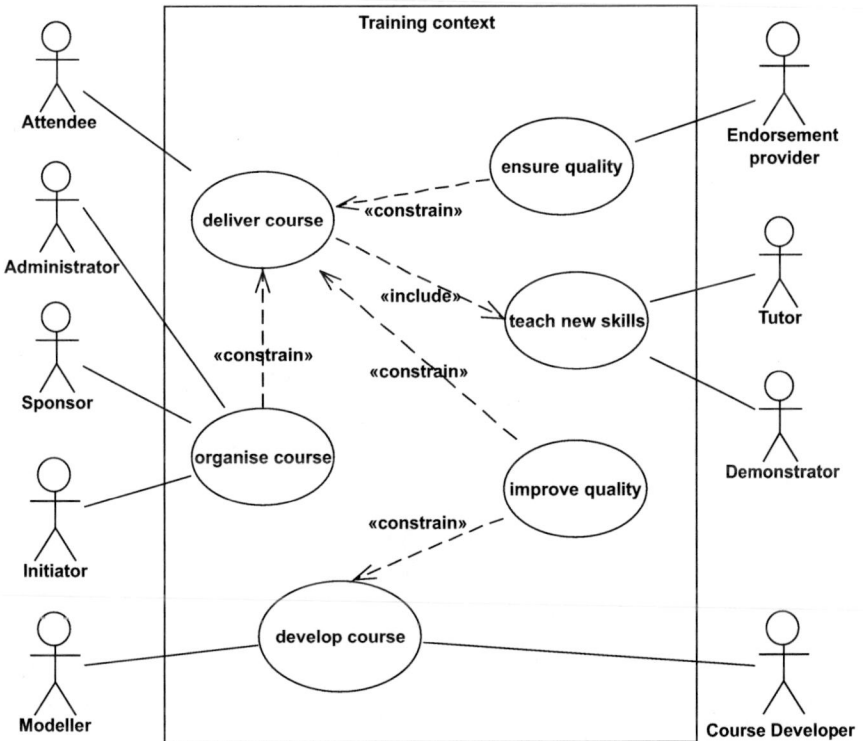

Figure B.23   Example use case diagram

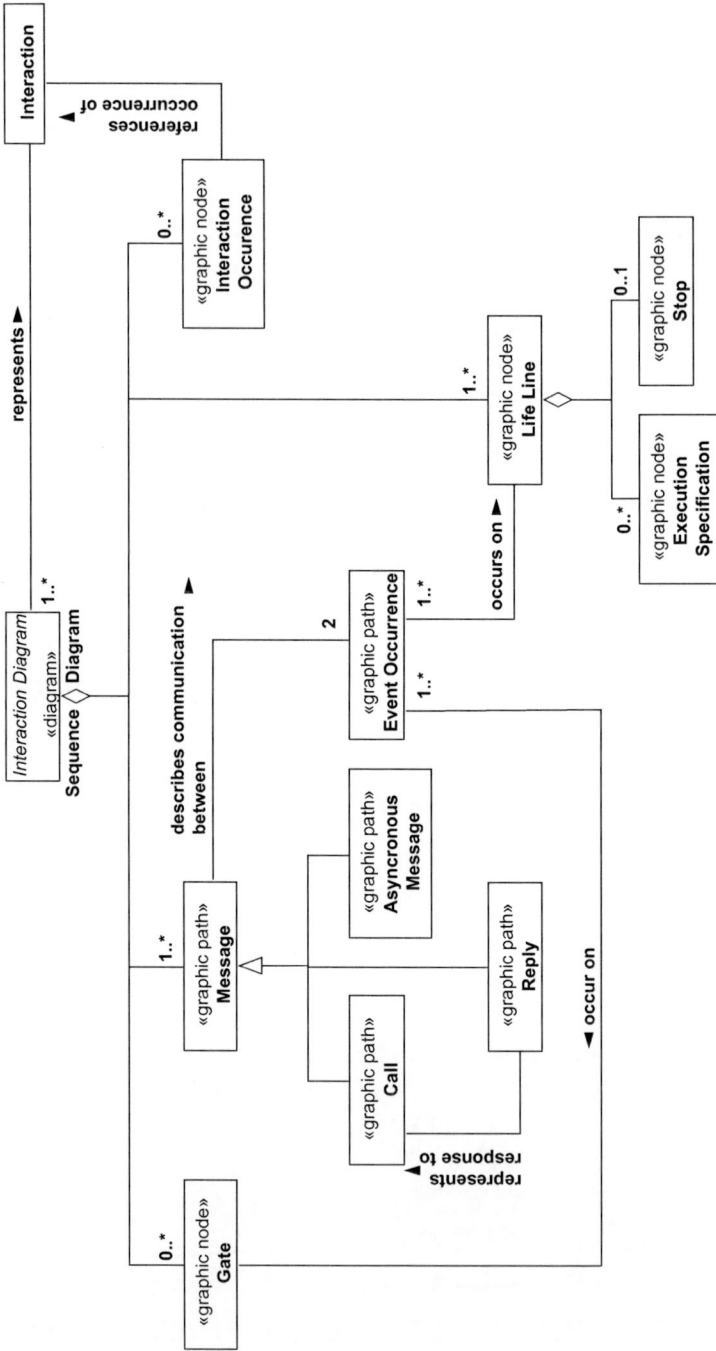

Figure B.24   Partial meta-model for sequence diagrams

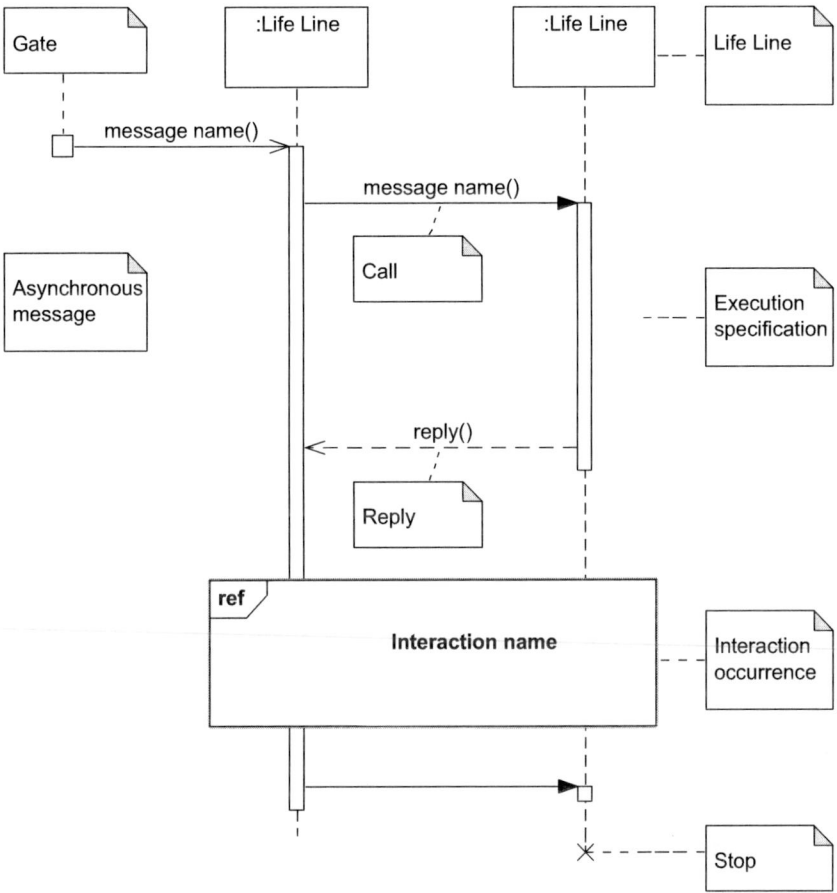

Figure B.25   Graphical symbols for elements in a sequence diagram

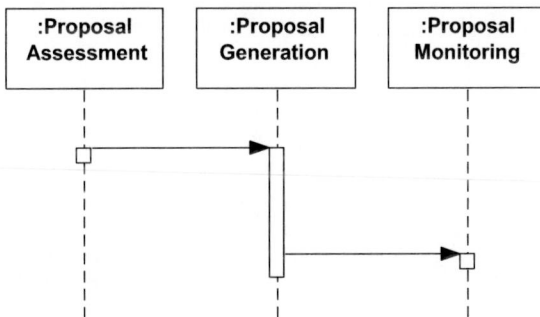

Figure B.26   Example sequence diagram

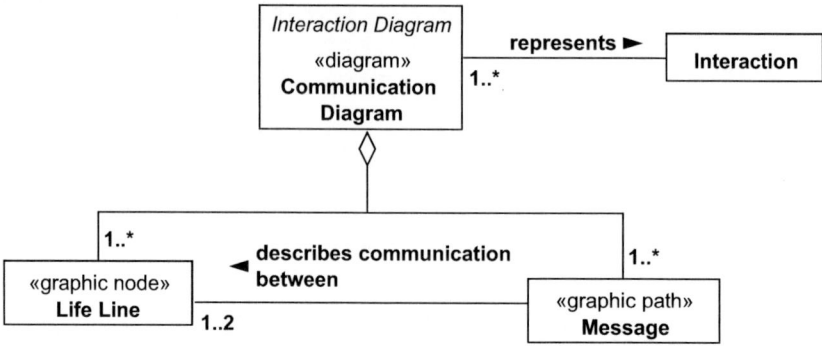

Figure B.27   Partial meta-model for communication diagrams

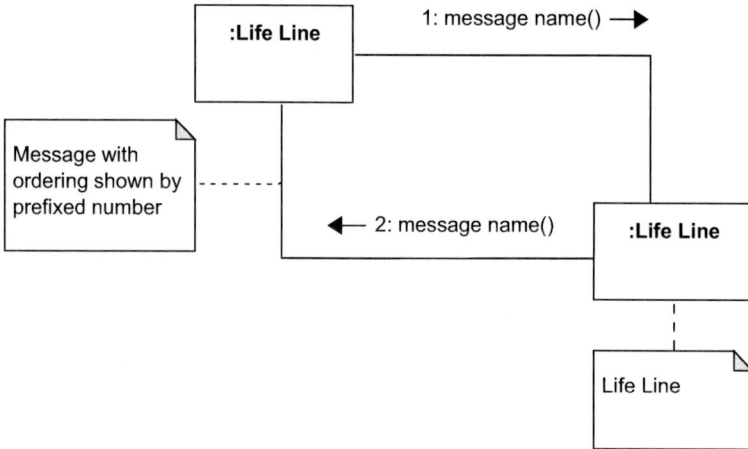

Figure B.28   Graphical symbols for elements in a communication diagram

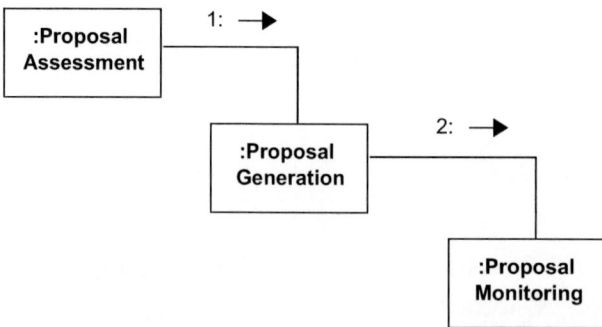

Figure B.29   Example communication diagram

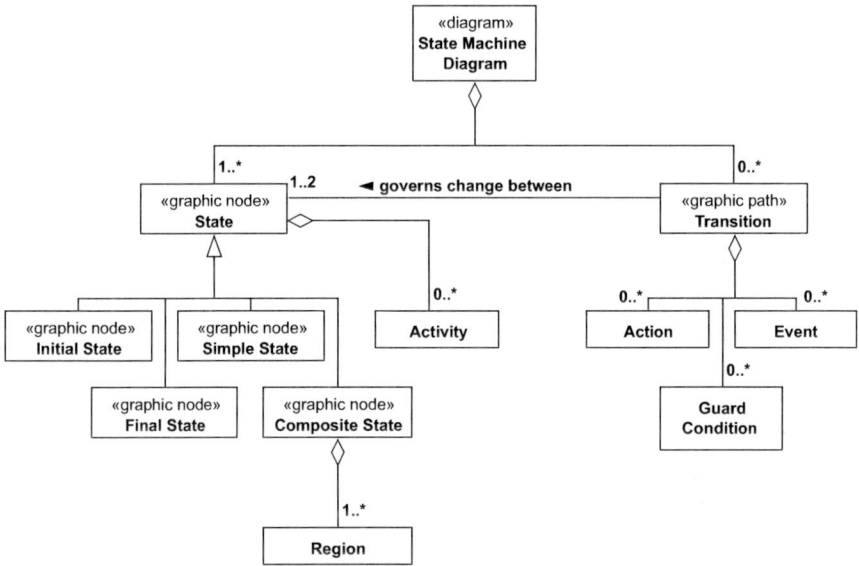

Figure B.30   Partial meta-mode for state machine diagrams

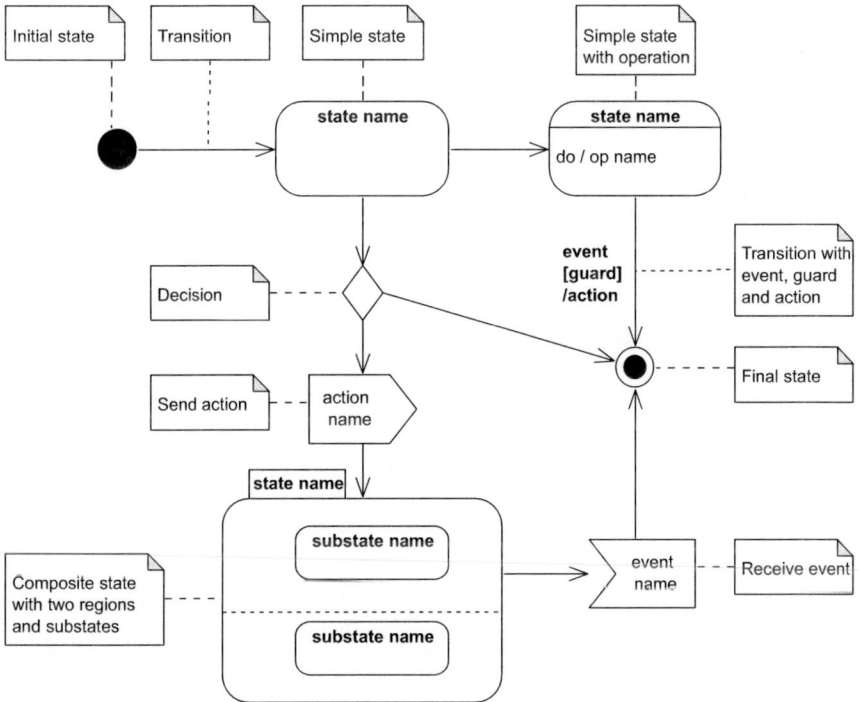

Figure B.31   Graphical symbols for elements in a state machine diagram

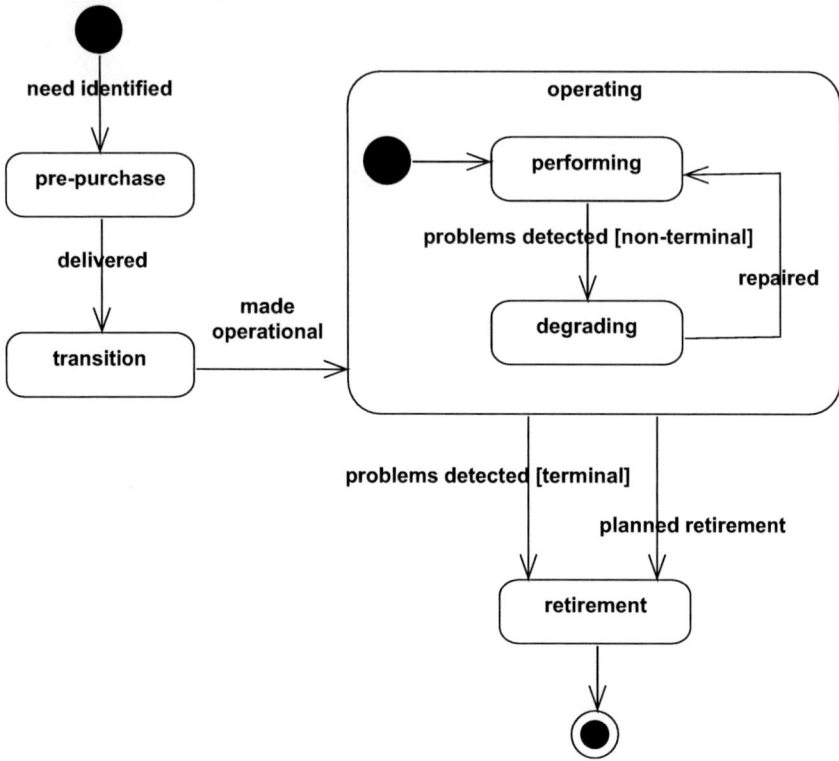

Figure B.32   Example state machine diagram

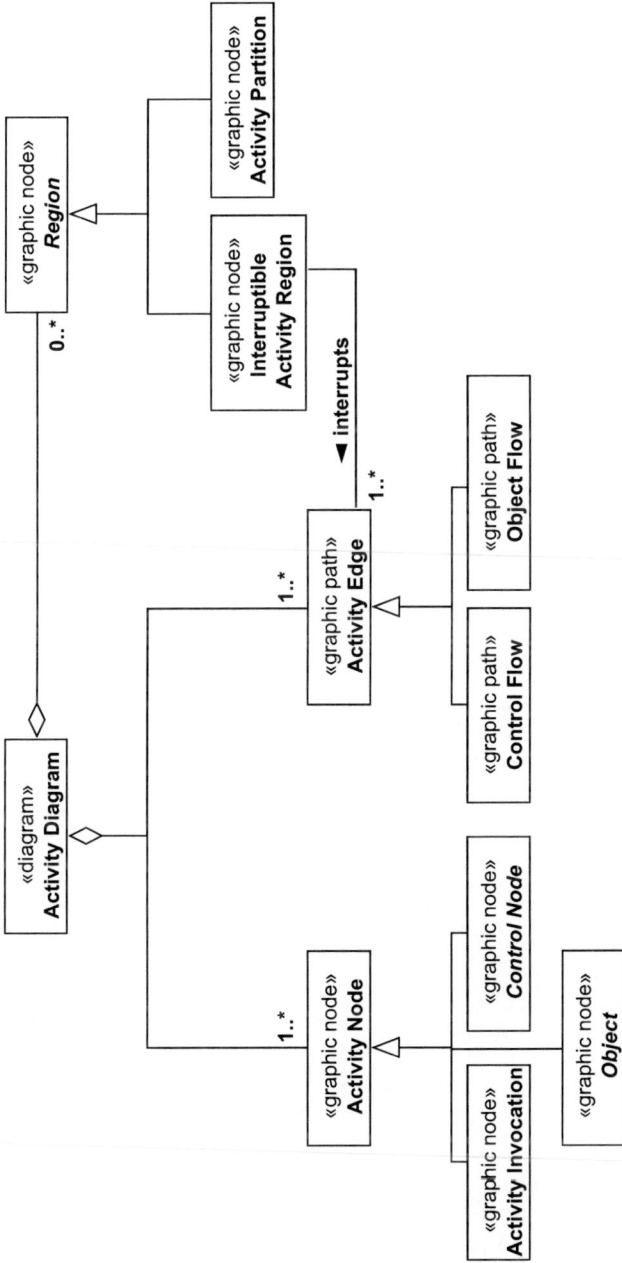

Figure B.33   Partial meta-model for activity diagrams

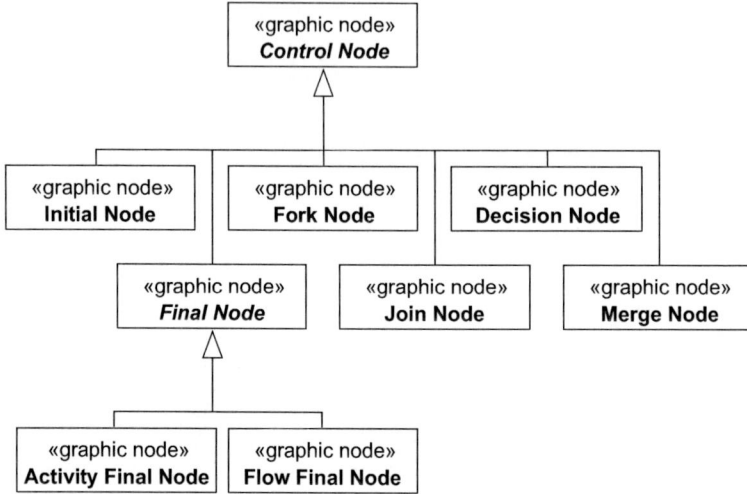

Figure B.34   Expanded partial meta-model, focusing on 'Control Node'

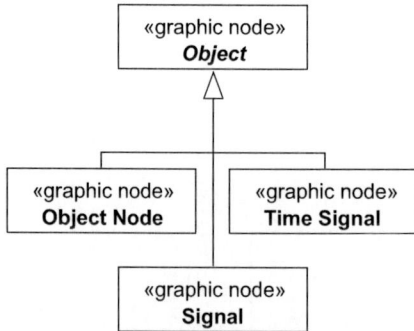

Figure B.35   Expanded partial meta-model, focusing on 'Object'

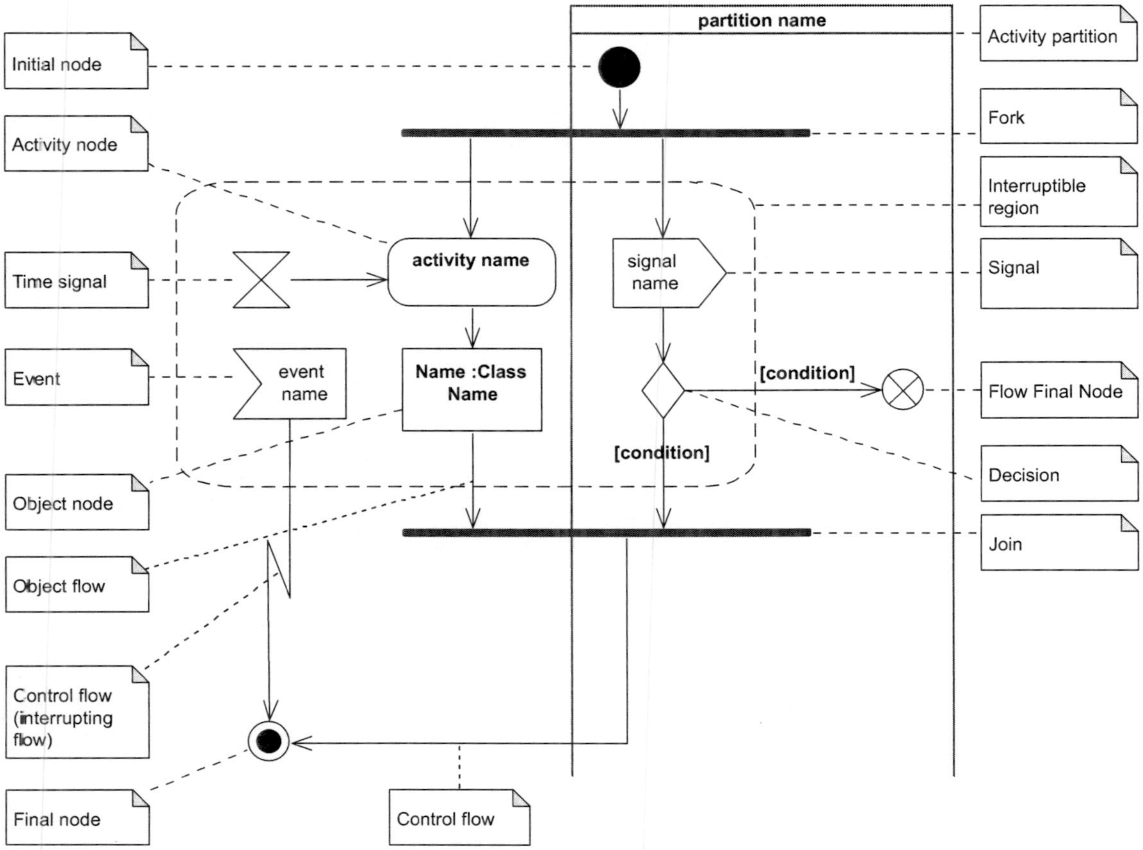

Figure B.36   Graphical symbols for elements in an activity diagram

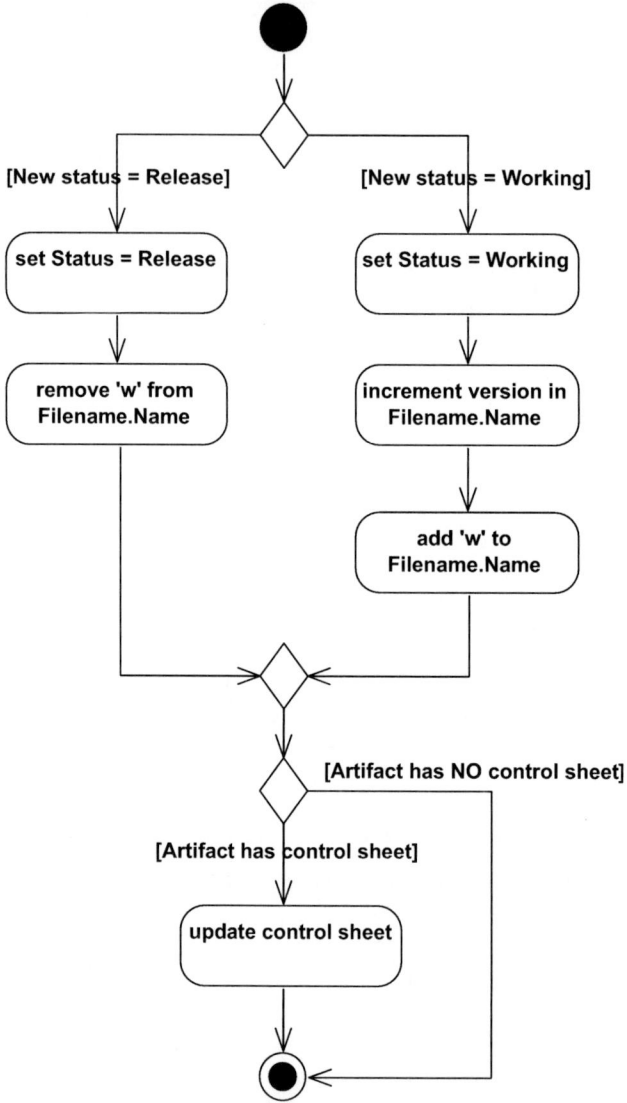

Figure B.37   Example activity diagram

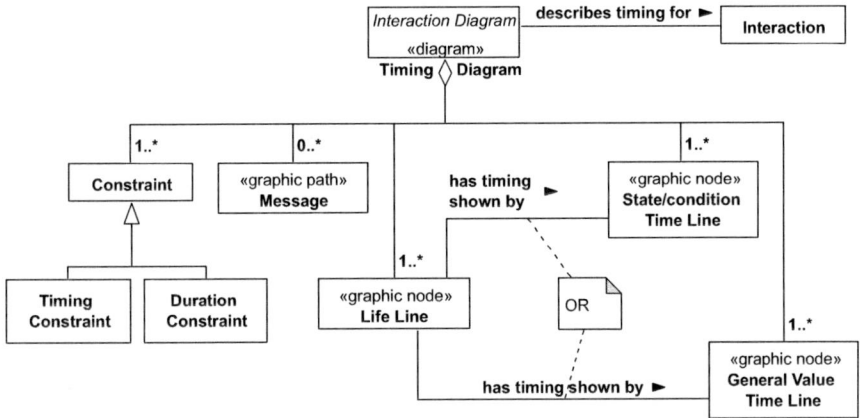

Figure B.38   Partial meta-model for timing diagrams

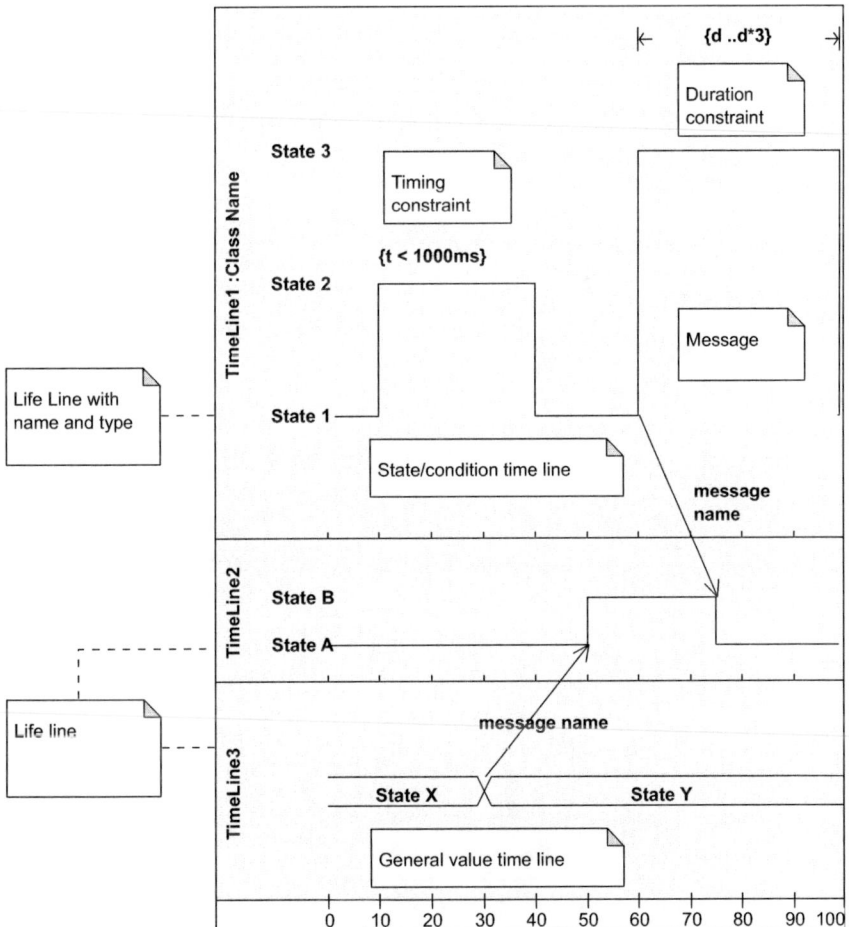

Figure B.39   Graphical symbols for elements in a timing diagram

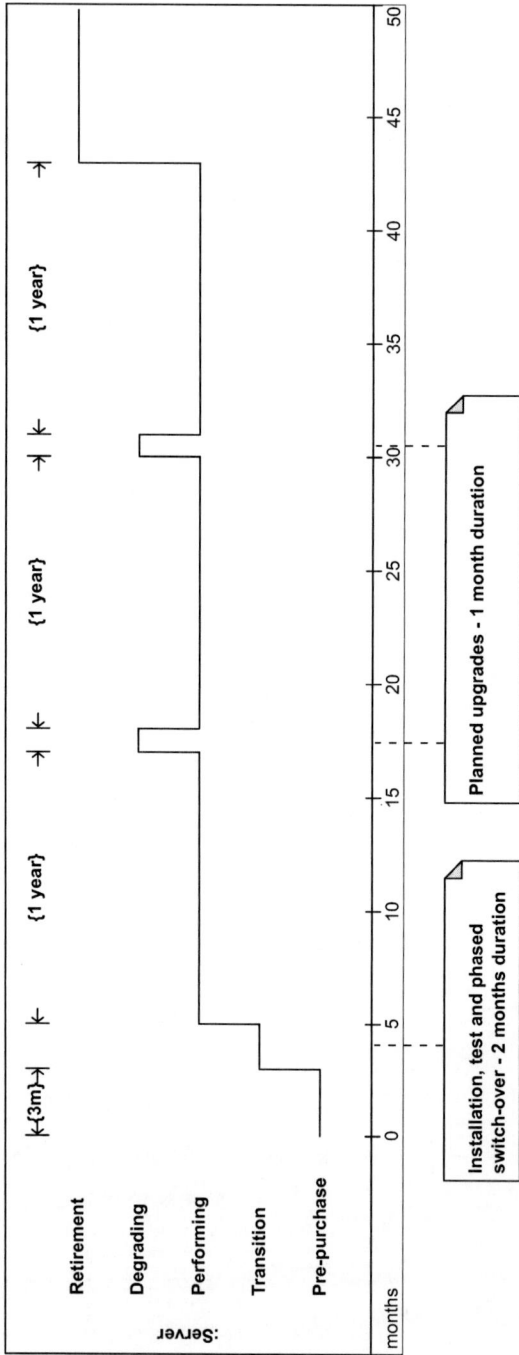

Figure B.40 Example timing diagram

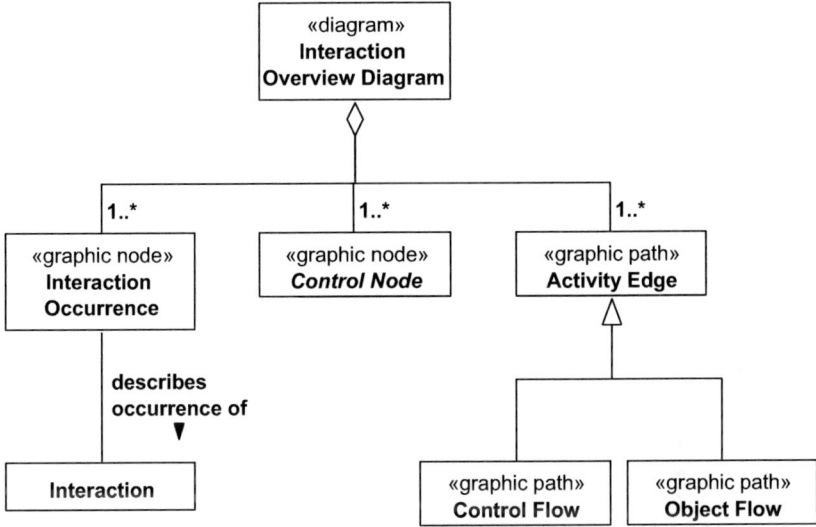

Figure B.41   Partial meta-model for interaction overview diagrams

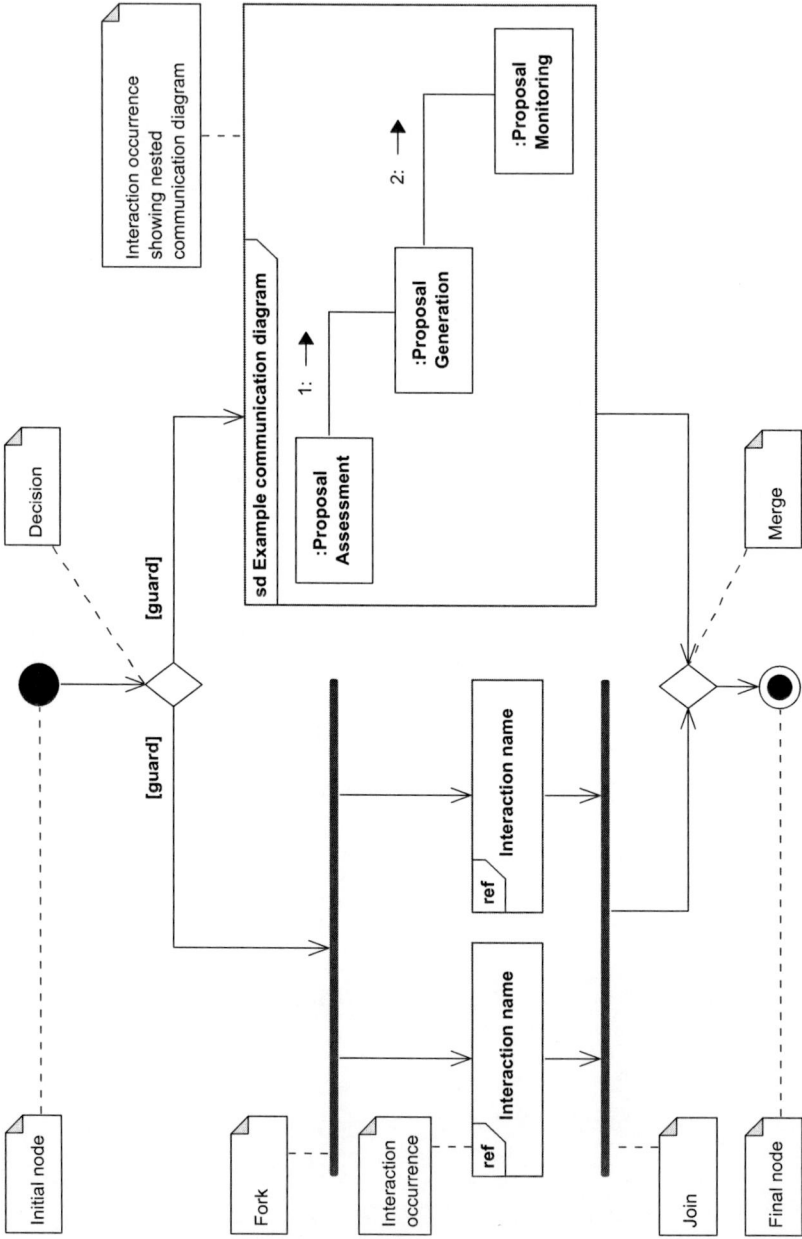

Figure B.42 Graphical symbols for elements in an interaction overview diagram

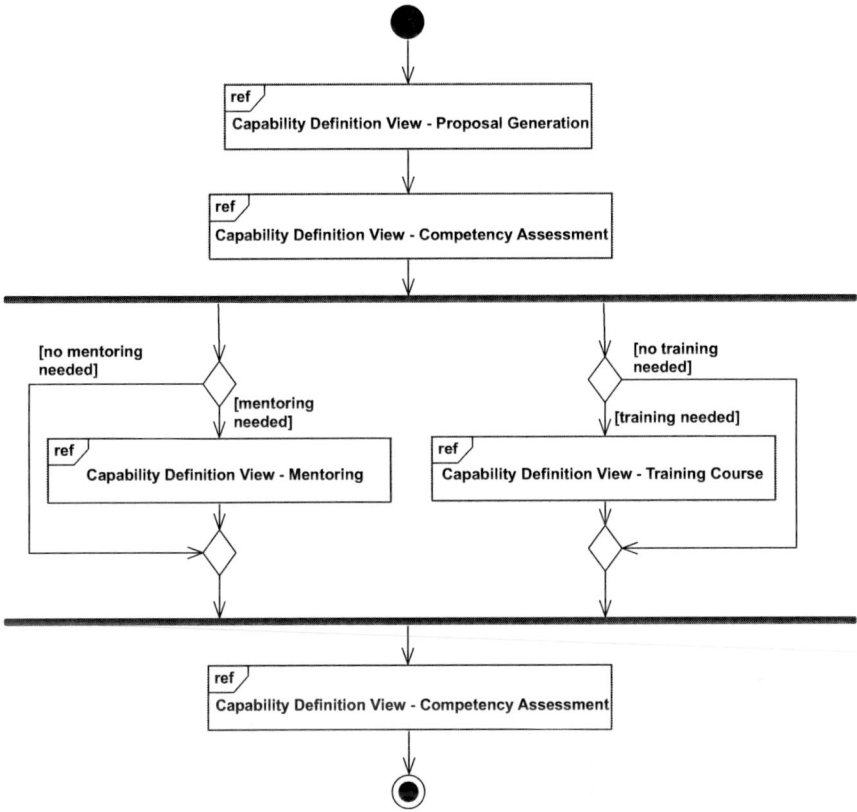

Figure B.43   Example interaction overview diagram

Index